The Old Contemptibles

Other books by the author

The Old Contemptibles

The British Expeditionary Force, 1914

ROBIN NEILLANDS

JOHN MURRAY

© Robin Neillands 2004

First published in Great Britain in 2004 by John Murray (Publishers)
A division of Hodder Headline

1 3 5 7 9 10 8 6 4 2

A CIP catalogue record for this title is available from the British Library

ISBN 0-7195-5646 5

Typeset in 11.75/14.75 Monotype Sabon by Servis Filmsetting Ltd, Manchester
Printed and bound in Great Britain by Clays Ltd, St Ives plc

Hodder Headline policy is to use papers that are natural, renewable and recyclable
products and made from wood grown in sustainable forests. The logging and
manufacturing processes are expected to conform to the environmental regulations
of the country of origin.

John Murray (Publishers)
338 Euston Road
London
NW1 3BH

This one is for Professor Michael Biddiss and Dr Frank Tallett of the Department of History, University of Reading, who may find parts of it strangely familiar.

Contents

Illustrations

The author and publishers would like to thank the following for permission to reproduce illustrations: Plates 2 (Q54990), 3 (Q51151), 4 (Q51471), 10 (Q51475), 11 (Q51478), 12 (Q33010),

Acknowledgements

One of the most enjoyable parts of writing a book is thanking the many people who made it possible – few books are written by the author alone. First among these must be Eric Garner, my most able researcher and master of the Internet, who has proved invaluable in tracking down references and finding information I had to include. Thanks also to Terry Brown, an old Royal Marine 'oppo', for the maps and his company on many visits to France and Belgium. Thanks also to Grant McIntyre and Caroline Westmore of John Murray for their help in bringing this project to fruition.

Next I must thank my tutors in the Department of History at the University of Reading, Professor Michael Biddiss and Dr Frank Tallett, for encouraging me to complete my MA dissertation on Henry Wilson and the BEF's move to France in 1914, and my own students on the First World War Studies course at Rewley House, Extramural Studies Department, University of Oxford – Richard Ashmore, Dr Paul Garnerus (Germany), Arthur Hall (USA), Mike Hodgetts (Australia), Paul McNicholls (Canada), Noriko Roberts (Japan), plus Barbara Topley, Tom Taylor, Bill Thompson and Mike Smith – for their enthusiasm, their extensive research into Great War studies, their various helpful contributions, and their willingness to argue.

Thanks also to William Spencer, Military Specialist at the PRO, Kew, the officers of the King's Troop, Royal Horse Artillery (RHA), Lt.-Col. Will Townend of the Firepower Museum, Woolwich, Alan Rooney of Midas Tours, the Historial Museum, Peronne, France, and museum staff in Ypres and Albert, together with those of the Library and the Department of Documents at the Imperial War Museum, most notably for help with the diaries of Henry Wilson, the Royal United Services Institute (RUSI) in Whitehall, and the London Library. Lastly to Judy, my wife, who endures all this.

Maps

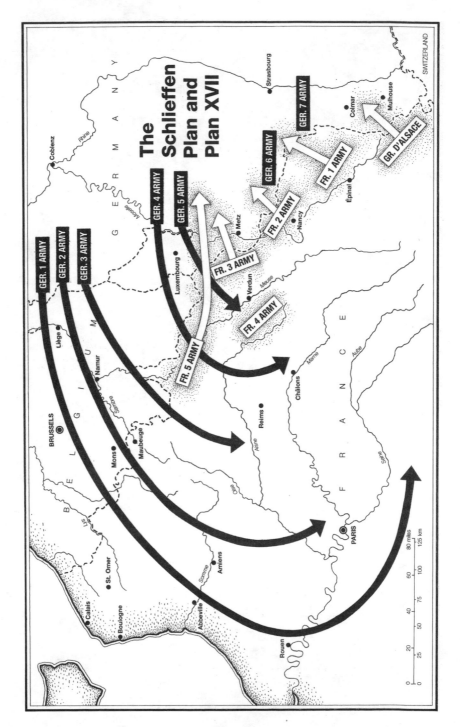

Map 1

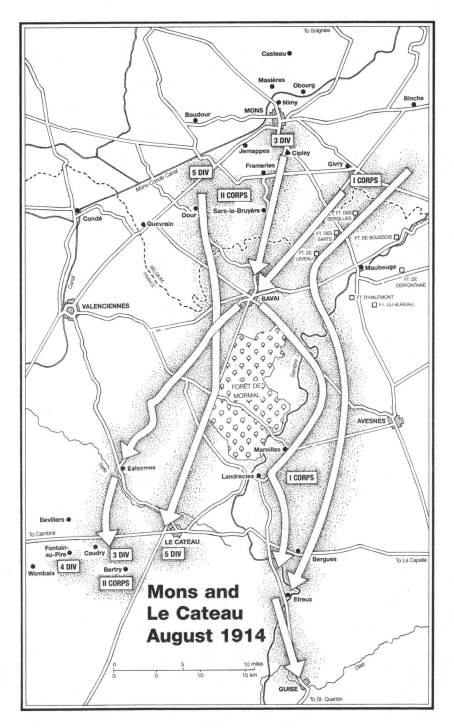

To Soignies

Casteau

Masières
Obourg

Nimy
MONS
Binche

Baudour

3 DIV

Jemappes · Cipley

5 DIV
Frameries
Givry

II CORPS
I CORPS

Condé · Quevrain
Dour · Sars-la-Bruyère

FT. DES
BERSILLIES

FT. DES
SARTS
FT. DE BOUSSOIS

FT. DE
LEVEAU

Maubeuge
FT. DE
CERFONTAINE

BAVAI
FT. D'HAUTMONT
FT. DU BORDIAU

VALENCIENNES

Sambre

FORÊT DE
MORMAL

BELGIUM
FRANCE

AVESNES

Maroilles

Solesmes

Landrecies
I CORPS

Bevillers

To Cambrai

Fontain-
au-Pire · Caudry **3 DIV**
LE CATEAU
5 DIV
Bergues
To La Capelle

Wambaix
Bertry
4 DIV
II CORPS

Mons and
Le Cateau
August 1914

Etreux

0   5   10 miles
0   5   10   15 km

GUISE
To St. Quentin

Mons-Condé Canal

Canal

Map 2

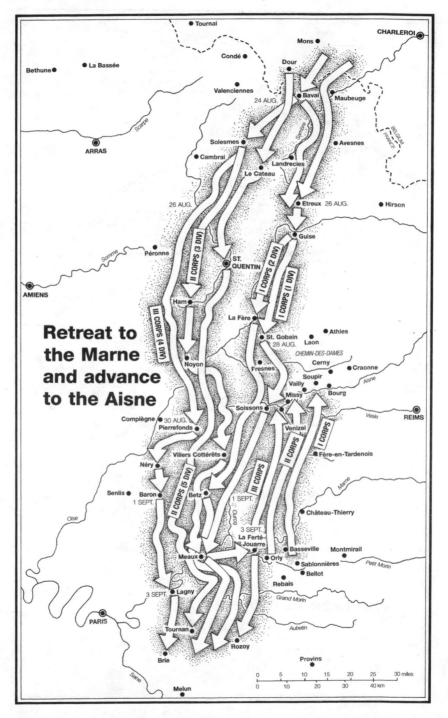

Retreat to the Marne and advance to the Aisne

Map 3

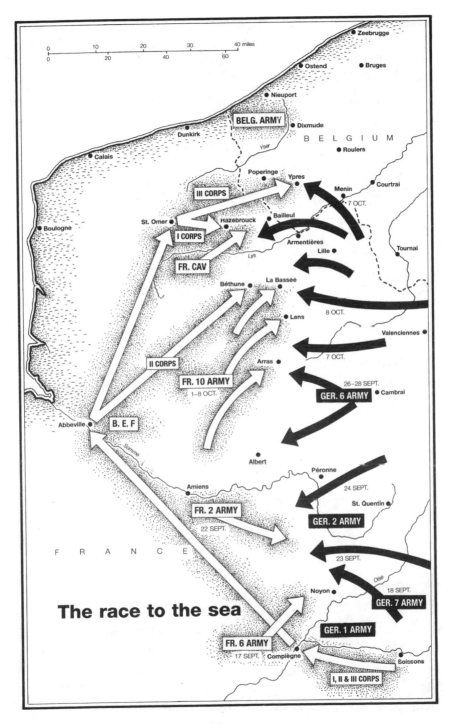

The race to the sea

Map 4

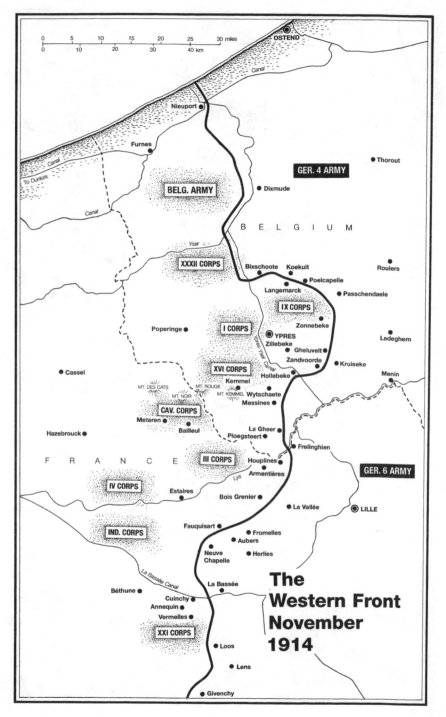

The
Western Front
November
1914

Map 5

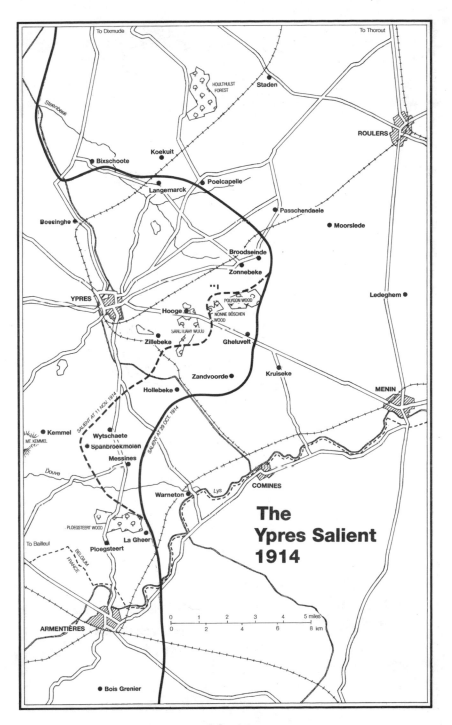

Map 6

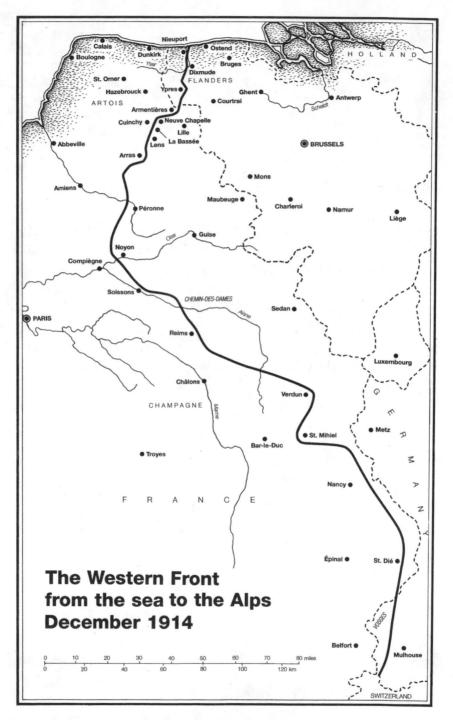

Nieuport
Calais
Boulogne
Dunkirk
Ostend
Bruges
HOLLAND
Yser
St. Omer
Dixmude
FLANDERS
Hazebrouck
Ypres
Ghent
Antwerp
ARTOIS
Courtrai
Scheldt
Armentières
Cuinchy
Neuve Chapelle
Lille
Lens
La Bassée
Abbeville
BRUSSELS
Arras
Mons
Amiens
Maubeuge
Charleroi
Namur
Péronne
Liège
Oise
Guise
Noyon
Compiègne
Soissons
CHEMIN-DES-DAMES
Sedan
Aisne
PARIS
Reims
Luxembourg
Châlons
Verdun
CHAMPAGNE
Marne
St. Mihiel
Metz
Bar-le-Duc
Troyes
G
E
R
Nancy
M
F   R   A   N   C   E
A
N
Épinal
St. Dié
Y
The Western Front
from the sea to the Alps
December 1914
VOSGES
Belfort
Mulhouse

0   10   20   30   40   50   60   70   80 miles
0   20   40   60   80   100   120 km

SWITZERLAND

Map 7

With the BEF, France, 1914

When the troops arrived, singing *'It's a long, long way to Tipperary'* at Maubeuge, after forced marches in the dark, it was one of the most tremendous moments I have ever experienced. *The most tremendous.* They swung up – or the tune swung them up – a very steep hill over the singing pavement and the French came out and threw them flowers, fruit and cigarettes, and they looked so young, so elastic and so invincibly cheerful, so unmixedly English, so tired and so fresh.

And the thought of these men swinging on into horror undreamt of – the whole German Army – came to me like the stab of a sword and I had to go and hide in a shop for the people not to see the tears running down my cheeks. I couldn't let my mind dwell on it for days without the gulp in my throat coming back.

I went to Mass this morning and in was nice to think that I was listening to the same words, with the same gestures that Henry V and his 'contemptible little army' heard before and after Agincourt, and I stood between a man in khaki and a French *poilu* and history flashed passed like a jewelled dream.

Lt. Maurice Baring, 25 October 1914

Introduction

This is the third book I have written about the First World War on the Western Front. The First World War or the Great War, or, as the French call it, the *Guerre de Quatorze*, has exercised a constant fascination for historians and the general public for decades and books on every aspect of the struggle continue to appear, ninety years after the conflict began. The reason for this enduring interest is quite simple. The Great War was a human tragedy on an epic scale, and large tragedies merit close study. If we can understand how that war started and why it endured beyond the point of reason we may reach some kind of understanding about ourselves and why the human race periodically indulges in such bloodbaths.

The Great War – which did not become the First World War until the Second World War began in 1939 – is also redolent with myths. My first Great War book examined the popular, public, British myth that the Great War generals were, without exception, a group of callous, incompetent cavalry officers who sent a whole generation of young men up the line to death, thereby causing a human catastrophe from which Britain has never recovered. This is not a view I share.

That book, *The Great War Generals on the Western Front*, was followed some years later by *Attrition: The Great War on the Western Front, 1916*, which examined the battles of Verdun and the Somme and speculated on why all the generals on the Western Front – German and French as well as British – abandoned their 1915 strategy of attempting a breakthrough in favour of a strategy based on pure attrition. My opinion here is that any doctrine based on attrition is insanity.

This present book, on the early months of the war – but also on the years preceding it – covers a shorter period and a smaller canvas and is somewhat short on myths – with the possible exception of the 'Angels of Mons'. This book is about the British Regular Army of 1914 – the British Expeditionary Force, the BEF or, as the survivors liked to call themselves, the 'Old Contemptibles', that well-trained, highly skilled, professional army which left Britain in August 1914. In the next four months the BEF was almost totally destroyed in the battles of Mons and Le Cateau, in the fighting on the rivers Marne and Aisne and, last of all, in the ferocious battle of 'First Ypres' in October and November 1914, where this little army of professional soldiers stood and fought and died, doggedly keeping their faces to the foe.

The survivors of the BEF took their curious nickname from the Kaiser's orders, allegedly issued at Aix-en-Chapelle on 19 August 1914: 'It is my Royal and Imperial command that you exterminate the treacherous English and march over General French's contemptible little army.'

There are some doubts as to whether Kaiser Wilhelm ever issued such an order. Other claims assert that even if he did issue such a command the German word means 'insignificant' rather than 'contemptible', that what he was actually referring to was a contemptibly *small* army – and small the BEF certainly was.

No matter. The name stuck and many 'Old Contemptibles' long outlived the Kaiser. Wilhelm II died in exile in 1940. The Old Contemptibles held their last parade at the garrison church of All Saints in Aldershot on Sunday, 4 August 1974, sixty years after the outbreak of the Great War, and took tea afterwards with Her Majesty Queen Elizabeth II. That done, they folded their standards and passed into history. There is no one left alive today who served in that famous little force.

The original intention was to concentrate on the exploits of that army in France but, as often happens, the course of research revealed that this narrow concentration would not do. The subject of the BEF in France had already been extensively covered and it gradually became evident that another equally interesting story underpinned the activities of the BEF in the field. This part of the story also examines the fundamental question as to what, after ninety-nine years of 'splendid isolation', the BEF was doing in France, taking part in this long-pending struggle between two continental powers.

That question clearly required an answer. The story told here therefore covers the BEF from before the moment of its conception at the end of the nineteenth century to its final demise in the water-logged trenches and misty woodlands around the Belgian town of Ypres in the autumn of 1914. Considerable attention is also paid to the actions and intentions of that wily officer Brigadier General Henry Wilson, Director of Military Operations at the War Office from 1910 to 1914, whose activities in the pre-war years deserve more attention than they usually receive.

The original BEF of 1914 was a very small army – it never amounted to more than seven divisions or around 160,000 men and the original force that sailed from Britain in early August numbered only half that – but it was a professional jewel among the much larger, conscript armies of continental Europe. It was also a very British army, composed of regular battalions drawn from the Guards and the Infantry of the Line, supported by famous cavalry regiments, still horsed at this time, and the dashing gun troops of the Royal Artillery, though it was later joined by one or two Territorial battalions and some splendid units of the Indian Army.

Essentially, though, in 1914 the BEF *was* the British Army, with all its faults and virtues. It was far too small and quite inadequately equipped for the job it was sent to do – but it did it anyway, soldiering on all the way from Mons to Ypres. Quality, not quantity, was the secret of its success, and that quality stemmed largely from the courage and skill of the officers and men, all professional soldiers, all fully determined to show the enemy – the Hun – what British soldiers could do. Telling what they did, and how they did it, and how and why the BEF was sent to France at all, is the purpose of this book.

1

The Continent Goes to War

1871–1914

The illusions with which the First World War began all stemmed from the belief that the war would be short.

James Joll, *Europe since 1870*, p. 193

This is the story of a small, professional British army and what became of it in the opening months of the First World War. In recent decades the story of the front-line soldiers in the Great War has tended to concentrate on the fate of the volunteers – the Territorials of 1915, the 'Pals Battalions' of Kitchener's armies in 1916 or those conscripts called to the Colours after 1916 who fell in such numbers on the Somme or at Arras, Passchendaele or Cambrai.

Less attention has been devoted to the soldiers of the old, pre-war, Regular Army, the one that held the line in 1914 until the Empire at large could muster and take the field. This hard duty has been the task of the Regular Army in all Britain's wars, but the army of 1914 – the British Expeditionary Force or BEF – was different from all other armies. This army was the product of a bygone Victorian age with all its faults and certainties. This was the first British army to take the field in Western Europe for almost a hundred years, an army that stood and fought and died at Mons and Le Cateau, on the Marne and the Aisne, and at First Ypres; a small, dauntless, *professional* army that deserves to be remembered.

It is necessary to put the actions of the BEF in the context of continental affairs. What were British soldiers doing on the continent of Europe in 1914, marching along the cobbled roads of northern France in August or dying in muddy Belgian trenches in December? What chain of events led the British nation into this terrible war after a century of disengagement from continental wars and disputes? To follow the events in Britain it is first necessary to discuss the drift to war in continental Europe.

There is a popular belief that the story of the First World War properly begins with the outcome of the Franco-Prussian War of 1870–71, and there is some truth in this conviction. The establishment of a united Germany under the first Kaiser after the Franco-Prussian War fatally altered the balance of power in Europe and led to the establishment of a large, well-populated and aggressive militaristic state in the very heart of the continent. This, coupled with French resentment over the provinces of Alsace and Lorraine, forcibly ceded to Germany in 1871, ignited the dangerous train of events that led to the general explosion in August 1914.

These events may account for the conflict between Germany and France, at least in part, but they do not explain why Britain found itself obliged to take part in this insanity. Britain had managed to stay out of direct military involvement on the continent since the Battle of Waterloo in 1815, and had been careful to avoid any firm, dangerous, continental commitment for the best part of a hundred years. Why had this policy been abandoned?

Again, popular belief holds that the British became involved in August 1914 because Germany had violated the neutrality of Belgium, a neutrality guaranteed by all the powers, including Britain and Prussia, in 1839. There is truth in this belief also but Britain's involvement in the Great War has deeper roots and less noble motives and began long before the German Army crossed the Belgian frontier in August 1914.

One of the great and most widespread delusions at the start of the First World War was that this new conflict would be short. In the UK it was widely believed that the British Army, less a few casualties, would be 'home by Christmas' or, as the Kaiser told the departing German regiments, 'You will be home before the leaves fall.'

Neither of these hopeful statements proved correct. In just four years the Great War killed 9 million soldiers and destroyed empires; slaughter and destruction on such a scale should have been foreseen before the armies were mobilized, for European industrialization and population growth – except in France – had strengthened the sinews of war and greatly increased the supply of cannon fodder in the years since 1871. Given these assets, the war was bound to be prolonged.

Knowing why the war began and putting the motives and actions of the various nations in context will help to explain why this war could not be stopped when it rapidly outran all previous projections of cost and loss. Viewed objectively, and with the precious benefit of hindsight, the war should have been terminated by the end of 1915, when the destruction of the first BEF and the countless losses to French and German soldiers on the frontiers, on the Marne and Aisne, at First Ypres, Second Ypres, Neuve Chapelle, Aubers Ridge, Festubert, Vimy and the Chemin des Dames – not to mention the slaughter on the Eastern Front – had already put 2 million young men in early graves; slaughter on this scale had never been anticipated and the nations' leaders might have recoiled from such a bloodbath.

Yet nothing happened. The war continued in spite of all the evidence that victory on the battlefield could only be achieved, if at all, at far too high a price. The inevitability of further killing was not denied but peace could not be contemplated, and so the war continued. This attitude – this political myopia – needs to be explained, and any explanation must begin with the politics of Europe *before* 1871.

Since the Congress of Vienna in 1815, a precarious European peace had been maintained by a 'balance of power' between the continental nations. There were local wars in plenty – in Spain and Italy, between France and Austria, between Prussia and Denmark, between Prussia and Austria, between Russia and an allied France and Britain in the Crimea – but the latter part of the nineteenth century witnessed no major conflagration on a Napoleonic scale, partly because no aggressive dictator had yet arisen, mostly because no one nation was able to overawe an alliance of the rest; power was defused and peace, albeit fragile, reigned. There was, however, a growing power in Europe, one aiming at a united Germany and so destabilizing this peace – Prussia.

The north German states – the Napoleonic Confederation of the Rhine and Prussia, amounting to some thirty-nine states in 1815 – began to unite through trade, most notably in the Prussian-dominated *Zollverein* or Customs Union, which came into being in January 1834 and comprised eighteen of the German states, some 23 million people.

This commercial union – a distant ancestor of the EEC – began to erode the ancient foundations of the Rhine Confederation and the remains of any former regal power. During the nineteenth century most of the European monarchs were related; many were descendants of Queen Victoria – the grandmother of Europe – and their domains were frequently linked. The King of England, for example, remained King of Hanover until 1837, when the accession of Queen Victoria broke that connection, and the King of Denmark was Duke of Holstein until as late as 1864.

There are strong echoes of Ruritania, Anthony Hope's fictional kingdom in nineteenth-century Europe.[1] This was a continent of kings and crown princes, archdukes and electors and serene highnesses, clinging on grimly to their traditional powers and influence as the world changed about them and new-fangled notions like liberalism, socialism, communism and constitutional democracy began to shake the ground around their thrones.

The dynamic for political change was civil unrest, industrial expansion – and war. The main power using war for political ends was Prussia, where the man most directly responsible was the Chancellor, Otto von Bismarck, a man who saw force, not argument, as the most useful catalyst of change.

The first application of this Prussian process came in 1864 with the violent settlement of the Schleswig-Holstein question. Schleswig and Holstein were two duchies on the edge of the Baltic and had been possessions of the kings of Denmark since the fif-teenth century. By the 1850s, however, the population of Schleswig was half German and the population of Holstein almost wholly German – and Holstein had been a member of that Napoleonic construct, the Confederation of the Rhine.

Irredentism – the nineteenth-century notion of reclaiming for-merly held land or that people of the same nation or race should live under national rule – made the Schleswig-Holstein question a hot political issue. The Danish king would not give up these valu-able duchies, so in February 1864 Prussian troops crossed the River Eider and occupied Schleswig. In October of that year, unable to get any help from the other European powers, Denmark capitulated and the two duchies were transferred to the joint own-ership of Austria and Prussia. There was, however, a long-term strategic aim here. The seizure of Holstein gave Prussia the terri-tory needed to construct the Kiel Canal, which enabled German warships to pass quickly and safely between German naval bases in the Baltic and the North Sea.

Prussia then turned on Austria. The intention was to gain full possession of the Schleswig-Holstein duchies – and dominate the other states of Germany. Bismarck cleared the ground for this step in 1865 by visiting the French Emperor, Napoleon III, and assuring him that while war was inevitable between Austria and Prussia, there was no threat to France. In fact, Bismarck's sole reason for meeting Napoleon was to prevent a Franco-Austrian alliance while Austria was crushed and so to clear the way for the subsequent step, an attack on France.

With the danger of a Franco-Austrian alliance averted, Bismarck played up differences with Austria over the Danish duchies, and in June 1866 the two countries went to war, Prussia calling on Austria's allies, the east German states of Saxony, Hanover and Hesse-Cassel, to demobilize or face invasion. These three states were occupied by Prussian troops in as many days, and the Austrian-Saxon army was crushed at Sadowa on 3 July – just two weeks after the declaration of war. Once again, Prussian violence had paid a rapid dividend.

Sadowa ended the Confederation of the Rhine and replaced it with a North German Federation dominated by Prussia. In effect, Prussia had now annexed Schleswig-Holstein, Hanover, Hesse, Frankfurt and Nassau. The next step was to take over the south German states, Bavaria, Wurtenburg, Baden and Hesse-Darmstadt. This takeover plan excluded Austria, the most populous German state, partly because Prussia wanted no rivals to her new-found dominant status, mainly because the Austro-Hungarian Empire contained a preponderance of Slavs. The Prussians were very intent on excluding non-Germans from their new creation; even in the 1860s racism was a factor in German politics.

The architect of this grand design was Bismarck and the catalyst for his next step, the takeover of the southern German states and their incorporation into a united Germany – the German Empire of the first Kaiser – was the Franco-Prussian War of 1870–71. This war was engineered entirely by Bismarck, notably by redrafting the notorious 'Ems Telegram', a missive from Napoleon III, and turning it from a conciliatory message into a cause for war.

War between Prussia and France began on 19 July 1870 and was over by 28 January 1871. Defeat cost France a colossal sum in reparations and the provinces of Alsace and Lorraine – and ended the reign of Napoleon III. From now on France would be a republic – the Third Republic – fired with the desire for *revanche* – revenge – against Prussia and a determination to reclaim these stolen provinces from the grasp of a united Germany – the southern German kingdoms and duchies now having also joined the Kaiser's Empire.

These events and their outcome, three major wars in six years propelling Prussia to mastery of a united Germany containing over 60 million people, were watched with alarm by the other nations of Europe. If force was to be the arbiter of European affairs, how could Germany be resisted? The obvious answer was the old one; a series of international treaties binding the smaller nations together to resist such aggression if or when it came.

In fact, fears of further German expansion were at first groundless. Bismarck had no wish to extend the territorial grasp of the German Empire in Europe or any interest in the acquisition of colonies overseas. After 1871 he devoted his life to consolidating those territories already gained and making Germany a great power through expansion of technical education and a move towards industrialization. In this he was extremely successful, but Bismarck also found it necessary to protect his new creation with a network of alliances, knowing that, sooner or later, the French would try to retake Alsace and Lorraine.

In 1872 Bismarck linked Germany with Austria-Hungary and Russia in the 'League of the Three Emperors' – the *Dreikaiserbund*. This proved a fragile alliance. Austria-Hungary and Russia were soon in dispute over the Balkans, where the Austrians hoped for territorial gains when the Ottoman Empire finally collapsed, while Russia saw itself as the protector of the Balkan Slavs, most notably the Serbs. Therefore, in 1879, Bismarck set up another alliance – the Dual Alliance – with Austria-Hungary. In 1882 Italy joined to form the Triple Alliance, which envisaged Russia as a potential enemy. However, to keep his options open, in 1887 Bismarck also signed a 'Reinsurance Treaty' with Russia. By the time he was forced out of office by Wilhelm II in 1890, Bismarck believed that he had constructed a firm basis for German security. This security was not to last. The other European leaders had eventually recognized Bismarck as a stabilizing force; now he had gone, who knew what might happen?

The third Hohenzollern Kaiser, Wilhelm II, a grandson of Queen Victoria, came to the Imperial throne in July 1888, aged twenty-nine. Having dismissed Bismarck, the Kaiser revoked the Reinsurance Treaty with Russia and proceeded to upset the fragile stability of Europe with a series of sabre-rattling declarations. The surrounding nations thereupon took appropriate steps to protect themselves against potential aggression, and in 1891 France formed an alliance with Tsarist Russia. This led to the Franco-Russian Pact of 1893, in which each nation promised to aid the other if attacked. The pact stated quite openly that the potential aggressor was Imperial Germany.

The problem for the smaller nations of Europe, and even for a half-European, half-Asian power like Russia, was not simply that the Kaiser was unpredictable. Imperial Germany also had a vast army and industrial muscle. Germany was now the leading industrial nation in Europe, and some sectors of industry, most notably Krupp of Essen, were devoting themselves to the manufacture of modern weapons for an army that could muster, at any one time, around half a million men. This already vast force could be rapidly expanded by the recall of trained reservists, and could have no other purpose but to overawe neighbouring states. In terms of location, population, industrial capacity and military strength, Germany was a force that had to be reckoned with, for if the German Emperor opted for territorial conquest he had the means to carry it out. Given the right catalyst, European peace might easily collapse into war.

The catalyst was Kaiser Wilhelm II himself. From the moment of his accession his behaviour increased the strains in Europe and set the continent on the road to war. His arrogance, his pleasure in military power, his suspicion of France, his contempt for Russia, his jealousy of Britain – especially the Royal Navy and his detested uncle, Edward VII – his threats, his interference in the affairs of other nations, combined to create a chronic instability in Europe. To give just one example of the Kaiser's behaviour, consider the following rant to his host, Leopold, King of the Belgians, during a visit to Brussels in 1904: 'I told him I could not be played with. In the case of a European war, whoever was not for me was against me. As a soldier I belonged to the school of Frederick the Great, to the school of Napoleon. As the Seven Years War began with the invasion of Saxony, and the latter had always, with lightning speed, forestalled his enemies, so should I, in the event of Belgium not being on my side, be actuated by strategical considerations only.'

Psychiatrists allege that arrogant behaviour often stems from a sense of inferiority. The Kaiser's actions seem to have been fuelled by a belief that Germany had been hard done by, that her obvious worth had not been fully appreciated by the other nations of

Europe. 'German *kultur* in German eyes was the heir of Greece and Rome and they themselves were the best educated and most cultivated of modern peoples, yet foreigners in their appreciation of this fact fell curiously short of perfect understanding,' wrote Barbara Tuchman.[2] 'Paris remained Europe's centre of art, pleasure and fashion, London of Society, Rome of antiquity and Italy the lure of travellers seeking sun and beauty.'

Nor was this all. Bismarck's desire to build the German empire from within had left Germany out of the late-nineteenth-century 'Scramble for Africa' and the subsequent acquisition of overseas colonies – it lacked what Wilhelm's Chancellor, Prince von Bulow, came to call 'a place in the sun'. The Germans were not content with economic dominance of Europe and the long-term benefits in political terms that must accrue to their growing industrial base. They wanted recognition of their worth *as a people*. They forgot that other nations also had interests that they would not willingly cede to German pressure or the Kaiser's ambitions.

The Kaiser inherited the Alsace-Lorraine problem along with his throne but he further upset France in 1905 by his interference at Tangier in Morocco, and did it again with the 'Agadir Incident' – again in Morocco – in July 1911, when the German gunboat *Panther* was dispatched to this Moroccan port in an attempt to intervene in French affairs. The British – following the *Entente Cordiale* of 1904 – supported France over the Tangier and Agadir incidents – by now the British also had long-standing problems with the Kaiser.

At the time the Kaiser's actions and attitudes could not be ignored or treated with the amused contempt they might now seem to deserve. Even those who regarded Kaiser Wilhelm as an arrogant blowhard had to face the fact that Germany was the major military and industrial power in Europe and, on the evidence of the recent past, one more than willing to employ force to get what it wanted. From 1900, the result was an escalating, European-wide arms race, each nation striving to protect itself from a situation it had played some part in creating – though the major player in this dangerous game was the Kaiser.

Smaller countries such as France clearly needed allies. In the last decades of the nineteenth century the populations of most European countries soared – Germany's rose by 10 per cent to 66 million – but for some reason, and in spite of state subsidies for mothers of large families, the population of France failed to expand; by 1914 it stood at only 37 million. Demographics alone dictated a bilateral defence treaty with another power, but the Franco-Russian Pact of 1891, which expanded to a full alliance in 1894, was regarded by the Kaiser as 'encirclement', a deliberate threat to the security of Germany and an excuse for further sabre-rattling.

The Imperial General Staff agreed with the Kaiser. Since 1871 they had been convinced that the French would one day attempt to take back Alsace and Lorraine. Now it appeared likely that when the French made their attempt their Russian allies would attack from the east. So the prospect of war grew – and tension increased in Britain from 1911 when the Germans began to widen and deepen the Kiel Canal, so threatening Britain's eastern coast and communications with the continent.

British attempts to stop an escalation in warship construction by mutual agreement were rejected by the Germans in 1912, so the British also began to modernize their fleet and look for allies. They came to an agreement with France whereby the French took charge of naval security in the Mediterranean and the British Navy guaranteed the security of the French Channel ports and the Channel entrance from the North Sea. The Kaiser, inevitably, saw this agreement as another threat to Germany.

There is some basis for this belief; nations are not altruistic and Britain's wariness about Germany's long-term ambitions provided a far stronger motive than any desire to help the French. Britain could never let a potentially hostile power such as Germany gain possession of ports on the Channel coast, close to her shores. Britain's interest in Belgian neutrality had the same strategic roots – the Germans must not gain possession of the Belgian ports.

In fact, Belgian neutrality was already under threat. The Imperial German Staff were preparing a war plan to combat the perceived problems of encirclement – war on two fronts – caused by the Franco-Russian alliance. This plan had been prepared by Count Alfred von Schlieffen, Chief of the German Imperial Staff from 1891 to 1906. Von Schlieffen was sure that Germany would eventually have to fight a war in the west against France and another in the east against Russia; it would therefore be caught in a vice and could not survive.

Von Schlieffen's answer to this problem was a first-strike plan – the Schlieffen Plan – based on the geographical fact that, thanks to a central position in Europe and her modern railway network, Germany possessed the strategic benefit known in military circles as the 'advantage of interior lines' – the ability to shift forces rapidly from one front to another. Further strategic advantages lay in the sheer size of Russia, the inefficiency of the Russian Army and the inadequacies of Russia's railway system. Russian mobilization must inevitably take time and it would be weeks – von Schlieffen thought six weeks – before the Russian armies could endanger the frontiers of the Reich. In that time span he saw an opportunity – and two snags.

It would be possible, von Schlieffen argued, for Germany to fall on France in great force and defeat her *before* the vast but obsolescent Russian Army could move. Then the full might of the German Army could be rushed east by rail to win a second victory over the Slavic hordes. Clearly, this dual campaign would not be easy but, given the size of the German Army and the professional skill of the Imperial Staff, it was feasible. The plan took years to develop but it stood up to critical examination and the facilities needed to make it work – the roads, the railways, the sidings – and, above all, the logistical aids and marching qualities of German soldiers – were all developed during this time.

The Schlieffen Plan required that while some German forces repelled any French invasion from the west into Alsace-Lorraine and across the Rhine, and opposed any Russian build-up in the east, the bulk of the German Army – consisting in fact of five armies – should be massed in the west, on the right wing, and sweep into France from the north-east – through Luxembourg and

Belgium. Once across the Franco-Belgian frontier, these armies would move west of Paris and swing to the east, south of the city, isolating the French capital and catching the French forces in the rear, hustling them against the fixed defences along the Franco-German border. This strategy would require great speed and mobility – and the violation of Belgian neutrality.

The first snag in the Schlieffen Plan was that speed and mobility were not adequately available in the horse-powered armies of 1914. The second was that invading Belgium would probably bring Great Britain and her empire into the war. This was something the Germans were fully aware of and most anxious to avoid, but a move through Belgium was the only way to bypass the fixed French defences on their common frontier and gain the necessary time.

The Schlieffen Plan passed through various drafts but was finally adopted in 1905. The French also had a plan, Plan XVII, which will be discussed later, but understanding the Schlieffen Plan is crucial, for it escalated progress towards war – and ensured British involvement. The crucial element in the plan was time, and there was not enough of it. Germany must mobilize *quickly* and strike *first* in order to defeat France completely in just six weeks, before the Russian armies could take the field. This time factor introduced a political dimension, for if Russia or France mobilized or started to mobilize Germany must declare war – waiting for arbitration or intervention from any quarter, say Britain or the USA, would eat into that precious, limited amount of time. Mobilization, in short, was not a step towards war or a precautionary gesture – in 1914 mobilization *was* war.

The broad details of the Schlieffen Plan were soon known abroad, and the details came out in 1909 when von Schlieffen, now retired, published an article in the *Deutsche Revue* magazine, criticizing his successor, General Helmuth von Moltke, the new Chief of the Imperial General Staff, for reducing the forces committed to the right wing. Von Schlieffen died in 1912; his last words were, allegedly, 'Remember, keep the right wing strong.'

Von Moltke did not heed this advice. He felt that Germany

could execute the Schlieffen Plan – given a few amendments – declaring in 1912, when army ranks were full and work on the Kiel Canal was almost complete, that 'War is inevitable, and the sooner the better.' Von Moltke then became worried that the eastern frontier was not fully secure. Therefore, while it is hardly fair to say that he weakened the right wing, it is true to say that he did not increase the forces destined to invade Belgium and France, preferring to devote more divisions to the east. Essentially, however, the Schlieffen Plan, Germany's once-and-for-all bid to win the war in six weeks and prevent the disaster of a conflict on two fronts, was still in place in August 1914.

So much for Germany. What of the Kaiser's principal European ally, the Austro-Hungarian Empire? The empire, a union resulting from the *Ausgleich* (Compromise) of 1867, when Hungary broke away and became a separate kingdom under the imperial crown, was already starting to crumble, though the major splits had yet to appear. Austria-Hungary in 1914 was that post-1920 ideal, the multiracial state, one where a great number of races lived in apparent harmony. The roots of internal conflict for the Austro-Hungarians lay in the Balkans, most notably in Serbia.

Serbia was an independent Balkan state, outside Austro-Hungarian hegemony, but a large number of ethnic Serbs lived in the newly annexed provinces of Bosnia and Herzegovina, which Austria-Hungary had taken over in 1908. These 'ethnic Serbs' wished to join these provinces with Serbia to create a 'Greater Serbia', and were pressing their case with demonstrations and acts of terrorism inside Austria-Hungary. A further complication was that Tsarist Russia, which regarded itself as the protector of Slav interests, had offered guarantees of support to Serbia in the event of Austro-Hungarian intervention. Austria-Hungary, on the other hand, had no intention of relinquishing the annexed territories – the Empire could not survive if parts of it were allowed to break away at will.

This, in broad outline, is the European powder keg of 1914. Examine the situation of all the major powers and the same scenario prevails – rising tensions and problems increased rather than reduced by an interlocking series of alliances which, if invoked, must surely escalate any local issue into a major European war. All it needed was a spark to touch off the powder.

That spark was provided on 28 June 1914, when a Serbian student, Gavrilo Princep, shot the Archduke Franz Ferdinand, the Austro-Hungarian heir, during a state visit to Sarajevo, the capital of Bosnia. From the moment the archduke and his wife fell dead, that long-established interlocking network of continental alliances was duly invoked and Europe began its rapid descent into war.

If Austria-Hungary had simply invaded Serbia the day after the assassination, when the shock waves from these murders were still reverberating around the chancelleries and palaces of Europe and there was a great deal of sympathy for the Austrian position, it is arguable at least that the conflict would never have spread outside the Balkans. However, weeks were to pass before any military action was taken, time for each side to muster their allies and broaden the base of the war but not, apparently, to consider exactly what sort of war it might be – a 'total war' – or to find ways to prevent it.

No one, least of all the Kaiser, really wanted war. Now that prospect was starkly before them, the impetus to war was spurred by a general feeling that a brief European war might clear the air, resolve issues and offer a fresh start. Nor was the prospect of war unwelcome to the electorates. In Berlin and Paris, Moscow and Vienna, even in London, crowds singing patriotic tunes took to the streets, cheering the arrival of a long-expected event, glad that the waiting was over.

Immediately after the assassination, Austria-Hungary demanded that Serbia hunt down and punish the assassins. This was understandable but the demands were made in a language that no independent nation could accept – which was their entire purpose. Austria-Hungary was set on war and needed a Serbian rejection of these demands in order to justify it.

Sensing this objective, the Serb government in Belgrade appealed to the Tsar for support and Russia duly warned Vienna that she would protect Serbia's interests if Austria's demands went too far. This led, inevitably, to the next step, for Austria duly called on her German ally for support. On 5 July 1914, Germany assured Austria-Hungary of her 'faithful support', the so-called 'blank cheque' of military assistance if Austria found herself drawn into war with Russia.

This assurance promptly escalated the tension. On 23 July Austria-Hungary issued an ultimatum to Serbia, demanding that the Serb authorities arrest or proscribe any individual or local organization demanding independence for the Austrian Serbs. This demand included a requirement that Serbia admit Austrian policemen to supervise the local investigation into the archduke's assassination. Even to Kaiser Wilhelm, who was then on holiday, cruising off Norway on the imperial yacht *Hohenzollern*, the Serbian reply was so conciliatory that it 'dissipated any cause for war'. The Kaiser therefore continued his cruise, clearly believing that any danger of conflict had passed. This belief proved false. The Austrians rejected the Serb response on 26 July and two days later declared war on Serbia. The following day Austrian ships were sailing down the Danube to shell Belgrade – and another step had been taken towards a general European war.

On 28 July Russia mobilized her own forces on the Austrian frontier, at that time her southern border. This order alarmed the German general staff; their entire strategy was posited on the requirement that Russia would still be mobilizing her forces while France was crushed. If the Schlieffen Plan were to be implemented, the Russians must not be given time to mobilize ahead of Germany.

Military escalation therefore continued. Austria promptly mobilized her own forces along the Russian frontier and on 31 July both Russia and Austria ordered total mobilization. Germany then entered the fray, the Imperial General Staff demanding that Russia demobilize within twelve hours. This ultimatum was ignored, so on 1 August Germany ordered a general mobilization. Their intention was to declare war on Russia and France and then implement the Schlieffen Plan – the basis of their entire strategy.

At this crucial juncture the Kaiser – or the Supreme War Lord, as he now became – hesitated. He had rushed back to Berlin, knowing that if Germany declared war on Russia, France would immediately strike at Germany's western frontiers and implement their war plan, Plan XVII. The French plan was well known in German military circles and required the bulk of the French Army to advance across the German frontier with great force and retake Alsace and Lorraine before crossing the Rhine and invading the Reich. Germany would immediately be faced with a war on two fronts, the ultimate result of 'encirclement', and the Kaiser was by no means sure that the outcome of these two plans – Schlieffen's and Plan XVII – would be favourable to Germany. Sabre-rattling was one thing, all-out war quite another – and war on two fronts a recipe for disaster.

There was, perhaps, one way of avoiding a two-front war. The German ambassador in London had already informed the Kaiser that the British Foreign Secretary, Sir Edward Grey, was offering to mediate between Austria-Hungary and Russia and keep France out of the war . . . or at least, so the ambassador alleged. The Kaiser grasped at this straw, and more precious hours were wasted while Berlin attempted to find out what Sir Edward was actually proposing.

Kaiser Wilhelm was also tinkering with the Schlieffen Plan. Desperate to limit the impending conflict, he told von Moltke that if the British could keep France out of the fighting, Germany could turn all her might against Russia. 'All we have to do,' claimed the Kaiser, 'is march the whole of our forces against Russia.' Von Moltke flatly rejected this proposal. 'A plan prepared and rehearsed over many years cannot be dismantled in a few hours. If we do as Your Majesty proposes we will send nothing more than an armed mob against Russia.'

Historians are divided as to the truth of this assertion, but military men are convinced that von Moltke was right and the sheer scale of Germany's military preparations supports that belief.

'On August 6', writes Basil Liddell Hart, 'the great deployment began; 550 trains a day crossed the Rhine bridges and by the 12th the seven German armies (totalling 1,500,000 men) were ready to advance. Over the Hohenzollern bridge in Cologne, a train passed every ten minutes during the first fortnight of war.'[3]

Perhaps Germany could have used that first-rate railway network to move her armies east, but that would have left her western frontier open to the temptations of Plan XVII, an opportunity the French could not have resisted. Besides, the Schlieffen Plan dictated that France was the main enemy and must be defeated first. Therefore the railway junctions in Luxembourg must be seized within hours of a declaration of war. Von Moltke pleaded with the Kaiser for permission to proceed that far, knowing that once the move towards France began it could not be halted.

The Kaiser refused. Wilhelm was not entirely a fool and he was much more widely travelled than his military advisers. They saw this conflict as a war on the frontiers, a chance to crush French and Russian aggression; the Kaiser was worried that the war might quickly consume the entire continent. He had, albeit belatedly, begun to grasp where the conflict was heading and what any failure in the Schlieffen Plan might mean for the Hohenzollern dynasty. However well prepared and planned and rehearsed, the Schlieffen Plan was, in fact, a gamble. It placed Germany's fortune and future on the outcome of one six-week campaign. If that campaign failed, then Germany would face the kind of war that, as the Plan asserted, it would certainly lose. Faced with this uncertain prospect, it is hardly surprising that the Kaiser hesitated.

Another telegram from the German ambassador in London then revealed exactly what the British Foreign Secretary was proposing. Sir Edward was offering to keep France neutral if Germany promised not to go to war with *either France or Russia*. The aim was to give Sir Edward time to seek a solution to the conflict between Austria and Serbia and extinguish this spreading conflagration at source.

Once again the issue was a matter of time. Grey was well meaning but it was already too late for outside mediation. The Russians were mobilizing and had refused to stop; for the Schlieffen Plan to succeed the German armies must move – at once. The Kaiser read the British telegram several times and then handed it to von Moltke. 'Now you can do what you like,' he said, and left the room. As the door closed behind him, Helmuth von Moltke picked up the telephone and started the First World War.

2

The British Go to War

1898–1914

*Cool bravery, chivalry, discipline . . . these were the qualities
which the British possessed at Waterloo and on the Somme, and
at almost every engagement in between. It must not be forgotten
that in this quixotic, eccentric and peculiar army, these qualities
existed to a very high degree.*
> Byron Farwell, *Mr Kipling's Army*, 1981, pp. 243–4

What were the reasons that impelled the British government to
send an Expeditionary Force to France in 1914, after ninety-nine
years of deliberate disengagement? This part of the story begins,
curiously enough, in the swamps of the Sudan, sixteen years
before the BEF went to France.

On 4 September 1898, two days after his victory over the Dervishes at Omdurman, General Sir Horatio Herbert Kitchener
received some disturbing news. A Dervish gunboat had docked at
Khartoum and the crew were anxious to report a recent encounter to the new ruler of the Sudan. Some days previously, European
troops occupying the fort at Fashoda on the upper Nile had
engaged them with rifle fire. General Kitchener was immediately
concerned. There were no British troops south of Khartoum, so
these troops could only be from Captain Marchand's Trans-Africa
Expedition – and that was especially disturbing, for Captain Jean-
Baptiste Marchand was French.

Apart from crushing the Dervishes and ending the Sudanese slave trade, the British conquest of the Sudan was part of a grand imperial design. The strategic aim was to create a swathe of British-controlled territory across Africa, from Cairo to the Cape. Only physical difficulties – the distance, the climate, the terrain and hostile tribes – now stood in the way of this strategy, unless the French succeeded in *their* grand design – creating a block of French-controlled territory, west to east across Africa, so barring Britain's progress to the south. Marchand's intrusion into a territory Britain regarded as her own was therefore not to be borne. Kitchener embarked a battalion of Sudanese infantry and a battery of artillery in two gunboats and sailed upstream to confront the French.

At Fashoda, Kitchener found Marchand's expedition firmly entrenched under the French flag, anticipating another Dervish attack but equally willing to fight the British. The size of Kitchener's force made the outcome of such resistance obvious, but Marchand declared that he had no intention of hauling down the French flag and intended to proceed with the annexation of the upper Nile. Should Kitchener use force to confound this aim, the effect on Anglo-French relations would be disastrous – a fact of which both officers were well aware. Kitchener delivered a formal protest at this French military presence on the Nile and declared that he now intended to hoist the Egyptian flag over what had always been Egyptian territory. That done, the two officers and their staffs sat down to an enjoyable lunch.

When the news of this meeting at Fashoda reached Paris in October 1898, there was public outrage. Once again, '*l'Albion perfide*' had come between France and her fair share of glory and territorial conquest. While the deputies debated what to do, the press seethed. '*Le duel sans merci est commencé*,' declared *La Patrie*, and other papers adopted a similar tone. 'France's honour is at stake,' declared *Le Figaro*; 'there could be no surrender and something must be done'.[1]

Something was done. Channel-based ships of the French fleet sailed for the Mediterranean. The French Army was put on a war footing and prepared to call up reservists. In public and political circles all the old familiar, Anglo-French animosities, dating back to the time of Napoleon or the Hundred Years War, were revived.

Nor were the British any less pacific. The French had been caught red handed attempting to sneak across the Nile, annex a territory under British protection and thwart a cherished imperial strategy. There was no room for negotiation on this issue. 'The elements of compromise do not exist,' stated *The Times*;[2] the French must withdraw forthwith. Where these hostile rumblings might have led is hard to say. War was certainly not impossible over this confrontation at Fashoda, but two factors combined to prevent it.

The first obstacle was the state of French society and the French Army in 1898, which can best be described as chaotic. For the last three years France's military and political elite had been locked in a public dispute over *'L'Affaire'* – the debate as to whether a Jewish staff officer, Captain Alfred Dreyfus, had or had not been passing military secrets to Germany, a crime for which Dreyfus had already been dismissed from the service and sentenced to a lifetime's imprisonment on Devil's Island. Following Zola's famous rebuttal – *J'Accuse* – and the investigation that followed, the Dreyfus Affair was about to reach a conclusion – the Court de Cassation called to review the Dreyfus verdict met on the day Marchand was ordered to withdraw from Fashoda,[3] but the effect of the affair was to split France in two, politically and socially.

At such a time a quarrel with Britain might have seemed useful, a good way of uniting the nation, so creating a situation in which internal political disputes could be put aside and the Dreyfus Affair forgotten. The French government wisely chose to ignore this option. France was in no state to engage in a major war that the British were clearly quite willing to fight – not with the army divided and imperial Germany on the eastern frontier.

Besides, there was no real *casus belli*. Kitchener handled the meeting with great courtesy, hoisting the Egyptian flag rather than the British one, and no shots had been exchanged. The French had no reason to be offended unless they chose to take offence: their national honour had not been impugned; their flag had not been insulted.

The subsequent discussions between Kitchener and Marchand are of no great relevance to the story of the British Expeditionary Force of 1914. The outcome of their talks at Fashoda was that the future of the upper Nile should be settled between their respective governments, not by an exchange of fire. What is relevant to our story is this: had Kitchener not handled the 'Fashoda Incident' with tact and charm – two qualities not normally attributed to this dour soldier – war between France and Britain might have followed. The *Entente Cordiale* would never have been signed in 1904 and the long process that created an Anglo-French alliance in the First World War would not have begun. Fashoda, in short, was a turning point. It marked the end of a centuries-old mutual animosity and a new beginning in Franco-British affairs; the road to Mons began at Fashoda.

The next step on the journey began in October 1899, with the outbreak of the second Boer War – the South African War. In this struggle Britain quickly found herself at odds with the rest of Europe, which was solidly in support of the Boers. This support was not merely vocal; the Boer artillery came from Krupp and Creusot, and many of the Boer gunners were French or German. Nor did the war go well; it began with a series of defeats, notably during Black Week, between 10 and 15 December 1899, which delighted Britain's opponents in Europe. 'The war exposed Britain to humiliation in the eyes of her European rivals, especially France and Germany,' writes Thomas Pakenham,[4] and Barbara Tuchman records that 'With Black Week went the last time Britons felt themselves unquestionably masters of the earth.'[5]

There can be no doubt that the South African War dented the confidence of the British military and political class. Coupled with these military worries, there were doubts about the handling of Britain's foreign policy. Her nineteenth-century 'splendid isolation'[6] was beginning to look rather less splendid by the end of the South African War. As Lord Salisbury's grip on foreign affairs slackened, his successor at the Foreign Office, Lord Lansdowne, 'began a quest for alliances and understandings with other powers to give Britain useful allies'.[7]

Another authority, John Keiger, endorses this view: 'The traumatic experience of the Boer War was a major cause of Britain's changed attitude towards France. It showed up a number of British military weaknesses and it underlined her diplomatic isolation. On the diplomatic front the popularity of "Splendid Isolation" was anyway on the wane and Britain began to look towards the Continent for support. British public opinion was growing increasingly hostile to an arrangement with Germany whose *Weltpolitik* was beginning to threaten Britain in the colonies and, by the expansion of the German Navy, at sea.'[8]

Keiger's comment introduces the third element into this evolving situation; apart from Britain's strategic concerns, the growing amity with France was matched by a decline in British relations with Imperial Germany. The underlying cause of this decline was economic, a growing and massive increase in German industrial power at a time when Britain's nineteenth-century industrial lead was declining in the face of competition from the United States – and Germany.

Paul M. Kennedy confirms this point: 'Historians grappling with the overall alteration in Anglo-German relations have before anything else to confront the fact that whereas Britain produced over twice as much steel as Germany at the start of this period it produced less than half at the end of it', adding that 'steel output is a very selective criterion but not a totally unreasonable one in an age of Dreadnoughts, field cannon and locomotives'.[9]

An economically powerful nation could certainly compete for markets with the United Kingdom but there was more to Anglo-German rivalries than trade. The creation of the German empire by Bismarck in 1871 had radically altered the balance of power in Europe. While Bismarck was in power his energies were concentrated on developing German industrial power and protecting his creation by a series of alliances – including, in 1889, the offer of an alliance with Britain. According to Kennedy, 'Bismarck's proposal for an open Anglo-German Alliance, to last for a fixed number of years and be directed ostensibly against France, was turned down, politely but firmly, by the British Prime Minister.'[10]

Matters changed radically in 1890 when Wilhelm II dismissed Bismarck from office. From that time on German foreign policy took an erratic course in which periodic attempts to reach an alliance with Britain were interspersed with actions calculated to annoy and alarm her government and people.

Wilhelm II could have been a potent source of Anglo-German amity; he was Queen Victoria's grandson, the nephew of Edward VII, a British Field Marshal, Colonel of the Royal Dragoons and an Admiral of the Fleet. Had he so wished, the Kaiser could have been a revered member of the British Establishment. Indeed, from time to time he did so wish; his relationship with Britain was one of love and hate, admiration and envy, imitation and rejection.

This volatility caused alarm, for the Kaiser was also the ruler of a large European country, which possessed a powerful industrialized economy, a very large army and a network of political and military leaders who intended to deploy that power in the not too distant future. These facts alone obliged all Germany's neighbours to be wary but posed little immediate threat to Britain; that threat took shape with the German Naval Law of 1900.

This was not the first sign of conflict. In 1896 the Kaiser sent what became known as the 'Kruger Telegram' to Paul Kruger, the president of the Transvaal, congratulating him on repelling the recent Jameson Raid and assuring the Boers of German support. When the South African War broke out in 1899, Germany again supported the Boer republics – as indeed did many other European nations – but the Kaiser's fatal mistake, certainly in the eyes of the British, was the German Naval Law of 1900.

More than any other single action, more than all the Kaiser's provocations in Europe over the last twelve years, the German Naval Law of 1900 brought Great Britain out of her century-old isolation from European affairs. 'It convinced Britain that she needed friends,' wrote Barbara Tuchman. 'In 1901 the Hay–Pauncefote Treaty cemented good relations with the United States. In 1902

Britain concluded a formal alliance with Japan, in 1904 the *Entente Cordiale*.'[11] These diplomatic moves would continue.

In 1907, three years after the *Entente Cordiale*, the Foreign Secretary, Sir Edward Grey, signed another conciliatory document, the Anglo-Russian Convention, which ended decades of dispute between the two countries over Afghanistan and India. It is important to stress that both these agreements, the *Entente Cordiale* and the Anglo-Russian Convention, were intended simply to resolve issues raised by Britain's imperial expansion. There was no military element in either agreement or any commitment for the future; Britain did not become a member of the 1894 Franco-Russian alliance or make any formal military alliance with France. Even so, these measures were watched uneasily by the Kaiser and added to his conviction about encirclement, an ingrained, neurotic belief that the other powers in Europe were gathering like jackals around the frontiers of the Second Reich.

However, the German Naval Laws of 1897 and 1900 underlined Britain's need for allies. The Reichstag bill of 1897 authorized the building of sixteen 'ships of the line' (battleships or cruisers) by 1900, and this programme went ahead quickly. Then, in October 1899, immediately after the outbreak of the Boer War, when, not coincidentally, Britain's attention was otherwise engaged, the Kaiser demanded another increase in the size of the High Seas Fleet. The bill introduced in 1900 proposed building three battleships a year for the next six years, and was seen in London as a direct threat to Britain's maritime supremacy and the security of the British Empire.

One result of this was a naval arms race following Britain's decision to outbuild the German yards and maintain a two-nation maritime supremacy. Another was the Anglo-Japanese Alliance signed on 30 January 1902. The terms of the alliance – that each party would support the other if it was attacked by two or more powers but remain neutral if the attack came from only one power – were not likely to involve either party in an aggressive war. The advantage from Britain's point of view was a reduction in the threat to her possessions in the Far East, enabling the Admiralty to withdraw capital ships from Hong Kong and Singapore to reinforce the Mediterranean and the Grand Fleet.

Paul M. Kennedy argues that 'the Anglo-Japanese Alliance, by lessening Britain's links with Germany and by strengthening the Japanese in their determination to stand up to Russia, was to provide one of the causes for the creation of the Anglo-French *Entente*'.[12] Perhaps, but the creation of that *Entente* received its greatest public boost in 1903 when Edward VII made a state visit to Paris. 'Though Edward neither initiated nor influenced his country's policy', writes Barbara Tuchman, 'his personal diplomacy made the change possible.'[13]

Edward had made many private visits to Paris during his days as Prince of Wales but this state visit was both public and political and made against diplomatic advice that the King of England would not be welcome in the French capital. At first this seemed to be true. Again according to Tuchman: 'On his arrival the crowds were sullen and silent except for a few taunting cries of "*Vivent les Boers*" or "*Vive Fashoda*" which the King ignored. When an aide muttered, "The French don't like us", Edward replied, "Why should they?" and continued bowing and smiling from his carriage.'[14]

King Edward's charm offensive against the general flow of French public opinion continued for the next four days. He attended troop reviews and the races at Longchamps, he lunched at the Quai d'Orsay and waved to the audience from his box at the theatre; everywhere he was smiling and gracious and full of compliments, about the French, French culture and the pleasures of the *ville lumière*, and gradually the public mood changed. 'When he left', writes Tuchman, 'the crowds now shouted "*Vive notre Roi!*"'[15] Tuchman appends the comment of the Belgian ambassador to France: 'Seldom has such a complete change of attitude been seen as that which has taken place in this country. He has won the hearts of all the French.'[16]

The King had achieved more than a merely personal success; his visit had altered the public mood and made political change possible. Within a year this change became official in the form of the

Anglo-French *Entente Cordiale*. The *Entente* quickly came to have much greater significance for Anglo-French relations than its clauses would suggest.[17]

Article 1 and Article 2 of the *Entente* confirmed that the French would not interfere with British control of Egypt and the British agreed that they recognized French interests in Morocco. Both countries confirmed that they had no intention of altering the political status of either country; the sum total of nine articles signed on 8 April 1904 was the settlement of any dispute, present or pending, between France and Britain along the North African coast; the Secret Articles, five in number, dealt with procedures for the settlement of any future dispute.

The *Entente* actually served a more fundamental purpose. It put an official end to centuries of Anglo-French animosity. It agreed, as in the quoted cases of Egypt and Morocco, that the two countries' national interests should be complementary rather than competitive, that there was room for the diplomatic settlement of disputes. The *Entente* implicitly conceded that the two nations needed each other and must unite in their common interest – not least in resisting any challenge from Imperial Germany.

All this represented a complete volte-face in Anglo-French relations, and was seen as such by the other countries of Europe, not least Germany. Neither the Kaiser nor his closest advisers had believed that Britain would ever come to terms with France and announce that fact in a formal declaration. In fact, between the 'Fashoda Incident' of 1898 and the signing of the *Entente Cordiale* in 1904 British relations with France underwent a complete transformation, moving from outright hostility and threats of war to a formal declaration of friendship. In the ten years after the signing of the *Entente* this process would continue, but many other obstacles, military and political, would have to be removed before the BEF sailed for France in 1914.

The first decade of the twentieth century diverted Britain from nineteenth-century notions of 'splendid isolation', rocked any reliance on a 'blue water' maritime strategy for national defence based on the world wide deployment of the British fleet, and increased national concern for the security of the empire – and Britain. Between 1900 and 1914 Britain had to face the centuries-old problem of the balance of power in Europe, a balance fatally upset by the establishment of the German empire in 1871.

Fashoda was a turning point in Franco-British relations; it changed old enemies into potential allies. The core of that alliance would be military. In considering the development of the British Army up to the outbreak of the First World War it is necessary to revert briefly to the time before Fashoda and acknowledge that the BEF that went to France in 1914 was, essentially, a Victorian army, manned and staffed by soldiers steeped in the rigid beliefs of the Victorian period.

Throughout the nineteenth century the British Army was the poor relation of the Royal Navy. Both had been greatly reduced in size at the end of the Napoleonic Wars, but the Royal Navy had embraced the century's expanding technology and the 'wooden walls' of England had gradually been replaced by the most power-ful battle fleet in the world, a force instilled with Nelsonian ardour and buttressed by considerable public esteem.

For some reason – and in spite of the fact that Napoleon's downfall came at Waterloo rather than at Trafalgar – this public regard did not extend to the soldiery. Although the British Army had not been engaged on the Continent since 1815 it was far from idle and retained its fighting spirit in a long series of campaigns. During the nineteenth century, the British Army fought no less than seventeen separate wars, in countries as far apart as Canada and New Zealand, South Africa and Afghanistan. These years had seen a mixture of victory and defeat in various colonial cam-paigns, the general shambles of the Crimea War in the 1840s and some truly startling demonstrations of incompetence during the South African War of 1899–1902. However, although all Britain's wars ended eventually in victory, one notable feature of the British military during this period was stubborn resistance to change.

For at least half a century after Waterloo the British Army remained in a Napoleonic time warp; the Duke of Wellington could have risen from his recent grave to command the army that sailed for the Crimea and found it much the same as the one he had last commanded at Waterloo in 1815. Fortunately, the avoidable tragedies of the Crimean War could not be concealed from the British public and, after the Crimea, change clearly had to come, in spite of the stout resistance put up by the then Commander-in-Chief of the army, the Duke of Cambridge. The duke was a cousin of Queen Victoria and had commanded a division – with no particular distinction – in the Crimea. He became Commander-in-Chief after the campaign and was not finally levered out of that position until 1895, after more than forty years in the post – and at the age of seventy-two. While in office, the duke regarded army reform not simply as unwise but as a potential threat to the state.

Bolstered by Her Majesty's approval, the Duke of Cambridge fought change for the rest of his life, and his influence in curtailing progress should not be underestimated. The chief advocate of reform was his deputy, General Sir Garnet Wolseley, the Adjutant General of the army, but change would result only as a consequence of political pressure. That came from three Secretaries of State for War, Edward Cardwell (1868–74), his immediate successor Hugh Childers, and R. B. Haldane, later Lord Haldane, who was Secretary of State for War between 1905 and 1912 and founded the army – and the BEF – that marched off to France in 1914.

In the late nineteenth century Army reformers were faced with one crucial problem: how to change command and control of the Army, how to transform it, root and branch, from an eighteenth-century relic into a twentieth-century fighting force without destroying the ethos that made the British Army such a wonderful and – when it reached the battlefield – such a powerful and courageous institution. The core of that problem was the regimental system.

The regimental system is not peculiar to the British Army but it is certainly arguable that nowhere else in the world is the notion of the regiment so deeply rooted in the Army and the nation at large. Essentially the regiment is a family; as in any family, members will make any sacrifice to preserve the lives of other members and not let the family as a whole down. The regiment transcends self. In the end – and whatever comforting illusions are cherished in Downing Street or Buckingham Palace – the British soldier does not fight for vague abstractions like 'Queen and Country'; he stands and fights – and dies if need be – because he cannot let his comrades and his regiment down. The soldiers at Mons and Le Cateau, the Aisne and the Marne, the gunners at Néry, that stubborn infantry who beat off the Prussian Guard at Messines and Ypres, were holding their ground because they were riflemen, fusiliers, guardsmen, gunners, Sherwood Foresters, Worcesters . . . men fighting for their comrades and their regiment. At that time and place only the regiment mattered because only the regiment was *there*; the regimental spirit was all they had to hang on to in that nightmare of noise and fear and death.

This ethos – regimental spirit or morale – takes time to build. It is founded on tradition, discipline, sound training and sensible handling in the field – plus that intangible notion of the 'regimental family', that barrack-home in which some families serve for generation after generation. Tinkering with the regimental family can be dangerous and difficult, but it had to be done and, fortunately, Cardwell and his successors handled the matter with considerable tact.

Cardwell struck first at 'purchase', the system by which commissioned ranks and promotion could be bought and traded between officers. For example, the Earl of Cardigan, notorious for his part in the Charge of the Light Brigade at Balaclava, purchased command of the 11th Hussars for the then considerable sum of £25,000 and regarded it as a good investment, which indeed it was. The command added to Cardigan's social prestige, and when he led his regiment to destruction at Balaclava the British government replaced it. The snag was that purchase barred promotion to officers of ability but slender means, and it had to go. At the same time Cardwell removed another obstacle to progress, promotion by seniority, and replaced it with a system popularly known as 'get on or get out', by which an officer had to attain promotion after a certain period in one rank or leave the army. None of this endeared

Cardwell to the officer corps, but it greatly improved the army by allowing talent rise to the top.

Cardwell's next reform – the Army Enlistment Act, which introduced short service – was even more controversial. Previously a soldier had enlisted for twenty years, and this caused several problems. Recruiting was difficult as good men were unwilling to sign on for such a long time and were middle aged by the time they drew a pension, so the system did not produce a trained reserve. Cardwell therefore introduced a twelve-year term of service in which seven years would be spent with the Colours and five on the reserve. The benefits of this system, said Cardwell, were obvious – 'in peace time the Army will feed the Reserve, in war the Reserve will feed the Army' – and he was right – more than 60 per cent of the soldiers in the 1914 BEF were recalled reservists.

Now came that really delicate matter, the regimental system. The very idea of tinkering with the old regiments – bringing in a territorially-based, linked-battalion system – caused uproar, and the matter was settled only under Childers in 1881, after Cardwell had left the War Office – and was never imposed on the aristocratic ranks of the cavalry. At the time most battalions had numbers and adopted names – the 3rd Foot, for example, were also known as 'The Buffs'. Now the old 'Buffs', who had held the line under Wellington's eye at Talavera during the Peninsular War and fought on a hundred dreadful fields, would become the two-battalion 'East Kent Regiment', which no one had ever heard of, and lose its proud position in the line. Locally recruited – in East Kent for this particular infantry regiment – one battalion would serve at the depot on garrison duties and in training recruits and the other would be on active service abroad. Periodically these roles would be reversed – and the regiment would also acquire a number of militia battalions of part-time volunteers.

It made good sense, but the old sweats hated it. Their regimental number was a source of pride and élan. Were not the 1st Foot, destined to become the Royal Scots, equally well known as 'Pontius Pilate's Bodyguard' from their long-standing position as the senior regiment of the line? Were they not therefore obviously superior to, say, the old 49th Foot? Perhaps so, but that obvious distinction would vanish when the 49th Foot became the Royal Berkshire Regiment or the 43rd and 52nd Foot combined to become the Oxfordshire and Buckinghamshire Light Infantry. All this may not matter much in the first decade of the twenty-first century, but British soldiers at the end of the nineteenth century thought it mattered a great deal. They loved their regiments, and the rank and file fought this particular change every step of the way.

In fact, as the soldiers soon discovered, the change produced a substantial number of benefits. It improved recruiting, forged family links in the recruiting area and did wonders for the private soldier's reputation. That much despised 'Tommy Atkins' about whom Kipling wrote was now a cousin or a brother or a member of the family down the road. When the drums beat and the sound of the regimental march echoed through the streets of the county town, the local populace turned out to line the route and cheer the soldiers as the battalion marched to the station, bound for the troopship and some distant war. This was now *their* regiment; its exploits in the field were followed with attention and anxiety – and the crowds turned out to cheer again when the boys came marching home, or shed a tear or two for those that were missing.

There were other changes. The red coat finally went out – other than for ceremonial occasions – and in came khaki. In 1903, the artillery ordered the 18-pounder gun for the field artillery – which supports the infantry – and the 13-pounder gun for the Horse Artillery – which supports the cavalry. Both guns would be widely employed by the BEF in 1914. The Martini-Henry single-shot rifle was replaced by the Lee-Metford magazine rifle, which gave way to the long Lee-Enfield, which was in turn replaced by the Short Magazine Lee-Enfield, the accurate and much loved 'SMLE' which the BEF used to such effect at Mons and First Ypres and which stayed in service in the British Army until the end of the Second World War.

The cumulative effect of these Cardwell–Childers reforms was to make the British Army a far more efficient fighting force, but it remained small in European terms. Continental armies were raised by conscription and were numbered in hundreds of thousands, even millions. Without conscription, which was not introduced until 1916, Britain's army relied on a supply of volunteers, but enough volunteers came forward for the size of force the politicians deemed sufficient for Britain's home defence and imperial needs. Before August 1914, the regular army's home establishment consisted of six infantry divisions and one cavalry division; none of these was up to strength and they had to be brought up to establishment on mobilization by the return of reservists – the BEF that went to France in 1914 mustered around 160,000 men. There were another four divisions overseas, giving the British Army the grand total of just eleven infantry divisions and a cavalry division.

This was about the same size as the army of Serbia – and these 'divisions', either at home or abroad, were not actually in existence as formed units. The army was deployed in garrisons or separate battalions or, here and there, as on the North-West Frontier of India, in operational brigades. In 1914 the home establishment also contained fourteen divisions of Haldane's newly created Territorial Force, totalling some 300,000 men, but none of these part-time volunteers could be sent overseas unless they volunteered to go. Even when fully mustered, the British Army was *small*.

In comparison the French Army in 1914 could muster 1,071,000 men in five armies,[18] and the Germans had 850,000 men with the Colours and could mobilize a total of 4,300,000 trained men in twenty-five active army corps in a matter of days,[19] plus 55 reserve, Ersatz and Landwehr divisions, and no fewer than eleven cavalry divisions – all as a result of conscription. Even the small Belgian Army, of six divisions and a cavalry division, could muster 350,000 men, if all the garrison and fortress troops were included.[20]

One answer to Britain's manpower problem was conscription, a course strongly urged by Lord Roberts and the National Service League, which campaigned for the creation of a larger army, but conscription did not suit Britain's pre-war military requirements.

Men could be conscripted only for a limited period, and quite apart from the general unpopularity of forced service, by the time a conscript had been trained and posted abroad it would be time to bring him back for demobilization.

However, the major problem facing the government and the army as the new century opened lay in the critical area of command and control. Britain's limitations in these particular skills had been brought harshly into focus by the various defeats and disasters of the South African War. That apart, the growing political tensions in Europe and elsewhere indicated that the army must be put on a more efficient footing, and above all provided with a General Staff of the kind that had organized Germany's rapid victory over France in 1870.

In 1900 St John Broderick was appointed Secretary of State for War. Early in 1901 he decided that, apart from home defence, the country 'ought to be ready at any moment to send abroad three Army Corps with the proper cavalry division, in fact a force of 120,000 men'. To supply such a force would be costly, so nothing was done to put this scheme into practice.

Broderick was much more successful with another scheme, persuading the Prime Minister, Arthur Balfour, to set up a committee to study the problems of imperial defence; the Cabinet Defence Committee was established in December 1902. This committee consisted of the Prime Minister, the Lord President of the Council, the First Lord of the Admiralty and the Secretary of State for War, all political figures, plus four serving officers, the Commander-in-Chief of the army, the First Sea Lord and the heads of military and naval intelligence. The purpose of the committee was to 'survey as a whole the strategical military needs of the Empire'. It was not designed to consider the prospect of a major war in Europe.

In October 1903, Hugh Arnold-Forster, a man who had little understanding of the army but plenty of ideas, replaced Broderick as War Minister. During his brief tenure in office he asked Lord Esher to examine the current structure and organization of the army and suggest improvements. Esher's committee, the War Office

(Reconstitution) Committee, began work in November 1903 and filed the first part of its report in January 1904; two further parts followed in February and March. The full Esher Report provided the Army with a blueprint for change at the highest level, which was the entire purpose of Esher's deliberations. In the first part of his report, which dealt with high command, Lord Esher stated that 'The object is to secure for the British Empire, with the least possible derangement of existing machinery, the immense advantages which the General Staff has conferred on Germany.'[21]

In this task Esher was very successful. Indeed, as Correlli Barnett has stated, 'Without the Esher Report and its acceptance by the Government of the day it is inconceivable that the mammoth military efforts in the two world wars could have been possible, let alone so successful.'[22]

However, here as elsewhere there was no gain without pain. One of the report's first proposals was to abolish the office of Commander-in-Chief of the army and replace it with an Army Council – later known as the Army Board – and a General Staff. The current commander-in-chief was a much loved figure, Lord Roberts of Kandahar, the famous 'Bobs' of Afghanistan and South Africa. Fortunately, 'Bobs' was a stout advocate of reform. He had been pressing the Government and the Army hard to introduce compulsory military service and raised no objections to the termination of his office.

A Committee of Imperial Defence, or CID – so called because Dominion ministers were invited to attend when in London – replaced the Cabinet Defence Committee. This committee included the nucleus of what became the General Staff, five officers each charged with some specific task – considering all matters relating to imperial defence; obtaining and collating relevant data from all official departments; preparing papers for the prime minister and the Defence Committee; furnishing advice on defence questions, especially those involving more than one department – so ending, for example, the compartmentalization of War Office and Admiralty. The CID was also charged with keeping records for the use of the current Cabinet and its successors.

The Army Council was created on 4 February 1904 and was followed three months later, on 4 May, by the formal establishment of the CID. The first task of the Army Council was the setting up of a General Staff under the first Chief of General Staff (CGS), General Sir Neville Lyttelton. This title was changed to Chief of the Imperial General Staff (CIGS) following the Imperial Conference of 1909.

To help him in his tasks the CGS was given three new directorates – Military Operations (DMO), Staff Duties (DMS) and Military Training (DMT); intelligence matters were included in the remit of the DMO. This new General Staff formed the second arm supplying the government, via the CID, with advice on strategy, the other arm being the Admiralty, both arms competing for official attention and funding.

This reorganization of the army command came at a fortunate time, for in 1905 two events shook the world's fragile stability. The first was Japan's defeat of Russia in the Russo-Japanese War, and in particular the destruction of the Russian Navy at Tushushima. Then came the Moroccan Crisis – the 'Tangier Incident' – in which the Kaiser displayed a remarkable resentment of France's activities in the western Mediterranean and which underlined the need for France and Britain to review their defence arrangments – by sea in the case of Britain, by land in the case of France. This was a year after the signing of the *Entente Cordiale*, and although this dispute was settled at the 1906 Algeciras Conference, the idea of extending Anglo-French cordiality into something more specific was soon mooted.

From its inception the CID had been dominated by the forceful character of Admiral Sir John 'Jackie' Fisher, the First Sea Lord. Fisher was relentless in pursuing the interests of the Royal Navy and the merits of a maritime or 'blue water' strategy for imperial and national defence; Fisher regarded the Army as 'a missile to be fired by the Navy', with no need for any separate function. Now, following the election of a new Liberal government in 1905, the CID was joined by the new War Minister, Richard Haldane, later Lord Haldane, a man who would not be browbeaten by Fisher and proved a strong advocate for the expansion of the army and its role in continental affairs.

This was useful, because following the Moroccan Crisis two separate strands of thought were emerging at the CID. Fisher and his Naval Staff considered that in the event of war between France and Germany the Royal Navy should rely on blockade and the army should launch amphibious assaults on the German North Sea and Baltic coasts. The army, on the other hand, considered that in the event of war the place of the British Army – assuming the government chose to commit it – would be in Belgium, both in support of Belgian neutrality, of which all the major European nations were guarantors, and to extend the northern flank of the French Army, should it deploy along the Franco-German frontier.

Major-General James Grierson, the DMO at the War Office, also averred that the idea of an amphibious operation in the Baltic was unsound since the Germans could reinforce their troops far more quickly than the Royal Navy could ship reinforcements and supplies to the landing force. This was quite true and everyone knew it; most people also knew that Fisher's amphibious strategy was simply his maritime strategy in another guise, a further plea for more resources and more Dreadnoughts.

For the moment all this was theory, a discussion of possible eventualities. There was no agreement of any kind that would lead Great Britain into a continental war. The *Entente Cordiale* had been a settlement of Franco-British colonial disputes and the setting up of spheres of influence with no hint of close military or naval involvement. Now, gradually and post-Tangier, all this was to change.

The Tangier Incident had long-term repercussions in Britain. According to the Cabinet Secretary, Maurice Hankey: 'About this time grave trouble arose between France and Germany over Morocco, and there were communications between the French and British General Staffs. In the case of the Admiralty these took the form of direct communications between Fisher and the French Naval attaché. In the case of the War Office they seem to have been conducted to some extent through the medium of Repington, the brilliant military correspondent of *The Times* – a somewhat irregular channel.'[23]

'Colonel Repington' was the pen name of Lieutenant-Colonel Charles à Court Repington, who, by virtue of his *Times* connections, was a well-known and influential figure in military and political circles. Again according to Hankey, in January 1906 the Foreign Secretary, Sir Edward Grey, 'yielded to the desire of the French Government for military "conversations" between the General Staffs of the two nations'.[24]

Grey agreed to these talks on the understanding that these 'conversations' were to be 'entirely non-committal in character, were to involve no promise of support in war and were not to restrict either Government if war should come to decide whether or not to assist the other by armed force'.[25]

A further requirement was that the talks were to be kept secret – even from most members of the British Cabinet – and it was this need for secrecy, plus the other essential requirement – that the 'conversations' were not to be seen as any form of military commitment – which obliged Grey to keep his distance and employ the good offices of Colonel Repington. As a result, the process of setting up these early Staff 'conversations' became somewhat convoluted.

After private talks with Lord Esher and Sir George Clark, the secretary of the CID, on 5 January 1906 Repington addressed eleven questions to Major Victor Huguet, the French military attaché in London.[26] The first question was: 'Have the *Conseil Supérieur de la Guerre* considered British co-operation in case of war with Germany? In what manner do they consider this co-operation can best be carried out, (a) by sea, (b) by land?'

The French answered this question in reverse order, and only the part concerning the Army need be covered here: 'The question of co-operation with the British Army has been studied – it is considered that, to be most useful, its actions should (a) be joined to that of the French Army, that is to say placed under the same direction, whether the two armies act in the same theatre of operations or in different theatres, (b) make itself felt at the opening of hostilities, because of the considerable moral effect that would result from that.'

In other words, the British Army should enter the war as soon as the French did and be under French command *wherever it served*. As a quid pro quo, the French would allow their fleet to serve under British command. Repington requested clarification on this point, and to the question 'Should we establish it as a principle . . . that the English shall command at sea and the French on land?' the French reply was: 'Yes; unity of direction being absolutely essential whether on land or sea.'

Repington's other questions requested French views on Allied action should Germany violate Belgian territory and the disposal of any captured German colonies, but having elicited the official French view on the use of the British Army in war – and a rather alarming view at that, since it implied handing over control of the British Army 'wherever it served' to the French – Colonel Repington reported back to Sir Edward Grey and responsibility for continuing these 'conversations' was handed over to Major-General Grierson. To pursue the matter, General Grierson had to meet the French attaché, Major Huguet, and to maintain secrecy, 'a few days later Grierson met Major Huguet, as if by chance, while riding in Hyde Park'.[27]

These somewhat torturous proceedings had an underlying purpose relating to the British Government's two prime needs. First, it was only wise to conduct staff talks with the French on how the two countries might cooperate in the event of war. Effective arrangements for military cooperation could not be created overnight or with the enemy at the gates. On the other hand it was also essential that there should be no 'mission creep' in these conversations. The French must be left in no doubt that these staff talks were not, must not become and must not be taken to imply any kind of British commitment to military action.

That this was a major British concern is borne out by the fact that this latter point appears again and again when the subject of these 'conversations' appears in contemporary accounts or subsequent memoirs. However, in his later reference to these 'conversations',

Winston Churchill, then Home Secretary and later First Lord of the Admiralty, makes a significant point: 'However much the two Governments might agree and affirm to each other that no national or political engagement was involved in these technical discussions, the fact remained that they constituted an exceedingly potent tie.'[28]

The British Government's position was understandable but naive. It was understandable because current circumstances did indicate that Imperial Germany was a potential threat to Britain as well as to France. If France were attacked, the chances were that without British support Germany would triumph – and what Germany would extract from that victory could only be to Britain's disadvantage. In any event, Britain could not tolerate either the violation of Belgian neutrality or a hostile and aggressive naval power – which Germany was rapidly becoming – gaining possession of Channel ports 20 miles from the Kent coast. In fact, German ambitions in the event of military victory would go far beyond mere naval interests, but that alone made Britain listen attentively during these 'conversations'.

The naivety stems from the point that these 'conversations' did not indicate the possibility of intervention. It was quite unrealistic to suppose that two nations could conduct military debates at the highest Staff level without the tacit admission that they did concern military action at some future date. If that was not the subject of these 'conversations', what were the General Staff members talking about?

Barbara Tuchman comments that: 'The [British] Government maintained the disingenuous position that the military "conversations" were, in Lord Haldane's words, "just the natural and informal outcome of our close friendship with France"'.[29] That was one man's opinion. Lord Esher, on the other hand, maintained that 'the plans worked out by the Chiefs-of-Staff have certainly committed us to fight whether the Cabinet likes it or not'.

The Cabinet at large were in no position to object to or approve of these 'conversations' because they did not know they were taking place. Knowledge of the talks was restricted to the Prime Minister, the Foreign Secretary and the Secretary of State for War.

The other Cabinet members were kept in ignorance for years, and were understandably peeved in 1912 when they finally found out what had been going on for years behind their backs. A final point was that these talks were taking place with a foreign power – France – that was fully determined to involve Britain in any coming war and transform the *Entente* into a full-blown military alliance.

Over the years after 1906 the French convinced themselves that the British were planning to join them on the outbreak of war. This conviction was established in spite of a letter of agreement, drawn up in 1906 by Sir Edward Grey and signed by Ambassador Cambon, that both parties were free to decide 'whether or not to assist each other by armed force' in the event of war. The later Anglo-French Naval Pact of 1912, an agreement by which the British fleet was to protect the Channel and the French fleet the Mediterranean, was also concluded on the understanding that it was 'not based on an engagement to co-operate in war'.

There is also a debatable political point. Had these 'conversations' become common knowledge, would they have alarmed Germany, increased the Kaiser's fear of encirclement and brought war closer – or would they have confronted Germany with a powerful alliance and made the Kaiser think twice about the direction of his policy? Unable to decide, the British Government elected to keep the talks secret.

Secrecy was easier to maintain because there is little evidence that the talks were leading anywhere. Jackson and Bramall comment that 'The military staff talks . . . were conducted intermittently from 1906 onwards on a contingency basis without political commitment on the British side', adding that 'Fisher [the First Sea Lord] refused to reveal any of the Admiralty war plans to the French and did his utmost to obstruct the General Staffs' intervention planning by refusing to authorise Admiralty staff co-operation in working out shipping schedules for the hypothetical movement of the BEF to France'.[30]

This matter of naval–military cooperation was partly resolved by a CID subcommittee, set up in 1908. According to Hankey: 'It defined the respective responsibilities of the War Office and the

Admiralty and laid down the broad lines of policy on which their plans would have to be based . . . and brought our leading sailors and soldiers into intimate personal contact, to their mutual advantage.'[31]

This last point is debatable. Another CID subcommittee decided in 1909 that the question of if and where the BEF should be sent was a policy matter that could only be decided 'by the Government of the day'. In other words, there would be no formal alliance with France and the decision to support her or not would be left until the opening of hostilities. On the other hand, it was clearly necessary to have some operational plans in place should some commitment be necessary.

The snag was that without a policy there could be no agreed plan – and so it proved. The General Staff continued to tinker with a scheme for sending a force to France but, again according to Hankey, 'The Admiralty, however, took a different view, Fisher remaining opposed to military adventures on the Continent. He had his own ideas on the subject and did not wish to see the British Army committed to a European campaign at the outset of a war. Consequently the Admiralty came forward with a counter-proposition.'[32]

The Admiralty proposed relying on economic pressure – a naval blockade – in the event of war with Germany. Fisher also stated – again – that any British military presence on the continent should take the form of a landing on the Baltic coast of Schleswig-Holstein, from where the landing force could threaten Prussia and so ensure the withdrawal of German units from France. The various difficulties attendant on this proposal – how the landing force could even reach the Baltic without running into the High Seas Fleet or the fact that, should it even land, the Germans could certainly supply and reinforce their armies far more quickly than the Royal Navy could bring aid to the British troops, or that France would be overrun by the German Army long before a British naval blockade could take effect – were not even discussed.

Between 1906 and 1910, the creation of an 'Expeditionary Force' became one of the prime functions of the Army Staff but, partly through Admiralty intransigence, but mainly for reasons of economy, little was done to give this force the transport, training or manpower it required. Even the establishment of a divisional system languished; the Home Army was organized on a command basis – Southern Command, Northern Command, and so on – and the battalions and regiments at home continued to pursue their original functions, the training of recruits and the dispatch of troops to battalions overseas, while at the War Office Haldane was mainly concerned with the creation of the Territorial Force and political arguments over conscription. The creation of an Expeditionary Force – or at least the notion of its prime role in support of France – might have been abandoned but for a succession of small but significant events overseas.

Following the Algeciras Conference of 1906, Germany's sense of grievance grew, notably in 1907 when Britain and Russia patched up their differences over Afghanistan and India and signed the Anglo-Russian Alliance. William Carr confirms that 'the agreement was not directed against Germany . . . though no doubt alarm at the growth of the German navy and resentment of Germany's blustering and arrogant diplomatic methods played some part on the British side; but first and foremost, this remained a colonial agreement, designed to reduce British commitments overseas'.[33]

Even so, the agreement exacerbated German resentment; Carr notes that 'German newspapers complained in 1907 of the ring closing around Germany',[34] though the signing of the Anglo-Russian Alliance did not commit Britain to membership of the current Franco-Russian *Entente*. Britain fully intended to keep continental affairs at a distance – a resolve that became increasingly difficult to sustain as the years passed and European tensions grew.

In Cabinet, defence debate was still concentrated on the Anglo-German naval race. This race accelerated in 1909 when the First Lord of the Admiralty, Reginald McKenna, demanded the construction of six new dreadnought battleships to compete with the latest German increases under the German Naval Law of 1908.

This demand led to widespread comment in the press, alarm among the public and disputes in cabinet. As Winston Churchill remarked later: 'Genuine alarm was excited throughout the country at what was for the first time widely recognized as the German menace. In the end, a curious and characteristic solution was reached. The Admiralty had demanded six ships; the economists offered four; and we finally compromised on eight.'[35]

The British Government and the general public then became concerned by the attitude of the Kaiser. On 28 October 1908 the Kaiser compounded his other diplomatic errors with the United Kingdom by calling the British 'as mad as March hares' in an interview with the *Daily Telegraph* newspaper. In what was later described in the German newspapers as 'one of the great diplomatic blunders of the century', the Kaiser stated that the German people had little time for the British: 'What has come over you that you are so completely given over to suspicions unworthy of a great nation? I have said, time after time, that I am a friend of England and yet your Press, or a considerable section of it, bids the people of England refuse my proffered hand and insinuates that the other hand holds a dagger.

'The prevailing sentiment among large sections of the middle and lower classes of my own people is not friendly to England. That is another reason why I resent your refusal to accept my pledged word. You retort that I am your arch-enemy and you make it hard for me. Why is this?'

The Kaiser also alleged that the French and Russians had tried to push Germany into conflict with Britain during the Boer War, and claimed that the rapidly expanding High Seas Fleet was aimed at Japan rather than Britain. These last comments proved particularly unwise. The Kaiser's remarks in this interview managed to alienate Britain, France, Russia and Japan, led to furious diplomatic exchanges, an acrimonious two-day debate in the Reichstag and the resignation of Prince von Bulow, the German foreign minister, who was blamed for failing to stop the Kaiser's outburst.

After this spectacular rant the Kaiser was obliged to endure a short period of silence, but his arrogance usually shielded him from the problems he created and from any sense of responsibility for the steps other nations felt obliged to take in response to such statements. 'We Hohenzollerns are the bailiffs of God,' he once declared, as if his words and actions enjoyed some form of divine sanction. The steps taken by other countries – forging defensive alliances, extending conscription, building dreadnoughts to match the expansion of the High Seas Fleet – only convinced the Kaiser that he was taking the prudent course in expanding his fleet and army to protect his people against aggression and encirclement.

In the autumn of 1908 trouble broke out in the Balkans with the Austrian annexation of Bosnia and Herzegovina. This action raised tension between Austria-Hungary and Britain's new ally, Imperial Russia. While making it clear that Britain would not be drawn into this dispute, Sir Edward Grey offered full support to Russia, and when Germany in turn supported Austria-Hungary political tension rose yet again. In the end Russia gave way but, said Churchill, 'This Teutonic triumph was a victory gained at a perilous cost . . . Russia in 1910 made an enormous increase in her already vast army and both Russia and France closed their ranks.'[36]

The French were not satisfied with either the Russian alliance or the existing *Entente* with Britain. They were determined to turn the *Entente Cordiale* into a full-blown military alliance, and their original agreement with Sir Edward Grey, reserving the decision on any BEF deployment to 'the Government of the day', did not deter French ministers from pressing this point with their British colleagues on many occasions. In April 1908, for example, the French premier, Georges Clemenceau, met Richard Haldane at Downing Street. 'I had an hour's talk with him and found him very well informed,' wrote Haldane. 'He had been following our Army reforms closely but he wanted much more from us.'[37]

Clemenceau wanted the British to introduce conscription and make a formal military alliance with France, but received no satisfaction on either point. Nor was the embryo BEF as yet either ready or equipped for such deployment. The plans for Anglo-French military cooperation in the event of war had made little progress since there was no political commitment to such activity. Steps to alter that situation began only in August 1910 when Brigadier General Henry Wilson became Director of Military Operations at the War Office.

3

Wilson at the War Office

1910–1914

Dined with the King. Also Prince of Wales and Standfordham.
Had little talk with the King but much with Standfordham who
said that I was more responsible for England joining the war than
any other man. I think this is true.

Diary of Major-General Henry Wilson,
4 December 1914[1]

If the Kaiser can be regarded as the man mainly responsible for involving Europe in a disastrous war, Brigadier General Henry Wilson can be seen as the architect of Franco-British military cooperation in the years before the war. As he himself admits in the above diary extract, if any one man was responsible for sending the BEF to France in August 1914, that man was Henry Wilson. But to understand why this relatively junior officer should be so directly concerned with matters of high policy and Britain's continental strategy in the pre-war years, it is necessary to understand the man.

Henry Hughes Wilson was born in Ulster in 1864, a product of that province which, says Correlli Barnett, has provided Britain with its closest approximation to a *Junker* class. However, the most significant thing about Wilson was not his background but his Francophilia: a long succession of French governesses and childhood visits to France provided the young Henry Wilson with a love of all things French. As he grew up, the food, the wine, the history, the towns and countryside of France became his abiding love, aided by a sound grasp of the French language, a rare asset in the pre-war British Army – though Kitchener and Douglas Haig were also proficient French speakers.

It is impossible to stress Wilson's Francophilia too strongly. Writing a warning letter to Reginald McKenna, the First Lord of the Admiralty, over the Agadir question in 1911, that astute observer, Cabinet Secretary Maurice Hankey, states:

> It is of course notorious that the DMO [Director of Military Operations] General Wilson, who has brought this question to the front, has a perfect obsession for military operations on the Continent. He spends his holidays bicycling up and down the Franco-German frontier; he has preached this gospel at the Staff College for years and packed the War Office with staff officers who share his views. He holds the view not only that military action is indispensable in order to pre-serve the balance of power in Europe, but that we require a conscript army for this purpose. If he can get a decision in favour of military action at this juncture he will endeavour to commit us up to the hilt.[2]

All this was very true, but to trace the development of Wilson's involvement with the BEF we must go back to the beginning of his military career. Wilson always intended to join the Army but failed the entrance exam for Sandhurst and Woolwich no fewer than five times, and finally entered the army 'by the back door', with a commission in the Irish Militia. Once in the army, though, Wilson flourished. He was gazetted into the Rifle Brigade in 1884 and served in the Burma campaign of 1887, receiving a wound in the face that scarred him for life. Wilson was generally popular in the army; he had copious amounts of Irish charm, was cheerful in adversity and considered brave in an army that took courage for granted – and no mean soldier in the field. His problems arose from his character, for Henry Wilson was a compulsive intriguer; his peers liked him but his superiors did not trust him.

Wilson attended the Camberley Staff College from 1890 to 1892 and during his time there made several visits to the battlefields of the Franco-Prussian War and the eastern provinces of France, a practice he would continue in future years. After graduation he was posted to the Intelligence Department of the Army, which took him back to France from time to time for discussions with the French commanders – those post-1906 'conversations' had deep roots. On some of these visits he was accompanied by a close friend, Captain à Court Repington, a man who later became the military correspondent of *The Times* – and one of Wilson's most devoted enemies.

In the British Army service on the Staff alternates with periods of regimental duty. In 1899 Wilson became brigade major of a light infantry brigade and went to war in South Africa, where he fought at Colenso, the Modder river and at Spion Kop; all were disasters of various kinds and did little to instil a favourable view of his superiors' competence in Major Henry Wilson.

When Lord Roberts replaced General Redvers Buller as commander-in-chief in South Africa in 1900, Wilson became 'Bobs' military secretary, the man responsible for postings and appointments, a post that greatly widened his range of acquaintances and contacts. Wilson returned to the UK in 1901 as a brevet Lieutenant-Colonel with a DSO, a man clearly marked for advancement. His time in South Africa may also have convinced Wilson that when something needed doing, he was the man to do it. He had seen enough to persuade him that many senior officers were hidebound, inefficient dinosaurs with no understanding of the modern world; when time presented him with the opportunity to intervene in strategic or political affairs, he would not be deterred by any respect for rank.

Wilson was arrogant, opinionated and not short of conceit, but he was no fool. He fully supported the reforms introduced by successive war ministers and by 1907 he was a Brigadier General. From 1907 to 1910 he was the Commandant of the Staff College at Camberley, and in December 1909, while on a visit to Paris, he decided to pay a courtesy call on his opposite number at the *Ecole Supérieure de la Guerre*, General Ferdinand Foch.

This proved a fateful meeting, one with far-reaching consequences. Wilson declined the usual rapid VIP tour of the facilities.
He asked permission to sit in on the classes and at some point
during the day he became smitten with Foch's intellect and grasp
of military matters. That this was so is a cause for wonder, for
Foch's reputation hardly stands up to close critical inspection.

Foch was one of the architects of the pre-1914 French tactical
doctrine of 'offensive à outrance', the result of French deliberations on the disasters of 1870–71. Harking back to the successes
of the great Emperor Napoleon, the doctrine meant abandoning
any notion of defensive tactics or the husbanding of reserves in
favour of an all-out attack on the enemy, regardless of loss. This
doctrine was total tosh in the face of twentieth-century firepower,
and should have been seen as such by the French general staff
before it led to the slaughter of French infantry and much of their
officer corps in the early weeks of 1914. To be fair, Foch also
emphasized the need for commanders to understand the elements
of defence and withdrawal, but these requirements were overwhelmed by the alleged benefits credited to the offensive. Critics
might argue that this view is based on hindsight, but if senior officers creating a tactical doctrine for a coming war cannot see where
that doctrine will lead, what use are they?

Foch is also on record as saying, after Blériot had flown across
the English Channel in 1909, that the aeroplane was 'good for
sport but useless for war', another opinion that did not survive the
first weeks of the Great War when aerial reconnaissance became
vital and the growth of tactical air power began.

Lacking these reservations, Henry Wilson found Foch entranc-
ing. Invited for a chat before lunch, Wilson stayed on throughout
the afternoon and insisted on returning the next day for more discussions with his French colleague. He returned to Camberley
declaring that his encounter with Foch was a meeting of minds,
'Foch's appreciation of German moves through Belgium are completely the same as mine,' he recorded, 'the important line being
between Verdun and Namur.'[3]

A month after this visit Wilson was back in Paris for further talks. He was already exceeding his official brief, for his job at this time was training British officers in staff duties, not discussing military strategy with the French. In May 1911, Foch visited Wilson at Camberley, and in June Wilson accompanied Foch on an Ecole staff tour. Although they became close friends – Wilson was even invited to the wedding of Foch's daughter – there is little doubt that Foch was the master and Wilson the disciple in this budding professional relationship – Foch's well-known ability to wind British generals round his finger was never more apparent than at this time.

Nor was Wilson reticent in declaring where this friendship was leading, for their talks clearly ranged far beyond the day-to-day routine of staff training duties. After a lunch at the War Office in 1911, Wilson took Foch to the Royal United Services Institute (RUSI) and told the secretary, 'I've got a French general outside – General Foch, and mark my words – this fellow is going to command the Allied Armies when the big war comes.'[4]

Both men were vocal advocates of Britain's commitment of an Expeditionary Force to France immediately on the outbreak of war. There was one telling exchange during Wilson's second visit to Paris in 1910 when he asked Foch to define the smallest military force that the French would find useful. Foch's reply was illuminating: 'A single British soldier . . . and we shall see to it that he gets killed.'[5]

During his time at Camberley Wilson nipped across the Channel at every opportunity to immerse himself in Anglo-French affairs, but his big chance to shape events came in August 1910 when he was appointed Director of Military Operations at the War Office – the very position from which his predecessor, General Sir James Grierson, had started the staff 'conversations' with the French four years previously.

On his first day in the post Wilson sent for the files on these 'conversations' – and was appalled by what he found. In four years nothing of any practical value had emerged. There were no plans, no draft orders, no estimates, no proposals or counter-proposals, no railway timetables or shipping schedules; nothing had been done of any practical nature to order or transport a British Expeditionary Force to France.

Wilson was still digesting these facts when the French military attaché in London, Colonel Victor Huguet, was ushered in, hot-foot from the French Embassy, urging Wilson to take action and breathe fresh life into these moribund 'conversations'. This Wilson proceeded to do, with considerable energy and no little success. He arrived at the War Office with one aim – to get the Expeditionary Force organized for rapid mobilization and deployment in the event of war, and to ensure that deployment was to France, in support of the French Army – and nowhere else.

By March 1911, seven months later, Wilson and his staff had worked out a plan for moving six infantry divisions and a cavalry division – the entire British Army in the United Kingdom – to France, with great speed, immediately on the outbreak of war; the infantry divisions on the fourth day after the mobilization order – M4 – the cavalry on the seventh day – M7 – the artillery on the ninth day – M9.

Now Britain had an outline plan, but that plan still had to be worked out in detail – and obtain Cabinet approval. This last task would be difficult, for in 1908 a subcommittee of the CID had prepared a report[6] on *The Military Needs of the Empire* and reached the following conclusions:

A. The Committee in the first place desired to observe that in the event of an attack on France by Germany, the expediency of sending a military force abroad or relying on naval means alone is a matter of policy, which can only be decided by the Government of the day.

B. In view, however, of the possibility of a decision by the Cabinet to use military force, the Committee have examined the plans of the General Staff and are of the opinion that in the initial stages of a war between France and Germany, in which the Government decided to assist France, the plan to which preference is given by the General Staff is a valuable one and the General Staff should accordingly work out all the necessary details.

In short, there would be no formal military alliance with France at any time short of war. The staff were to work out a plan to assist France in case, and then only when the crunch came, the 'Government of the day' elected to approve of such assistance. This turned the normal process of government decision-making – political approval first, executive action later – on its head, but it suited the political needs of the moment. Undeterred by this caveat, Wilson's first task on taking up his post as DMO was to cross the Channel for further conversations with General Foch and members of the French General Staff.

In view of what follows it is important to understand Wilson's official position at this time. He was not an important figure in the War Office or among the military establishment. He was one of three officers on the third rung of the War Office ladder, below the CIGS, the Adjutant General, the Quartermaster General and the Master General of the Ordnance, far below the Secretary of State for War.

There were three directorates at the War Office – Military Operations, Staff Duties and Military Training; the other two directors were on the same level as Wilson and his equals in rank. Wilson was a Brigadier General, the lowest grade of general officer, and had neither the rank nor the appointment, let alone the official backing, to engage in high-level discussions on the deployment of British forces with the representatives of a foreign power. Given these facts, Wilson's actions and the latitude he was granted in pursuing his aims can only be described as remarkable.

However, given his aims, the question arises as to what the state of the British Army and the British Expeditionary Force was when Wilson took up his post as DMO in August 1910.

Writing in his diary in April 1908, R. D. Haldane records having assured the French Prime Minister, M. Clemenceau, that 'We have a force ready to co-operate with an ally on the Continent if necessary', adding that 'this force was fully equipped and so organised as to be capable of rapid mobilisation and transport'.[7]

Wilson's diary for 27 October 1910, two months after he

became DMO, disputes this claim and records the following: 'Long day in office. I am very dissatisfied with the state of affairs in every respect. No rail arrangements for concentration and movement of either Expeditionary Force or Territorials. No proper arrangements for horse supply, no arrangements for safe-guarding our arsenal at Woolwich. A lot of time spent writing beautiful but useless minutes.'[8]

Since both cannot be right, what was the true situation at this time? The answer lies in a War Office memorandum[9] issued late in 1911 and entitled 'Action taken since 1906 in preparing a plan for rendering military assistance to France in the event of an unprovoked attack on that power by Germany'. A pencilled note on the memorandum refers to the 'WF' (Wilson–Foch) scheme.[10] The memorandum details the progress of the plan and begins:

> After due consideration, and taking into account the requirements of home defence, the General Staff were of the opinion that our military resources would admit the formation of an Expeditionary Force for the purpose in view consisting of four divisions and a cavalry division . . . But if the scheme were to be of any value should the occasion arise for carrying it out, it was necessary to go further and to collect and formulate information regarding the ports of embarkation and railway transport thereto, transport by sea across the Channel, the ports of disembarkation, and railway transport therefrom to the assumed area of operations.

Then follows a brief account of steps taken from 1906, but the sum total of the report supports Major-General Sir Percy Radcliffe's allegation in the same War Office file that:

> When he [Wilson] took over the appointment as DMO, there were certain tentative schemes in the War Office pigeon-holes, but these were entirely academic. Not a single, practical step had been taken to give effect to them, no such thing as a railway timetable on our side of the Channel had even been attempted, nor would the QMG [the Quartermaster General, the staff officer officially concerned with transport and logistics] touch the business.

Wilson therefore faced an uphill task when he arrived at the War Office in August 1910. The government remained adamant that these Staff 'conversations' with France were not to be regarded as a firm commitment to military action and defence expenditure was concentrated on the Royal Navy, then engaged in its dreadnought race with the High Seas Fleet. Few practical steps had been taken to mobilize Britain's reserves in the event of hostilities, bring the divisions allocated to the BEF up to strength or make arrangements to ship them to France.

Wilson's diary for the next few months is full of notes on the difficulties he encountered in attempting to alter this situation. On 28 October he 'got off my detailed queries to the QMG in regard to horses for mobilisation'.[11] His queries came back the next day with the statement that the QMG's department were 'quite unable to give me the information I want and . . . no one can tell me where the horses are coming from nor when they will come. This is as I thought, but what a scandalous state of affairs! I'll push this to the end.'[12]

On 28 November Wilson writes: 'I had a long talk with the DST [Director of Staff Training] about horse mobilisation. He is taking my papers and will find out from the C-in-Cs when they expect to be mobilised; but the fact is clear and is this – that at the end of 1910 no one knows how long it will take us to mobilise. A disgraceful state of affairs.'[13]

On 2 January 1911, Wilson sums up the situation: 'Ever since last August I have been trying to find out when the four divisions (1, 2, 3, 5) of the Expeditionary Force will be ready to move and up till now (5 months), have been quite unable to do so.'

On 9 January Wilson writes, 'I told Nick [General Sir William Nicholson, the CIGS] he must support me in my endeavour to force Mills [the QMG] to make detailed arrangements for railing the Expeditionary Force to the ports of embarkation. At present absolutely nothing exists, which is scandalous.'[14]

Similar entries continue into the summer. Then Wilson's hand was strengthened on 1 July 1911 when the Kaiser sent the gunboat *Panther* to the Moroccan port of Agadir, allegedly to protect

German interests. At this, says Churchill, 'All the alarm bells throughout Europe began immediately to quiver.'[15]

The arrival of the *Panther* at Agadir seemed to promise a rerun of the 1905 Tangier Incident, and tension duly mounted between Berlin and Paris. British interests were affected, partly because the Moroccan question had supposedly been settled at Algeciras in 1906, but mainly because Agadir was a newly built port on the Atlantic coast of Morocco which might become a base for the High Seas Fleet. On 5 July Sir Edward Grey asked the German ambassador for an explanation and informed him that 'until Germany's intentions were known, the British Government's attitude remained one of reserve'.[16]

No reply was received from the German government and tension increased until 21 July when the Chancellor of the Exchequer, David Lloyd George, speaking at a dinner in the City of London, told the audience that 'if Britain were to be treated where her interests were vitally affected as if she were of no account in the Cabinet of Nations, then I say emphatically that peace at that price would be a humiliation intolerable for a great country like ours to endure'.[17]

These words produced a swift reaction from Berlin. The first response was a note to Sir Edward Grey so stiff that it seemed to suggest the possibility of war, and refusing to account for the presence of the *Panther* at Agadir. The Fleet was put on alert, the German note met with an equally stiff reply, and it was some weeks before the *Panther* left Agadir and tensions relaxed.

These alarm bells had also alerted Henry Wilson, and on 20 July he departed for Paris and further talks with the French general staff. Samuel Williamson comments: 'That this trip had Haldane's approval is not certain; that it did not have the Cabinet's sanction is certain.'[18]

In Paris, on 20 July 1911, after the usual disclaimer that this military agreement was not to be confused with any political intention, Wilson and General Auguste Dubail, Chief of the French General Staff, drew up a specific memorandum which provided for the dispatch of a British Expeditionary Force of six infantry divisions and a cavalry division to France in the event of British intervention in any Franco-German war. Wilson and Dubail both signed this memorandum,[19] Brigadier General Henry Wilson thereby committing the British government to a course of action that had no prior cabinet approval *whatsoever.*

This Wilson–Dubail memorandum was no vague declaration of intent. The terms were specific: the total BEF would consist of some 150,000 men – and 67,000 horses – and would come ashore at Boulogne, Le Havre or Rouen between the fourth and twelfth day after mobilization and proceed to concentrate near Maubeuge. Therefore, when war came, and if the British entered it, their course of action had already been proscribed; they would form part of the French Army, charged with protecting the left flank of that Army from envelopment by the German Army.

This was certainly the view taken by a delighted Colonel Huguet, who alleged that the French had persuaded Wilson and the British general staff that there should be no 'secondary theatre of operations' but common action in 'the main theatre, that is to say, the French'.[20]

If the French had indeed persuaded Wilson to support this deployment it must have been a simple task, for Wilson needed little persuasion. On his return from Paris he did not hesitate to present the Foreign Secretary and the Secretary of State for War with his fait accompli, even telling them what they had to do if – when – war came about. 'First, we must join the French. Second, we must mobilise on the same day as the French. Third, we must send all six divisions.'[21]

Why these senior politicians should let themselves be lectured by a fairly junior army officer is hard to say, but Wilson's position was strong at this time, not because of his rank, position or reputation, but because of his convictions. He knew what to do at a time when everyone else seemed to be dithering, and this conviction – that he alone knew what to do – carried Wilson along. Rather than being an adviser to the Chief of the Imperial General Staff, he became the quasi-official spokesman for the Army view on Franco-British military cooperation – though the views he presented were those he shared with Foch and the French General Staff, not with his British colleagues and superiors at the War Office.

British views he tended to dismiss: 'I was profoundly dissatisfied with the grasp of the situation possessed by Grey and Haldane,' he wrote in his diary on 9 August 1911, commenting on Kitchener and General Sir John French the following day that 'neither of [them] knows anything at all about the subject'.[22] In other words, when it came to Franco-British affairs, the Foreign Secretary and the War Minister as well as Britain's senior field marshal and most experienced general must take the advice of a Staff brigadier. Hubris could hardly be greater.

There were, of course, other views on how British strength might be deployed in war, not least those of the Royal Navy. Since the Army and Navy views differed somewhat, on 23 August the Prime Minister, Hubert Asquith, called a special meeting of the CID to consider what should be done in the event of war between France and Germany. Asquith and the Foreign Secretary, Sir Edward Grey, were privy to the staff 'conversations' and believed that an Expeditionary Force should be sent to France. Wilson had already moved the issue forward by concluding the agreement with Dubail – the question was not should Britain intervene, but where and how? To ease matters along, several ministers known to oppose any continental intervention – and blissfully unaware of the existence of these Anglo-French 'conversations' – were not invited to this meeting. Those present included Asquith, Sir Edward Grey, the War Minister, R. G. Haldane, Lloyd George, the Chancellor of the Exchequer, Winston Churchill, then Home Secretary, and two known opponents of intervention, the First Lord of the Admiralty, Reginald McKenna, and the First Sea Lord, Admiral Sir Arthur Wilson.

The meeting lasted all day. Asquith proposed that Brigadier General Wilson should present the army's argument in the morning and Admiral Sir Arthur Wilson should put the Royal Navy's case in the afternoon. This 'Battle of the Two Wilsons', as it came to be called, was a triumph for Henry Wilson, who came to the meeting well prepared and wiped the deck with his unfortunate namesake.

'I put all my big maps on the wall,' Wilson wrote in his diary, 'and lectured for one and a half hours. Everyone very nice. Much questioning, especially from Winston and Lloyd George.'[23] Wilson began by explaining the military position on the Continent. He demonstrated convincingly that unless the BEF was sent to France immediately on the outbreak of war, it would arrive too late to prevent the French armies being outflanked and overrun – and that if these armies were overrun before Russia could mobilize, German victory was certain.

The crux of the matter was *time*. The BEF must mobilize when the French did. Whether the BEF went to Belgium or fell in on the French left – northern – flank, it must be shipped across the Straits of Dover where the troop transports would be safe from German naval attack. That done, the French would transport the BEF to Maubeuge, from where it could be sent either to Belgium or into position alongside the French. It should be noted that at no time during this presentation did Wilson mention his recent meetings with the French general staff or the Wilson–Dubail agreement. At the end of this tour de force Wilson sat down and turned the floor over to the admiral.

Admiral Sir Arthur Wilson's effort has been described as 'a pathetically inept presentation of sketchy naval plans for amphibious landings on the German coast, aimed at drawing troops away from the Western Front'.[24] Wilson was, in fact, regurgitating Admiral Jackie Fisher's old scheme of putting troops ashore in Schleswig-Holstein, calculating that a landing there – less than 100 miles from Berlin – would oblige the Germans to rush back from France to protect the Reich. That argument would have failed even had it been well presented, for the original counter-arguments still held good. Britain did not have the amphibious shipping or expertise to land a large force in the Baltic and the Germans could reinforce the defending units in Holstein far faster than the Royal Navy could ferry troops ashore from Britain.

The next logical action for Asquith was to set the CID secretariat to examining both plans and providing the Cabinet with some sound advice. Nothing could or would be done unless the Cabinet gave its approval – and most of the Cabinet, and some important members of the CID, did not know that the Staff 'conversations' had taken place since 1906, let alone about the Wilson–Dubail accord. Asquith therefore did nothing, hoping, as he told Haldane in a letter, 'that we may not have again to consider the contingency'.[25] Had the Agadir crisis of 1911 blown up into a full-scale war, Britain would have been entering the conflict without any pre-arranged political direction, but fortunately the crisis passed. Nerves jangling, the politicians returned to the policy of hoping for the best, and Henry Wilson continued to hone his preparations for mobilizing the BEF and sending it to France.

In the following months Wilson continued to commute across the Channel for more meetings with the French chiefs, interspersing these trips with the submission of advice, some of it requested, some not, to the leaders of the British government. Wilson's diary at this time makes interesting reading, demonstrating that his position as international *éminence gris* was doing nothing for his modesty. The entries for August 1911, for example, contain the following passage: 'After lunch Winston Churchill came to my room and discussed the present situation which, according to him, has become critical. He remained three hours with me . . . I was rather pleased with Winston.'[26] On the following day Wilson records: 'A despatch from Fairholm, MA [Military Assistant] in Paris, describing an interview he had with General Joffre, the new Chief of Staff in Paris. In the main, Joffre seems to agree with me.'

If Wilson's diary is accurate, his position at this time resembles that of a spider at the centre of a web; nothing happens of which he is unaware, no action is taken unless he is consulted – and all this, be it remembered, when Wilson was merely one of three directorate heads at the War Office and a brigadier, the lowest rung on the general officers' ladder. Nevertheless, at least according to Wilson, senior ministers – Churchill, Grey, Lloyd George – come to visit him, asking his advice, seeking his opinions.

Wilson also maintained close contact with the French military attaché, Colonel Huguet. On 9 September 1911, his diary records:

> Huguet spent an hour with me in the office. I impressed on him the value of Belgian active support. He went back and told Cambon [the French ambassador] who is going to Paris tomorrow and will lay this out before the Ministers. I showed him my maps with German and French troops on them. He was immensely struck with all the work and knowledge this meant. He told me where the French General Staff wanted us to go and what their plans are. This is the first time I have been told. He told me also that if I had gone to the manoeuvres, M. Massigny [the French war minister] was himself going to invest me with the Legion of Honour.

It does not seem to have occurred to Wilson that this information on the intentions of the French should have been passed to his superiors in the War Office or that Royal – not merely official – permission is needed before a British officer can accept a foreign decoration. Wilson had effectively taken full charge of Anglo-French military plans; the Wilson–Dubail memorandum may have contained the usual reservations about political approval and no firm commitment, but these were negated when Wilson handed over the BEF's order of battle and agreed with French proposals for the deployment of the BEF. As always, actions speak louder than words, and Wilson's involvement with the French General Staff continued.

When Wilson is invited to consult with the French General Staff on 28 November 1911, he goes to Paris. It never seems to occur to him that a more senior officer might be more appropriate, or that he should ask the CIGS's permission; he simply goes. Moreover, once there he is clearly accepted as Britain's plenipotentiary – no one questions his ability to make decisions or commit his country's armed forces to a continental struggle.

'They showed me papers and maps,' he writes, 'copies of which they are giving me, showing in detail the area of concentration for all our Expeditionary Force. Intensely interesting. We had a long discussion. Afterwards we went through many other matters.'[27]

Quite what the French staff were doing, blithely drawing up detailed plans for the concentration of the British Army in France, is neither questioned nor examined.

Wilson's diary contains no indication that on his return to London he passed on the details of these 'intensely interesting' discussions to his superiors in Whitehall or Downing Street. Indeed, after a few days he is off to France again, this time to make a cycle tour of the roads along and behind the eastern frontier, from the Belgian border to Verdun and Mars-la-Tour, where a most curious incident took place.

Mars-la-Tour had been one of the battlefields of 1870 and was now dominated by a statue of 'France', 'looking as beautiful as ever,' says Wilson, 'so I laid at her feet a small bit of map I have been carrying, showing the areas of concentration of the British forces on her territory'. As John Terraine remarks, 'This was an odd procedure on many counts – not least that of security . . . but its significance lay in the fact that when war came Wilson's plan for the British Army was the only one in existence.'[28]

By the time he returned to London in October, Wilson's plans had received a most welcome boost. The obstructive Reginald McKenna had gone from the Admiralty and Winston Churchill was now First Lord. This was wonderful news; up to now the Admiralty had been less than helpful in supplying Wilson with the shipping schedules and the transport ships necessary to get the BEF to the French ports. With the dynamic Churchill – a man who shared Wilson's vision – now in the post, this part of the plan would surely forge ahead.

There was then a small problem in Cabinet – actually a 'serious difference', according to Wilson, because those Cabinet ministers not present at the CID meeting, the 'non-interventionists', those opposed to any formal alliance with France, had now been told – probably by McKenna – of what had transpired at the August meeting and of the five-year course of the secret Franco-British conversations. The Cabinet outsiders were naturally furious and, again according to Wilson, were 'opposed to all idea of war and especially angry with me'.[29] Wilson survived the non-interventionists' displeasure and from January 1912 to August 1914 continued to work on plans to ship the BEF to France. The threat of war had faded after Agadir, but no one doubted that fresh causes would arise and there was a lot to do before the BEF could actually move – again, always supposing it was ordered to move by 'the Government of the day'.

Meanwhile, there were some changes in the British Establishment. General Sir William Nicholson left the War Office in March 1912 and was replaced as CIGS by Field Marshal Sir John French, and Richard Haldane, the Secretary of State for War, went to the Woolsack as Lord Chancellor and was replaced at the War Office by Colonel Jack Seeley – a member of parliament as well as an army officer. Neither Colonel Seeley nor Sir John French was any match for Wilson, who had no difficulty convincing them of the validity of his plans.

One political step taken at this time was the completion of the Anglo-French Naval Agreement of 1912, by which the Royal Navy undertook to protect the Channel coast – and therefore any troop convoys to France – while the French fleet took over the main burden of defending the Mediterranean. This agreement came about because the Kaiser, yet again, had overplayed his hand. In February 1912 Asquith sent Haldane to Berlin to urge the Germans not to proceed with further warship construction; if the Kaiser would desist from building more dreadnoughts it would greatly ease British fears and lead to a general relaxation of tension. The Kaiser would agree to this only if Britain in turn agreed to remain neutral in the event of war between Germany and France. Britain refused to accept this bargain and Haldane returned from Berlin convinced that war was only a matter of time.

By the end of 1912 Wilson's plans for the BEF had reached the point where Joffre could tell the French Cabinet that 'L'Armée W'– so called after their stoutest ally – would consist of 145,000 men and be ready for action in France on M15; no mention was made of the necessary approval from the British Cabinet. During 1913 the process of consultation continued. Wilson was in Paris every month, 'tightening and perfecting his arrangements with the French',[30] and by the spring of 1914 these arrangements were all in place. Then came a sudden distraction.

Ireland had been a thorn in the side of Britain's body politic for most of the nineteenth century. For the last few years it had been moving towards Home Rule, which the majority Catholic population wanted but to which the Ulster Protestants in the North, led by Sir Edward Carson, were totally opposed. Declaring that 'Home Rule meant Rome Rule', Carson had imported rifles and ammunition into Ulster and made ready to contest the Catholic majority's claim to a united Ireland, if need be by force. The British Government were determined to get the Home Rule bill through and be shot of the Irish for ever, and had no intention of letting Carson and his Orangemen get in the way.

Therefore, in March 1914, Brigadier General Hubert Gough, commanding the 3rd Cavalry Brigade at the Curragh camp near Dublin, was ordered to issue live ammunition to his troops and prepare to march on Belfast to suppress any Loyalist attempts to resist Home Rule. Naval units were ordered into Belfast Lough, and it was hoped that this display of force and firmness would nip any trouble in the bud.

The soldiers and sailors did not like this order. On 21 March an Army conference in Dublin discussed this order, noted the officers' objections and stated that any officer from the North could go on leave until the crisis was over. This was a limited concession; officers from any other part of the UK who opposed this act of coercion would be obliged to comply or resign their commission. The Army liked this suggestion even less, and most of the officers in the 3rd Cavalry Brigade promptly sent in their papers; they would neither take up arms against the Protestants nor support any government attempt to bully Ulster into a united Ireland. In taking this action the cavalry officers were quite right; soldiers must obey all lawful orders but no order can oblige a British soldier to deliver his fellow citizens by force into the power and jurisdiction of another country.

The 'Curragh Incident' rumbled on for months and caused

considerable dissension in Parliament and the Army until Field Marshal French, Colonel Seeley and the Adjutant General of the Army, Sir John Ewart, were obliged to resign. Prime Minister Asquith took over the War Office portfolio, but the incident led to a complete if temporary breakdown in relations between the Cabinet and the War Office.

The incident was still at the top of Britain's political agenda on 28 June 1914, when a Serbian student shot the Archduke Franz-Ferdinand, heir to the Austro-Hungarian thrones. From that moment Europe slid inexorably towards war – and the British Government was dragged ever closer to that dreaded moment of commitment with France.

Churchill recalls that on Friday, 24 July 1914, the Cabinet were still discussing the Irish Home Rule bill and attempting to fix the boundaries of Fermanagh and Tyrone when 'Sir Edward Grey's voice was heard, reading a document which had just been brought to him from the Foreign Office. It was the Austrian Note to Serbia.' Churchill continues: 'This Note was clearly an ultimatum,' and its arrival in Grey's hands marks the point where the British Government first realized that Europe was on a path for war.

On 1 August, France declared war on Germany, and the situation predicted in the report of the CID subcommittee in 1909[31] had now come to pass. The decision on whether or not to aid France had then been reserved for 'the Government of the day', which, it now transpired, was still essentially the Government of 1909. The 'necessary details' required of the General Staff in 1909 had been worked out by Henry Wilson and the moment of decision could be put off no longer. Would the British Government send the BEF to France or not?

The Government hesitated. This hesitation, however understandable in retrospect, infuriated many people at the time. M. Cambon, the French ambassador, was soon asking Sir Edward Grey whether England was 'going to wait until French territory was invaded before intervening?' . . . in which case, he added, British help might be 'very belated'. As tension mounted and nerves frayed, M. Cambon's demands became ever more shrill. Reminded that the British 'commitment', in so far as it existed at all, was no more than a matter of honour, he retorted, *'Et l'honneur? Est-ce que l'Angleterre comprend ce que c'est l' honneur?'*[32]

Asquith's problem was that the Cabinet was split. On 1 August, twelve out of eighteen Cabinet members declared themselves totally opposed to giving the French any assurance of British support, and there were signs of similar opposition in the House of Commons. Even so, some moves in support of France were being made. On 28 July the British Grand Fleet, assembled at Spithead, was ordered by Churchill to sail for its war stations at Scapa Flow, and other naval units were put on a war footing. However, on 1 August, when Grey asked for authority to implement the naval agreement and seal off the Channel, four members of the cabinet resigned.

To muster Cabinet support and gain parliamentary approval, Asquith and Grey needed something more fundamental than a desire to help France in her hour of need. This was found in the 1839 treaty guaranteeing Belgian neutrality, to which Britain, France and Germany were signatories; if Germany violated the frontiers of Belgium, Asquith and Grey would have the justification they needed to put Britain in the field with France.

Asquith's problems in Cabinet and the House of Commons were not appreciated by Henry Wilson. His plan called for the BEF to mobilize on the same day as the French Army, and as the hours and days went by Wilson became, in Callwell's words, 'seriously disturbed'.[33] On 1 August Wilson and Nicholson, Chief of the Imperial General Staff, went to see Grey, and Wilson spent the rest of that day moving ceaselessly between the War Office, the French Embassy and the Foreign Office – by the evening he was 'very pessimistic, all countries mobilising except us'.

On that day Germany declared war on Russia, Belgium mobilized her army and General Joffre went to the French Minister of War and asked permission to begin a general mobilization at midnight. Britain then asked the French government if the French Army would respect the neutrality of Belgium, and a similar query went to Berlin. The French replied that no French soldier would cross the Belgian frontier. Germany made no reply at all, knowing that her advance brigades were in Luxembourg and already close to or over the Belgian frontier.

Brigadier Wilson was by now frantic. Everyone knew – for had he not told them? – that Britain must mobilize *at the same time as the French*; now the French reservists were rushing to their depots and Asquith still refused to order the BEF to France. The Royal Navy would protect French shipping and Channel ports against aggression but the French wanted the *immediate* commitment of a British Expeditionary Force and muttered about British perfidy when the troops did not arrive. The hours and then the days went by, and still the BEF did not move.

With the rest of Europe mobilizing, diplomatic attention now turned to London, where Asquith and the Cabinet were still deliberating. The Foreign Secretary was coming under considerable pressure from the French ambassador, M. Cambon, while in Berlin the British ambassador, Sir Edward Groschen, was coming under similar pressure from the German Chancellor, Theobald von Bethmann-Hollweg. M. Cambon wanted the British to come out in support of France and send troops to the Continent at once. Germany, said Bethmann-Hollweg, wanted Britain to stay neutral, declaring that Britain should not intervene in a continental quarrel 'just for a word, neutrality – just for a scrap of paper' – his term for that 1839 treaty that guaranteed Belgian neutrality.

On the afternoon of 3 August Sir Edward Grey went to Parliament and presented the government's position to the House of Commons. His task was difficult for he was, says Barbara Tuchman, 'committed to support France by virtue of something that was not a commitment'.[34] Therefore, in presenting his case to Parliament, Grey wisely decided to come clean about past actions and events.

He told members about the long-running staff 'conversations' and about the British naval agreement with France. He admitted that there was no treaty requiring Britain to aid France in the event of war but urged consideration of 'British interests, British honour and British obligations', asking the House whether Britain could stand by while Belgium was overrun. Finally, Grey presented members with a choice – the issue was the neutrality of Belgium, the choice was to intervene or do nothing. Amid loud applause and the waving of order papers, the House signified its support for war if the German Army did not withdraw from Belgium within twenty-four hours.

This support was not unanimous. Two leaders of the Labour Party, Ramsay MacDonald and Keir Hardie, spoke out against further involvement, MacDonald opting for neutrality, Keir Hardie taking the line adopted by many European socialists at this time – total opposition to war on any grounds. Nevertheless, Grey carried the day; two of the four Cabinet members who had resigned that morning agreed to return and an ultimatum was sent to Berlin, requiring Germany to halt the invasion of Belgium by midnight Continental Time on 4 August – 11 p.m. in Britain – or face war with Great Britain.

On 4 August, Germany informed the Belgian government that German troops would march through Belgium, using force if necessary to clear their path. In fact this move had already begun; German troops were already exchanging fire with Belgian troops and would soon be shooting Belgian civilians allegedly for acting as guerrillas – *francs-tireurs* – and slowing their progress through the country. That afternoon the British government ordered general mobilization and sent out telegrams recalling all reservists to the Colours. No reply was received to Britain's ultimatum, and at 11 p.m. (2300 hours) on 4 August 1914, Britain was at war with Germany.

The delivery of the ultimatum, the general mobilization and the declaration of war led to an immediate flurry of activity – closely resembling panic – in both Downing Street and the War Office. Britain had entered the war or was about to do so, but what would happen now and what action should be taken? Fortunately, the chief secretary to the cabinet, Maurice Hankey, had long since prepared a 'War Book', a fat volume covering the actions every Government department needed to take on the outbreak of war.

This War Book went into the greatest detail. It included proclamtions that needed only the King's signature, detailed plans for the dispatch of telegrams to reservists via the Post Office, orders for the immediate requisition of trains and boats – and horses – and warrants for the arrest of known spies. Nothing had been neglected, and every department of state knew what to do, but inevitably there were flaws. The most notable was in the orders for the dispatch of the BEF to France. These ordered the troops 'to mobilise' but failed to add the words, 'and embark'.

This flaw enraged Brigadier General Wilson. According to his plan, the BEF should already have mobilized and be on its way to the ports. Now it could not even begin to move until 5 August at the earliest – five days behind his long-prepared schedule – and in military matters delay is often followed by dissent. So it was here. Wilson's plan dictated that the BEF should consist of six divisions – the entire British Army in the United Kingdom, less the Territorial force. Now the Government prevaricated yet again, unable to face the prospect of totally denuding the country of its prime means of defence – though Winston Churchill was sure that the Royal Navy alone could deter any possible aggressor.

The lack of a War Minister since Seeley's resignation four months previously was resolved on 4 August when Lord Kitchener – Kitchener of Khartoum, Britain's most distinguished soldier – was located boarding a ferry at Dover on his way back to Egypt, and was summoned back to London and offered the post of Secretary of State for War. Kitchener accepted and took up his new position on 6 August – so adding another opinion to the BEF debate.

Although the post of Secretary of State for War was a political appointment, Kitchener was on the active Army List. His selection as War Minister was to cause problems, not least for Wilson and the newly-appointed commander of the BEF, Field Marshal Sir John French, who had now been recalled to duty. Kitchener was an autocrat, a soldier rather than an administrator, and a poor conciliator of opposing views. On the face of it he was ill suited to his task, but he took up his new duties at once and flung himself into the job of expanding the British Army and the munitions industry that supported it. His first decisions as War Minister showed sound judgement, and the decisions he took in his first weeks in office would serve Britain well in the years ahead.

His first proposal was to keep two Regular divisions in Britain – a decision that naturally infuriated Henry Wilson. Kitchener was also one of the few people in Britain to realize that this war would be a long one – Haig was another – and that Britain would need to raise and train armies running into millions, create a munitions industry and prepare for a conflict that might last for years. Trained soldiers, officers and NCO instructors were essential for this process and must not all be sent to France. In both these conclusions Kitchener was quite correct. His next decision, that the Territorial force was not a suitable medium for the raising of vast new armies, was at best debatable and probably wrong.

The final decisions in this eight-year-long, pre-war saga, were taken at a War Council meeting in Downing Street at 4 p.m. (1600 hours) on 5 August. Those present included almost everyone with a point of view, including the elderly Field Marshal Lord Roberts and Henry Wilson, whose diary gives some idea of the proceedings:

> Asquith stated that he had summoned the great soldiers at the earliest possible moment. Then a lot of platitudes on the situation and strategy generally. Winston said the Dover Straits were now completely sealed. Jimmy Grierson spoke up for decisive numbers at the decisive point. Sir John French said we should go over at once and decide destination later. Haig asked questions and this led to our discussing strategy like idiots.
>
> Johnnie Hamilton plumped for going to Amiens as soon as possible. Then desultory strategy (some thinking Liege was in Holland) and idiocy. Kitchener plumped for Amiens but wanted to get in closer touch with the French; suggested they should send over an officer.
>
> Question then arose on what strength the BEF should be. Winston in favour of sending 6 divisions as naval situation most favourable owing to our having time to prepare. Lord Bobs agreed. Decision

taken that we should prepare at once for all six (infantry) divisions. All agreed. A historic meeting of men, mostly entirely ignorant of their subject.[35]

Wilson's opinion of his colleagues and superiors did not change in the next few days. Kitchener assumed charge at the War Office on 6 August and promptly revoked the order for the dispatch of all six divisions. Now only four would go, plus the cavalry division, with a fifth to follow later; embarkation would begin on Sunday, 9 August.

Wilson, now appointed Sub-Chief of Staff at BEF headquarters and promoted to major-general, continued to deal directly with the French. On 7 August, Colonel Huguet returned from Paris, where he had been in discussions with Joffre. He went directly to see Wilson, who briefed him on the War Council meeting and let him go back to Paris – without meeting Kitchener. The Secretary of State was naturally anxious for some direct contact with the French, and Wilson's action provoked a flaming row. Kitchener, wrote Wilson, '. . . was angry because I let Huguet go and angrier still because I had told Huguet everything about our starting on Sunday. I answered back, as I have no intention of being bullied by him, especially when he talks such nonsense as he did today.'[36]

Callwell's comment on this exchange is interesting. Normally sycophantic towards his subject, Callwell now writes, 'It must be allowed that even on his own showing, Wilson adopted a tone towards a superior that any superior would be justified in resenting and which to a man of Lord Kitchener's record and temperament was bound to give serious offence.'

Falling out with his superior officer hardly mattered now. Wilson's work was done and his time at the War Office was over. A week later, on 14 August, Henry Wilson crossed to France with Sir John French's Expeditionary Force Headquarters.

The bulk of the BEF had already preceded him, the front-line units and supply trains following the plans Wilson had worked out in such detail since 1910. His arrangements stood up to the test of war and delivered the BEF to that place on the left wing of the

French Army where Wilson and Foch had agreed it should go years before.

The role of Henry Wilson was crucial to the dispatch of the BEF to France in 1914. The course of Anglo-French relations is clear from 1898; Fashoda was a turning point. Both nations felt in need of friends as the new century dawned and ancient enmities were put aside with the 1904 *Entente Cordiale*. A subsequent series of crises – Tangier in 1905, Agadir in 1911 – kept the British interest in the *Entente* alive and inspired the French desire to turn it into a firm and open military alliance.

At this point British and French interests began to diverge. The British position is laid out most clearly in that subcommittee report of 1909 which concluded that any decision on British involvement in a continental war would be left to 'the Government of the day', but because that Government might indeed decide to get involved the staff 'conversations' started in 1906 were valuable and should continue.

This policy reflected the British position until the outbreak of war: sitting on the fence, putting off the day of decision while hoping that it might not arrive – while allowing for a degree of preparation in case it did. However, implicit in continuing the 'conversations' post-1909 was the point endlessly reiterated since 1906: that the 'conversations' were not, and must not become or be seen as steps towards, a formal alliance.

Given the French determination to overturn this latter point, maintaining the British position was always going to be difficult. Even so, it might have been managed and the BEF deployment remained a dusty plan in some War Office pigeon-hole but for the advent as DMO of Brigadier General Henry Wilson. Wilson's weight tipped the scale in favour of the French position. Indeed, had the British Government deliberately intended to undermine its own policy it could not have done more than appoint Henry Wilson to the post of DMO and keep him there when his intentions became plain and his methods obvious. Lacking any firm control or political direction, Wilson took over the show and built his DMO job into a position of influence.

Williamson quotes a 1911 comment by Sir Arthur Nicholson, Permanent Under-Secretary at the Foreign Office, to the effect that 'although there had been a certain amount of desultory talk with the French', Nicholson doubted that 'a concerted plan of action will ever be settled'. Williamson then comments that 'Nicholson, like his superiors, had misjudged the character, ability and ambitions of Henry Wilson'.[37]

Bramall and Jackson endorse this point, stating that after Wilson's triumph at the CID meeting in August 1911 'British strategic policy in the run up to the First World War was thus to be based upon one brilliantly partisan exposition by Henry Wilson'.[38]

The conclusion has to be that Henry Wilson played a major, indeed a decisive, part in the departure of the BEF to France in 1914. Why he did so is fairly clear: an engrained Francophilia, an overwhelming admiration for Ferdinand Foch, contempt for his political and military superiors in Britain, personal arrogance, and a sense of mission.

These were Wilson's convictions and characteristics. They provided a personal motivation, but that alone would not have achieved Wilson's desired objective. For that he needed the context of European affairs, post-Fashoda, and that chronic dichotomy in the British Government's position. From these he gained the freedom to develop and implement a logistical plan for moving the BEF to France on the left wing of the French Army – and nowhere else.

The WF plan and Wilson's preparations to implement it, described earlier, were a miracle of organization. The plan worked perfectly; the BEF move to France was accomplished swiftly and without problems. Moreover, the existence of a complex, workable, logistical plan gave Wilson a great deal of influence in the pre-war period. His actions from 1910 and their outcome in 1914 provide a classic example of the effect one determined individual, even in a relatively junior role, can have on a government's political and strategic policies.

Whether Wilson was right is another matter. It can be argued that if France and Germany were to go to war Britain must inevitably become involved, if only to protect her strategic position.

That being so, preparations for a full commitment of the BEF were both necessary and wise.

This view now seems correct, but fails to make Wilson's case, that the BEF should mobilize at the same time as the French and form up on the left wing of the French Army to help stem the German advance towards Paris. The British Army was too small to make any decisive intervention and in the event did little to impede the progress of the German armies to the Marne – losing many good men in the process.

There is one final point about the BEF deployment which strikes at the root of the British Government's pre-1914 position – and Wilson's actions during that period. The British Government's reluctance to face up to the prospect of a European war with all it might entail, and Wilson's determination to commit the BEF to France at the start of the struggle, combined to create a tragedy. The *British Official History* claims that the BEF that went to France in 1914 was 'the best trained, best organized and best equipped British Army that ever went forth to war'.[39] Then comes the qualification . . . 'except in the matter of numbers; so that though not "contemptible" it was almost negligible in comparison with continental armies, even of the smaller states. In heavy guns and howitzers, high explosive shell, trench mortars, hand grenades and much of the subsidiary material required for siege and trench warfare it was almost wholly deficient. Further, no steps had been taken to instruct the army in a knowledge of the probable theatre of war or of the German Army.'

Wilson's planning, so detailed and so central to his main ambition, left out these essential provisions. The result was the events that followed: the rapid destruction of the BEF, starting at the Battle of Mons in August, culminating with the terrible losses incurred at the First Battle of Ypres in October and November 1914. These losses and the destruction of that Army can largely be attributed to the pre-war actions of the British Government and Henry Wilson.

The Government was responsible for sending the BEF to fight the kind of war for which it was woefully ill equipped, and

Wilson's obsession with the French blinded him to the fact that the BEF was not designed for a continental struggle. If, instead of working hand in glove with French intentions, he had devoted his formidable energies to bringing the state of the BEF to public attention, or doing something about it in the War Office, matters might have gone differently after the BEF went to France in August 1914.

4

Mobilization, Transport and Logistics

1911– 1914

*In most military books strategy and tactics are emphasized at the
expense of the administrative factors . . . Bear in mind when you
study military history or military events the importance of the
administrative factor, because it is where most critics and many
generals go wrong.*
     General Sir Archibald Wavell, *Generals and Generalship*, p. 11

Before following the BEF to its first engagement at Mons it would
be as well to look briefly at the logistical arrangements that
brought these British soldiers to the firing line. As the previous
chapters will have indicated, the process of getting the BEF to
France took years and an immense amount of planning and preparation. This task tested Henry Wilson's capabilities to the limit,
and his achievement cannot be fully appreciated without an
understanding of logistics, that part of the military art concerned
with the problems of movement and supply.

    That this subject needs a closer look is revealed in an address by
Major-General Sir Percy de B. Radcliffe, KCMG, CB, DSO, following
the publication of the first volume of the *British Official History*:

> Certain passages in the *Official History* appear likely to give quite a
> false impression of the extent and thoroughness of the preparations
> made by the British Naval and Military Authorities for the embark-

ation of the British Expeditionary Force and its concentration in the theatre of operations.

On page 25, it is true, it is stated that a scheme had been elaborated between the General Staffs for the concentration of the British Expeditionary Force between AVESNES and LE CATEAU. On the other hand, from the account of the meetings at the War Office on the 5th and 6th August, the casual reader might infer that the whole plan of concentration was evolved and decided upon at these meetings.

It would be a very bad thing indeed if the idea should be allowed to gain ground that the movement of a large force from its place of mobilisation in the United Kingdom to the ports of embarkation – its transport by sea, its disembarkation in French ports and movements thence by rail to the concentration area, all within a period of 14 days, could be improvised on the spur of the moment.[1]

Major-General Radcliffe gives much of the credit for the rapid mobilization of the BEF to Henry Wilson as DMO and is clearly unaware that Wilson was acting without any official sanction, with a very small staff and obliged to keep these plans and preparations secret, not least from the Cabinet and Parliament.

At the start of the twentieth century the science of logistics was essentially new, though the problems of military supply had existed since armies were created. However rudimentary the supply structure, an army's logistical arrangements remain fundamental to military success. Without adequate supplies of men, food, ammunition and transport an army cannot function for long, and the advent of advanced technology at the end of the nineteenth century, the growing size of armies and the complexity of their equipment had only added to the problem. This much applied to all European armies, but the problems facing Henry Wilson when he decided to send the BEF to France – and nowhere else – in 1911 were more fundamental than mere supply.

To begin with the British Army of 1914 was small, fully volunteer, largely deployed overseas and composed of men on a twelve-year engagement. As explained earlier, seven years would be spent with the Colours and five on the reserve; the bulk of the Army consisted of reservists. Infantry regiments were organized on a two-battalion basis. One battalion would be fully up to strength – 978 rifles – and serve overseas. The other would remain in the UK depot, training recruits and sending drafts abroad to top up the ranks of the first battalion.

Periodically these battalions would change round, but the home battalion was always under strength, and it was these home battalions that had to provide the teeth of the British Expeditionary Force in war. To a greater or lesser extent, the same circumstances applied to the cavalry regiments and the artillery, where the mobilization problem was compounded by the need for an abundance of horses.

Each infantry division comprised three brigades, each of four battalions, plus 'divisional troops' – artillery, engineers, supply and transport lines, medical units and mounted troops – giving a division a strength of some 18,000 men, of whom 12,000 were infantry and 4,000 were artillery, manning the division's seventy-six supporting guns (fifty-four 18-pounders, eighteen howitzers and four 60–pounders). The machine-gun scale was two per battalion or twenty-four in a division. A cavalry division was smaller, consisting of four brigades, each of three regiments, plus 'divisional troops' as above; a cavalry division mustered around 9,000 men with 10,000 horses, twenty 13-pounder guns of the horse artillery and again twenty-four machine guns.

The first task for the army staff on receiving the cabinet order to mobilize was to recall the reservists and form the divisions. Across the army as a whole, 60 per cent of the BEF soldiers that went to France in 1914 were reservists, so each home infantry battalion needed around six hundred men to bring it up to strength on mobilization. This could take time, for even the home battalions were not necessarily at their depots.

To give just one example: the depot of the 1st Battalion The Gordon Highlanders was at Aberdeen in north-east Scotland, but in August 1914 the battalion was stationed in Plymouth in south-west England. The mobilization order was received at the Gordons' depot at 1720 hours on 4 August and telegrams went out to 531 reservists. These men had to travel to Aberdeen from all over Britain and pick up their kit before heading for Plymouth at the other end of the country. The battalion was not fully mustered for another four days.[2] This ate considerably into the twelve days allotted by the WF plan for the mobilization of the entire BEF and its arrival at the forming-up position in France.

The number of reservists who had to be recalled to their depots and clothed, armed and equipped before they could join their battalions to complete the 160,000-strong BEF amounted to some 98,000 men. This was a complicated administrative task, and none of these reservists could be recalled until the cabinet decided to mobilize the army – a political decision over which Wilson had no control.

However, the most pressing need on mobilization was for horses; without horses the army could not move. Horses were not on any War Office list and could not be kept in reserve, but they were essential for early-twentieth-century warfare, not least for the movement of guns across country. An account of the logistical problems facing Wilson and the BEF should therefore begin with a study of the artillery, and in particular of the artillery's dependence on horses.

In 1914 the majority of European armies relied on horse transport. Horses were needed for pulling guns and transport wagons, for mounting the cavalry, much of the artillery, some infantry officers and most of the staff. The strength of the British Expeditionary Force on a six-division scale is shown in the table on page 84,[3] which notes an immediate need for 60,368 horses.

According to Robert Grey,[4] in August 1914 the British Army had only 25,000 horses, a fact confirmed in the *British Official History*;[5] the rest had to requisitioned from riding schools, hunts, private individuals and public companies. The official pre-war estimate was that, allowing for casualties, the Army would need 165,000 horses in the first three months.

During the first two weeks of the war the British Army purchased some 140,000 horses – including all the tram horses from Morecambe and many other seaside towns[6] – and within twelve

The Strength of the Expeditionary Force on a Six-division Basis – May 1913

	Officers	Other ranks	Horses	Guns	Machine guns	Horsed	Motor cars	MT vehicles	Motorcycles	Bicycles
							VEHI	CLES		
FIELD ARMY										
Cavalry division	467	9,412	10,327	24	24	582	23	–	18	371
6 divisions	3,558	108,342	36,750	456	144	5,034	54	–	54	1,662
2 mounted brigades	208	4,405	4,901	12	12	263	10	–	6	132
Royal Flying Corps (4 sqdns & depot)	98	685	55	–	–	9	2	94	4	22
Other army troops	219	3,847	2,285	–	2	286	24	8	35	48
Total at the front	4,550	126,691	54,318	492	182	6,174	113	102	117	2,235
LINE OF COMMUNICATION										
Details left at the base of the field army	130	12,742	1,088							
L. of C. units	1,068+759 nurses	20,713	4,962	–	8	1,025	74	1,083	62	258
GRAND TOTAL	5,748+759 nurses	160,146	60,368	492	190	7,199	187	1,185	179	2,493

days had distributed 120,000 horses to the units. But simply finding horses was not the complete answer – not all horses were suitable for army use, and some units had particular requirements.

Every gun in the horse artillery – which in war supported the cavalry – was pulled by six horses. Guns and limbers have no brakes and the horses work in three pairs; the two 'leaders' have to be bigger and faster than the rest for they set the pace; the two 'centres' provide stability and keep the gun team balanced; and the two 'wheelers' have to be smaller and stronger for they are responsible for stopping the gun and slowing the entire team. Clearly, just any horse will not do, and once recruited these horses had to be trained.

According to Captain Neil Cross, a section commander with The King's Troop, Royal Horse Artillery, the last unit in the British Army equipped with horse-drawn guns,[7] finding suitable troop horses is not easy. They have to be selected for size and temperament, and in 1914 training a troop horse would have taken between one and three months, depending on the horse and what it had been doing before enlistment.

This brings the matter back to the question of numbers. The pre-war army ran its artillery batteries on a 'low establishment', with four guns to a battery. The 'higher establishment', when units were brought up to strength in preparation for war, called for six-gun batteries, and the 'war establishment', while still employing six guns, needed more men and more horses. A field artillery battery in 1914 had 119 horses on low establishment, 158 on high establishment and 198 on war establishment. These would include fifty-four draught horses, towing guns and ammunition wagons, eighteen riding horses for the NCOs and other ranks, plus six officer horses and one draught wagon for general stores (GS), tents, bedding and baggage. To this can be added other horses for towing food, troop stores, fodder, cooking equipment, the battery office and farrier equipment.[8] Battery commanders were always very anxious to keep up their horse strength. Captain Cross of The King's Troop estimates that a battery on war establishment might have up to 250 horses, since the officers would bring their own riding mounts, some of them hunters, and retain any issued horses they could get.

When horse requirements are calculated across the BEF as a whole, the scale of the problem is apparent. In a lecture on horse mobilization given to the Royal United Services Institute for Defence Studies (RUSI) and published in the *RUSI Journal* in November 1921, Brigadier General T. R. F. Bate reveals the extent of the problem: 'In 1914 the Expeditionary Force had a Peace Establishment of approximately 19,000 horses. Its War Establishment included 55,000 horses so the first task was to produce 36,000 horses and this was done successfully in 10 days.[9] Ninety per cent of these horses were provided by impressment. However, the mobilization of the Territorial Force as it stood in 1914 required another 81,000 horses while recalled reserve units required another 18,000 horses bringing the total number up to 135,000 in round figures.'

With the problem of horses comes the problem of fodder. Horses cannot do heavy work like pulling guns and ammunition limbers while fed on grass. They need hay and grain, which, again according to Captain Cross of The King's Troop, meant a large supply of oats and cereals. The BEF consumption of fodder was truly prodigious, the horses requiring many hundreds of tons of hay, oats and cereal every day. If the fodder ran out the horses died and the guns and ammunition had to be abandoned.

Wilson's anxieties over horses, so often expressed in the previous chapter, are therefore understandable; horses were hard to find, could not be maintained on a wartime scale in peacetime, were difficult to look after, and took up a great deal of shipping space, not least as regards the transport of fodder.

A further illustration of the supply problem comes from *Supplying the Front Line*,[10] which gives the stores requirement for the actual BEF of four infantry divisions and one cavalry division that went to France in 1914. In August 1914, this force of 120,000 men and 53,000 horses required: 3,600,000 lbs of meat, 4,500,000 lbs of bread, 5,900,000 lbs of horse fodder and 842,000 gallons of petrol (including aviation spirit).

The weight of fodder is nothing compared to its bulk; the BEF's fodder needs occupied an immense amount of rail and shipping space. One answer was to increase the amount of motor transport, but the automobile was in its infancy in 1914, vehicles were underpowered and unreliable, and very few people could drive; it was usual to impress the vehicles and recruit their drivers at the same time. The war establishment shown in the table (see page 84) lists just 1,185 MT (motor transport) vehicles; of these ninety-four were attached to the Royal Flying Corps and most of the rest (1,025) were in the lines of communications, engaged in moving supplies from the railheads to dumps closer to the front.

This transport echelon was for the army as a whole; the BEF was far less well endowed. According to Ian Malcolm Brown,[11] the BEF motorized logistical support in 1914 amounted to a mere eighty trucks, twenty automobiles and fifteen motorcycles, most of these attached to GHQ.

No MT whatsoever was attached to the infantry or cavalry units, which relied exclusively on horse transport. Here too plans had been made to collect motor transport committed to the army on the outbreak of war through a pre-war subsidy scheme. This produced only eighty lorries, and the bulk of the BEF's motor transport was obtained either by requisition from private companies – like the London furniture store Waring and Gillow – or through donation by individuals.[12]

In the event, 40,000–50,000 horses were quickly collected and distributed to units, and as PRO/WO 339/14401 records, 'this was a wonderful testimony to the preparations made in peacetime by the QMG's Branch'. It adds that, 'It was after the completion of mobilization that the chief difficulties began because from that moment we were dealing with unknown quantities as nothing was definitely certain as to ships, and embarkation, disembarkation and entrainment across the Channel.'

The problem of guns can be related to the problems of ammunition. Ammunition is heavy and bulky and needs careful handling, but the big issue, and one that was not given sufficient consideration, was how much ammunition would the BEF need to fight in this continental war? The short answer was that nobody knew, and the estimates based on ammunition consumption in the South African War proved completely inadequate for the demands of the Western Front – an inadequacy that culminated in the notorious shell shortage scandal of 1915.

The pre-war rifle ammunition scale per soldier was 100 rounds per man in the cavalry and 150 per man in the infantry (carried in pouches or bandoliers) plus 100 rounds for each man in the regimental (or battalion) reserve. With divisional reserves, the total number of rounds available per man at the front came to 370 for each cavalry trooper and 420 for each infantry soldier. Each battalion also had two medium machine guns (MMGs) – Maxim or Vickers – with a cyclic rate of fire of 600 rounds per minute.[13]

The BEF had four types of artillery piece: the 13-pounder Quick Firer, used by the Royal Horse Artillery, the 18-pounder used by the Field Artillery, which supported the infantry, and for general bombardments the 4.5-inch field howitzer and the 60-pounder. The average number of rounds per gun held forward of the advanced depot was calculated at 528 rounds, which compared well with the French artillery's 579 rounds per gun (mostly of the rapid-fire 75mm shell) and the German artillery's average of 386 rounds per gun.[14]

This ammunition scale seems adequate, but looking back at ammunition expenditure in the Russo-Japanese War of 1904–05 – a conflict that much resembled the Great War and deserved closer study than it usually received after 1905 – it was discovered that at times the Russian guns were firing up to 360 rounds of ammunition *per day*. Before the 1904 war the Russians thought that 500 rounds per gun was enough for all emergencies, but afterwards they concluded that 1,000 rounds per gun was the minimum requirement. Getting the quantity of artillery ammunition right was crucial; without ammunition the most powerful gun is little better than a heavy piece of scrap iron. As we shall see, the BEF was soon woefully short of artillery ammunition.

In fact, all the armies of the Great War entered the conflict with far too little artillery ammunition. The French, for example, calculated that their guns would use around 100,000 shells a month;

between August and December 1914 their guns consumed almost 900,000 rounds a month, and this quantity would soon grow. During the First Battle of Ypres in October 1914, Sir Douglas Haig had to withdraw one third of his guns from the field and send them to the rear, as he had no ammunition for them. In the early weeks of 1914 the British artillery fired more shells than it had expended during the entire South African War.

Shipping was another problem. The Admiralty did not keep troop transports on call, waiting at anchor for an emergency. In the past, when shipping was needed, it was simply hired, or the troops were embarked on ships making regular peacetime sailings. That would not do for shipping such a large Expeditionary Force. For that it would be necessary to requisition merchant shipping. These vessels were known as STUFT (Ships Taken Up From Trade) transports, but their availability depended on the ships in port at any one time – and not every ship would do.

The Admiralty solved the first part of this problem by taking a census of available vessels over a twelve-month period during 1912, so arriving at a total and breakdown of types for ships that should be available for STUFT purposes on any particular day. In the event this worked very well. The ships would be available; whether they could work to the tight BEF timings was another matter.

WO 339/14401 remarks [15] that in 1890 the War Office asked the Admiralty 'How long it would take to ship 40,000 men and 7,900 horses to the Continent. The answer was 4 to 5 weeks. The gap to be bridged between this and the completion of the concentration on the Belgian frontier by the 12th day of 185,804 men and 60,368 horses was thus a pretty big one.'

Putting the practical details of the mobilization plan together took several years and was almost entirely the work of Henry Wilson. By the end of 1913 he had drawn up a list of movement schedules and priorities and backed these with the appropriate administrative and transport arrangements.

Before the troops could move they must be mobilized, and the timings for this phase were as follows, based on 'M1', the day of mobilization:

1. English infantry stationed in England could mobilize by 1159 hours (midnight) on the third day (M3).
2. English and Scottish infantry stationed in Ireland could mobilize by 1159 hours on the fourth day (M4).
3. Cavalry could mobilize by 1159 hours on the fifth and sixth day (M5 and M6).
4. Artillery could mobilize by 1159 hours on the sixth day (M6).
5. Motor transport could mobilize by 1159 hours on the fourth day (M4).

This mobilization and transport schedule was detailed in a number of separate instructions, contained in three fat files, WO106/49A/6 (Entrainment and Move to Areas of Concentration), WO106/49A/9 (Mobilization Appointments) and W106/49B/1 (Instructions for Entrainment of the British Expeditionary Force). Having mobilized, the units must then be moved to the docks, where certain limitations materialized.

All tables for railway movements[16] were made out by the various army commands – Southern Command, Northern Command, Western Command, etc. – the movement order including the trains for the collection and distribution of horses. Since the main embarkation ports were in the South of England, the final arrangements were worked out by the movements staff at the War Office – MO(1) – and the QMG's department. These liaised with the London and South Western Railway (LSWR), the latter being the medium of communication with the other British railway companies.

The routine was that the MO(1) collected the information from the commands with the units already sorted into trainloads, and noted the day they had to move according to the WF plan, and their destination. From this information the railway companies worked out the timings and the LSWR provided the coordination and linked the trainloads to the ports. The main limiting factor here was the number of trainloads that could run into the principal embarkation port, Southampton. The rail capacity in 1912 was around thirty trains a day but extensions to the rail yards in the pre-war years had greatly increased that capacity by 1914.

The BEF also embarked from a number of other ports: Newhaven, Avonmouth, Liverpool, Belfast, Dublin, Queenstown, Cork and Glasgow. These had been selected in 1912 by a joint War Office–Admiralty committee under Admiral Slade, and were chosen for the suitability of their berthing facilities, tidal range, warehouses, lifting cranes and wharves. A similar transport and embarkation organization was then created in each location. From the completed railway timetables, which showed the time of unit arrivals, the MO(1) compiled another table showing the 'allotment into ships', that is the sorting out of trainloads into shiploads, depending on the type of unit – infantry, cavalry, artillery – and the number of ships and ship movements possible each day. This was dependent on tides and the port facilities in France, where 'the port capacity was definitely limited'.[17]

Page four of this War Office file (WO 339/14401) also refers to another problem, Admiralty ignorance of what is now called 'combat loading' – the need for military equipment to be stowed in ships in reverse order so that kit needed first is landed first and is not at the bottom of the hold. 'At the outset they needed a certain amount of education as to Army requirements for their first instinct was to bundle men, horses, transport etc. on in bulk, into different ships, regardless of unit organisation, but they quickly tumbled to our necessities.'

The disembarkation ports and their berth capacities were: Le Havre – thirty ships a day; Rouen – twenty ships a day; Boulogne – eleven ships a day.

This was not the end of the problem; every port had its own limitations. Boulogne had a narrow entrance and was difficult to enter in bad weather. Rouen was far up the Seine and difficult for ships of more than 18-foot draught or 300 feet in length at most states of the tide. Crane power was none too good anywhere, and there were navigation difficulties in the Seine between Le Havre and Rouen.

One point that affected all mobilization and transport arrangements in the pre-war years was the need for secrecy. Callwell records:

Quite apart from the uncertainty which was caused by the lack of any definite policy on the part of H.M. Government – and uncertainty that made the basis of the whole scheme a matter of conjecture – it had been necessary throughout to perform the work with the utmost secrecy. The fact that Wilson and his staff were in communication with the French had to be kept concealed. The whole of the clerical labour – the typing and duplication of railway timetables and so forth – was in the hands of half a dozen officers, who alone at the War Office knew of what was in progress. Maintaining profound secrecy, and limiting the time that the operation would take as a whole, were the dominating factors in the transaction throughout.[18]

WO 339/14401 expands this point when it comments: 'The provision of the necessary ship fittings was a difficult fence to get over involving spending much money on services which could not be defended in the House of Commons. It is remarkable that in these circumstances Mr Asquith's Government did provide considerable sums for these purposes and also for improving the railway communications with Southampton.'

As this extract indicates, there were a number of technical problems affecting these arrangements, and the first, inevitably, concerned horses. Ships carrying horses needed special cranes or gangways and had to be fitted with stalls and 'horse-brows' for loading and tethering points, and once so fitted could not be readily used for anything else. It was also important that the horses should be accompanied by grooms and other shipping containing water and fodder.

Once the BEF arrived in France the arrangements to send the men, horses, guns and equipment up to the mustering area at Maubeuge, and the BEF's subsequent supply, were the responsibility of the Inspector General of Communications (IGC). The IGC would work closely with the Quartermaster General (QMG). 'Close coordination between the IGC and the BEF's QMG who would select railheads and refilling points in accordance with the army's operational requirements was mandatory if the system were to perform efficiently.'[19]

The IGC had to rely heavily on help and support from the French port and railway authorities, for the BEF had no control of the railways and in the crisis conditions of 1914 the BEF could not be a French priority. Again according to WO 339/14401, 'the outflow from the French ports was limited to a total of 60 trains per day from the 7th day onwards.'[20] The normal train distribution was: from Le Havre, twenty-five trains daily; from Rouen, fifteen trains daily; from Boulogne, twenty trains daily.

There was, however, a problem. French trainloads were not consistent and bore no relation to British trainloads; it was not possible to put, say, two trainloads of British troops on a ship, transport them to France and hope that they would fit comfortably into two French trains. Since the outcome was more important than the input – units must arrive at the concentration area together and with their equipment – it was necessary to reallocate all units to French trainloads and accept that the component parts of a French trainload might travel in different ships; some elements would have to be held at the French port until the rest arrived.

There was also the matter of transport capacity. A British battalion made two British trainloads but one French trainload, though WO 339/14401 remarks that: 'Some of the French trainloads were a very tight fit and this made it impossible to add a single pair of wheels to the War Establishment of a unit without upsetting all the French train tables. Consequently all such alterations had to be very carefully scrutinised by the MO(1) in the War Office and if necessary the trainloads adjusted to suit.'

These organizational difficulties were being tackled by 1912 with the appointment of a base commandant and staff to each French port. They were responsible to the IGC for the reception and accommodation of troops and liaison with the French railway authorities, who were in turn organized via a 'Commission de Port', composed of French naval and military personnel and harbourmasters, together with the necessary workmen, dockers, crane operators, etc.; the French also undertook the provision of water, lighting and fuel.[21]

Movement from the port to the concentration area was entrusted to the French railway system (SNCF) and its staff. The BEF were allocated a total of seventy-five daily departures from all ports, controlled via the main railway junction or bottleneck at Amiens, through which the lines from every port passed. It was anticipated (correctly) that only about sixty departures would actually be used. Overall control was exercised by a French officer, the *Commissaire de Ligne,* who met every day with his British and French colleagues and made out a return of arriving units to be railed to the concentration area the following day. This return was then sent to the ports and to Amiens, where arrangements were completed for the departure and reception of trains.

The system, though logical, was inevitably complicated. Fortunately, the plans were completed and issued by the end of 1913, and arrangements were made early in 1914 for the British and French staff to meet at the French ports and try out the arrangements, ironing out any potential snags in the process.

A final paragraph on the working of the WF scheme comments:

> It is fair to say that all details of the plan of movement had been worked out beforehand as completely as it was possible to do so. In the latter part of June 1914 a Staff Ride was held at Amiens, attended by British officers of the MO(1) in which the entire railway movement plan was tested very thoroughly. The entire *Commission de Ligne,* including French staff officers and technical railway officials with their representatives at ports, occupied their war stations. Every sort of mishap was practised such as tunnels being blown in, trains derailed etc., and alternative routes organized to meet the emergency. In the previous winter British officers had witnessed French units entraining at war strength and frequent conferences had been held at the French War Office.

All was therefore ready when the mobilization order arrived and the four infantry divisions and one cavalry division of the BEF, with all their impedimenta, set out for France. The first four infantry divisions were formed into two corps; I Corps, consisting of the 1st and 2nd Divisions, would be commanded by Lieutenant-

General Sir Douglas Haig; II Corps, consisting of the 3rd and 5th Divisions, would be commanded by Lieutenant General Sir J. M. Grierson. The cavalry division would be commanded by Major-General E. H. H. Allenby, and the entire force would be under the command of Field Marshal Sir John French, with Lieutenant General A. J. Murray as his chief of staff, Major-General Henry H. Wilson as sub-chief and Major-General Sir William Robertson as quartermaster general.

The BEF were extremely fortunate to have Sir William Robertson as QMG. Robertson had joined the army as a cavalry trooper and is still one of the few private soldiers to have risen through the ranks to field marshal. Commissioned in 1888, he had gained promotion through sheer ability, attended the staff college and later been the college commandant. A soldier to his fingertips, Robertson knew how to tackle a complicated logistical task and, rather more to the point in August 1914, how to cope when matters went awry. As he wrote in his memoirs:

> It was necessary that the Quartermaster-General's staff should examine the situation from every point of view, and introduce such elasticity into the supply arrangements as would promptly afford the Commander-in-Chief the greatest possible choice of action. In short, it should be prepared to meet any and every reasonable contingency, for no matter how skilful the plans of the Commander-in-Chief might be, they would almost certainly fail in execution if the troops were not properly fed, quartered and kept supplied with ammunition.[22]

It is noticeable – and curious – that Robertson's memoirs make no mention whatsoever of his colleague Henry Wilson, the sub-chief of staff.

The total force under Field Marshal French's command amounted to around 150,000 men, a puny force perhaps when compared to the vast armies of France and Germany, but a well-trained, efficient and completely professional one. Haldane and Wilson had done wonders in creating the BEF and preparing it to move, but the problems facing it had only just begun in August 1914. As related – and in view of what follows the point is worth stressing – Wilson had spent years getting the BEF ready to move, but he still had to work with the ration strengths and equipment scales drawn up and funded by his military and political superiors. Had the Government been willing to admit in Parliament the progress of the 'conversations' and Wilson's close links with the French General Staff, it is at least possible that the Government and staff, working together, would have devoted more thought to the kind of fighting a European war would involve and created a BEF equipped to continental standards in both size and equipment.

As it was, they had got a colonial army, small, mobile and lightly equipped – the sort of army Britain had needed to fight the South African War back in 1899. What was needed in 1914 was a continental army, massive, largely conscripted, armed with heavy artillery, howitzers and machine guns, equipped with motor transport and backed by ammunition scales suitable for heavy usage and a long war. In the event, since the British Army was small, the munitions and armaments industry that supported it was equally small and proved itself unable to meet the demands that would shortly come from the divisions in the field and the new divisions training at home.

Nevertheless, on 4 August, the BEF reservists began to muster at their regimental depots and proceed from there to their battalions and the docks. The troops in Britain went to Southampton, those in Ireland to Cork, Dublin and Belfast. The motor transport went to Avonmouth, military stores and supplies to Newhaven, food to Liverpool. In the first five days of mobilization 1,800 trains ran to these ports. At the ports the men and stores were embarked on four classes of ships: Class 1, Personnel; Class 2, Horses and Vehicles; Class 3, Motor Transport; Class 4, Stores. Each day an average of thirteen fully loaded ships sailed from the UK.

These ships sailed to Boulogne, Le Havre and Rouen, escorted across the Channel by the Royal Navy; not a ship, man or gun was lost on the voyage.[23] Henry Wilson's plan had worked to perfection. The WF scheme finally came to fruition on 23 August 1914 when the infantry of the British Expeditionary Force opened fire on the German First Army to begin the Battle of Mons.

5

The BEF Advances

9–22 AUGUST 1914

*To the north, outlined against the sky, countless fires were
burning. It was as if hordes of fiends had suddenly been released,
and dropping on the distant plain, were burning every town and
village.*

Edward Spears, *Liaison, 1914*, p. 103

While the British Army was mustering troops and sending them
to France, the German armies were pouring into Luxembourg and
Belgium and French forces were surging across the eastern frontiers of France into the Ardennes and the lost provinces of Alsace
and Lorraine. The French deployed their First Army in the South
and their Fifth Army in the North; the German armies mustered
in reverse order, with the Seventh Army in the South and the First,
Second and Third, set to move in a great scythe-like thrust into
Luxembourg, Belgium and northern France, in the North. All
these forces were working to a pre-war plan; the French armies
were following the dictates of Plan XVII and pushing east, and the
Germans were enacting the strategy drawn up years before by the
late Count Alfred von Schlieffen, Chief of the German General
Staff from 1891 to 1906.

The famous Schlieffen Plan had the aim of avoiding the ultimate
peril for any nation, a war on two fronts. When faced with an array
of enemies, the wise general will try to defeat the strongest force

first, and the strongest enemy facing Germany, post-1871, was France. Von Schlieffen calculated that the vast, slow-moving Russian armies would take six weeks to muster, and this period provided his 'window of opportunity' – the German armies must defeat those of France in no more than forty-two days, before the Russians could take the field. That done, the German armies would be rushed eastward on Germany's well-developed railway system and inflict a similar blow on the armies of the Tsar.

The Germans had to move quickly, avoiding any delay caused by the mighty French forts along the Franco-German frontier by attacking France through Belgium, overwhelming the French armies in just *six weeks*. Germany's entire strategy for victory in the First World War was based on this long-prepared plan and these tight timings – and it is therefore at least arguable that when the French, far from being defeated, struck back on the Marne on 6 September 1914, thirty-seven days after the invasion of Belgium, Germany had already lost the war.

Von Schlieffen worked on his plan for years, but most of his work was refinement; the essence of the plan did not change. By the time he retired in 1906, his plan called for just one German army – the Eighth – to contain the Russians in the East. The Sixth and Seventh under Crown Prince Rupprecht of Bavaria, totalling 345,000 men, were to hold the French assault by the First and Second Armies in Alsace and Lorraine, even giving ground if need be. At the same time the First and Second German Armies, 320,000 and 260,000 strong respectively, under the overall command of General von Bulow of the Second Army, were to advance into northern France via Belgium, scooping up the Belgian Army, most of the French Army and – should they be so foolish as to intervene – any British force in their path.

This sweep should go as far west as possible; ideally, von Schlieffen had decreed, 'when you march into France the left-hand soldier should brush the Channel with his sleeve'. Meanwhile the German Fourth (180,000 men) and Fifth Armies (200,000 men) were to advance through the Ardennes, conforming with the movements of the armies on either flank and holding the German line together. It will be noticed that the German armies grew progressively stronger from south to north; von Kluck's First Army on the right wing, mustering 320,000 men, was the strongest of all.

Having overrun Belgium and reached France, these armies would press south to envelop Paris. Von Kluck's First Army would move south of the city before all three armies turned east to press the French armies attacking Germany against their own eastern fortifications. Von Schlieffen based his confidence in this part of the plan on prior knowledge of the French strategic plan, Plan XVII.

As with the Schlieffen Plan, Plan XVII had taken years to prepare. The plan adopted in May 1913 was actually the seventeenth draft of the original, much altered since the French staff sat down to discuss what they could do to recover the lost provinces of Alsace and Lorraine in the 1870s, and tinkered with most recently by General Joffre. Brooding over the losses and humiliations of 1870–71, the French looked back to their days of *la gloire* under the great Napoleon – and eventually decided that the answer to their problems was staring them in the face. It lay in resurrecting the first Emperor's principles; there they would find a method – a tactic, perhaps even a strategy – that would guarantee success when the struggle with Germany began again.

During the first Emperor's campaigns, a combination of artillery and infantry, the latter surging forward to the sound of drums, had given the French armies victory over a host of foes for more than a quarter of a century. Here, then, lay the solution to all military difficulties – the offensive; abandon all other possibilities and concentrate on attack, all-out attack, '*l'attaque à outrance*', a constant, no-holds-barred assault on enemy forces wherever found. Forget defence, forget withdrawal, above all forget reserves; only attack and victory would be yours. This doctrine was expounded in the years up to 1914 by Colonel de Grandmaison, chief of the Troisième Bureau (Operations Branch) in the French general staff, aided by the chief of the Ecole Supérieur de Guerre, Henry Wilson's confederate and boon companion, General Ferdinand Foch.

With the advent of modern weaponry, the French doctrine of *l'attaque à outrance* was, to put it bluntly, insane. Times had changed since Austerlitz and Wagram. In the face of new technology, such as magazine rifles, automatic weapons, shrapnel and heavy guns, plus the use of entrenchments – all of which had made their appearance in the US Civil War fifty years previously and had been greatly refined since – the thought that troops could storm enemy positions and carry all before them, relying on courage and the sudden force of their attack – *l'attaque brusque* – was stark lunacy.

The French general staff did not see it that way. They based their strategy on the ancient *furia frances,* the power and élan of the French infantry soldier, the *cran* – guts – of the officer corps, backed up by the new 75mm quick-firing gun. Let those soldiers see the enemy, let the *Soixante-Quinze* do its work, and all would be well.

It might therefore be argued that if the BEF of 1914 was a Victorian army, the French Army that entered the First World War was a Napoleonic army – at least in matters of training and doctrine. In appearance it dated from 1870, from the red pantaloons worn by the infantry and the helmets, breastplates and plumes adorning the cavalry troopers, to the white gloves worn into battle by the officers. Attempts to introduce the less visible 'horizon-bleu' uniform to the infantry was resisted by all ranks until the fields of France were carpeted with gloriously clad heaps of dead in the late summer of 1914. Nor were the French over-blessed with modern weaponry. The cavalry had a carbine as well as sword and lance, but with the exception of the excellent 75mm field gun, the famous *Soixante-Quinze*, most of the French guns were obsolete; as with the BEF, there was a shortage of heavy guns and high-explosive shells. In 1914 the German Army had 3,500 heavy guns, the French 300 heavy guns and several hundred *Soixante-Quinze*, the BEF just 480 guns of every calibre.

The '*offensive à outrance*' was the doctrine driving Plan XVII. Essentially, the French armies would all push east for the Rhine, driving the enemy before them. Five armies would be deployed in the East, running north from Belfort in Alsace to Hirson on the Franco-Belgian border. The area to the west, from Hirson to the North Sea, would be left wide open – unless covered by the British Expeditionary Force or the Belgians.

If, as was rumoured in Berlin and reported by French spies, the Germans *really* intended to attack through Belgium, west of Hirson, and surge south across the Meuse into France, so much the better. They could not possibly have enough men to carry out the Schlieffen Plan *and* defeat Plan XVII . . . or so it was thought. Moreover, brooded the Troisième Bureau, if they were strong on the two flanks they must be weak in the centre and therefore vulnerable to an attack through the Ardennes by the French Third and Fourth Armies. In brief, says the *British Official History*, before the war: 'Joffre's first object was to break the enemy's centre and then fall on the right, or western wing of the German Armies'.[1] Deep down, however, Joffre did not really believe that the Germans would come into France via Belgium.

The Germans were equally content with their enemy's tactics. The farther the French armies pushed east, the easier it would be for the German right wing to get in behind them. To aid this process, the commander of the German left wing, Crown Prince Rupprecht of Bavaria, a very competent soldier, was ordered not to put up too much resistance to the main French thrust. When the French advanced he was to fall back steadily, causing heavy casualties but doing nothing to hinder the French advance until the encirclement of French forces was complete. Nor were the Germans worried by any lack of numbers; they fully intended to employ their Reserve Corps in their field armies – a decision that would provide the German staff with more than enough troops to carry out their entire strategic plan.

By August 1914, seven German armies, seventy divisions containing over 1,500,000 soldiers, had been mustered along Germany's western frontier. These armies were divided into three wings. The left wing, defending Alsace and Lorraine, was comprised of the Seventh and Sixth Armies – smaller than the other two wings with a total of sixteen divisions. Then came the centre – the Fifth and

Fourth Armies – totalling twenty divisions, and finally the right wing, made up of three armies, the Third, Second and First. This wing contained thirty-four infantry divisions and a mounted corps of three cavalry divisions. The first part of the BEF story is largely concerned with the actions of the German First Army (von Kluck), the Second Army (von Bulow) and the Third Army (von Hausen), the three armies on the German right wing – though other German armies will become involved later.

Von Schlieffen never ceased to press the merits of his strategy. Unfortunately, his successor as Chief of the General Staff, General Helmuth von Moltke, was much less certain that he should denude the Rhine and Russian frontiers to provide the maximum possible strength for Schlieffen's push into Belgium and France. To von Moltke, the Schlieffen Plan seemed just a touch too risky; it flew in the face of that old English proverb about not putting all the eggs in one basket. Von Moltke therefore proceeded to tinker with the plan, first by allocating newly raised divisions to the Rhine, then by actually transferring divisions from west to east.

It is possible that von Moltke's action fatally undermined the plan. The slow-moving Great War armies had weight rather than momentum; by reducing the weight of the main attack, von Moltke reduced the chances of it succeeding. On the other hand, it is equally possible that the Schlieffen Plan simply demanded too much of the soldiers. The armies of 1914 relied on feet and hoofs – and it is doubtful that the German armies, especially the First and Second Armies on the western flank, which had the farthest distance to travel, could have marched the hundreds of miles from the Luxembourg frontier to the outskirts of Paris and still been fresh enough to fight a major engagement. It is also possible that von Schlieffen was well aware of this problem; since nothing could be done about it, it was simply ignored.

This is only a brief outline of the strategic plans with which the two continental enemies entered the war. The essence of both plans is simple, and that is sound strategy for, according to Clausewitz, in war only the simple succeeds. A broad understanding of these plans is essential, both in order to understand what was going on in France between August and December 1914 and to see where the BEF fits into the overall situation; the image to bear in mind is that of the revolving door, with two forces pushing in opposite directions about the pivot of Paris, and a timescale of just forty-two days. If anything delayed or disrupted that timescale the Schlieffen Plan would fail and Germany might lose the war.

Germany's belief in the prowess of her armies was not without foundation. With the possible exception of the fully professional British Expeditionary Force of 1914, the German Army outclassed every other army on the Western Front for much of the war. It was the powerful and efficient product of a society steeped in militarism and dedicated to the subjection of neighbouring states. In such a role it proved itself invincible against more numerous opponents – until those opponents also became powerful and efficient under pressure of necessity. Germany was, however, obliged to pay a stiff price for such military efficiency – despotism at home and tyranny abroad.

Countries with a democratic system of government – such as Great Britain – go to war reluctantly and only when forced to do so; their armies consequently suffer both heavy losses and disasters in the early days. Such countries are more interested in the maintenance of civilised values – and less of a threat to their neighbours – but there is a price to pay, and when war comes the soldier pays that price. Britain's failure to prepare for a modern European war cost the British Army – and the British Empire – a great number of lives after August 1914.

In 1922 Rudyard Kipling, the Imperial poet, noted that the British Army's general unpreparedness for a continental war in 1914 'has been extolled as proof of the purity of this country's ideals, which must be a great consolation to all concerned'. Kipling's only son, Jack, was killed at the Battle of Loos in September 1915, so the bitterness in that comment is understandable. Even so, professionalism is not everything in military affairs. The German Army was highly professional but its conduct in the first weeks of the war, during the advance into Belgium, was disgraceful. As they advanced, the German generals implemented a deliberate policy of terror to quell any spirit of resistance in the towns and villages the army overran.

The path of the German armies in 1914 was marked by atrocities, the shooting of civilians and the wilful destruction of towns and villages. Hostages were taken, collective punishments imposed and fines levied on the civilian population, either for their having had the temerity to oppose the German advance or for no reason but the need to create terror. The fruits of this policy can be seen to this day in the towns and villages of eastern Belgium. On 21 August the Germans shot 211 civilians in the village of Andenne near Namur and burned the village to the ground. On the same day, another fifty Belgian civilians were murdered in the village of Seilles. On 22 August, German soldiers looted and burned the town of Tamines where – according to the existing memorial in the town cemetery – 384 men, women and children were massacred, some by firing squad, others with the bayonet. Two days later, at Dinant, no fewer than 612 civilians were done to death in the streets. These events are only the major atrocities. The shooting of men, women and children went on in every hamlet, village, town and city as the German armies surged into Belgium and northern France.

The German excuse for this barbaric behaviour was that *francs-tireurs,* irregulars, descendants of those lone riflemen who had harassed the German advances in 1870, had been at work in Belgium and thus had brought down reprisals on their towns and villages. Even if this were true – and the evidence is scanty – it is hard to accept that the actions of a lone peasant armed with a rook rifle can justify the slaughter of hundreds of innocent people. The truth is that under the constant time pressure of the Schlieffen Plan the German generals intended to stamp out anything or anyone that delayed their advance, and did so by the naked application of terror.

These atrocities were not isolated incidents perpetrated by undisciplined or drunken troops but the result of orders issued by the army commanders. General von Bulow ordered the shootings in Andenne and the taking of hostages in Namur. Von Kluck was implicated in the murder of Belgian civilians in Vise and General Max von Hausen, commander of the Third Army, was actually present when his soldiers carried out the massacre at Dinant.[2]

The Kaiser's much vaunted Officer Korps was implicated in mass murder at the highest level – and no action was taken to bring the culprits to book or curb their behaviour. Their conduct destroys many of the arguments against British involvement in the war and provided the *Entente* powers with considerable propaganda, not least in the USA. After this advance through Belgium the German military machine – and the political will that drove it – was seen as a threat to civilized rule in western Europe. The Germans had to be resisted and the Belgians paid a terrible price for the tenacity of their resistance.

The Germans needed to destroy the Belgian defences along the River Meuse, which, though not so numerous as those in eastern France, were still extremely strong. The first obstacle to the German advance was the fortress cities of Liège and Namur. Liège, the most easterly fortress, stood on a hill on the left bank of the Meuse and was protected by a ring of twelve forts constructed from 1880 onwards. Liège was regarded in military circles as the finest fortified position in western Europe, and for the Schlieffen Plan to work it had to be taken quickly. Liège was therefore attacked by six infantry brigades supported by special siege artillery, a force detached for the purpose from General von Bulow's Second Army and commanded by General Otto von Emmich.

The Kaiser and the German High Command had hoped that the Belgians would either submit to their first demands for a free passage across Belgium into France or, if pressed, put up only token resistance. Anticipating a rapid surrender, and reluctant to slow their advance with a ponderous siege train, von Bulow's army had therefore left its heavy artillery behind. This included Skoda 305mm (12-inch) mortars and Krupp 420mm (16.5-inch) cannon, the largest guns then in service anywhere, massive ordnance fully capable of reducing the Liège defences to rubble. Without these guns, the first German attempt to take Liège took the form of an infantry assault supported by field artillery. This attack went in on 5 August and met with a crushing reverse.

King Albert, the Belgian monarch, was determined to defend his tiny kingdom against any aggressor, and when the German armies crossed the frontier the Belgian Army put up a stout resistance. The light German field guns did little damage to the Liège forts and when they advanced to attack on 5 August the German infantry were met with machine-gun and rifle fire and a deluge of shrapnel from the Belgian guns. 'They made no attempt at deploying', wrote a Belgian officer later, 'but came on line after line, shoulder to shoulder until, as we shot them down, the dead and wounded were heaped on top of each other in an awful barricade of dead and wounded that threatened to mask the fire of our guns.'[3]

This first attack was broken off at dusk but at midnight Major-General Erich Ludendorff took charge of the 14th Infantry Brigade and ordered a renewal of the assault on Liège at dawn on 6 August. This attack was driven home in spite of losses, and by mid-afternoon on 7 August the German brigades had penetrated the line of forts and entered the city. The Belgian field army then fell back to take up fresh positions in front of Louvain, but the garrisons of the Liège forts continued to hold out. They were still holding out five days later, on 12 August, when the great German siege guns arrived.

The bombardment of the eastern forts began that afternoon. Twenty-four hours later three of the forts had fallen, shattered by shells, and by the following day all the forts east and north of the city were in German hands. The guns were then dragged through Liège to engage the western forts. On 17 August, the last of the Liège forts, Fort Loncin, was taken. With the fall of Liège, the advance of the German Second and Third Armies down the Meuse towards Namur could begin.

The German juggernaut began to roll forward again, its way marked again by the bodies of dead civilians and burning Belgian towns. These latest crimes culminated in the sacking and burning

The fatal friendship: Ferdinand Foch and Henry Wilson in 1918

Lieutenant-General Sir Charles Monro inspects troops of 2nd Division, I Corps, 1914

Arrival of the BEF in France: train carrying the 11th Hussars stops at Rouen

Draft horses unshipped in France, August 1914

Lieutenant-General Horace Smith-Dorrien, Commander of the II Corps: arguably the best of the BEF generals in 1914

Lieutenant-General Sir Douglas Haig, Commander of the I Corps: his dour courage saved the day several times at First Ypres

General Joseph Joffre, Commander-in-Chief of the French Army, victor of the Marne

Field Marshal Horatio Kitchener, Secretary of State for War, 1914–16; founder of the 'New Armies' which took the field on the Somme in 1916

An infantry battalion of the BEF marching through a northern French town before the Battle of Mons. Within three months most of these men will have been killed or wounded

'B' Company, 1st Bn The Cameronians, marching to the line, August 1914

1st Bn, The Cameronians resting after the Battle of Mons, 27 August 1914

A British munitions factory produces shells for the field artillery – but not enough to keep up with demand

of the university city of Louvain on 25 August, an act of savagery and vandalism unparalleled until that time. Five days earlier, on 20 August, von Kluck's First Army had entered Brussels and the Belgian Army fell back towards the port of Antwerp and its strong defensive outworks. For the next three days the divisions of von Kluck's First Army marched through Brussels, the citizens closing their ears to the sound of the German bands and the chanting of the marching infantry; the rear elements of the First Army were still in the city when their advance units ran into the BEF at Mons on 23 August.

Meanwhile, Field Marshal French's force had started landing in France on 9 August and, having been railed to the north and assembled around Maubeuge and Le Cateau, was marching towards the Belgian frontier to take up its designated position on the left – or western   flank of the French Fifth Army.

The reception accorded to the BEF at this time was little short of rapturous. Crowds flocked to the quaysides and lined the roads to watch the British soldiers come ashore and march to their camps, offering fruit and bottles of wine, begging for souvenirs; within hours of landing most of the private soldiers were without their cap badges and brass regimental shoulder tags. Lord Kitchener had distributed a written order to the troops, instructing that it should be pasted into every soldier's paybook before they embarked. The order concludes:

> Be invariably courteous and kind. Never do anything likely to injure or destroy property and always look on looting as a disgraceful act. You are sure to meet with a welcome and be trusted; your conduct must justify that welcome and that trust. Your duty cannot be done unless your health is sound. So keep constantly on your guard against any excesses. In this new situation you may find temptations both in wine and women. You must entirely resist both temptations and while treating all women with perfect courtesy, you should avoid any intimacy.

The last few lines were wishful thinking, as Lord Kitchener was probably well aware. The ladies of France were eager to meet these

English soldiers and vice versa; inevitably one thing led to another and a good time was had by all.

'I believe we were the first infantry battalion to enter Rouen,' wrote Frank Richards of the Royal Welch Fusiliers,

> and the inhabitants gave us a wonderful reception and cheered us all the way from the docks to our billets in a convent. On arrival at a new station we pre-War soldiers always made enquiries as to what sort of a place it was for booze and fillies. If both were in abundance it was a glorious place from our point of view. We soon found out we had nothing to complain about as regards Rouen. Each man had been issued with a pamphlet signed by Lord Kitchener warning him about the dangers of French wine and women; they may as well not have been issued for all the notice we took of them.[4]

The BEF's assembly at Boulogne and Rouen was complete by 14 August and over the next few days they began to move north via the rail junction at Amiens to concentrate in the area between Maubeuge and Le Cateau. This move was effected by train or route march, but the aircraft of the Royal Flying Corps (RFC) flew to the airfield at Maubeuge, where four squadrons, with 105 officers, 755 men and fifty aircraft, were assembled by 18 August.

And so, delighted with their welcome, somewhat hung over, shedding badges, brass shoulder tags and caps, the infantry battalions of the BEF, singing heartily and surrounded by a crowd of young women and children, set off for their position on the Belgian frontier.

When in position, the BEF would have General Charles Lanrezac's Fifth Army on its right flank but their left flank would be 'in the air' or completely open. Except for General Sordet's three-division-strong cavalry corps, which had been making a forward reconnaissance into Belgium, and some French Territorial troops around Cambrai, there was nothing between the BEF's left flank and the Channel coast, 115 kilometres (70 miles) west of Mons.

Field Marshal Sir John French arrived at Boulogne on the evening of 14 August. From there French and his staff drove to Paris, where the field marshal met the President of the Republic, M.

Poincaré, and the Minister of War, M. Adolphe Messimy. On 16 August they drove to the French Army headquarters, the Grand-Quartier-General or GQG, at Vitry-le-François, where French met the French Commander-in-Chief, General Joseph Joffre.

French was clearly much impressed by his first sight of Joffre. Even speaking via an interpreter, he got the impression that the French generalissimo was a man 'of firm mind and steadfast intent, not easily moved from a position he had adopted or an opinion he had formed'. French was quite right in this assessment, though whether such entrenched characteristics are of real benefit in an army commander is rather less certain. French adds that 'History will record him as one of the supremely great commanders',[5] a comment not borne out by later comments or wiser observers.

Joseph Jacques Césaire Joffre was born in the Pyrenees in 1852, one of eleven children of a small-town barrel cooper. His was an unusual background for an officer in the class-conscious French Army of the Third Republic, where Napoleon's pledge – that every French soldier carried a field marshal's baton in his knapsack – had long since been forgotten. As a student in Paris during the Franco-Prussian War, Joffre found himself serving a cannon during the siege of Paris in 1871. This experience gave him a taste for the military life and he was commissioned into the artillery, transferring to the engineers before being sent to Indo-China in 1873.

Joffre spent most of his military career in outlying parts of the French Empire. He took part in the Timbuktu Expedition of 1894 and served for several years in Madagascar, becoming Director of the Engineer Corps in 1904. Needing field command experience, he then spent the years from 1906 to 1910 commanding an infantry division and then an army corps, both in metropolitan France. In 1910 he became a member of the French War Council, and in 1911 Chief of the General Staff, the designated commander-in-chief of the French Army in the event of war. He supported the introduction of three-year conscription in 1913, increased the work being done on the fortifications along France's eastern frontiers and, with the assistance of his intellectual and aristocratic colleague and subordinate General Noel de Castelnau, finalized the details of Plan XVII, introducing the idea of an attack on the German centre through the Ardennes.

Various traits stand out in Joffre's character. One modern historian has described him as 'a man with immense patience, enormous strength, great courage and few nerves; he was not an intellectual but he had intellectuals in his entourage and he listened to them'.[6] The one aspect of Joffre's character that attracted the greatest amount of comment at the time was his prodigious appetite; he ate gargantuan meals, followed by long siestas, and woe betide any officer or courier who interrupted either of these events, even with a vital dispatch. Alistair Horne has described Joffre as 'a true viscerotonic, a man who thought with his belly rather than his mind'.[7]

Joffre was certainly single-minded. He did not study strategy before the war and showed no interest whatsoever in how the war had been fought after the armistice in 1918. His attention was devoted to the here and now and the immediate future. Joffre's great contribution to the famous victory on the Marne and the survival of the French nation in the early months of the war can be attributed to his possession of some basic military assets, a feeling for the battlefield and a sense of the developing situation – plus a stubborn refusal to panic. When all seemed lost and chaos was reigning, Joffre remained calm. Whether this calm was due to a sense of destiny or his inability to grasp the seriousness of the situation hardly matters now. At the time, Joffre's dour nature and his refusal to let his strategic decisions be swayed by subsequent events saved his country from disaster in the late summer of 1914 and gave it victory on the Marne.

It is fortunate that French formed a good opinion of Joffre. The two commanders would have to work together and French's orders from Field Marshal Kitchener were somewhat less than helpful on the question of Anglo-French cooperation. The crucial passage come in the fourth paragraph of his instructions:

. . . while every effort must be made to coincide most sympathetically with the plans and wishes of our Ally, the gravest consideration will devolve upon you as to participation in forward movements where large bodies of French troops are not engaged and where your Force may be unduly exposed to attack. Should a contingency of this sort be contemplated, I look to you to inform me fully and give me time to communicate to you any decision His Majesty's Government may come to in the matter. In this connection I wish you distinctly to understand that your command is an entirely independent one and you will in no case come in any sense under the orders of any Allied general.[8]

Advice on how the field marshal should follow these conflicting instructions was not provided, and they were to provide the BEF commanders with considerable headaches in the months and years ahead.

Nor was French's faith in Joffre's judgement of long duration. Indeed, within hours of meeting the French generalissimo Field Marshal French found fault with one of Joffre's opinions, that General Charles Lanrezac, commander of the Fifth Army, was one of the finest officers in the service. French drove directly from Vitry-le-François to Lanrezac's headquarters at Rethel for a meeting that was to affect the BEF considerably in the days ahead. French records that Lanrezac was 'a big man with a loud voice and his manner did not strike me as very courteous.'[9] The field marshal's comment was an understatement; at this first meeting between the two commanders, General Lanrezac was very rude indeed.

It was 17 August and Lanrezac was a very worried man – with good reason. The French Army was poised to implement Plan XVII, which called for four out of the five French armies, a force totalling around 800,000 men, to surge into Germany across Alsace and Lorraine with the aim of dislocating the German war machine before it could swing into action. Plan XVII was taking shape, but for some days past Lanrezac had been forming the impression that something formidable was building up in the

North and threatening his left flank along the Belgian frontier on the rivers Sambre and Meuse. He had passed this worry on to GQG, where his views had been totally ignored.

This was more than normally worrying, for his left flank was at present 'in the air', as the BEF had not yet arrived, as promised. As noted, the British Army had *not* mobilized with the French Army on 1 August and had therefore not yet taken up position on Lanrezac's left, so the general felt both let down and fully entitled to be furious. His attitude had historic roots. Like many French officers, General Lanrezac was an Anglophobe and endowed with the common and enduring French notion that French officers – the heirs of Napoleon – were superior to the officers of any other armies and infinitely superior to the officers of the British Army. The exploits of Lieutenant-General Sir Arthur Wellesley, later Lord Wellington, victor of Vimeiro, Salamanca, Vittoria and Waterloo, were not much talked about at the Ecole Supérieure de la Guerre.

One must sympathize with General Lanrezac's position at this time. Try as he would, he could not persuade Joffre, or anyone else at GQG, to pay any attention to his fears that the Germans now rampaging across Belgium were intent on encircling his left flank. Joffre had allowed Lanrezac to realign some of his troops along the Sambre, just in case there was some substance in these fears, but Lanrezac had not received any reinforcements for this action and was therefore obliged to thin out his centre in order to strengthen his left, a process known as 'taking ground to the flank' – and that flank should by now have been covered by the BEF. This thinning out of his strength reduced his ability to repel any attack from the north, and he was therefore getting steadily more peeved with the still-absent British. As a result, when French and his staff drove into Lanrezac's headquarters on the morning of 17 August, they met a frosty reception. As they got out of their cars, Lanrezac's Chief of Staff, General Hely d'Oissel, greeted them with, 'Well, here you are, and about time too . . . If we are beaten, it will be thanks to you.'

Fortunately, this remark was made in French. Only Henry

Wilson and Lieutenant Edward Spears, the British liaison officer with the French Fifth Army, understood it, for Field Marshal French's language skills were extremely limited. In spite of this, French and Lanrezac then withdrew into a side room for a private discussion, only to re-emerge swiftly when they realized that they could not understand each other. The two generals then consulted the war map, while a French staff officer gave an assessment of the situation, including the Fifth Army view that the Germans had reached the River Meuse. French traced the course of the Meuse and, putting his finger on one of the bridges at the town of Huy, he asked Lanrezac, in stumbling French, what he thought the Germans were doing there. Lanrezrac replied that he supposed the Germans 'had gone there to fish'.

French did not understand this reply but he caught the tone of it and realized that Lanrezac was being deliberately insulting. The atmosphere in the room became tense, and after twenty minutes Field Marshal French said a brief goodbye and withdrew. 'I left General Lanrezac's headquarters believing that the Commander-in-Chief had overrated his ability.'[10]

Spears records this French–Lanrezac meeting as 'a complete fiasco',[11] and it certainly had the most unfortunate repercussions. It was vital that the two armies, Lanrezac's Fifth and the BEF, should cooperate closely in the hard days ahead, but the commanding generals had already formed an unfavourable impression of each other and French had no particular desire to meet Lanrezac again. He hurried on to Le Cateau, where his own head-quarters were being set up; there he would be surrounded by his own officers, men with manners, gentlemen who knew more about war than any arrogant French upstart. When he arrived at Le Cateau, still not in the best of spirits, he received some bad news; the II Corps commander and his close friend, Lieutenant General James Grierson, had collapsed and died from a heart attack, another blow to this beleaguered commander.

Like Henry Wilson, Field Marshal Sir John French was an Ulsterman. He was sixty-two years old in 1914 – rather old for a field command – and had never commanded any field force larger than a cavalry brigade. The young French had hoped to be a sailor but, having no head for heights or scaling masts, he left the Royal Navy in 1874, transferring first to the 8th Hussars before moving to the fashionable 19th Hussars. It took money to maintain the expected lifestyle of a cavalry officer and French had none, a chronic problem that eventually got him into debt. He was also very fond of the ladies, maintaining a string of mistresses and marrying twice. On the other hand, he displayed a deep interest in his chosen profession, studied strategy and was a great admirer of Napoleon. French served in India and was with Kitchener in the Sudan in 1885, fighting with distinction at the Battle of Abu Klea. By 1895 he was a colonel and Assistant Adjutant General at the War Office.

So far his career had followed the path taken by many officers, but he made his name and ensured more rapid advancement when commanding a cavalry brigade during the South African War. French took part in the relief of Kimberley, remained in South Africa until 1902 and was one of the few commanders who returned from that disastrous war with an enhanced reputation. This led to his advancement to the rank of major-general and his appointment to the prestigious Aldershot command.

Unfortunately, in an age of increasing firepower, General John French's field experience was as a cavalry commander. He had little interest in the other arms of service, and in spite of ample evidence from the Boers that the days of sword and lance were over, French came back from the veldt a vocal advocate of *arme blanche* (sword and lance) cavalry tactics, regarding with contempt anyone who pressed the advantages of mounted riflemen, infantry tactics and the deployment of new-fangled machine guns. For the next few years, while the lessons of South Africa were gradually being digested, French continued to argue that there was no substitute for sword, lance and the cavalry charge. In 1907 this passion for sharp points and cold steel was to bring him into conflict with his successor at the Aldershot command, Major-General Sir Horace Smith-Dorrien – and this was to pose another problem for the BEF, for in August 1914 Smith-Dorrien was the man chosen by Kitchener to replace General Grierson as commander of II Corps.

Horace Smith-Dorrien was an infantry officer of considerable experience and known ability. He was also one of the few British officers to survive the massacre at Isandlwana in 1879, when a Zulu impi destroyed the 24th Regiment of Foot – later The South Wales Borderers. Smith-Dorrien was born in Hertfordshire in 1858 and was fifty-six years old in 1914. He entered the Royal Military College, Sandhurst, in February 1876, and was commissioned into the old 95th Foot (later the 2nd Battalion, Sherwood Foresters) in January 1877. His first overseas posting was to South Africa for the Zulu War of 1879, and he then served in Egypt under Sir Garnet Wolseley, taking part in the 1882 Arabi campaign. He spent some time in India before being seconded to the Egyptian Army for the Suakin campaign against the dervishes. In that campaign he took part in the Battle of Ginnis, the last occasion on which British soldiers wore their red coats in battle.

He attended the staff college from 1887 to 1889 and returned to India, where he saw further action in the Tirah campaign of 1897–8. In 1898 he took command of a Sudanese battalion for Kitchener's Nile campaign and fought at the Battle of Omdurman, after which victory he accompanied Kitchener up-river to meet Commandant Marchand at Fashoda.

Smith-Dorrien's promotions came slowly. By the outbreak of the South African War in 1899 – after twenty-two years' service – he was only a lieutenant-colonel, commanding the 1st Battalion, Sherwood Foresters. However, in February 1900 he took command of the 19th Infantry Brigade and was quickly promoted to the rank of major-general. Smith-Dorrien saw a great deal of active service in South Africa, where he served with Sir John French, and by all accounts the two men got on well. From 1903 to 1905 he commanded the 4th Division of the Indian Army, and in 1907 he succeeded French at the Aldershot command, a highly prestigious post at the home of the British Army. This was Smith-Dorrien's first posting in the United Kingdom for twenty-seven years, and during it he fell out decisively with Sir John French.

Smith-Dorrien was noted for his ferocious temper and for taking good care of his men. When he took over at Aldershot in 1907 his first tasks were to cancel the military police patrols around Aldershot town that harassed the men in their off-duty hours and to order the cavalry regiments in garrison to start learning infantry tactics and improve their performance with rifle and carbine. Sir John French took this abrupt departure from his own *arme blanche* methods as a slap in the face and conceived a dislike for Horace Smith-Dorrien that soon amounted to hatred.

On leaving Aldershot in 1910, Smith-Dorrien was offered the South African command, but preferred to take over the Southern Command in the UK. Here he became acquainted with Britain's newly formed Territorial Force troops, whom he came to admire for their enthusiasm and intelligence. By now knighted and a lieutenant general, he was still in charge of Southern Command in August 1914 when Kitchener offered him the chance of a field command in France – under Sir John French. Smith-Dorrien was fully aware of French's antipathy towards him – indeed, the entire Army was aware of it – but what was he to do? He was a professional soldier and a fighting man; the only place for a British officer in August 1914 was with the army in France.

John French provides the classic example of an officer promoted above his level of ability. He had been a good brigade commander in South Africa – where the competition was admittedly not great – but he peaked at that level. His advocacy of lance and sword in an age of the magazine rifle and automatic weapons was more than short-sighted, and his reaction to Smith-Dorrien's implied criticism in his abandonment of obsolete cavalry tactics was disgraceful. To find the reasons for this – and for why French was allowed to get away with it – it is necessary to look briefly at the military mind.

The military mind is essentially conservative. It dislikes new and unfamiliar methods, weapons and tactics. It prefers to stick to the old ways, even when advances in technology have clearly rendered those methods and tactics out of date, if not positively dangerous. The horse – that noble steed – had stood the aristocracy in good stead since the Battle of Hastings in 1066, and it seemed churlish to abandon it now simply because someone had invented the magazine rifle. Many senior officers were former cavalry officers; they were reluctant to give up cavalry tactics because cavalry tactics were what they knew and the basis of their professional reputation. But there is no reason to assume that because a man was a cavalry officer he was automatically a fool; the best of them had already realized that while the horse could provide the means of rapid transport to the battle, it no longer had a place on the battlefield. They saw the future of the cavalry in the tactics employed so successfully by the Boers – as mounted riflemen. Sir John French, on the other hand, regarded the mounted rifleman as an abomination.

However, it was not French's blinkered approach to modern war which caused the BEF so many problems in 1914; the problems arose from French's character rather than his competence. As the Lanrezac incident illustrates, Field Marshal French was quick to take offence and enjoyed bearing a grudge. He was vindictive, touchy, volatile, indecisive and, when confronted with the German Army in 1914, completely out of his depth. He was also weak willed; he tended to heed the advice of the last man he had spoken to; he was only too willing to listen to Henry Wilson and putty in the hands of Ferdinand Foch.

The Field Marshal's relations with the French were not helped by the instructions he had received from the Secretary of State for War, Field Marshal Kitchener. The dichotomy in his orders would have been difficult for any commander to square and the situation was made even more difficult because the Allied generals involved were French and fully determined to bend the British to their wishes. French did not speak French and had no understanding of French methods or intentions; for that he had to rely on Henry Wilson, who was not the best man to ask for impartial advice. It is also probable that French was too old for such a heavy responsibility, far beyond anything he had experienced so far; sixty-two is not the best age to take an army to France and engage the full might of the German Army.

While awaiting the arrival of his new and unwanted subordinate, French held a conference at Rethel and outlined the current situation, in so far as it was known, to General Allenby, commanding the cavalry division in the BEF, and General Haig of I Corps. Most of the news he had to give came via Henry Wilson or Colonel Victor Huguet, now the French liaison officer at French's headquarters, from the French GQG. The burden of this intelligence was that some five German corps – ten divisions – were about to move across the northern French frontier on a line between Brussels and Givet. In fact this was only a part of the force so deployed, but that the Germans were massing in the north did not seem to be causing Joffre any undue alarm. Nothing ever did, but on this occasion Joffre's chronic calm was leading him into error – and exposing the Anglo-French forces in the north, the BEF and Lanrezac's Fifth Army, to an overwhelming attack.

On 18 August Joffre concluded that 'The enemy may engage only a fraction of his right wing north of the Meuse. While his centre is engaged frontally by our Third and Fourth Armies, the other part of his northern group, south of the Meuse, may seek to engage the flank of our Fourth Army.' In making this assessment Joffre appears to have assumed that von Moltke was as obsessed with Plan XVII as he was, and deploying his forces in the north with the sole purpose of taking the French armies in the flank as they pushed to the east. That the Germans were preparing a great thrust, south and west into France from Belgium, had not occurred to him, and any intelligence reaching GQG indicating such a move was simply ignored. Joffre told Lanrezac that the BEF and the Belgians were 'quite capable of dealing with the German forces north of the Meuse and Sambre', an optimistic forecast in view of the forces involved, but for the moment Field Marshal French, informed by this GQG intelligence, held to the same opinion and ordered his forces north as soon as they assembled.

August 20 was a significant day on many sections of the Western Front. On this day the German First Army entered Brussels. RFC patrols reported long columns of German infantry and artillery heading south and west, straight for an area north of Le Cateau, where the British were destined to form up on the left flank of the French Fifth Army. These RFC reports were quickly rejected by Henry Wilson, the Sub-Chief of Staff who was in charge of intelligence at GHQ. Relying on GQG intelligence, Wilson declared that the RFC information was 'somewhat exaggerated . . . only mounted troops or jägers are in your area'. Here is another example of wishful thinking; there is no point gathering intelligence if you do not pay attention to what it says.

Farther south, the French armies pushing into Alsace and Lorraine were met and counter-attacked by the German armies – the Sixth and Seventh under the command of Crown Prince Rupprecht of Bavaria. This counter-attack was to have a grave effect on the operation of the Schlieffen Plan, for the German armies were supposed to make a fighting retreat, drawing their opponents east, deeper into the Schlieffen trap. The counter-attack happened because the French tactic of '*l'attaque à outrance*' did terrible damage to the French forces in the first days of August and presented Rupprecht with an opportunity he was unable to resist. When his guns were carpeting the ground before them with tens of thousands of French dead, it seemed insane to retreat.

Therefore, from 16 August Rupprecht was bombarding von Moltke with requests that he should counter-attack and move on Nancy, the capital of Lorraine, declaring that the French armies could be equally well contained by an attack – a claim which, though true, was exactly contrary to the Schlieffen Plan.[12] The telegraph wires between von Moltke and Rupprecht grew hot, but on 18 August German Supreme Headquarters (OHL) passed the buck back to Rupprecht. They would neither forbid him to attack nor order him to do so; the decision was up to him.

Rupprecht's decision can hardly have been in doubt; the Sixth and Seventh German Armies were ordered to stop retreating and prepare for a counter-attack,[13] and that attack too went in on August 20. The 'revolving door' had been stopped and was about to go into reverse. As a result the Schlieffen Plan promptly started to unravel; the French front would start to firm up as her armies, rather than pushing deeper into the trap, were forced to retreat and able to stay in contact.

On 20 August French reported to General Joffre that the BEF had formed up and was ready to march north towards the Belgian frontier and take up position on the flank of the French Fifth Army. This march commenced on 21 August. On that day the new commander of II Corps arrived, the general Field Marshal French cordially detested – Lieutenant-General Sir Horace Smith-Dorrien. From then on French found some relief from his other worries by pursuing his long-held vendetta against Smith-Dorrien – so creating one of the great personal tragedies of the war.

The two men met that day at Bavai; all seemed friendly and the BEF movement forward continued. However, by this time the effects of the German counter-attack in Lorraine and the advance from the Meuse were being felt – on 22 August, Lanrezac's army was being pushed back across the Sambre by the German Second Army and the French Fourth and Third Armies farther south were being driven back by the Germans in the Ardennes. The 'Battle of the Frontiers' was not going France's way; the French armies were in trouble and worse, much worse, was to follow.

The Schlieffen Plan had always depended on time. Liège – the blocking point on the main German 'axis of advance' down the Meuse valley – fell on 16 August, but Belgian resistance there had put the first crimp in the plan. So too had Rupprecht's decision to counter-attack in Lorraine, an entirely avoidable and unforced German error. The next, totally unexpected obstacle the advancing German armies would encounter was the 100,000 strong BEF, which appeared in front of the German First Army along the canal at Mons on 23 August.

The BEF had assembled around Maubeuge, 24 kilometres (15 miles) south of Mons, on 20 August. Orders were then issued for the advance north towards the Belgian frontier, and on that day the RFC and cavalry made their first reconnaissance forays towards Binche. They saw no sign of the enemy south of Louvain, where a large column of German infantry from von Kluck's First Army was spotted by the RFC. Von Kluck also had his troubles and was now obliged to detach two corps – the III Reserve and later the IX Reserve, the equivalent of five divisions – to pen the Belgian Army in Antwerp while the rest of his force marched through Brussels, which was entered on 20 August.

The *Official History*[14] describes 20 August at 'as fateful day in many respects', a comment that seems entirely justifiable. As we have already noted, a lot happened on this day, less than three weeks into this war: the Belgian Army retreated to Antwerp, the Germans marched up to Namur in the Meuse valley, and Joffre gave the order for a general advance on the German forces to their front, an instruction that obliged the BEF on the left of the French Fifth Army – which was in fact already falling back under the pressure exerted by the German Second Army – to advance to the north-east. This meant that while the BEF were marching north towards the German First Army, the Fifth Army was retreating south before the German Second Army.

Although neither side knew it, this forward action from 20 August set the BEF and von Kluck's army on a collision course; on the other hand, it was possible that von Kluck's army, still edging west in a bid to outflank the Allied line, would pass the left flank of the BEF and offer Field Marshal French the chance for a flanking attack – should the field marshal become aware of the situation. To support and screen the BEF advance, GQG ordered General Sordet's Cavalry Corps to take up position on the left of the BEF while General d'Amade's three Territorial infantry divisions, positioned still farther west, were to push north as well and see what they could find.

The BEF advance began on the misty morning of 21 August and went well, the troopers of the 2nd Cavalry Brigade entering Mons before noon. There was no opposition in the town but enemy cavalry patrols were spotted by the 9th Lancers and the 4th Dragoon Guards approaching the bridges over the Mons–Condé canal (see map 2) at Obourg and Nimy, while the local peasants described seeing large German forces at Soignies, 16 kilometres (10 miles) north-east of Mons, the previous evening. By that evening the 9th Infantry Brigade were in position west of Maubeuge, 10 miles or so south of the Mons Canal, overlooking Marlborough's battlefield of Malplaquet. That night the BEF outpost line was formed by battalions from two regiments – the Lincolnshire Regiment (10th Foot) and the Royal Scots Fusiliers (21st Foot), which had fought against the French at Malplaquet in 1709.

This first march, although short by comparison with those that were to follow, was not easily accomplished. The weather was hot and the cobbled roads of northern France proved a hardship to soft feet in stiff, newly issued boots. Smith-Dorrien's II Corps led the way with the 3rd Division on the right and the 5th Division on the left, followed by Haig's I Corps, 1st Division on the right and 2nd Division on the left, both corps screened by regiments from Allenby's Cavalry Division. During the afternoon the weather cleared and RFC patrols – already proving their worth – spotted a large German cavalry formation, with some infantry and guns, moving through Nivelles, 32 kilometres (20 miles) north-east of Mons. These were later identified as coming from the 9th Cavalry Division of von Kluck's army, and during the day two more cavalry divisions were spotted, the 2nd and 4th, the three making up General von der Marwitz's 1st Cavalry Corps.

If this information was correct it implied that von Kluck's First Army was now coming south in force – a theory validated when von Bulow's Second Army was confirmed as being in action against the Fifth Army on the BEF's right. A total of seven German regular corps with four reserve corps were now somewhere to the north of the BEF, but in which direction were they heading? Von Bulow's men were in action against Lanrezac's forces to the east, but it seemed probable that as von Kluck's units came on the fighting would spread west, round that half-open flank. This being so, Field Marshal French was anxious to take up position west of Mons on the line of the Mons–Condé Canal, a waterway that offered a good defensive line – though the orders issued on the night of 21 August assumed that the BEF would cross the canal the next day, following Joffre's orders to advance to the north.

The BEF's first encounter with the enemy came soon after dawn on 22 August. A patrol of the 4th Dragoon Guards of the 2nd

Cavalry Brigade bumped into a German picket north of Obourg; after a brief exchange of fire the enemy fled. The dragoons followed up this success, bumped into a still larger enemy force and again engaged it, killing four and capturing three of the enemy before they were driven back by rifle fire. British and German cavalry continued to bicker north of the Mons–Condé canal for the rest of the day and although none had been seen, the British cavalry were left with the strong impression that large bodies of enemy infantry could not be far away; the cavalry had clearly been scouting the ground for the infantry. Later reports from Sordet's French cavalry and RFC patrols to the north confirmed this impression. Strong enemy forces were coming on; just how strong they were and where exactly they were heading remained to be seen – the best estimate on 22 August was that a full infantry corps was out there somewhere, heading in a south-westerly direction via Soignies.

Meanwhile, screened by the cavalry, the infantry of the BEF's I and II Corps were advancing north. By the evening of 22 August the BEF was in position around Mons, the I Corps on the right, Smith-Dorrien's II Corps on the left; this put the II Corps in Mons itself, with its brigades and battalions spread out along the south bank of the Mons–Condé Canal, occupying a front of some 18 kilometres (11 miles), with Allenby's Cavalry Division covering their flank to the west.

During the day the position on the northern French frontier gradually became clear. Two German corps – one of them the formidable Guards Corps – plus a Guards cavalry division from von Bulow's Second Army were engaged with the Fifth Army along the line of the Sambre, and the Fifth Army was in the process of being driven back. Sordet's French cavalry corps on the BEF's left, or western, flank had also fallen back and were now some 16 kilometres (10 miles) to the rear of the BEF line. This was a far from happy situation; if the Germans arrived now the British would be caught in an exposed salient and open to attack on the left, right and centre.

Moreover, the Germans *were* coming on; some 50,000 German soldiers of the VII Corps were between Nivelles and Charleroi.

Another corps, probably the IX Corps, was south of Soignies, and yet another, the II Corps, was moving on Landeuse, north-west of Condé. This force, plus two cavalry divisions, was closing inexorably on the BEF.

This information did not arrive at French's HQ in one intelligence estimate; it trickled in over the day. Some of it was of doubtful provenance, some of it was speculative and some of it was duplicated, but the overall impression was accurate; a large German army was rolling south and the BEF was now 16 kilometres (10 miles) – a day's march – ahead of any French help and right in the German path.

That evening Field Marshal French held a conference at his headquarters in Le Cateau. The position was fully discussed and the decision made that no further advance was possible at this time. General Lanrezac had meanwhile requested that the British attack into the right flank of the German forces currently attacking the Fifth Army, a request to which the field marshal was unable to accede, although he did agree that the BEF should hold its present positions for another twenty-four hours.

The BEF's peril was eased somewhat by the fact that von Kluck was equally confused about the strength and position – even the very presence – of the BEF, whose appearance on the First Army's front that morning had come as a complete and unpleasant surprise. That surprise would intensify the following day when von Kluck's advancing battalions ran into the BEF, entrenched and well concealed in positions around the Belgian town of Mons.

6

The Battle of Mons

23 AUGUST 1914

The battalion is a mere wreck, my proud, beautiful battalion.
Our first battle is a heavy, an unheard of heavy defeat, and
against the English, the English we laughed at.

Hauptmann Walter Bloem, *Vormarsch,* 1919

Mons is a small Belgian town, close to the northern frontier of France and capital of the province of Hainault. With a population of around 30,000 people, in 1914 it served as the business and market centre for the surrounding villages, where most of the population were involved in coal mining. As a result of this long-established industry, the main physical feature of the Mons area was numerous, towering slag heaps – *crassiers* – and the Mons–Condé canal, an industrial waterway 20 metres wide and 2 metres deep, which runs through the town from the River Sambre and west for 24 kilometres (15 miles) to the town of Condé.

The country around Mons is flat, partially wooded, scattered with hamlets and isolated farmhouses, seamed with ditches and streams and dotted with ponds. Visibility in any direction is restricted by clumps of woodland, with only a limited amount of high ground on the tops of the slag heaps offering observation points for artillery observers. Mons is, in short, a bad place in which to fight a battle.

The *Official History* describes Mons as 'one huge unsightly village, traversed by cobbled roads and overlooked by pit heads and slag heaps, often over 100 ft high. It is a close and blind country such as no army had yet been called upon to fight in against a civilised enemy in a great campaign.'[1]

One point the *Official History* neglects to make is that the real problem for the BEF on 23 August was a shortage of troops to defend such a long front along the Mons–Condé canal – over 32 kilometres (20 miles) when their line was extended east to circle Mons itself. In addition, the Condé canal, curving round to the north of Mons, puts any troops lining the south bank into a salient which an enemy coming from the north could bring under rifle and artillery fire from three sides.

On coming up to visit his forward troops, Horace Smith-Dorrien saw immediately that, in spite of the canal, the 'Mons salient' was not defensible. He therefore proposed preparing a second, shorter defence line, a mile or so south of the canal, and digging in there. Field Marshal French, on the other hand, regarded the canal as a useful barrier that should not be quickly abandoned. Both were correct but, clearly, the canal position, and especially the Mons salient, could not be held for long if attacked by a superior force.

To protect the II Corps' left flank, the newly formed 19th Infantry Brigade, made up of the 2nd Royal Welch Fusiliers, 1st Scottish Rifles, 1st Middlesex and 2nd Argyll and Sutherland Highlanders – battalions originally tasked to work on the lines of communication, while remaining under force command, the commanding brigadier reporting to French rather than Smith-Dorrien – was therefore attached to II Corps and positioned to provide the link – a rather loose link – with the French 84th Territorial Division farther west. II Corps then dug in along the canal and around the Mons salient, while Haig's I Corps extended the BEF line east and south from Mons, their trenches and positions facing east between the Bois Haut position and the village of Grand Reng, where they formed another loose link with the French Fifth Army to the east.

The Fifth Army was already in trouble. When the BEF arrived

on their flank the Fifth Army divisions were engaged in what became known as the Battle of Charleroi, opposing the advance of von Bulow's Second Army, and ignoring Joffre's orders to join the Third and Fourth Armies in an all-out attack on the German line. Writing of the events of 21 August, Edward Spears, the British liaison officer with the Fifth Army, records:

> I was in the 2ème Bureau, going through the most recent intelligence reports, when General Lanrezac walked in. He began to talk of what the Germans were doing and he was always interesting when he talked like this for he was a brilliant speaker.
>
> Presently he went on to talk of the situation of his own Army . . . he had not been speaking long before my interest changed to amazement and my amazement to incredulity. Pointing to the line held by the Fifth Army south of the Sambre and expatiating on its strength, he was saying it would be madness for troops in such strong defensive positions to abandon these and attack . . . From that moment I felt that whatever orders he might receive, General Lanrezac would be most unwilling to attack.
>
> I was aghast as I thought of how this would affect the British . . . that the enemy's corps believed to be slipping across its front would fall with full force on the British, who numbered some 80,000 men, whilst General Lanrezac, commanding a quarter of a million men, stood by with folded arms.[2]

Spears is being a little unfair to General Lanrezac. His army was already being threatened by von Bulow's force, and Lanrezac knew that von Kluck was out there to the north and about to enter the fray; at such a time it would have been hard for any general to pay too much attention to the problems of his tardy allies.

Several points need to be considered here. First, the composition of the 19th Infantry Brigade, made up of the 1st and 2nd Battalions of some famous regiments; the other BEF brigades were also composed of regular battalions. Second, the so-called Mons salient – this would prove to be the crux of the Battle of Mons; if the salient fell or holding it proved too costly, II Corps would have to pull back from the line along the Condé canal. Finally, the distance and communications problem; from Smith-Dorrien's advance HQ at Sars-la-Bruyère, eight kilometres (five miles) south of the canal, communication with units along the canal and with Field Marshal French's GHQ at Le Cateau, 40 kilometres (25 miles) to the rear, was poor, other than by staff car or motorcycle courier.

There had been no time for the Royal Engineer sappers – the Signals Corps had not yet been formed – to lay out land lines and establish field telephone links either along the 32-kilometre (20-mile) front held by II Corps or between the divisions, corps and GHQ – and the French telephone network was neither extensive nor reliable in 1914. The chronic problem of battlefield communications, which would dog the actions of army commanders for much of the First World War, made an early appearance here during the BEF's first engagement.

Intelligence was also poor, not least on the strength and movements of the enemy. The BEF marched up to the canal on Saturday, 22 August, arriving in position in the early afternoon, the first BEF encounter with the enemy taking place at dawn that day when a patrol from 'C' Squadron of the 4th Royal Irish Dragoon Guards, led by a Captain Hornby, charged a group of Germans from the 2nd Kuirassiers near Casteau, killing several.

This skirmish attracted little attention. The troops that marched on to the canal had little idea of what lay before them and were not greatly worried about the future anyway. Arriving around Mons they dug in, screened their positions from view, cleaned their rifles, examined their feet, treated their blisters, lit their pipes or cigarettes and awaited further orders or the arrival of the enemy; what would happen now was a problem for Field Marshal French and his divisional commanders.

This brief pause before the enemy arrived gave French time to work up the first of many resentments against both his superior officer, Field Marshal Lord Kitchener, and his newly arrived subordinate, Horace Smith-Dorrien, both of whom now provided a focus for his ever simmering anger. French was jealous of his position as commander-in-chief of the BEF and regarded the right to choose his own corps commanders as a perquisite of command. Kitchener had not only ignored his particular request for Lieutenant General Plumer but had sent out an officer French personally detested. The first indications of French's deeply ingrained enmity towards Smith-Dorrien would appear shortly, but for the moment he was more concerned with the actions of his latest enemy, General Lanrezac.

As the BEF marched towards the canal on 22 August, Lanrezac's Fifth Army on their right flank had begun to withdraw, forced back from the Sambre by the weight of von Bulow's Second Army. There was no alternative to this, and the withdrawal was not Lanrezac's fault; his army had been forced back by enemy pressure on his front and right flank. The result of this pressure was the curious situation of the BEF marching north and the French Fifth Army moving south. German pressure was clearly building up from the north and east on both the BEF and the Fifth Army, but information reaching the Allied HQs – Joffre's, Lanrezac's and French's – was scanty, often confused and frequently ignored. On the evening of 22 August, having declined the request from Lanrezac that the BEF should advance and attack the flank of the Second Army, French told his corps commanders that while there would be no further advance he had agreed to hold the BEF on the canal for another twenty-four hours until the position was more clear.[3]

However, there are indications that the Germans were equally in the dark over the dispositions, or even the presence, of the BEF in France and Belgium. A German General Staff intelligence estimate on the evening of 22 August stated that 'disembarkation of the English at Boulogne and their employment from the direction of Lille must be reckoned with . . . but the opinion here, however, is that large disembarkations have not taken place'.[4] The following day, 23 August, German intelligence reported the presence of an English cavalry squadron at Casteau, 10 kilometres (six miles) north-east of Mons, and an aircraft of the 5th Squadron, RFC, was shot down near Enghien.[5] The intelligence report concludes that 'the presence of the English on our front was thus established, although nothing was known of their strength'.[6]

Von Kluck's main fear at this time was that the British would appear on his flank as the First Army surged south and west into France; the possibility that they would appear to his front, entrenched and ready to give battle, had not occurred to him. Indeed, when the 2nd Battalion of the 12th Grenadier Regiment of the German III Corps reached Badour, three kilometres (two miles) north of the Mons–Condé canal, at noon on 23 August, they reported that there was no enemy within 50 miles. This impression did not last; shortly afterwards two German hussars galloped into their lines, covered with blood and shouting that the enemy occupied the line of the canal to their front.

It therefore appears that on the morning of 23 August the fog of war was affecting both sides on the Belgian frontier. Allenby's troopers, moving on the left flank of the BEF, had already bumped into German cavalry and were reporting back that strong German forces seemed to be somewhere to their front, but their reports, like those received from RFC observers, were either ignored or discounted at French's HQ. French was waiting to hear from either Fifth Army HQ or Joffre at GQG – and until he had firm orders to the contrary he intended to stay where he was along the canal, neither advancing nor retreating.

In fact, his situation was already grave. The left flank of the BEF was now largely 'in the air', fully open to the enemy with nothing to screen it but a division of French Territorial troops and General Sordet's small but willing French cavalry corps. This force had entered Belgium on 6 August to check on German moves south of the Meuse and had ridden as far as Liège before turning back, the troopers wearing their horses out in the process; unlike the British cavalry, the French rarely dismounted to march on foot. Sordet was also sending back reports of strong German forces crossing the Sambre. All this should have rung alarm bells at the Field Marshal's HQ, alerting him to strong enemy forces to his front and on his left flank.

No such bells rang. French was far more concerned with the situation on his right flank, where the BEF was now 16 kilometres (10 miles) ahead of the French Fifth Army . . . and the more the

Fifth Army withdrew or the BEF advanced, the wider that gap would become.

For the BEF to wheel right into von Bulow's Army, as Lanrezac had requested, meant exposing its flank to the advancing Germans coming in from the north. This would have been a risky man-oeuvre at any time, but on the night of 22/23 August Lanrezac informed Joffre that, far from being fourteen kilometres (nine miles) out in front, with German forces lapping at its flanks, the BEF was actually 'echeloned in rear of 5th Army'. This statement, which was obvious nonsense, indicates either that chaos was rife or that communications were non-existent between the BEF and Lanrezac's HQ. This situation was about to get worse as the German threat became a reality.

In his diary entry for 22 August, Wilson writes: 'There is no doubt we are a little in the air; but Maubeuge on our right rear relieves from anxiety. How badly the [French] X Corps has been handled we don't know, but rather badly we gather. When they fell back they lost touch with Namur. Reports today said Namur would fall tomorrow but I can't believe it. Altogether the day has not been satisfactory, although nothing serious has happened. I wish I could have got Sir John to go and see Lanrezac. It is of great importance that they should understand each other.'[7] On the fol-lowing day Callwell records that 'the BEF held its ground at Mons while the French Fifth Army gave way along the whole of its front'.

The growing perils of the current situation were not the fault of Field Marshal French. He had been ordered to cooperate with the French Army by following the wishes of General Joffre, and that was what he was trying to do. Joffre had ordered him north, to take up the long-planned position on the left flank of the French Army, and he had tried to do that as well. What had not been fore-seen was the vast open flank between the BEF and the sea on the left – and German pressure forcing the French Fifth Army back on the BEF's right.

The BEF was supposed to protect the left flank of the Fifth Army but who was protecting the left flank of the BEF? Only one weak French Territorial division, the worn-out troopers of Sordet's corps and some of Allenby's cavalry regiments. This was hardly enough to stem the advance of the powerful German First Army now coming down from the north, which, thanks to that growing gap between the BEF and the Fifth Army – a gap now fourteen kilometres (nine miles) wide – was perfectly positioned to split the Allied forces in two. Should that happen, one or other – or both – of these forces would be destroyed.

The error lay partly with the French Fifth Army and partly with GQG, and the problems were not only affecting the BEF. Lanrezac's retreat was also allowing the German Third Army to push itself forward at Charleroi into the gap between the Fifth Army and General Langle de Cary's Fourth Army on Lanrezac's right, so creating a gap that Lanrezac was desperate to close. Like Field Marshal French, General Lanrezac was far more worried about his right flank and was fully prepared to abandon the British on his left in order to stay in touch with French Fourth Army.

The only answer to the problem lay in close inter-Allied co-operation and the maintenance of a common BEF–Fifth Army–Fourth Army front against this developing attack from the northeast. Joffre, the effective generalissimo of the Allied armies, issued no orders to that effect, and since the relevant generals were no longer communicating – French and Lanrezac were barely even on speaking terms – this did not happen. In sum, therefore, on the evening of 22 August, the BEF was being abandoned by its allies. Unable to grasp what was happening, either through poor intelligence, a lack of information or an inability to read the situation, Field Marshal French elected to hold his ground along the canal and give battle to the enemy at Mons.

At dawn on the morning of Sunday, 23 August, another misty, rainy morning, Field Marshal French called a corps commanders' conference at Smith-Dorrien's HQ at Sars-la-Bruyère. French was clearly in good spirits, telling his subordinates that 'at most' two enemy corps – four divisions – and perhaps a cavalry division were advancing on the BEF. This estimate of the enemy forces was a gross miscalculation. According to *Die Schlacht bei Mons*, an account of this action published by the German General Staff in

1919, six divisions attacked II Corps, three and a half divisions attacking the positions of the 3rd Division and two and a half divisions attacking those of the 5th Division; other units engaged Haig's I Corps. Von Kluck had four corps – the IX, III, IV and the II Cavalry Corps – to the BEF's front, a force which together mustered six infantry divisions plus three cavalry divisions. In numbers, the Germans had some 160,000 men with 600 guns compared with the BEF's 70,000 men with 300 guns.

Fortunately, at this time the Field Marshal was blissfully unaware of these odds and was therefore, according to Smith-Dorrien, 'in excellent form' at his conference on the morning of 23 August, ordering his commanders to prepare for another advance but also to strengthen their outposts and to prepare the numerous bridges on the II Corps front along the canal for demolition – this slight confusion in orders perhaps indicating some doubt over what to do next.

Smith-Dorrien pointed out the inherent weakness of his position along the canal, especially in the Mons salient, adding that he had already issued orders for the preparation of a second defensive line two miles south of Mons. The Field Marshal approved of this arrangement – yet a third alternative plan – and prepared to return to GHQ, which had now moved south to Valenciennes. The opening shots of the Battle of Mons were already being fired as this conference at Sars-la-Bruyère ended, and the sound of artillery and rifle fire could be heard from the north as the field marshal drove away.

The Battle of Mons was not a major engagement. Indeed, by the Western Front standards set only a few weeks later, Mons would hardly amount to a skirmish. It has gained its memorable place in British military history because it was the first British battle of the Great War, and because it was here that the well-trained soldiers of the British regular army – the old BEF – first displayed their traditional tenacity in defence and their superb skill with the .303 bolt-action rifle.

It has frequently been alleged, and there is some truth in the allegation, that the British soldier is not at his best in offensive operations. This may be due to the fact that the British are not an aggressive nation, or because their small armies have traditionally preferred to fight a defensive battle that goes some way to negate their usual shortage of numbers; as a rough rule, it takes three men to attack a position and only one man to defend it.

However, the traditional ability of the British soldier in defence may have more to do with the British soldier's equally traditional bloody-mindedness. Give the British soldier a piece of ground to defend and he will not lightly give it up – and will charge the enemy a heavy price when he attempts to take it. That has been the case on a hundred bloody fields in the long and glorious tradition of the British Army, and so it was here at Mons on the Belgian frontier on Sunday, 23 August 1914, just three weeks after Britain entered the war.

British outposts on the canal started bickering with German cavalry scouts around 0600 hours. This skirmishing continued for some hours while the German infantry came up and the enemy brought forward their artillery, which started to shell Mons and the British positions in the salient at around 0900 hours. At 1000 hours, when he was returning to his HQ from a visit to the forward positions west of Mons, Smith-Dorrien saw a shell burst on the road in front of his car. German artillery had been pounding Mons for about an hour before their infantry advanced and the fighting then spread around the Mons salient and westward along the canal, British riflemen in cover engaging German infantry in the open while their positions were probed and pounded by the German guns.

The main pressure at first came against the 4th Battalion, The Middlesex Regiment in the salient – where the Germans could not have found a British regiment traditionally less willing to budge. At the Battle of Albuhera on 15 May 1811, during the Peninsular War, Colonel William Inglis of the 57th Regiment of Foot, later the Middlesex Regiment, lay wounded among his soldiers as they fired their volleys into the advancing French, urging them on with cries of 'Die hard, 57th . . . die hard'.

'They could not be persuaded they were beaten,' wrote the

French commander, Marshal Soult, later. 'They were completely beaten and the day was mine but they would not admit it . . . and they would not run.' The British commander at Albuhera in his report of the battle recorded that 'Our dead, particularly of the 57th Regiment, were lying as they had fought, in rows, and every wound was in the front.'

The Middlesex Regiment was ever afterwards known as 'The Diehards', and the men of 1914 were as steady and determined as their ancestors of 1811. The *British Offical History*[8] records that the Middlesex were offering 'a stubborn resistance' to the German advance and that the German infantry were 'met by a shattering fire from rifles and machine-guns and were seen to suffer heavily'.[9]

The German infantry do not seem to have made any attempt to deploy or use fire and movement tactics in an attempt to suppress this fire and move forward. As with the French *'attaque à out-rance'*, this may be a result of a pre-war doctrine which declared that objectives must be taken at any cost and held at any cost, and if lost be retaken by immediate counter-attack. German infantry field instructions, issued in 1906, make this very clear: 'The actions of the infantry must be dominated by this one thought; forward on the enemy, cost what it may . . . an uninterrupted forward movement and the desire to get ahead of its neighbours should animate all units in the attack.'[10] This fact, and the German losses at Mons and elsewhere in 1914, should give the lie to the popular and deeply ingrained belief in many quarters that only the British generals sent their infantry forward across open ground to face decimation by enemy fire.

The Brandenburg Grenadiers from the German 5th Division attacked the well-concealed positions of the 1st Battalion, The Royal West Kents and the 2nd Battalion, The King's Own Scottish Borderers (2nd KOSB) along the canal. The Brandenburgers advanced in solid company formations, presenting a perfect target, and were swept with a fire so intense and so rapid that they believed that only machine guns were being used against them, the soldiers unable to accept that bolt-action rifles could produce such a weight of fire.

In 1914, even the average British infantryman could get off fifteen *aimed* shots a minute, and most of these soldiers could do far
better than that. The German tactic – massed infantry assaults
supported by artillery – provided these marksmen with excellent
targets. At Mons the German infantry came on 'in solid blocks,
standing out sharply against the skyline', and the British infantry,
recalling the painful lessons learned fighting the Boers in South
Africa, and firing from positions the enemy could not locate,
poured a barrage of fire into the German ranks.

This storm of rifle fire sorely dismayed the Germans. The writer
Walter Bloem, then serving with the Brandenburg Regiment,
recalls his battalion commander that night, lamenting the loss of
'my proud, beautiful battalion . . . shot to pieces by the English,
the English we laughed at'. Throughout the morning and for part
of the afternoon the German infantry continued to come on in
solid masses and were shot down in great numbers, not even seeing
where this fire was coming from. The German tactic at Mons was
both crude and ineffective; it amounted to little more than naked
attrition, an attempt to overwhelm the British line by force of
numbers, accepting heavy casualties as the price of success.

Nor was heavy rifle fire the only obstacle to the German
advance; the British infantry were using their brains in this engagement, another asset of the South African War. The soldiers waited
under cover until the advancing Germans were in range and fully
exposed before opening fire, and they picked their targets carefully.
The British officers and NCOs detailed the better shots in their sections to note the swords and stripes of the German officers and
NCOs and shoot them down; men without commanders will hesitate, mill about in the open, and become especially vulnerable. So
the slaughter across the canal and around the Mons salient went
on, hour after hour, throughout that long summer day, the enemy
death roll increased by stubbornness and considerable gallantry.

This fighting went on until evening, the last British units withdrawing from Mons at 1800 hours. The 'Battle of Mons' lasted
only about twelve hours, and on the British side involved just one
reinforced infantry corps – the two divisions of II Corps, the 5th

and 3rd, and the 19th Infantry Brigade. The *British Official History* notes that the strength of II Corps at Mons amounted to just under 36,000 men, about the same number as Wellington had commanded at Waterloo, ninety-nine years before.

Until his soldiers came under accurate rifle fire, von Kluck had no idea that British troops were in the line at all, and that first blast of musketry came as a distinct shock to both the general and his troops. Then, slowly, as more German troops filtered towards the canal and German guns began to shell the British positions, the fighting spread along the canal to the west and around the salient – and British casualties began to mount.

Two of von Kluck's corps, the III and the IX Corps – four divisions, plus a cavalry division – were soon heavily engaged, mainly with Smith-Dorrien's divisions. Haig's I Corps front, which faced the dividing line between the German First and Second Armies, remained quiet, largely as a result of the overall German strategy, which, as described, was designed to keep moving to the west and head for Paris. Throughout the day more German units came up and were sent towards Mons by brigade and battalion, all heading for the bridge at Nimy in the salient.

This should have been more than enough to swamp the British positions but the German troops were not well handled and their tactics were poor. At first they made little use of their advantage in artillery and sent in their infantry virtually unsupported – with predictable results. The carefully concealed and well-deployed British infantry had a clear view of these large German infantry formations advancing on their front and quickly turned the countryside north of the canal into a killing ground.

Being new to battle, inexperienced troops tend to cling together for mutual support; while understandable, this creates a large target for enemy fire. Old soldiers, wiser in the art of staying alive, much prefer spreading out, taking up hidden positions, digging in or going to ground to avoid concentrated fire. The only way the British could be winkled out of these positions was by rooting them out with the bayonet after scouring their ground with artillery. Both were tried, but separately; the first proved costly for the

German infantry but the second gradually became effective. The combination carried the Germans across the canal and into Mons – at a price.

One of the partially correct legends regularly revived about the British Army is that it is always ready to fight the last war. In South Africa the British infantry had learned – the hard way – that, when outnumbered, good infantry, such as the Boers, fought on the defensive, occupied concealed positions, and hit what they aimed at with their rifles.

The lessons taught by the Boers at Spion Kop and the Modder river had not been forgotten. These useful, complementary skills – fieldcraft and musketry – were skills that had to be maintained with constant practice. In pre-war years long hours had been spent on the depot rifle ranges, concentrating on rapid fire and accurate shooting, and the results were evident here in the casualties inflicted on the grey mass of German troops, stumbling forward unawares towards the British line at Mons.

Eventually, their ranks thinned by rifle fire from men they could not see, the German infantry faltered – and only then did the balance of the day begin to turn against the British, for German artillery then took over the weight of the battle. Enemy guns were in action from around 0900 hours but the German artillery only came fully into play from mid-morning, when their heavy guns began to probe the British line.

'All at once,' says one British account, 'the sky began to rain down bullets and shells.' At Mariette, five kilometres (three miles) west of Mons, the enemy manhandled two field guns forward and opened fire with high-explosive shell on the Fusiliers defending the canal bridge there. The first shell fell on a house containing a number of Fusiliers who were further confused when, in the midst of this action, a crocodile of Belgian children, making their way home from church, came filing down the road. The Fusiliers stopped firing and the enemy rushed forward to the banks of the canal, from where they could put the bridge defenders under enfilade fire.

The Great War was to become an artillery war – around 60 per cent of all British deaths and casualties between 1914 and 1918 would be due to shellfire – and if the shelling at Mons was trifling compared to the later bombardments at Ypres or the Somme it was still bad enough for troops that were not yet accustomed to it. It was the guns and not German infantry attacks which finally drove the British out of the Mons salient and back from the canal, where their line was anyway too long and their numbers too few.

This withdrawal began at around 1500 hours, after six hours of heavy fighting. The British battalions in the salient – the 4th Middlesex, the 4th Royal Fusiliers, the 1st Royal Scots Fusiliers, the 2nd Royal Irish – were engaged by a full German division. Farther west, pressure was building up along the canal until the defending battalions blew up the vital bridges at Nimy, Jemappes and Mariette and fell back, company by company, to the position Smith-Dorrien had prepared two miles behind Mons.

The German units attacking along the canal had been held off without great difficulty, but once the salient had gone the entire canal position could be outflanked. German strength was steadily increasing in the early afternoon, and Smith-Dorrien had no reserves to put into the line. The Germans had more and heavier artillery and a greater number of troops; sooner or later they would cross the canal, turn his flank and trap the battalions in Mons. Before that could happen, he had to withdraw.

Fortunately for the BEF, General Horace Smith-Dorrien – and his troops – knew their business. The 4th Royal Fusiliers, the forward battalion defending the bridges inside Mons, withdrew first, blowing the bridges before they fell back. Then the whole of the British line, starting on the right and shifting steadily left – or west – began to pull back, again after destroying the bridges on the battalion fronts. At Jemappes, just west of Mons and Mariette, a mile farther west, the first demolition charges failed to detonate. Therefore, while some infantry sections stayed in position, keeping up a steady fire to hold the Germans back, Captain T. Wright of the Royal Engineers crawled back to replace the detonators at the Mariette bridge. Captain Wright was severely wounded on his first attempt but tried again, winning the Victoria Cross for his efforts, but still failing to destroy the bridge. At Nimy, Lieutenant M. J. Dease and Private S. F. Godley of the 4th Royal Fusiliers won the Victoria Cross for manning two machine guns and holding off the enemy while their company withdrew. At Jemappes, another sapper, Lance-Corporal G. E. Jarvis, aided by a private soldier, worked under the bridge for over an hour to place fresh explosive charges and gained a well-earned VC when the bridge collapsed.

The British withdrawal from Mons was not a sudden, coordinated movement across the entire front — poor communications prevented that. It was a piecemeal process as companies and platoons and sections found themselves able to briefly beat down the enemy fire to their front and fall back, or noted men falling back on their flanks and elected to follow, or were ordered back by their officers. Withdrawing from a position when under direct attack is among the most difficult of military manoeuvres, but these soldiers were skilled and disciplined troops who quickly grasped what was happening and knew what to do when their chance came to move — many had withdrawn under fire before when closely pressed by Pathan tribesmen on the North-West Frontier of India. Fortunately they found plenty of cover among the gardens and houses in the suburbs of Mons, so the withdrawal was effected without undue difficulty and was in no sense a rout. The blowing of the canal bridges was the signal for a general withdrawal, and by 1700 hours most of the British line had disengaged and was moving back to Smith-Dorrien's previously prepared positions south of the canal.

Only in the Mons salient, where some battalions of the 8th Infantry Brigade were surrounded by German forces, was there any significant loss. Here some platoons of the 4th Middlesex — pinned down by shellfire, their rifles jammed by sand and running out of ammunition for their machine guns — were overrun, though the soldiers continued to engage the enemy until their positions fell. The rest of Smith-Dorrien's corps withdrew from Mons and the canal line, turning to face the enemy again a mile or so farther south. Pinned down by British shellfire in their first attempt to carry this second position, the Germans put in another attack about 1730 hours and were hurled back by rifle fire from the 2nd Royal Scots, the 1st Gordon Highlanders and the 2nd Royal Irish Regiment. The Germans then broke off the attack; in the early evening their bugles sounded the ceasefire, ending any further advances that day. The German Army had discovered what professional British infantry could do in a defensive battle and had not enjoyed the experience.

This was the famous Battle of Mons. It lasted twelve hours, and apart from a few tactical decisions during the day and the order to pull back later that night, none of the senior officers had a lot to do. From the moment the first shot was fired, the outcome at Mons depended on the shooting and fieldcraft of the soldiers and the tactical skills of the battalion commanders; both were well up to the task.

Total casualties in II Corps were just over 1,600 men, killed, wounded and missing; the Corps also lost two guns along the canal. The largest battalion casualties were in the 4th Middlesex, which lost 400 men, and in the 2nd Royal Irish Rifles, which lost over 300; both of these units were in the 8th Infantry Brigade in the salient. Haig's I Corps, which was barely engaged at all, lost just forty men and Allenby's Cavalry Division even fewer. German losses, largely from rifle fire, exceeded 5,000 men.

The Battle of Mons was largely fought by the two divisions of Smith-Dorrien's II Corps, and they should get the credit for it. The *Official History* comments that: 'Altogether the British commanders were not dissatisfied with this day's work. The unsatisfactory position on the canal had been imposed on them fortuitously; but it had been held for a sufficient time and had been evacuated, without great disaster or difficulty, in favour of a second position only a mile or so in rear. The men too were in high spirits, for they had met superior numbers of the most highly renowned army in the world and given a good account of themselves.'[11]

There was, of course, a hidden error here, a failure in the senior command. But for the skill of those riflemen a heavy price would have been paid for committing the BEF against so many German divisions. The finger of blame here must point at General Lanrezac and to a certain extent at Field Marshal French. French had failed to keep a grip on the campaign so far, had declined to consult his allies and insist on an obviously essential conference with Lanrezac. As a result, he had let the BEF march on unsupported towards the advancing Germans. Good generals have to be lucky but Field Marshal French was pushing his luck too hard and it soon began to run out.

At nightfall on 23 August, II Corps were pulling back from direct contact with the enemy and taking up defensive positions three kilometres (two miles) south of the canal. They had been in action all day, had withdrawn by platoon and company under shell and rifle fire and were naturally in some disorder. The men needed to sort themselves out and receive fresh supplies of ammunition, a hot meal and, if possible, some rest. The brigades of the 3rd and 5th Divisions had to reform while General Smith-Dorrien received reports and casualty and ammunition returns from his commanders. That done, he would have to contact Field Marshal French, report on the situation and obtain fresh orders.

While Smith-Dorrien was doing all this, he pulled his men back to the hastily prepared defensive position three kilometres (two miles) south of the canal and ordered them to dig in there for a renewal of the battle on the following day. The weary soldiers of II Corps were carrying out this order at 2300 hours on 23 August when a message arrived from Field Marshal French, ordering Smith-Dorrien to send a staff officer at once to GHQ and receive fresh orders. The essence of these orders was that there would be no stand south of Mons. With a strong German force to his front and the French on his right falling back, Field Marshal French had decided to retreat.

This decision had not been reached without some furious debate at GHQ. Wilson's diary entry for August 23 states: 'During the afternoon, I made a careful calculation and I came to the conclusion that we only had one corps and one cavalry division (possibly two corps) opposite us. I persuaded Murray and Sir John that this was so, with the result that I was allowed to draft orders for an attack tomorrow by the Cavalry Division, 19th Brigade and II Corps, to the North East, pivoting on Mons.'[12]

Given the fact that II Corps and the 19th Infantry Brigade had been in close action all day with large forces of the enemy, one can only wonder where Wilson was getting his information from or what might have happened had this order to attack been implemented. Fortunately, this was not the case. Wilson's account continues: 'Just as these [orders] were complete, a wire came from Joffre to say we had two and a half corps opposite us. This stopped our attack and at 11 pm came the news that Fifth Army were falling back still further. Between 11 pm and 3 am we drafted orders and made arrangements for a retirement to the line Maubeuge–Valenciennes. It had been a day of sharp fighting and severe disappointment.'[13]

The withdrawal of the BEF from Mons to the Marne duly began in the small hours of 23/24 August, only to stop again two days later when Smith-Dorrien's now battle-hardened II Corps turned on its pursuers at Le Cateau.

7

The Battle of Le Cateau

26 AUGUST 1914

Very well, gentlemen, we will stand and fight.
Lt.-Gen. Horace Smith-Dorrien

The order to withdraw the BEF from Mons came not a moment too soon. Not only were the French on their right continuing to withdraw from the engagement around Charleroi, but von Kluck's forces were still moving round the British left, continuing their march towards the west of Paris while hoping to drive their opponents, French and British, into the elusive safety of Maubeuge.

According to the *Official History*, after the fight at Mons von Kluck 'resolved to continue the attack next day, enveloping the [British] left flank with the intention of cutting off the enemy's retreat to the west'. It adds, 'the attack will be so directed as to force the enemy into Maubeuge'.[1] If the Anglo-French forces in the north could be penned in Maubeuge the general German advance on Paris could continue unimpeded.

These twin aims produced a certain ambivalence in von Kluck's actions. Convinced that the British would fall back south and west, down their line of communications towards the Channel ports, he sent the entire II Cavalry Corps, three divisions under General von der Marwitz, to cut them off while a further four infantry corps – eight divisions – were tasked to push south and drive the BEF and at least part of the Fifth Army into Maubeuge.

These actions thwarted Field Marshal French's first firm intention of abandoning any further attempt to liaise with the detested Lanrezac and withdraw towards the Channel ports down the route of the BEF's advance.

Up to a point, this was a sensible intention. By retreating down his established lines of communication, French would enjoy the advantage of organized rail links for the movement of supplies and reinforcements to the front and the evacuation of the wounded, as well as the availability of supply dumps. However, with the enemy trying to edge round his left flank, this withdrawal to the south and west was no longer an option – and would anyway have created a gap between the BEF and the French Fifth Army that the Germans would surely exploit.

French therefore elected to pull back towards the south, and Joffre asked the Field Marshal whether he might care to consider withdrawing in the direction of Cambrai. Map 2 shows the location of these places and the positions of the BEF as the retreat from Mons began.

This decision to retreat was providential for intelligence errors continued, and, as noted, on the evening of 23 August Wilson had persuaded French to order a fresh advance. Fortunately new information then arrived from GQG and the BEF attack was shelved. French then received news that the Fifth Army were still falling back, so the BEF were ordered to retreat towards a line between Maubeuge and Valenciennes. This order had to be relayed to the BEF's corps and divisional commanders; this took time and caused further confusion.

It is essential to bear in mind the problems of telephonic communication in northern France in 1914. Haig's HQ was in telephone contact with GHQ but Smith-Dorrien's was not, so a II Corps staff officer, Brigadier General Forrester-Walker, was sent back 35 miles to GHQ at Le Cateau to receive the new orders. The time taken for this 115-kilometre (70-mile) round trip caused further delay. It is hard to see why these orders were not sent directly to Smith-Dorrien for execution.

When Forrester-Walker arrived back at Smith-Dorrien's HQ, it was discovered that the orders contained no coherent plan for the BEF retirement. Instead, French stated that the arrangements for withdrawal were to be 'worked out between the two Corps commanders', but seemed to suggest that Haig's I Corps should cover the retreat of II Corps. It was now 0300 hours on 24 August, the day after the engagement at Mons. Dawn would come at 0500 hours, the men had not slept for two nights, and the German attack was sure to be renewed as soon as it was light enough for their artillery commanders to spot the fall of shot. There was no time for the two Corps commanders to work things out, and they were not, in fact, able to meet until noon on 24 August, when German artillery had been firing on II Corps positions for several hours and an infantry attack was clearly pending. By that time Haig's Corps was already on the move – the 1st Division's retreat had started at 0400 hours and the 2nd Division moved out shortly afterwards – and if Smith-Dorrien's corps were to manage another successful disengagement they must move quickly.

French had not indicated a destination for the withdrawal, as he had not yet made up his mind where to go. He had already assured Joffre that he would withdraw the BEF towards Valenciennes and had abandoned the idea of a retreat south-west towards Amiens, but he was also toying with the notion of pulling back inside the fortress of Maubeuge, a second-class French fortress with defensive bastions stretching for 32 kilometres (20 miles), a position that was close to his right rear, well provisioned and, perhaps, defensible.

The idea of a retreat into Maubeuge was, French admitted, 'a terrible temptation'.[2] Fortunately, recalling the example of Marshal Bazaine, who had been penned in Metz in 1870 and forced to surrender by the Prussians, French resisted this alluring prospect. Had the BEF withdrawn into Maubeuge German siege artillery deployed at Liège would have arrived within days to enforce surrender; in the face of modern heavy artillery, these fortress cities had lost their value in the first weeks of the war. The only remaining option was retreat, so the BEF got wearily to its feet and began to pull back to the south, the first leg of their retirement taking them towards Le Cateau.

As noted – and in spite of French's previous intention – it was Haig's corps which moved first while II Corps stayed back to cover their move. Smith-Dorrien's men were therefore still in position when the German attack was renewed at 0700 hours, and they greeted it with a storm of rifle and machine-gun fire. This briefly checked the German advance and Hamilton's 3rd Division got clear, the 2nd South Lancashires and the 1st Lincolns, backed by the field guns of the 109th Battery, RFA, punishing the German troops pushing into the village of Cipley and the small town of Frameries, though suffering heavy losses in return.

An officer of the 24th Brandenburg Regiment, Captain von Brandis, who served later at Verdun and was no stranger to hard fighting, wrote in his post-war memoirs that: 'A continuous stream of gun and howitzer shell hurtling and howling overhead falls on Frameries. No human being could possibly live there. If we thought the English had been shelled enough to be "storm ripe" we were fairly mistaken. They met us with well-aimed fire and as we went forward only dead and wounded were to be seen in our firing line. Tommy seems to have studied our tactics and waited for the moment of assault, and only when we were fully in the open did he fire with his machine-guns.'[3]

The British infantry were actually making very little use of machine guns – currently only issued on a scale of two to a battalion – and most of this drenching fire came from the 'ten rounds rapid' opened on the enemy by the soldiers of the 1st Lincolns. The German assault failed and was resumed only after another half-hour of artillery fire, but when the Germans finally entered Frameries the British had slipped away; 'from their experience in small wars', wrote von Brandis, 'the English veterans knew how to slide off at the last moment'.[4]

The British battalions had not disengaged before causing the enemy considerable casualties. Von Brandis records that his battalion alone had lost one third of its men, three company commanders and half the other officers; the British tactic of identifying and picking off the officers was clearly taking effect. The losses, however, were not all on one side; the 2nd South Lancashires, waiting too long before slipping away, were caught in enfilade by machine guns and lost over 200 men.

At dawn, three German divisions, one from III Corps and all of IV Corps, engaged Fergusson's 5th Division, attempting to out-flank the left of the British line. The tactics employed here repli-cated those used against the 3rd Division. Fergusson's brigades were first pinned in position by artillery fire and then hit with a massive infantry attack. In response, riflemen of the 1st Dorsets and guns of the 37th Battery, RFA, scorched the advancing German line with fire and, having checked the first German attack, began to retire. The withdrawal was not made without loss; the 2nd Duke of Wellington's Regiment, not having received the order to retire, was surrounded by the enemy and lost some 400 men before it could disengage.

Problems then arose on Fergusson's right flank. This should have been covered by the 19th Infantry Brigade and Allenby's cav-alry division, but the cavalry had ridden out on reconnaissance before dawn and the 19th Brigade, which was still taking its orders from GHQ and not from II Corps HQ, had been ordered back long before dawn, leaving the left flank of the 5th Division com-pletely 'in the air'. The Germans discovered this fact before noon, and IV Corps promptly came in from the west to roll up the British front.

Fortunately, the cavalry division came back from its foray just in time to re-enter the fray. Fergusson, realizing the danger to his left flank, had already formed a small rearguard consisting of the 1st Norfolks and the 1st Cheshires, supported by the 119th Battery, RFA. He gave command of this force to Colonel Ballard of the Norfolks and ordered him to hold the ground around Quiévrain that offered a good field of fire to the north-west. When the German infantry tried to cross this ground soon after noon they received the usual violent pummelling from BEF rifle and artillery fire.

This action was under way when the 2nd Cavalry Brigade under Brigadier de Lisle appeared on the scene, assessed the situation and elected to participate with a charge. Charging the enemy in the open was tantamount to suicide, but the cavalry could rarely resist the opportunity and the 9th Lancers, backed by two squadrons of the 4th Dragoon Guards, swept into the fray, catching and spearing a few German soldiers in the open before sweeping across the front of the British infantry.

The horsemen were now under fire from no fewer than nine German batteries and every German soldier in the area, fire that emptied saddles and brought horses crashing down in mid-stride. When they reformed behind the British infantry, cavalry losses in those few hectic minutes were found to be high; around 250 cavalrymen and many horses had been shot down. The only solid gain from this charge by the 9th Lancers and the 4th Dragoon Guards – one of the last such exploits in modern war – was that it enabled the cavalry to extricate some guns of the 119th Battery, RFA, which were in danger of capture – a feat for which Captain Francis Grenfell of the 9th Lancers was later awarded the Victoria Cross.

Although this action and the presence of Ballard's force foiled von Kluck's first attempt at envelopment, this did little to improve a steadily deteriorating situation. A fresh German division, the 8th, was now deploying and moving in on the two infantry battalions, and fire from the horse artillery and RFA batteries could do little to stop them; once again it was time to go, and at 1430 hours Colonel Ballard ordered his units to withdraw.

The cavalry duly fell back and the 1st Norfolks also managed to slip away; not so the 1st Cheshires. Three separate orders to break off the action failed to reach the battalion commander, by now wounded, and the Germans gradually closed in on the Cheshires until the battalion was completely surrounded. The Cheshires kept up the fight for three hours before the handful of survivors ran out of ammunition and were forced to surrender.

In this action the 119th Battery lost thirty officers and men, the 1st Norfolks lost over 250 officers and men, and the 1st Cheshires, which had started the day with almost 1,000 men, were reduced to just two officers and 200 men when the battalion remustered the following day.

All in all, though, 24 August, the first day of the retreat from Mons, had gone very well; von Kluck's attempt at envelopment had been defeated and the BEF had successfully disengaged. Smith-Dorrien's corps had beaten off all attacks, though at some cost; BEF losses for the day, mostly in II Corps, amounted to around 2,000 men, killed, wounded or missing. Most of these casualties were in the rifle battalions, which had now lost some 3,500 men in two days of action, but II Corps was still confident, rightly proud of what it had achieved – and full of fight. Haig's corps again saw very little fighting on 24 August, casualties not exceeding 100 men; with total casualties of 4,000 men, the BEF was virtually undamaged. The main problem was weariness; the men had been without rest for three days and were very tired, in urgent need of rest, sleep and food. These casualty figures must also be placed in context; the bulk of them fell among the infantry battalions, the cavalry units and the artillery, the 'teeth' of the force. While the 'ration strength' of the BEF remained impressive, the losses among the fighting men were rising steadily and would shortly rise again.

The condition of the troops was not helped by the weather, which was extremely hot, or by the hard cobbles of the French roads, which caused agony to feet blistered by stiff new boots. Food was running out and thirst a problem, but the men kept moving, their third day of long marches interspersed with plenty of action for II Corps and very little rest for anyone. Morale remained high; various accounts recall that at the end of the day, when they arrived at their billets around Bavai, the troops 'marched in singing'.

If so, the singing was probably due as much to the need to stay awake and keep moving as high spirits. The troops were now so tired that they could hardly put one foot in front of the other and fell asleep in the road the second their column halted . . . and this was only the first day of the long retreat to the Marne.

This weariness may have accounted for some of the tales that sprang up about the 'Angels of Mons', the legend that during the retreat from Mons the ghostly figures of English archers, armed and clad as for Agincourt or Crécy, had appeared in the sky to support their descendants in this present struggle. An investigation in calmer times revealed that these alleged sightings were pure fiction, the invention of a journalist. Nevertheless, the story of the Angels of Mons and reports of sightings continued to flourish, although Private Frank Richards of the Royal Welch Fusiliers reports: 'We retired all night with fixed bayonets, many sleeping as they marched along. If any angels were seen on the retirement, as the newspaper accounts said they were, they were seen that night. March, march, for hour after hour without no halt; we were breaking into our fifth day of continuous marching with practically no sleep in between. Stevens said, "There's a fine castle there, see?" pointing to one side of the road. But there was nothing there. Very nearly everyone was seeing things, we were all so dead-beat.'[5]

Field Marshal French spent most of 24 August at his advance HQ at Bavai, sending messages to Lanrezac and Joffre. He went to visit Haig, finding him marching south with his corps, and had a meeting with General Sordet, commanding the French Cavalry Corps, which, with d'Amande's Territorial divisions, was the only force covering the open country between the BEF and the Channel coast, a force that would shortly be joined by the garrison evacuated from Lille. French then went off to greet General T. d'O. Snow, GOC of the newly arrived 4th Division, elements of which were detraining and coming forward to link up with the retreating battalions of the BEF, where Snow's division would soon become part of Major-General W. P. Pulteney's III Corps. At 1500 hours on 24 August French issued orders directing the retreat to continue on the line Le Cateau–Cambrai.[6]

On this day the field marshal appeared to be in full command of the situation, issuing orders, liaising with his allies and visiting his troops. It is very noticeable, however, that he apparently made no attempt to contact Smith-Dorrien or visit II Corps. This is strange, for Smith-Dorrien was commanding the only corps to be heavily engaged with the enemy at Mons and during the first day of the retreat, and surely warranted closer attention. It is the practice in the British Army for a commander to go forward and visit his subordinates during difficult times, to assess the situation on the ground, receive reports and offer support and advice. French did not do this; instead Smith-Dorrien appeared at GHQ in the late afternoon of 24 August and asked the Field Marshal for instructions – specifically, should he hold his ground on the following day or continue the retirement?

Perhaps this was the question that rekindled French's latent animosity towards Smith-Dorrien. On 24 August, for all his apparent sangfroid, French was a very worried man, fully aware of the peril of his position. It was apparent that four German corps were advancing on his force and that the Fifth Army was in full retreat, leaving a 16-kilometre (10-mile) gap on his right. French was rapidly becoming convinced that the campaign was a disaster and that, unless he was very lucky or very astute, the BEF was lost. And now here was Horace Smith-Dorrien, badgering him for a decision about II Corps.

According to Smith-Dorrien, French told the II Corps commander that 'he could do as he liked'.[7] If this is true – and since it has never been denied there is no reason to doubt it – French's attitude toward his subordinate and his overall command responsibilities can only be described as remarkable. French's memoirs, which give a detailed account of his actions on this day, make no reference to this meeting with Smith-Dorrien, who adds in *his* memoirs that French had mentioned that Haig intended to start retreating again with his corps at 0500 hours on the following day, 25 August.

From 24 August until the opening salvoes of the Battle of the Marne two weeks later, French's main concern was to save the BEF. This was understandable; the BEF was the only trained army Britain had and he had been instructed to take good care of it. The other element of his orders, to cooperate closely with the French, was subordinate to this prime requirement.

Anxious to avoid yet another dawn struggle with the German Army, Smith-Dorrien told French that he intended to get his men on the move by midnight and be across the Valenciennes–Bavai road before daylight – a requirement that would deny his weary men yet another night's sleep. French had learned that all three French armies on his right – or eastern – flank were now retiring, so after a brief delay while Sordet's cavalry corps crossed their line of retreat, the BEF began to march south again early on 25 August, French shifting his headquarters from Le Cateau to St Quentin.

Joffre had now realized that the Germans were using reserve corps alongside their active formations, so increasing the size of their armies in the field. 'This', said Joffre, 'explained how they were able to extend the length of their front.' With that realization came another one; the Germans were fully capable both of holding up the French advance in Lorraine *and* sweeping south to envelop Paris, cutting off any French armies that got left behind on the northern frontier. Plan XVII, which had always been based on a belief that the Germans could not be strong everywhere, had clearly collapsed. This being so, Joffre's main task now was to keep the French forces in being, shore up any breach and prevent his armies being surrounded and reduced. To achieve this aim there was no option, for the moment, but further retreat. Under German pressure the French armies north and east of Paris began to bend back like a bow, pivoting on Verdun.

However, on 25 August Joffre issued his second General Order of the war. In this he proposed creating a new French army, the Sixth, formed from divisions taken from the still-intact front in Lorraine where Crown Prince Rupprecht's Army Group were making no progress against the stubborn resistance put up by the armies of de Castelnau and Dubail. The Sixth Army, when formed, would take up a position on the extreme left flank of the French line, beyond the BEF, which would therefore be sandwiched between the Sixth and Fifth French Armies.

This move served three purposes. First, it recognized, at last, that the main German thrust was from the north, an attempt to get round the French western flank and encircle the armies defending Paris. Second, it created a force of three French armies – the Sixth, the Fifth and General de Langle's Fourth, which, together with the BEF, should be able to stem this German advance and then launch a counter-attack. Finally, it placed a force on the

French left wing to which Joffre could give direct orders, knowing they would be obeyed. Negotiating with his British allies over what they would or would not do was not an option at this critical time. Joffre anticipated that the Sixth Army would be formed, in position on the left wing and ready to fight by 2 September.

With the benefit of hindsight, it is possible to see that the French situation was not as grave as it then appeared. The Third and Fourth Armies in the Ardennes had not yet been seriously engaged and the Second and First Armies in Lorraine, albeit shedding men in great numbers, were still in being and holding up the German attack. On the northern front the Fifth Army and the BEF had not been enveloped and destroyed. Although off balance and in full retreat, nowhere had the French armies been defeated; they were still in line, still fighting hard and taking a toll of their enemies. The main danger lay in the situation now developing in the north, where a wide turning movement by three German armies, advancing on a front 120-kilometres (75 miles) wide, was threatening to destroy the BEF and the French Fifth Army. Both now had to pull back out of the trap as quickly as possible while maintaining a united front against the foe.

It is important to understand that the French were still full of fight, if only to put the BEF's part in this campaign in context. While the BEF were in battle with von Kluck at Mons on 23 August, Lanrezac's army had been hotly engaged by von Bulow's Second Army at Charleroi, where the Germans had attempted to send three corps across the Sambre. The town of Charleroi straddles both banks of the river, and the Second Army forced the French III Corps back into the town and began to fight its way towards the river, street by street, house by house. Losses on both sides mounted quickly, the German formations decimated by the quick-firing 75s, the French defences and much of the town shattered by the plunging, high-explosive fire of German artillery. By the evening of 22 August the corps of the Fifth Army had suffered severely, with a particularly heavy toll among the officers.[8]

The fighting at Charleroi continued unabated during 23 August – on a far larger scale than that currently raging at Mons – and by the evening von Hausen's troops had established a bridgehead over the Sambre south of Dinant and Lanrezac's III Corps was forced out of Charleroi. Then came even worse news; the French Fourth Army, on Lanrezac's right flank, was being forced back from the Ardennes. To save his army from encirclement, Lanrezac decided to retreat – and made this decision without consulting Joffre or advising Field Marshal French; the retreat from Charleroi and the Sambre began on 24 August, even as the British pulled back from Mons.

On 25 August, marching south from Bavai, the BEF encountered another problem. Across its path lay a thick wood, the Forêt de Mormal, 22,400 acres in extent with good roads across from east to west, and roads on either side, but no roads directly through it from north to south. It was clearly desirable to keep the BEF together, but one road could not support four divisions; the only solution was for the corps to divide, I Corps passing to the east of the forest, Smith-Dorrien's corps to the west.

Having passed the forest, the two corps were supposed to swing inward and join together again, but this did not happen. A gap of some miles opened up between Smith-Dorrien's troops and Douglas Haig's command which was not to be closed for another six days. Smith-Dorrien records that, as the march began, 'Communication with I Corps was a matter of supreme difficulty . . . I heard nothing from I Corps throughout the day . . . and no information was sent to me by GHQ concerning it. I imagined we would meet up at Le Cateau in the evening, according to orders.'[9]

During the day Haig's formations became seriously entangled with elements of Lanrezac's Fifth Army retreating from Charleroi, with the French 53rd Division and Major-General S. H. Lomax's 1st Division of bone-weary men competing for the same road – which was also clogged with thousands of refugees. After another hard day's march and some mild skirmishing with the enemy, by 1800 hours I Corps were moving into billets at Landrecies and Maroilles, two villages on the south-east corner of the Forêt de Mormal. This last village was the forward supply base for two French divisions, the 53rd and 69th, a fact which caused still more confusion and congestion as French supply wagons clogged the roads. So far Haig's Corps had seen little of the enemy and lost very few men, but constant marching and lack of sleep were taking a heavy toll of officers and men.

II Corps, with the 19th Infantry Brigade and Allenby's cavalry division attached and moving west of the Forêt de Mormal, had a much more difficult time. Delayed at the start by the passage of Sordet's Cavalry Corps across their rear, they were then continually engaged by elements of the German First Army, still attempting to either cut off II Corps or drive the entire BEF into Maubeuge. Smith-Dorrien and Allenby were able to beat off these German thrusts but the need to deploy and take up defensive positions time and time again meant that II Corps and its supporting elements became strung out over many miles of road.

'It will be difficult to realise the fog of war which surrounded us that night,' writes Smith-Dorrien.

> Communication was most difficult and although the Corps signallers performed miracles with their wires and cable it was impossible to find out the position of units until hours after they had reached them. It was not only as if I had II Corps to deal with, for mixed up with them was the Cavalry Division, the 19th Infantry Brigade and the 4th Division, none of which were under me but were reporting their movements and getting their orders from GHQ, twenty-six miles to the rear. It is true that GHQ issued an order at 1pm [1300 hours] 25 August, placing the 19th Brigade under II Corps, but it was then with the Cavalry Division and heaven knows when it got the order . . . I only succeeded in collecting them next morning when they were starting south from Le Cateau.[10]

These skirmishes on 25 August were small affairs in comparison with the actions of the two previous days but they still cost II Corps another 450 men, mostly from the 3rd Division, and tired the men still more. The men perked up when they went into action, but when the firing died down and the march resumed their weariness returned, each time worse than before. By the evening of 25 August II Corps was scattered, somewhat disorganized and, to complete their general misery, just before dark a heavy thunderstorm drenched the marching troops, who arrived at Le Cateau both wet and weary.

Over to the east, German patrols began probing I Corps positions at dusk, appearing first at Maroilles, where a skirmish with the 1st Royal Berkshires of the 6th Brigade in the 2nd Division cost the latter some 60 casualties while defending the bridge over the Sambre. After dark there was another flurry of activity when the 4th (Guards) Brigade in Landrecies fought a brief engagement with an uhlan patrol on the outskirts of the town. Haig was with this brigade during the fight and afterwards he made his way to GHQ, arriving there some time after midnight on the night of 25/26 August to tell French that the situation at Landrecies was 'very critical'. He therefore requested that II Corps, then trailing into Le Cateau, eight miles south-west of Landrecies, should be ordered at once to the Guards Brigade's assistance.

There was no need for such action. The action at Landrecies was a minor affair, between the 3rd Coldstream Guards and infantry from the German III Corps. Skirmishing began at dusk and apparently went on until 0400 hours on the following morning, but the casualty figures – 120 from the Coldstream Guards and 125 Germans, killed, wounded or missing – confirm that the engagement at Landrecies was no real cause for alarm.

Haig thought otherwise. He was quite convinced his Corps had been attacked in strength and at 0350 hours on the morning of 25 August he sent an urgent message to GHQ, demanding assistance from II Corps. Field Marshal French went farther. At 0500 hours the field marshal sent Colonel Huguet, the French liaison officer at GHQ, hurrying to Lanrezac's HQ with the message that 'I Corps has been violently attacked in its billets between Le Cateau and Landrecies and is falling back – if it can – on Guise to the south; if not, south-east in the direction of La Capelle. Tomorrow the BEF will continue its retreat towards Peronne. Can Fifth Army come to FM French's aid by sheltering I Corps until it can rejoin the main body of the British forces?'[11]

In his memoirs French goes even farther, claiming in a letter to

Kitchener sent on 27 August that the Coldstream Guards had been attacked by at least a German Brigade, that 'a frightful panic ensued and in a very few minutes no less than 800 or 900 dead and wounded Germans were lying in the streets'.

None of this was necessary and not all of it was true. I Corps had not been seriously attacked and was not falling back on Guise, and there was very little panic outside Corps HQ. Haig was not well at this time and it may be that the sudden outburst of night firing brought this normally phlegmatic Scots officer close to panic. According to his Intelligence Officer, Brigadier General John Charteris, 'D. H. ordered the whole town into a state of defence, wanted barricades erected across the streets with furniture or anything handy and ordered all official papers burned, saying, "If we are caught, by God, we will sell our lives dearly."'[12]

The action at Landrecies was brisk enough but a minor skirmish compared with the heavy fighting on the II Corps front in previous days. However, since there was no way of quickly finding out what had actually happened, fears escalated, not least at Fifth Army HQ, where French's message spurred Lanrezac into offering assistance. It also created the impression that Haig's Corps had been broken and was in full retreat towards the safety of the French lines, while a German host poured into the gap so created. This impression was no less alarming for being totally untrue, and fears that the entire BEF was collapsing were spread to Joffre at GQG by Colonel Huguet. In fact, by dawn on 26 August, the Germans had been driven out of Landrecies and I Corps resumed its retreat unhindered.

Meanwhile the 4th Division, commanded by Major-General T. d'O. Snow, the first element of what would become III Corps, was taking position on the left of II Corps, on a line between the villages of Fontaine au Pire and Wambaix. The first battalion to come up, the 2nd Inniskilling Fusiliers, marched into Bevillers, where they immediately encountered a troop of German cavalry followed by six lorries full of German infantry – a rare example of the Germans using motor transport at this time. The Inniskillings promptly opened fire and the enemy quickly retreated.

When dawn arrived on 26 August it was clear that there was no major danger at Landrecies but the I Corps retreat continued. The only effect of this alarm was to deprive the soldiers of yet another night's sleep, but as Haig's soldiers marched south they heard the sound of artillery and rifle fire coming from the direction of Le Cateau, where II Corps, the 4th Division and Allenby's cavalry were now heavily engaged.

To pick up the developments that led to the II Corps battle at Le Cateau it is necessary to go back to the evening of 25 August. When Smith-Dorrien's staff reached Le Cateau at around 1730 hours they were aware that Haig's corps was some thirteen kilometres (eight miles) away to the north-east and moving into billets. II Corps were less fortunate; Smith-Dorrien's units had become dispersed during the day and units of the 3rd Division were still trailing into Le Cateau at midnight or later, many of the battalions in some disorder, all the men weary beyond description. Other units were equally tired; the cavalry were exhausted, horse and man, and the men of the 19th Infantry Brigade, who had been marching with Allenby's cavalry, were quite worn out. With the exception of Snow's battalions, the BEF had now been marching or fighting or digging trenches for three days and nights with very little sleep and not much in the way of food.

There was, however, nothing wrong with their morale. No soldier enjoys retreating, but these were professional fighting men who had quickly realized the gravity of the situation confronting the BEF and their French allies; in the circumstances a retreat was sensible and they did not let it depress them. They also knew that they could give the enemy a bloody nose whenever the opportunity arose, and even if they had ceased to cheer or shout 'Are we downhearted? No!' their spirits were high; all they needed to restore them to full fighting trim was a good night's sleep and a hot meal.

Smith-Dorrien established his HQ in Bertry, a village five kilometres (three miles) south-west of Le Cateau, where he received a message from Henry Wilson, telling him that orders would shortly be issued for a continuation of the retreat. This order duly arrived at 2215 hours, when the situation of II Corps was as described above; the units were scattered, some battalions were just coming in and the location of many others was still unknown. Smith-Dorrien therefore had a problem; how could he distribute this order to his widely dispersed and weary forces when their location was often unknown . . . and were the units he could locate in any state to continue marching?

Units continued to trickle in all night, their commanding officers reporting to Smith-Dorrien's HQ. None of these officers was eager to carry on retreating and all confirmed that their men were exhausted and some companies or battalions incomplete. At 0200 hours General Allenby arrived to tell the II Corps commander that his cavalry brigades were widely scattered and his men and horses were also 'pretty well played out'. This being so, said Allenby, with only the 4th Cavalry Brigade intact, he would not be able to occupy the high ground at Viesly overlooking Solesmes and the proposed II Corps line of retreat the next day. He therefore urged Smith-Dorrien to get away in the dark, for strong German forces would certainly attack Le Cateau at daylight.

Smith-Dorrien then consulted his two divisional commanders, Hamilton and Fergusson. Both confirmed Allenby's views but added that their men were tired out and their battalions were still coming in. The general conclusion was that II Corps could not move as a body before 0900 hours next morning – and that was the optimistic prediction.[13]

Smith-Dorrien wisely took a little time to make a full assessment of the situation and consider the difficulties and alternatives. His corps was in grave danger, tired, hungry, dispersed and short of support. If he continued the march the men would grow even more exhausted, many units would never catch up, and it seemed highly probable that from the high ground around Solesmes the enemy would be able to bar the retreat and catch the scattered BEF units on the move; it might be better to stay put and muster his forces against the enemy.

On the other hand, he had been ordered to continue the retreat. If he did not do so and II Corps were caught by the enemy and destroyed, the BEF would lose a large part of its strength – and the full weight of Field Marshal French's wrath would surely fall upon him. So, what to do? The loneliness of command can rarely have been more apparent, but Smith-Dorrien did not flinch from the only possible decision; his units could no longer retreat, therefore they must stand and fight.

Before announcing this decision Smith-Dorrien asked Allenby whether he would act under his command should he make a stand at Le Cateau. 'Allenby replied in the affirmative,' says Smith-Dorrien, 'and I remarked, "Very well, gentlemen, we will stand and fight and I will ask General Snow to act under me as well." '[14]

General Snow also agreed to put the 4th Division under Smith-Dorrien's command, and with that much decided the troops began to prepare for battle, their weariness falling away at the prospect of action. If less tired than the other units, Snow's force was not without problems; his division was still without its cavalry, heavy artillery, ambulances and engineers – and its ammunition train. With luck, this would not matter; Smith-Dorrien was not planning a long engagement. He intended to strike the enemy hard – dealing them 'a stopping blow' in military parlance – and slip away before they could recover. He sent a note of this decision by staff car to GHQ at St Quentin, explaining the circumstances that required his forces to stand and fight rather than continue the retreat.

Field Marshal French's reply came back at around 0500 hours: 'If you can hold your ground the situation appears likely to improve. 4th Division must co-operate. French troops are taking the offensive on right of I Corps. Although you are given a free hand as to method, this telegram is not intended to convey the impression that I am not anxious for you to carry out the retirement and you must make every effort to do so.'

This somewhat equivocal communication cheered Smith-Dorrien up considerably. It appeared that the Field Marshal understood his reasons for making a stand and fully approved of this decision. Smith-Dorrien's intention, as he told Henry Wilson later that day, was to 'give the enemy a smashing blow and slip away before he could recover', and he felt he had a good chance of doing that. Wilson's reply was fully in support of this intention: 'Good luck to you . . . yours is the first cheerful voice I have heard in three days.'[15]

As at Mons, the fight at Le Cateau did not last long or make any great demands on the generals; Le Cateau was a soldier's battle. It required the British soldier to do what he does best, occupy a position and defy eviction, taking a toll on the attacking enemy, forcing them to halt and deploy. Once the enemy had been halted, and hopefully somewhat damaged, Smith-Dorrien would break off the action and get his men away before the enemy counterattacked. This was his sole intention at Le Cateau and he succeeded brilliantly.

The British position at Le Cateau was not unlike that taken up at Mons, a long front facing north with a bend at the small town, which had a population of around 10,000 people in 1914 and stands at the junction of the east–west road to Cambrai and the north–south valley of the River Selle, and a shorter front facing west along the river valley. The 3rd Division faced north along the Le Cateau–Cambrai road while the 5th Division occupied the town and held the high ground along the Selle, their front extended by Snow's brigades. Sordet's French cavalry kept the open, western flank covered and beyond that a French Territorial division under General d'Amande held the town of Cambrai. Allenby's dismounted cavalry brigades were in support, taking up positions to the rear of the infantry or on the flanks. The eastern flank was wide open, for Haig's corps was now too far away to give any assistance and was given no orders to halt or turn back. Smith-Dorrien's men therefore held a thin, curving line, some 16 kilometres (10 miles) in length, facing north or along the Selle, and they cannot have expected to hold it for long.

Von Kluck attacked the British employing much the same tactics he had employed at Mons. The greatest German asset was a superiority in numbers and plenty of artillery, but instead of pounding the British positions with his guns, to which the BEF had no viable response, and then sending in a single, massive infantry attack, von Kluck sent in four army corps, the IV, IV

Reserve, Cavalry Corps and III Corps, in separate attacks against the British line, while his II Corps engaged General d'Amande at Cambrai.

The *Official History*[16] reminds the reader that 26 August was the anniversary of the Battle of Crécy in 1346, another occasion when a British – actually an Anglo-Welsh – army stood its ground in France against a superior force. The 7th Division of the German IV Corps attacked Le Cateau and quickly forced the defending soldiers, from the 1st East Surreys and the 1st Duke of Cornwall's Light Infantry (1st DCLI), out of the town on to the higher ground to the south. There, backed up by dismounted troopers from the 3rd Cavalry Brigade, the rapid rifle fire of the British infantry stemmed any German progress up the slopes.

The morning of 26 August was misty, promising another hot day, and under cover of a thin fog the Germans managed to infiltrate through the 5th Division positions and proceed down the valley of the River Selle. As more and more German units came up and were engaged by the British field and horse artillery and infantry, the fighting gradually spread west, as the Germans attempted to find a way round the British line. German artillery fire had been the main problem for the British since Mons, and heavy shellfire took a steady toll of the exposed artillery batteries and the soldiers of the 2nd Suffolks and the 2nd King's Own Yorkshire Light Infantry (2nd KOYLI).

The main thrust of the German attack on the right flank was made against the infantry battalions in Le Cateau and along the Selle. These units broke up attack after attack with their rapid and accurate rifle fire, with the guns of the 11th Battery, RFA, in support of the Suffolks frequently engaging the enemy over open sights. The gunners stood to their guns throughout the morning, their ranks gradually thinned by rifle and artillery fire. By mid-morning, when a heavy concentration of German troops came forward west of Le Cateau, all the artillery officers had been killed or wounded and the 11th Battery had been reduced to one gun – that gun, however, remained in action.

This repulse of the German infantry was a considerable feat of arms, particularly when it is remembered that the troops involved were hungry and tired and many battalions were much reduced in numbers. The infantry brigades on the right flank held off the German attack for six full hours and the troops in the centre – the 13th Brigade of the 5th Division and the 3rd Division – held up any advance there until well into the afternoon.

On the left flank, however, the Germans enjoyed greater success. Here they were moving against the units of Snow's 4th Division. This attack began at 0600 hours when the 1st King's Own of the 12th Brigade were hit by machine-gun fire while still in column-of-route and lost around 400 men before they could scatter; the survivors quickly remustered and fought on for the rest of the day. Other units of this brigade, the 1st Hampshires, the 2nd Lancashire Fusiliers and the 2nd Inniskilling Fusiliers, then came up to join the fight.

Snow's battalions displayed great tenacity in holding their ground at Le Cateau under heavy artillery fire and frequent infantry attacks. They endured the artillery fire in the open, having had no time to dig trenches, but they repulsed the German infantry and dismounted cavalry with rifle and machine-gun fire, taking a heavy toll on their attackers. By mid-morning, in spite of their advantage in numbers and artillery, the German attacks had come to a virtual standstill while the enemy regrouped and rethought his tactics.

When recalling the weariness of the BEF, it has to be remembered that the German infantry had also been marching and fighting since they crossed the German frontier. They were equally weary, none more so than the troops of von Kluck's First Army, which had marched the greatest distance and been in action for the last three days. One of the fundamental flaws in the Schlieffen Plan was now about to become evident; the plan had always relied heavily on the marching ability and physical fitness of the German infantry soldiers, and those soldiers were now tired out.

Von Kluck's aim was now to envelop the British line, and shortly after noon it gradually became apparent that on the right flank this tactic was starting to work. Fergusson's 5th Division was being gradually outflanked, and by early afternoon Fergusson found it advisable to start withdrawing some of his units.

The weak point in the British line at Le Cateau was the right flank, left uncovered by the retreat of Haig's corps, now withdrawing to the south. Field Marshal French seems to have taken no interest in the events at Le Cateau on 26 August; one might wonder why, instead of harassing Smith-Dorrien to break off the action and continue the retreat, he did not order Haig to stop his withdrawal and either support II Corps or create some diversion to relieve the pressure on those BEF units fighting at Le Cateau. John Terraine records a comment made by Henry Wilson to Smith-Dorrien after the latter had requested help from I Corps: 'Troops fighting Haig cannot fight you',[17] a remark which ignores the fact that very few Germans were actually fighting Haig on 26 August 1914.

Eventually, around midday, the relentless German pressure on the II Corps position began to tell. Though the Germans were suffering losses and being held along the line, fresh units were coming up and extending the line of their attack in a bid to envelop the entire II Corps position. It was clearly time to go, and Smith-Dorrien therefore ordered a general withdrawal, commencing on the right flank.

The first problem was to extract the guns, many of which were now well forward, deployed in close support among the infantry positions. Here the soldiers of the 5th Division artillery showed the infantry what gunners could do, the gun teams of the 11th Battery galloping their horses up to the guns, hooking up guns and limbers and galloping away, all under heavy fire from the Germans; one team was shot down but the other five guns were retrieved, the gunners cheered by the infantry as they hurtled back to shelter over the rough ground.

The *Official History* records the extraction of the 122 Battery, RFA, supporting the 5th Division:

The teams . . . galloped through the lines of the West Kents, who stood up and cheered loudly as they dashed between the trenches and down the slope towards the guns. As they came in view of the enemy they were struck by a hurricane of shrapnel and bullets from machine-guns on the Cambrai road, but still they went on. One officer was killed, one team shot down in a heap before the guns were reached but two guns were carried out without mishap. A third gun was limbered up but the horses instantly went down. It was an extraordinary sight; a short, wild scene of galloping and falling horses, and then four guns standing derelict, one on the skyline, its pole vertical and dead men and dead horses everywhere.[18]

That horses are no longer employed on the battlefield is one of the few benefits of early-twenty-first-century warfare. Horses were essential to the armies until well into the Second World War, and the suffering of these willing and gallant animals throughout the First World War was terrible – and heartbreaking.

Further attempts to bring out the guns of the 123 and 124 Batteries, RFA were abandoned; twenty-five field guns and a howitzer were left on the field after their gun-sights had been smashed and their breech blocks removed. Considering that the guns were virtually in the front line it is astonishing that any at all were extracted. To quote the *Official History* again: 'the feat redounds to the eternal honour of the officers and men of the 5th Division Artillery'. Three of these gunners, Captain Reynolds and Drivers Drain and Luke of the 37th Battery, RFA, received the Victoria Cross for extracting the guns at Le Cateau.

The removal of the guns alerted everyone – including the enemy – to the fact that II Corps was about to pull out. Steadily, battalion by battalion and company by company, in perfect order, the infantry now began to fall back, in section parties and platoons, moving from one patch of cover to another, turning back at intervals to engage the enemy with rapid bursts of rifle fire, one company or platoon engaging the enemy while their comrades retired, entire battalions leapfrogging to the rear, held together by discipline and regimental élan. With the guns back and in position to cover a withdrawal, the infantry began to push its way past the advancing patrols of the German III Corps, which was moving in to cut off the II Corps line of retreat down the Selle valley.

The Germans had meanwhile assembled in strength along the Cambrai road and were making a heavy attack on two battalions of the rearguard, the 2nd Suffolks and the 2nd Argyll and Sutherland Highlanders. After a final vicious fight these units were finally overwhelmed at around 1500 hours, having stood off the enemy for nine full hours. The 3rd Division in the centre got away smoothly, though a battalion in the 8th Brigade, the 1st Gordon Highlanders, did not receive the order to retire and the soldiers fought on until they were overrun. The end of this fierce action at Le Cateau came at about 1800 hours when the 5th Division broke off contact with the enemy.

In general, the disengagement at Le Cateau went well and this efficient action did wonders for morale. Later that day Smith-Dorrien saw the men of his corps streaming down the road past his position and described the sight as 'like a crowd coming away from a race meeting, the men smoking their pipes and chatting over the events of the day, apparently completely unconcerned'. The Germans made no attempt at pursuit and, as II Corps withdrew into the gathering dusk, German shells were still falling on their abandoned positions.

That said, casualties at Le Cateau had been severe. According to the *Official History*,[19] they amounted to 7,812 men, killed, wounded or missing, and the *Official History* attributes some of this loss to the fact that the 4th Division had no ambulances in which to remove its wounded, many of whom therefore became prisoners. German losses cannot be computed as the German accounts include Le Cateau as part of the wider engagements that day around St Quentin; it seems certain that by pressing on with their tactic of massed infantry attacks they incurred far higher losses than the British.

Le Cateau was a neat little battle, planned in haste but professional in execution. The credit for the success of this engagement goes to General Smith-Dorrien, the troops of II Corps and of the two divisions, the 4th and the Cavalry Division, who gave them such unstinting support. Smith-Dorrien also records his debt to Sordet's French cavalry and d'Amande's men at Cambrai, who held up the German advance on the left flank throughout the day and used their 75mm guns to great effect against the German infantry.

In the words of the *Official History*, 'With both flanks more or less in the air II Corps had turned on an enemy of at least twice their strength; struck him hard and withdrawn – except on the right flank of 5th Division – practically without interference.'[20] Not without loss, alas, but the enemy had been stopped, and for some days the BEF retreat continued unimpeded. When the fight at Le Cateau was over, with his men marching south again, Smith Dorrien was naturally elated.

This elation did not last. On the evening of 26 August Smith-Dorrien went back to report the day's events to French at St Quentin and found that GHQ had shifted back to Noyon, 20 miles farther south. Smith-Dorrien arrived at GHQ at 0100 hours on the morning of 27 August – his fourth night without sleep – and found everyone in bed, slumbering peacefully and less than pleased at being aroused. Field Marshal French eventually appeared, in no very good humour, and when Smith-Dorrien reported on the success of the day rebuked him in front of the staff for being 'too cheerful'. It is hard to see why the good news was unwelcome; earlier that evening the general view at GHQ was that II Corps was lost and Colonel Huguet – no Anglophile at the best of times – had reported to Joffre that 'the English Army appears to have lost cohesion' and the battle at Le Cateau was a great defeat.

To be fair, Field Marshal French had just had a very bad day. Apart from his worries over II Corps – worries that did not seem to involve taking any interest in its affairs – he had been summoned to a meeting with Joffre and Lanrezac in which Joffre explained the thinking behind General Order No. 2, his plan for a counter-attack, and expressed the hope that the BEF would conform to it. French retorted that he had not yet seen General Order No. 2 and was less than happy with his treatment by the French so far; Lanrezac had retreated, exposing his right flank, his troops were exhausted, he was opposed by superior numbers and half his force was in danger of envelopment at Le Cateau even as they sat here, discussing an Order he had never received.

It then transpired that Henry Wilson, the Sub-Chief of Staff, had the order and had had it for some time. General Order No. 2 had arrived the previous evening but, said Wilson, it had not yet been translated into English – though why Wilson had not simply read the order to the Field Marshal is not immediately apparent. This failure to pass on at least an outline of the order to his commander rather negated the purpose of the meeting, which petered out after a couple of hours without any BEF commitment to conform with the French plan – and leaving Joffre in some doubt about the reliability of his British allies. Joffre went back to Chantilly to brood about the English and French went back to Noyon for his later confrontation with Smith-Dorrien.

When the battle is over, the controversy begins. In the case of Le Cateau, the argument began some time later and can be traced to French's virulent animosity towards Smith-Dorrien. In his September dispatch, covering the events of the retreat from Mons, French gave full credit for the engagement at Le Cateau to Horace Smith-Dorrien, but in his memoir, 1914, published in 1919, French withdrew his praise of Smith-Dorrien and set in train an argument that was to rock the British Army. 'In my despatch of September 1914,' he wrote, 'I refer eulogistically to the battle at Le Cateau . . . It [the dispatch] was completed, of necessity, very hurriedly, and before there had been time to study the reports immediately preceding and covering the period of that battle, by which alone the full details could be disclosed . . . I accepted without question the estimate made by the commander of II Corps as to the nature of the threat against him and the position of the German forces opposed to him . . .'[21] French withdraws the favourable comments in his dispatch entirely. The broad thrust of his later argument is that Smith-Dorrien had not deserved so much praise and needed cutting down to size. French's explanation for doing this does not bear close inspection, for his dispatch was not written hurriedly or amended in haste. Twelve days passed between the fight at Le Cateau and the issuing of the dispatch . . . and five full years and an entire war had passed before French saw fit to refute much of what the dispatch contained.

By then everyone knew that Smith-Dorrien was perfectly

correct in disobeying the order to retreat, indeed had a duty to do so. Actions of this kind are covered by Army Field Service Regulations.[22] 'If a subordinate, in the absence of a superior, neglects to depart from the letter of his order, when such departure is demanded by the circumstances and failure ensues, he will be held responsible for such failure.'

By any standards of accuracy or veracity *1914* is a most distressing work. It might well be ignored as a historical source or treated by historians with the contempt it truly deserves but for the insights it offers into the character of Field Marshal Sir John French, commander-in-chief of the BEF at a critical time in its history. The overall impression is that French was in a state of chronic paranoia over Horace Smith-Dorrien. His book gradually becomes a diatribe against his former subordinate and, as is so often the case, does far more damage to the reputation of the attacker than to that of the man attacked with its mixture of innuendo, distortion and downright lies.

For example, on page 80 of *1914* French writes: 'In more than one of the accounts of the retreat from Mons, it is alleged that some tacit consent at least was given at Headquarters at St Quentin to the decision arrived at by the commander of II Corps. I owe it to the able and devoted officers of my staff to say that there is not a semblance of truth in that statement.'

This is simply not true. French's message to Smith-Dorrien on 26 August – cited above – clearly gives tacit support to Smith-Dorrien's decision to stand at Le Cateau, even to the point of saying that the 4th Division must back him up. French then states: 'It was not until 8 am on the 26th that I knew that the left wing of the Army was actually committed to the fight . . . staff officers were sent to General Smith-Dorrien carrying peremptory orders to break off the action and continue the retreat forthwith.'[23] This is another lie. The reply sent from GHQ to Smith-Dorrien, giving tacit consent to his stand – the reply later refuted by French in his book – was timed at 0500 hours on arrival at Smith-Dorrien's HQ, three hours *before* French claims to have heard that Smith-Dorrien's corps was in action at all.

On page 84 of *1914* French refers to 'the shattered condition of the troops which had fought at Le Cateau', overlooking the fact that these same troops, though undoubtedly weary, marched more than 30 miles on the two days after the battle and had re-formed by the end of the second day. French contradicts himself on this point in his memoirs, for on page 89 of *1914* he records standing beside the road at Ham on 28 August, two days after the fight at Le Cateau, and watching the troops march by 'whistling and singing', adding that 'Their one repeated question was "When shall we turn round and face them again?"' and that they would add, '"We can drive them to hell."' These hardly sound like the comments of men in a 'shattered condition'.

French seems to have understood very little of what was going on in France at this time, but he knew how to bear a grudge. The Field Marshal kept his resentment simmering as the soldiers of the BEF trudged south from Le Cateau, the Germans snapping closely at their heels.

8

The Retreat to the Marne

27 AUGUST–5 SEPTEMBER 1914

I would never have believed that men could be so tired and so hungry and yet live.

British Official History, 1914, Vol. I. p. 260

The action at Le Cateau, brief as it was, proved very useful to Field Marshal French's weary little force. It was a full day before von Kluck could remuster his forces and renew the pursuit, and Smith-Dorrien records that his Corps was not seriously troubled, 'except by mounted troops and detachments which kept a safe distance,'[1] for the next week. Le Cateau was certainly not a major battle but it was the perfect example of a 'stopping blow', which is all that Smith-Dorrien intended.

This being so, 27 August, the day after that engagement, would be a good time to assess the BEF, after two small battles and at the start of a long retreat. Losses so far had not been severe; at Mons the BEF had lost 1,638 men, all but fifty from II Corps.[2] At Le Cateau II Corps lost 7,812 men, killed, wounded or missing, and thirty-eight guns. I Corps had lost very few men and the cavalry division even fewer, so total losses so far barely exceeded 14,000 men.[3] The problem was that these losses had fallen almost exclusively among the rifle battalions and artillery batteries, some of which had been virtually destroyed – all this in just four days. That enemy losses had been far higher is not relevant at this time; the enemy had more men to lose.

Even so, and as already described, losses in action were not the biggest problem confronting the BEF as it marched south from Le Cateau. The real problem was that the men were exhausted, the weather continued hot, the cobbled roads of France were purgatory to sore and blistered feet, and long marches, scanty food, a shortage of water and very little sleep were taking their inevitable toll. Many of the men were so tired they went to sleep on the march; whole battalions went to sleep whenever they stopped beside the road and had to be dragged to their feet or kicked awake by their officers and NCOs. In the main, though, discipline, unit pride, the support of their comrades and bursts of activity against the enemy kept the men on their feet. They did not enjoy retreating but orders were orders and the retreat continued.

Haig's I Corps had not been significantly engaged while II Corps made its stand at Le Cateau, but from 26 August on I Corps losses would start to mount – on 26 August Haig lost 405 men, on 27 August 874.[4] After the night skirmish at Landrecies, Haig had continued to withdraw towards the south, while keeping in loose contact with the Fifth Army on his right. On the night of 26 August, I Corps was in billets in and around the village of Etreux; the only significant event during the day was the loss of some 300 officers and men of the Connaught Rangers in a series of skirmishes with the enemy at Marbaix and Le Grand Fayt. By nightfall on 26 August, I and II Corps were 30 kilometres (18 miles) apart and Haig was entertaining justified fears that the enemy would soon be thrusting forces into this gap. It therefore seemed advisable to withdraw without delay; at 0100 hours on 27 August Lanrezac's HQ agreed that Haig's corps could use the only road south through Guise and I Corps marched on again at 0400 hours.

This was another day of hard marches and intermittent skirmishes, the largest involving the 2nd Royal Munster Fusiliers, now commanded by Major P. A. Charrier. This battalion formed part of Brigadier General Ivor Maxse's 1st Guards Brigade, the designated rearguard, and fought off the enemy for most of the morning until ordered to break off any contact with the enemy and withdraw. This proved difficult; the order went out at 1300 hours but failed to reach the Munsters, who continued to fight on while moving back towards Etreux, which the rest of the 1st Division had long since left. At around 1400 hours Maxse received a message from Charrier stating: 'We have two wounded German prisoners who say that about 2 regiments are opposing us and some guns,' adding that this force belonged to the German 15th Reserve Infantry Regiment of the Guards Reserve Division.[5] By 1735 hours the Munsters were surrounded and running out of ammunition.

Major Charrier led three charges against the German positions at Fesmy and was eventually killed attempting to blast a way through. All the other battalion officers being killed, wounded or missing, the command descended on Lieutenant E. W. Gower, who mustered the remaining men in an orchard, ordered them to take up any defensive position they could find and fight on. The Munsters continued to resist until 2115 hours when, out of ammunition, under fire from machine guns at very close range and down to fewer that 250 men, the battalion surrendered, having sustained the fight against great odds for over twelve hours – yet another outstanding example of what disciplined British infantry could do.[6]

While the BEF were trudging south towards the River Somme, events were moving to a close in Belgium. On 27 August a brigade of the Royal Marine Light Infantry came ashore at Ostend but stayed only three days, being too small a force to defend this port, before re-embarking on 31 August. The Belgian garrison in the Antwerp fortress was still holding out, their resistance obliging von Kluck to divert several divisions and a number of heavy guns to the siege, but it was clear that without assistance this resistance could not be prolonged.

The brisk actions at Etreux and Fesmy were followed by similar actions in the days that followed; the enemy were still coming on and it was necessary for the French and BEF rearguards to face about from time to time and beat the enemy back. The weather continued hot and as well as suffering from fatigue the men – and the horses – were increasingly short of food and frequently short of water. These shortages arose from the fact that they were not retreating down their line of advance to the south-west, on which lay their supply bases, but south towards Noyon, Compiègne and Soissons, Meaux and the Marne. In an attempt to provide the men with rations, Major-General Robertson started dumping supplies beside the roads, hoping the men could fill up their packs as they marched past, but most of these supplies fell into the hands of the enemy – and helped to convince the German commanders that the BEF was in desperate straits.

In fact the situation of the BEF was gradually improving. With every day of the march after 28 August the two corps drew closer together, and on that day even the chronically pessimistic Field Marshal French could see that, whatever their fatigue, the private soldiers, NCOs and officers of the battalions and regiments were in good spirits and getting fitter. All they really needed was a chance to rest, a square meal and an opportunity to hit back at the enemy. On 29 August the BEF, apart from the cavalry, enjoyed their first day of rest, a brief halt largely devoted to sleep.

Nor were the steady losses doing much to erode the BEF's fighting strength for new units were coming up and a trickle of reinforcements were arriving from the UK. On 30 August the 19th Infantry Brigade and Snow's 4th Division were formed into III Corps under Pulteney which, with the other two corps, continued the march south, crossing the Aisne later that day without any significant interference from the enemy.

The prospect of an Anglo-French counter-attack was now increasing, as the German supply lines lengthened and the German soldiers became ever more weary. On 26 August General Joffre completed his plans to form a Sixth Army on his left wing, west of the BEF. Joffre had informed French of his intention during a visit to French's HQ on 27 August, and by the following day the first units of this new army were detraining at Villers-Brettoneux, east of Amiens. On that day Joffre also ordered General Lanrezac to launch an attack against von Bulow's Second Army at St Quentin, hoping thereby to take some of the pressure off the BEF. By the evening of 28 August, Lanrezac was in position to mount this attack, a well-handled affair which became known as the Battle of Guise.

This attack at Guise provided Field Marshal French with an opportunity to score off his new enemy, General Lanrezac. Lieutenant-General Sir Douglas Haig had noticed that the German Second Army was now exposing its flank to the Fifth Army and offered to support General Lanrezac's attack with I Corps. Lanrezac accepted this offer, but on the evening of 28 August a message from French to GQG withdrew this support: 'Compiègne, 28 August, 1914. 6.55 pm. Marshal French regrets his inability to co-operate with you in tomorrow's general action in the measure desired by you. Troops very tired, must have at least one day's rest on the ground occupied tonight. After tomorrow they will be able to occupy the line of the Crozat Canal if necessary; if ultimately the French Army is victorious, the Field Marshal will place his troops at your disposal as a reserve.'[7]

Spears describes this message as, 'really amazing',[8] but the fact that Haig's corps had been forbidden to cooperate with Lanrezac was confirmed when a staff officer from Haig's Corps HQ arrived at Lanrezac's headquarters later.

Spears records that 'Lanrezac's anger was terrific' and that 'terrible things were said concerning Sir John French'.[9] Spears also adds that 'For the first time I felt that we were in the wrong . . . The great complaint of the British against General Lanrezac was that he could not be induced to attack. Now that he was about to do so, nothing would induce the British to co-operate. They were doing as they would be done-by.'

Clearly that disagreeable first meeting with Lanrezac ten days previously still rankled, and his reason for blocking Haig's participation, that the BEF soldiers were 'very tired and must have a day's rest', was a limp excuse indeed. All the soldiers, British, French and German, were equally tired, and the I Corps battalions were, if anything, rather less tired than many other BEF units – and very eager to engage the enemy.

French certainly had another reason – or another excuse – in that part of his orders from Kitchener told him to consider carefully before 'participating in forward movements where large bodies of French troops were not engaged and where your forces may be unduly exposed to attack'. However, large French forces *were* involved at the Battle of Guise on 29 August and Lanrezac can be forgiven for describing French's response as '*une félonie*' (a betrayal).[10]

To describe French's attitude towards Lanrezac as petty-minded is to seriously understate the case, but Field Marshal French and his principal subordinates, Lieutenant-Generals Haig and Smith-Dorrien, were putting up a varied performance at this time. Haig's I Corps had hardly been engaged so far, and while those units, such as the 2nd Munsters and the Guards, that had met the enemy had put up a creditable performance, very little generalship had been required and any judgement on Haig's command skills must wait. Haig was obeying orders, keeping his corps together, continuing the retreat and striking the enemy when the opportunity arose. His hour of trial had yet to arrive.

After a week in action Smith-Dorrien was clearly the star general of the BEF. He was handling his troops well and had twice met a stronger enemy in difficult circumstances and fought him to a standstill. That done he had extricated his men – or most of them – and got them away to fight another day. It could perhaps be argued that Smith-Dorrien was lucky; he was in command of superb troops and fighting the kind of mobile, small-scale, cut-and-run war in which the discipline, fieldcraft and marksmanship of his soldiers could be deployed to telling effect against larger enemy formations that, time and time again, presented themselves as targets. On the other hand, he was engaged with a much larger enemy force, one with an abundance of artillery and which seemed able to absorb any losses his troops were able to inflict. All in all though, full credit must go to Smith-Dorrien for conducting a retreat with considerable skill in very difficult circumstances and remaining cheerful. For some reason this combination of cheerfulness and competence did not endear Smith-Dorrien to the BEF commander.

Assessing the performance of Field Marshal French is more difficult. His responsibilities were outlined in the orders he had been given by Kitchener, and carrying those orders out in the present circumstances was far from easy – not least the part that obliged him to take good care of Britain's only fully trained field army while cooperating closely with the French. The situation was nothing if not perilous, and it was hardly surprising that the weight of command was gradually wearing French down. He was by no means the oldest of the Western Front commanders at this time but he was, perhaps, too old and too temperamental for such a delicate and dangerous appointment.

Any sympathy for French on these points must be tempered by the fact that he failed to perform well even within his previous limits of competence. He did not provide his men or his subordinates with adequate leadership or guidance and failed to exercise even the basic duties of command. On occasion days went by without any orders coming from GHQ; Operation Order No. 6 was issued on 21 August; Operation Order No. 7 did not appear for another three days – the day after the engagement at Mons, when, as noted, French had made no attempt to contact Smith-Dorrien. On 30 August, the day the BEF crossed the Aisne, he left the Corps commanders to decided on the moving-off time when every effort was needed to keep the three corps together.

A general is not obliged to bombard his subordinates with orders or send out messages when there is nothing to say but French carried reticence to extremes. He frequently left his Corps commanders to work out the best course of action, separately or together, on a day-to-day basis, and contact with his allies or subordinates seems to have been motivated largely by his personal likes and dislikes rather than by the demands of the situation. He only met General Lanrezac twice, having taken against him at their first meeting, when the two commanders should have been in close and frequent contact. As before with Smith-Dorrien, he continued to nurture his resentments, as if they were a welcome distraction from the pressure of current events.

While the BEF was trudging south from the Belgian frontier to the elusive security of the Marne, elsewhere on the Western Front the Schlieffen Plan was running out of time. According to the plan the French should have been beaten or be on the point of surrender in within forty-two days. On 28 August, when the first of Joffre's counter-attack force detrained, only fourteen days of the timetable remained – and the armies of France, albeit battered, were nowhere near defeat.

On the Eastern Front von Schlieffen's masterplan was suffering another reverse. The Russians had reacted with unexpected speed and, rather than falling back, as anticipated, to take advantage of Russia's wide open spaces, by 20 August Russian forces were advancing on Königsberg in East Prussia, with the German Eighth Army falling back before them. This Russian advance was causing the Kaiser considerable disquiet, and Helmuth von Moltke was obliged to take action. On 28 August, von Moltke ordered that two corps should be transferred from the west to the Eighth Army in the east.

The commander of the Eighth Army, Lieutenant-General von Prittwitz und Gaffron, was sacked and replaced by General Paul von Hindenburg, who came out of retirement at the Kaiser's call and took up this challenge in the east. As his Chief of Staff von Hindenburg took Major-General Erich Ludendorff, the officer recently credited with the taking of Liège. Von Hindenburg and Ludendorff made a formidable military combination that would endure until the end of the war.

Germany's failure to either defeat the French armies or stem the Russian advance on the Eastern Front was the first German reverse in this war – and arguably a fatal one. Since 1895 – for almost twenty years – German victory had been predicated on the avoidance of a two-front war and the rapid defeat of first France and then Russia. By the end of August this plan was falling apart and Germany's attempt to win the war quickly and get the troops home 'before the leaves fall' was clearly a pipe dream. If Hindenburg was not able to reverse the position in the east quickly, so getting the Schlieffen Plan back on track, von Moltke might be obliged to divert large forces from the Western Front – and that would be serious indeed, for the Schlieffen Plan was already behind schedule and that forty-two-day window of opportunity was closing fast.

This pending failure of the German master plan was not yet apparent to the French. Joffre and his commanders had also seen their plan – Plan XVII – dissolve under the German guns and were now in full retreat from the frontiers of France; '*l'attaque à outrance*' stood revealed as a nonsensical doctrine, most costly in lives.

Here is the first great paradox of the Great War. Although the French and their British allies were in full retreat and the news from every front was grave, hindsight reveals that it was the Germans who were actually losing the war at this time, for their strategy was either being abandoned or falling apart. This abandonment was a grave error; strategists should not lose track of their declared aims and divert their attention to winning battles, but that is what the Germans were doing as these precious days slipped away. Everywhere there is evidence of failure, evidence von Moltke ignored.

The Russians were not yet supposed to be in the field, yet there they were, advancing. On the Western Front the French armies were supposed to be pushing east towards or across the Rhine, each step of their advance exposing Paris and their own rear to attack; instead they were falling back, much reduced but still intact, to a position where they could re-form and come on again, with the new Sixth Army about to outflank the western end of the German line.

As for the situation on the Northern Front, where the BEF had made that surprising appearance at Mons, the Allies were in retreat but as yet undefeated. This again was not part of von Schlieffen's scenario. German hopes for victory in this war depended on avoiding a fight on two fronts. To do that it was necessary to destroy the French Army before the Russian armies could take the field. Now, some three weeks into the war, the Russian Army was in the field and the French Army was still undefeated. Although the war would go on for more than four years, it is at least arguable that the Germans lost it in the first three weeks.

The French retreat from the frontiers was not part of von Schlieffen's plan. Hard as it was for the Allied soldiers on the ground, slogging along those punishing cobbled roads under a blazing sun, periodically drenched by sudden rainstorms, their retreat kept the French armies together. In spite of terrible losses to individual units, and especially among the officers, too many of whom fell victim to the leadership demands of *l'offensive à outrance*, the French armies had not been crushed.

Nor had the small and gallant Belgian Army. This small army had now withdrawn into the forts defending Antwerp, where King Albert intended to hold off the advancing Germans until his French and British allies sent forces to his assistance.

The overall picture was the same on every front; nothing was going as planned for the German armies. In Alsace and Lorraine the French armies of Generals Noël de Castelnau and Auguste Dubail were falling back but fighting hard for every metre of ground, and General Ferdinand Foch, now commanding the French XX Corps – the Iron Corps – was stoutly defending Nancy. In the centre, astride the Ardennes, the Third and Fourth Armies of Generals Ruffey and Ferdinand Langle de Cary were regrouping their forces, while General Lanrezac, falling back from the Meuse with the BEF hanging on his flank, was resisting the temptation to seek the shelter offered by the fortifications of Maubeuge and keeping his army on the move. The Anglo-French forces, albeit in full retreat, were still in existence and presenting a common front to the foe; the situation was certainly grave, but it could have been a great deal worse.

It is important not to present too rosy a picture of the BEF at this time. If the units were not as disorganized and the soldiers' morale nowhere near as low as Field Marshal French from time to time believed, there were some reasons for disquiet. Haig had been obliged to unload supply wagons and send them to the rear loaded with exhausted soldiers. Major-General Robertson's action in piling supplies by the side of the roads, hoping that any passing British unit could avail themselves of the contents, supplied more Germans than British and gave von Kluck the idea that the BEF was on the run, throwing away supplies and on the brink of disintegration – an idea also held at Joffre's GQG, which was receiving regular gloomy reports from Colonel Huguet, their liaison officer at French's GHQ. Huguet was an Anglophobe, but there were indeed signs of collapsing morale among some BEF units.

On 27 August the remnants of two exhausted British battalions, the 1st Royal Warwicks, commanded by Lieutenant-Colonel Elkington, and the 2nd Royal Dublin Fusiliers, under Lieutenant-Colonel Mainwaring, lay down in the central square in St Quentin and flatly refused to move, declaring to the cavalry commander, Major Tom Bridges of the 4th Royal Irish Dragoon Guards, that their commanding officers had promised the town mayor that their troops would surrender rather than have the town destroyed in more fighting. Bridges managed to rouse the men by collecting a number of musical instruments from a nearby toy shop and creating a band. This scratch orchestra, playing marches and lively airs, eventually got the men back on their feet and the retreat continued, but both commanding officers were later cashiered and dismissed from the army. Colonel Mainwaring, who was sick at this time but roused himself sufficiently to lead his men away from St Quentin, was never reinstated. Colonel Elkington joined the French Foreign Legion as a private soldier and his gallant conduct with that unit led eventually to the restoration of his British commission.

The German armies, surging forward in apparent victory, were gradually slowing down. Smith-Dorrien's 'stopping blow' at Le Cateau had confused von Kluck, who, believing that the British would retreat south-west towards their base at Amiens and the Channel ports, set out in that direction. This was a miscalculation since the BEF was marching south, but it proved of great benefit to the Allied cause. Von Kluck's shift to the west – already dictated by the Schlieffen Plan – obliged Field Marshal French to abandon his first aim, to retreat down his line of communications towards Amiens and the Channel ports; to go that way would bring on another encounter with the enemy, so a retreat towards Valenciennes and the Marne was the best option.

The second Allied advantage was that von Kluck's shift west caused the German First Army to lose contact with von Bulow's Second Army on its right. On 27 August von Kluck and von Hausen, the commanders of the German First and Third Armies on the right wing, were released from the overall control of General von Bulow, commander of the centrally placed Second Army, who had been acting as an army group commander. Von Kluck's shift west of the First Army caused von Bulow considerable alarm, for it split the German front. That great, 115-kilometre (70-mile) wide *feldgrau* tidal wave, now sweeping down from Belgium, was starting to break up. After the fight at Le Cateau, von Bulow had ordered von Kluck's pursuit of the BEF to be continued 'in a south-westerly direction'; once free of von Bulow's control, von Kluck went off to the west and a gap of some 22-kilometre (14 miles) soon opened up between the German First and Second Armies.

Haig brought this situation to the attention of General Lanrezac, pointing out that the current direction of von Bulow's army was presenting the German flank to an Allied counter-attack. This German move had also been spotted by French aircraft and reported to GQG, from where – as noted – Joffre ordered Lanrezac to attack von Bulow at Guise and Haig offered to support him. Given the events described above, it is agreeable to record that Lanrezac's attack at Guise was a considerable success.

On 29 August, aerial reconnaissance suggested that von Kluck 'had reached the limit of his western advance and was wheeling south eastward, covering his southern flank with his cavalry'.[11] Further reconnaissance on 30 August confirmed this manoeuvre, and on that day the leading cavalry units of von Kluck's army crossed the River Oise, so exposing the First Army's flank to Lanrezac between St Quentin and Guise.

Lanrezac, so often derided as a cautious commander, handled his army with considerable skill and nerve in the battle that followed. As his Fifth Army advanced against von Kluck at St Quentin, von Bulow's Second Army came in on Lanrezac's right flank. Undaunted, Lanrezac swung his army about and soundly defeated von Bulow at Guise, driving the Second Army back five kilometres (three miles) on a 40-kilometre (25-mile) front – a far larger reverse than the 'stopping blow' at Le Cateau, and one with wide-ranging effects. Alarmed at this unexpected reverse and at the growing gap between their two armies, von Bulow called for help from von Kluck, who hastened to comply.

Basically, the presence of the BEF on his front presented von Kluck with a hard choice; he could either stick with the Schlieffen strategy and swing west of Paris, thereby splitting the German front, or he could shift east and keep in contact with von Bulow. Worried that pressing on to the south-west would expose his army or that of von Bulow to another attack, he elected to abandon the march south and west and keep in contact with the Second Army on his right flank.

This decision was in defiance not only of the original plan but also of fresh orders which arrived from the German High Command (OHL) on 28 August, orders that again directed von Kluck to advance to the Seine south-west of Paris, von Bulow to advance south, directly on Paris, while the Third, Fourth and Fifth German Armies were to advance to the Marne east of Paris as Crown Prince Rupprecht brought the Sixth and Seventh Armies in from the east – those vital timings might be falling apart, but on 28 August von Moltke at least was still sticking to the territorial requirements of the Schlieffen Plan. By 30 August von Kluck had torn the plan up and the German armies were set on a course that would carry them east, north of the city rather than south of it.

Though impressed by the need to maintain a united front, von Kluck's decision to shift east was also inspired by the belief that the BEF and the Fifth Army were on their last legs and could be rounded up without any need for more of this exhausting marching. He had succeeded in driving back the French forces on his right and come across those piles of abandoned British stores in the centre; why bother to hook round south of Paris, when all the current evidence suggested that the French and British could be rounded up by a swift hook north of Paris? The French and British were defeated, he told von Moltke in a cable – all that remained was a little mopping up.

Von Moltke was not entirely convinced of this; the wider intelligence sources open to OHL told him that the French armies were still united and fighting hard. Evidence of a Franco-British collapse was also scanty, said von Moltke; if the French and British armies were collapsing, he asked, where were the prisoners? Before this question could be answered, on 30 August von Kluck informed OHL that his First Army would start to wheel east, north of Paris, in order to keep in touch with von Bulow. This decision was in line with German military practice, which left the greatest possible latitude to the field commanders, a practice that often led to quick decisions and decisive results. Tactically this was sound doctrine; strategically it was disastrous – but von Moltke was already losing control of this campaign and let von Kluck have his way.

Lanrezac's victory at Guise–St Quentin was a great boost to French morale but Joffre believed, rightly, that the time was not yet ripe for a general counter-attack. The French armies and the BEF were still off balance and the German advance, if slowing down as the soldiers grew tired and their supply lines lengthened, was still grinding relentlessly forward. The BEF managed a rest day on 29 August while the French were engaged at Guise–St Quentin, and on that day Joffre paid a visit to Field Marshal French at the latter's newly established HQ at Compiègne, 64 kilometres (40 miles) from Paris. The purpose of this visit was to urge on French the necessity of keeping the BEF in the field, a point on which Joffre, alarmed by Colonel Huguet's gloomy dispatches, was less than convinced. This meeting on 31 August did not resolve the issue; Joffre left Compiègne without any certainty that French appreciated this point or would comply with his requests; French had decided that his force was exhausted and must be pulled out of the line for a complete rest and refit.

A brighter picture may have revealed itself to the Field Marshal the following day, in the great fight put up by the 1st Cavalry Brigade – the 2nd Dragoon Guards (The Bays), the 5th Dragoon Guards and the 11th Hussars – and 'L' Battery of the Royal Horse Artillery (RHA) at Néry on 1 September. The brigade and its artillery had camped overnight at the village of Néry and awoke to find the valley deep in mist. The march should have been resumed at 0400 hours, but since it was difficult to collect the column in such poor visibility the start was put back until 0500 hours and then until 0530 hours. Then, before the men could move, a storm of shellfire broke upon them from German artillery and machine guns, which had taken up position on the 200-metre (650-foot) high slopes around the village.

While the troopers attempted to find and mount their horses, Captain E. K. Bradbury of 'L' Battery succeeded in manhandling three of his guns into position and opening fire on the enemy. One gun, commanded by Lieutenant Giffard, was hit almost at once, a shell striking the muzzle and killing the entire crew except Lieutenant Giffard, who carried on firing the gun single-handed until all the ammunition in the limber had been used up; only then, wounded in three places, did Giffard seek safety. Scratch crews of officers and men manned the other guns and returned the enemy fire while the troopers from the cavalry regiments, the Bays and the 11th Hussars, took up position on the eastern edge of the village and prepared to beat off an infantry attack; surprised the cavalry may have been, dismayed they were not. As the battle got under way it became clear that the enemy was present in considerable force; in fact the 1st Cavalry Brigade and 'L' Battery were engaging the German 4th Cavalry Division – and holding it off.

Captain Edward Bradbury, Battery Sergeant-Major Dorrell and Sergeant Nelson were now manning the sole surviving gun of 'L' Battery and continued to do so until Captain Bradbury was hit and mortally wounded, after which the others kept up the fire until they ran out of ammunition. That was long enough for 'I' Battery, RHA, and the 4th Cavalry Brigade to come over from St Vaast and reinforce them, joined shortly afterwards by units of the 10th Infantry Division. The 11th Hussars, backed by infantry from the 1st Middlesex, charged the German guns and chased the enemy for more than a mile before they were recalled, bringing back seventy-eight prisoners from the 4th Cavalry Division. Losses were severe; the 1st Cavalry Brigade lost 135 men, including five officers and forty-nine men belonging to 'L' Battery, but, once again, discipline, professionalism and a willingness to stand and fight had paid dividends for an outnumbered British unit. Captain Bradbury, Battery Sergeant-Major Dorrell and Sergeant Nelson subsequently received the Victoria Cross for their action with the guns at Néry. Lieutenant J. Giffard received the Legion of Honour.

Nor was this all. On the same day, farther to the east, the 1st Guards Brigade of I Corps became hotly engaged at Villers-Cotterêts, where the Guards were covering the withdrawal of the 2nd Division. The action here involved the 2nd and 3rd Coldstream, the 1st Irish Guards and the 2nd Grenadiers, and took place largely in the thick woods of the Forêt de Villers-Cotterêts when the brigade were engaged by elements of the German III Corps and the 2nd and 9th Cavalry Divisions.[12] The action here began at about 1000 hours and went on until 1800 hours, when the Guards withdrew, having held off the enemy for most of the day, fighting against great odds and inflicting considerable casualties. The 4th Guards Brigade lost over 300 officers and men and the 6th Infantry Brigade, which covered the Guards' withdrawal, around 100 men. Two platoons of the 1st Grenadier Guards were surrounded at the Rond de la Reine in the middle of the forest and fought to the last man – Field Marshal French was quite wrong in assuming that his men were no longer able to fight.

French was taking council of his fears and had reached the decision that the Anglo-French situation on the Western Front was now critical. To be fair, there is some evidence to support this view; French attacks along the German frontier ordered under Plan XVII had been thrown back with losses and the German right wing had succeeded in forcing the French left wing and the BEF into full retreat. The German armies were now sweeping south, and in spite of the victory at Guise there seemed no way of stopping them in their headlong march towards Paris. Those who wanted to look on the dark side at this time could see more problems looming in the immediate future.

On the other hand, this was only one view; there were also some hopeful signs. The Allied soldiers falling back towards the Aisne, the Oise and the Marne were clearly exhausted and short of supplies, but then so were their adversaries. In spite of frantic efforts to repair the torn-up Belgian and French railway lines and link them with those of Germany, the German armies were outmarching their supplies and forced to live off the land – and all too often off the wine; many BEF accounts relate how any village retaken from the enemy was littered with empty bottles. German losses had been considerable and the troops were now bone weary, but German atrocities did not cease.

The German Army occupied St Quentin on the afternoon of 29 August, and within hours posted notices requiring all men aged between eighteen and forty-eight to register with the occupying authorities. A curfew was announced from 1900 hours to dawn each day, all movement from the city was stopped, and coal, factory equipment, wine and mattresses had to be handed in. These actions may have been excusable but the punishments for failure to comply were harsh. Two British soldiers found sheltering with French families were shot; the families were sent to labour camps. Three French soldiers found behind the German lines were also shot, and a French pensioner of the Franco-Prussian War was executed for the possession of an 1870 model rifle. The male population was then obliged to undertake forced labour, constructing defences, those who declined to do so being imprisoned or shot. None of this did any good to the reputation of the German Army, which was gradually running out of men.

Replacements were clearly needed, but where were they to come from? German reverses in the east had obliged von Moltke to send two corps from the west, and this was only one reduction among several. More forces had been detached to invest the port of Antwerp and others to besiege Maubeuge. Maubeuge, though battered by heavy guns, held out until 6 September, but every town, village, railway bridge or river crossing that had fallen into German hands since the war began required a guard or a garrison. And so, slowly, the strength of the German thrust leaked away, with every mile of their advance.

Plans are one thing, the reality of war quite another. It was now obvious, not least to von Moltke, that the Schlieffen Plan had been too ambitious. Von Schlieffen had arrived at his plan through a logical assessment of Germany's strategic position and the need, in view of the Franco-Russian Pact, to avoid a two-front war. But the plan was based on nineteenth-century logistical and transport arrangements that were simply not up to the burden the plan laid upon them. Basically, the German soldiers charged with marching and fighting their way into France and defeating the French armies in six weeks ran out of food and energy before they arrived on the Marne.

The other problem is that war is unpredictable. Campaigns rarely – perhaps never – go as planned. The Russians had mobilized far more quickly and put up a much better fight than von Schlieffen had anticipated, but there were also tactical errors on the German side, most notably the eagerness of the German commanders in Lorraine to counter-attack against the oncoming French and drive them back – an action that threw the 'revolving door' part of the Schlieffen Plan out of gear. And finally there were the setbacks caused by the resistance of the Belgians on the Meuse and at Antwerp, the appearance of the BEF at Mons, the stopping blow at Le Cateau, and the reverse at Guise. Taken singly, none of these actions presented a real reverse to German arms, but the effect was cumulative and paved the way for the major reverse on the Marne.

The Fifth Army's victory at Guise on 29 August jarred the Germans considerably. It also enabled the BEF to make good its escape unhindered, to the River Aisne, which it reached on 30 August, a day notable as that on which von Hindenburg shattered the Russian Army at Tannenberg. News of this setback in the east had not arrived by 31 August, when Field Marshal French took a decision that threatened to destroy the fragile fabric of the Anglo-French military alliance.

For the past week, ever since the full extent of the German threat had dawned upon him, General Joffre had been intent on reinforcing his left wing, protecting Paris and protecting his armies against the German attempt to roll them up from the west. He recognized the left flank as the weakest part of the entire French front – and the extreme end of that flank was occupied by the BEF, a force to which Joffre could not give direct commands. Any commander would have been concerned that the spot vital for national survival was in the keeping of an Allied army, but Field Marshal French's volatile conduct since his arrival in France had not added to Joffre's confidence.

Joffre naturally wanted to have French troops on this critical flank, commanded by reliable officers who were directly under his orders. He was therefore weakening his right flank in Lorraine and his centre in the Ardennes to find units for a new army, the Sixth Army, which was now being formed under General Maunoury and moving to a position on the extreme left flank of the line, beyond the BEF. The Sixth Army began to take up positions north of Paris even as the BEF retreated across the Aisne and south, into a position between the Fifth Army and the Sixth Army.

There is no need to give a blow-by-blow account of the remaining days of the BEF retreat. This finally ended on 5 September when the Sixth Army was ready to make the opening moves of the French counter-attack – the Battle of the Marne. Indeed, to labour the exploits and hardships of the BEF during the retreat from Mons is to take their actions out of context; they did well, but no better than their French comrades, and it took some days for the many stragglers to come in and rejoin their units. One account by a BEF medical officer recalls:

On arriving at Compiègne on August 28 we found we were to be stationed in a kind of sports ground with a small grandstand on one side. When we got there we found there were already about 300 BEF stragglers there who had rolled up on their own with no officers as yet. Instructions were received for our CO to take over as camp commandant and there was a constant stream of stragglers coming in, in parties of one or two or up to 30 at a time, mostly under NCOs, only about half a dozen officers. Each party was quite sure they were the only survivors of their battalion and while they were telling us that

another party of the same battalion rolled up. They were in rather a
state. Most of them, or quite half, had no arms or equipment of any
sort. All were footsore and some had slight wounds. How they found
their way was a bit of a mystery. The marvel will always be how many
of them stood up to the intense fatigue and fighting continuously for
days against hopelessly overwhelming odds.

Between 23 August and 5 September the BEF marched at least
320 kilometres (200 miles), in scorching heat and drenching rain
with little food and no more than two or three hours' rest per day.
When the retreat ended the BEF had apparently lost around 20,000
men, but troops continued to trickle in during the following days
and weeks and the final total of men lost – killed, wounded or
missing – was in the region of 15,000, plus forty-five guns, most of
the losses falling on the hard-pressed II Corps.

The *Official History* sums up the state of the BEF when the
retreat ended: "They were short of food and sleep when they began
their retreat; they continued it, always short of food and sleep, for
thirteen days and at the end they were still an army and a formidable army. They were never demoralized for they rightly judged
that they had never been beaten.'[13]

Not beaten, perhaps, but certainly disorganized. Writing to his
wife from Compiègne on 30 August, Henry Wilson records:

We are still here, gradually withdrawing our troops to the west under
cover of the R. Oise. No fighting for us today, and if we get ten days
of quiet we shall be able to get out of the really great confusion we
are now in. We have men of every battalion and battery scattered all
over the place, columns of ammunition, sappers, ambulances, parks
etc., mixed up in a most bewildering way. Still quite impossible to say
who has been killed, wounded or missing though a preliminary list
goes home today, I hope. We are still waiting for the 6th Division and
what on earth keeps the Cabinet from sending it here passes all understanding.[14]

The BEF would not get ten days of quiet. In spite of their
numerous problems the men in these units were more than ready

to fight, but on 30 August Field Marshal French informed Kitchener and Joffre that he intended to exercise the privilege of independent command. His men, he declared, were exhausted and short of supplies. He therefore intended to withdraw the BEF to a safe haven south of Paris and keep it there until it was refreshed, re-equipped and reinforced. Only then would he bring his force back to the battle.

Once again, as in his orders preventing BEF participation in the Battle of Guise, French's action seems to have been motivated by his early experiences with Lanrezac. 'I could not forget', French wrote:

> that the 5th French Army had commenced to retreat from the Sambre at least 24 hours before I had been given any official intimation that Joffre's offensive plan had been abandoned. Only due to the vast superiority of our cavalry and the marching and fighting powers of our troops had we been saved from an overwhelming disaster . . . It is impossible to exaggerate the danger of the situation as it existed. Neither on this day or for several subsequent days did one man, horse, gun or machine-gun reach me to make good deficiencies.[15]

Whatever the truth of these assertions, if Field Marshal French carried out his declared intention and took the BEF out of the line, a wide gap would be created in the Allied front and the Battle of the Marne would be fatally compromised before it had even begun.

9

From the Marne to the Aisne

5–12 September 1914

*It appeared to the Cabinet that Sir John French had determined
to retire so far out of the Allied line that he would frustrate their
policy of co-operating closely with the French.*
         British Official History, 1914, Vol. I, p. 244

To trace the origins of the next dramatic event in the BEF story it
is necessary to go back to 29 August, the day of the Battle of Guise,
and refer to the memoirs of Field Marshal French. Although
French's account is a masterpiece of obfuscation – and frequently
a tissue of lies – now and then it proves helpful, not least in revealing the thinking of the commander-in-chief of the BEF at critical
moments in its history.

By now it will be clear that from the very start of this campaign
the field marshal had been prone to doubt and subject to mood
swings. From 25 August he had become increasingly convinced
that his force had suffered considerable losses, that his allies were
unreliable and that the enemy was about to overwhelm him. The
field marshal maintains this position in his memoirs, while freely
admitting at the same time that his troops were still fighting hard,
were well disciplined and by no means disheartened. Even so,
when offered a choice between optimism and pessimism, the Field
Marshal usually took the gloomy view, and so it was on 29 August.

'Throughout the day', he writes,

reports, often contradictory and conflicting, reached me. It was quite clear that our position on the Oise was being dangerously threatened by superior forces and I felt that it would be impossible to stand on that line even until we could make good some of our heavy losses and I could not hope to get anything up for several days to come.

With great reluctance I ordered the retreat to be continued to the line of the Aisne from Compiègne to Soissons but in view of the knock given to the enemy at Guise by the Fifth French Army and the desire expressed by General Joffre that the Allied forces should hold their ground as long as possible and only retire when necessary I directed all commanders to carry out their marches with all deliberation and to take advantage of every opportunity to check the enemy's advance.[1]

If so, French was ordering his commanders to do no more than they were doing already, while Joffre, as French confirms in the next paragraph, was 'most anxious to take the offensive at the earliest possible moment'.[2] Therefore – and again according to French's own account – on the afternoon of 29 August Joffre came to see French at Compiègne to urge the Field Marshal to keep his force in the line and join the French in the forthcoming offensive.

French declined to do so. 'I remained firm in my absolute conviction that the British forces could not effectively fulfil their share in such action for some days and that, in so far as we were concerned, a further retreat was inevitable. I strongly represented to Joffre the advantage of drawing the German armies on still further from their base, even although we had to move south of the Marne.' In fact, again according to French, his intention was to withdraw the BEF even farther south, to somewhere between the Marne and the Seine.

The problem with tracking the course of the Field Marshal's decisions is that his account is frequently contradictory – as again here: 'The French Army was still in full retreat,' he writes. 'The French 6th Army on our left was not yet formed and the Commander-in-Chief had put no definite plan of attack before me, with an assigned role which he desired me to fulfil. All he asked me to do was to remain in the line and fill up the gap between the 5th and 6th Armies. This I had every intention of doing.'[3]

One must doubt this, if French's other statement on the same page – that a further BEF retreat was 'inevitable' – is anything to go by. Inevitably, French is incapable of making this latter, more positive declaration without a further swipe at his particular *bête noire*, Horace Smith-Dorrien. 'I am bound to say that I had to make this decision in the face of resistance from some of my subordinate commanders, who took a depressed view as to the condition of the troops. When I discussed the situation at a meeting of British commanders held at Compiègne, Sir Horace Smith-Dorrien expressed it as his opinion that the only course open to us was to retire to our base, thoroughly refit, re-embark and try to land at some favourable point on the coastline. I refused to listen to what was the equivalent of a counsel of despair.'[4]

This account, published in French's memoirs in 1919, is a lie. When it appeared, a furious Smith-Dorrien wrote to the other BEF commanders present at that Compiègne meeting – Haig, Allenby and French's chief-of-staff in 1914, Lieutenant General Sir Archibald Murray – asking whether they could recall him ever expressing such an opinion. Without exception they stated that they had no such recollection and, on the contrary, had found Smith-Dorrien 'full of optimism at all times'.

It will also be recalled that only three days previously, at Le Cateau, French had chided Smith-Dorrien, in front of his staff, for being 'over-optimistic'. The field marshal also neglects to mention that on 29 August he had given a warning order to Major-General F. S. Robb, the BEF's Inspector General of Communications – the officer responsible for transport and supply – advising him that he had decided to make 'a definite and prolonged retreat, due south, passing Paris to the east or west'.

The decisive point in the week-long retreat from Mons came on 30 August, when the Field Marshal informed Joffre and Kitchener that he intended to withdraw the BEF from the Allied line to somewhere south of Paris and keep it there until, in his opinion, it was rested and re-equipped and again ready for battle. His report to

Kitchener, justifying this decision, stated: 'I feel very seriously the absolute necessity for retaining in my hands complete independence of action and power to retire towards my base should circumstances render it necessary.'[5]

This blunt declaration caused considerable consternation in London and Paris. Joffre called on the French War Minister, M. Millerand, to intervene, and Millerand took this request to President Poincaré, who immediately contacted the British ambassador, Sir Francis Bertie, who passed on their appeals to London. Within hours, frantic messages from the French and British Governments came pouring into GHQ, urging French to keep the BEF in the line; should he carry out his stated intention, a wide gap would appear in the Allied front and the coming Marne counter-attack would be in serious jeopardy.

It would probably be unfair to attribute French's decision on withdrawal simply to pique with his French allies – though his memoirs give that as one of the reasons.[6] French certainly believed that the situation he imagined actually existed – that his army was unable to fight, was sorely tried and in need of rest and resupply. This situation took some time to remedy; writing of the situation a month later, Frank Richards recalls: 'Our clothes were beginning to show signs of wear, though, and some of the men were wearing civilian trousers which they had scrounged. A lot of us had no caps;[7] I was wearing a handkerchief knotted at the four corners, the only headgear I was to wear for some time. We looked a ragtime lot but in good spirits and ready for anything that turned up. About eighty per cent of us were Birmingham men; I never saw better soldiers or wished for better pals.'[8]

It is perfectly true that the troops were very tired after their gruelling march from Mons, were in less than perfect order and in need of rest and reinforcement. It is not true, as French apparently believed, that they were unable to fight or, indeed, in a worse state than their French allies or their German opponents. If anything, the men were fitter, their boots were 'broken in' and causing fewer blisters, the supply situation was improving and on 30 August Lieutenant General Pulteney arrived to form III Corps, which consisted initially of the 4th Division and the 19th Infantry Brigade, pending the imminent arrival of the 6th Division, which had now been ordered to France.

The Field Marshal discounted these encouraging facts and pursued his intention to withdraw in spite of numerous appeals to hold fast. 'The demand that we should stand and fight was not only urgently repeated', he writes, 'but was actually backed by imperative messages from the French President, and from Lord Kitchener and the British Government.'[9] There was also an appeal from General Joffre, startled out of his customary calm and busy preparing his counter-stroke against the enemy. Joffre begged the Field Marshal 'not to retire too rapidly and at least contain the enemy on the British front', but French's reply to all these appeals was a blunt refusal.[10]

Appeals having failed, some personal contact was called for. By now thoroughly alarmed, the Cabinet duly dispatched Field Marshal Kitchener, the Secretary of State for War, to Paris to confer with French – and change his mind. The situation was critical, so no time was lost; Kitchener arrived in Paris before dawn on 1 September and summoned French for an urgent conference at the British embassy.

Kitchener left no account of this meeting so again one is forced to rely on Field Marshal French's account, which proves damning enough. The meeting began with a typically petulant display of temper when French objected to Kitchener appearing in uniform. French chose to regard Kitchener's appearance in this dress as an attempt by the Secretary of State for War to overawe him and, he says, Kitchener, 'from the outset of his conversation assumed the air of a Commander-in-Chief'. That Kitchener was also a Field Marshal and fully entitled to wear uniform in wartime – and habitually wore uniform in London – did not impress the BEF's thin-skinned commander.

Then, again according to French, having heard the Field Marshal's assertion that his force was exhausted and short of equipment and supplies, Kitchener 'announced his intention of taking the field and inspecting the troops'. Given the situation and

French's claims, this seems a perfectly reasonable request but – again according to French – it aroused the ire of Lord Bertie, the British ambassador. French tells us that Bertie 'stated his views', but fails to tell us what these views were – presumably an endorsement of French's position – or why the ambassador chose to involve himself in a purely military matter that was none of his business, and was not equally concerned with the state of the troops. French's manner was now so close to insolence that Kitchener suggested they retire to another room and continue their meeting in private.

When the two Field Marshals were alone, according to French,

> I told him what was on my mind. I said that the command in France had been entrusted to me by His Majesty's Government and I alone was responsible for whatever happened and that on French soil my authority as regards the British Army must be supreme until I was legally superseded by the same authority which had put that responsibility on me. I further remarked that Lord Kitchener's presence in France in the character of a soldier could have no other effect than to weaken and prejudice my position in the eyes of the French and my own countrymen alike . . . and while I valued his advice I would not tolerate any interference with my executive command and authority as long as His Majesty's Government chose to retain me in my present position . . . we finally came to an amicable understanding.[11]

Assuming that any of this is true, the outcome was certainly an understanding; that it was amicable is extremely doubtful. Kitchener was a man who did not suffer fools at all, let alone gladly, and his ire when aroused was both fearful to behold and hard to endure. It is probable that he brushed French's objections aside and gave his subordinate a blunt order – to do as he was told or resign. Kitchener did not leave an account of this discussion, and by the time French's account came out in 1919 he had been dead for three years. However, the best indication of what actually happened in that meeting comes not from French's arrogant bluster in 1919 but from subsequent events in 1914.

At 1930 hours on 1 September, Kitchener cabled the Cabinet

with the news that 'French's troops are now engaged in the line and will remain there, conforming to the movements of the French Army'.[12] By the time that cable was dispatched French had already written to Joffre suggesting that the BEF take up a defensive line along the Marne and hold that 'for as long as the situation requires, provided our flanks are not exposed'. Two days later, on 3 September, French, having received a copy of Kitchener's cable to the cabinet, confirmed that: 'I fully understand your instructions . . . I am in full accord with Joffre and the French.'[13] Naturally, no mention of these later communications appears in the Field Marshal's memoirs, published in 1919, and the *Official History* did not appear until 1922, but all the evidence suggests that Kitchener overruled French's decision of 30 August and ordered the Field Marshal to keep his troops in the line – or else.

Kitchener should have gone farther; Field Marshal French should have been sacked on the spot. His arrogant assumption that once a general has been given command of an army he can do what he likes with it is ludicrous. That, plus his showing in command so far, should have been grounds for instant dismissal; by 1 September there was ample evidence that French was failing to provide the BEF with the necessary leadership and was reluctant to cooperate with his French allies.

Joffre was quick to sack any French general who failed to measure up to the demands of the situation. In spite of his successes at Guise and St Quentin, General Lanrezac was sacked on 3 September and replaced by General Franchet d'Esperey, and the same harsh but necessary measures should have been taken against Field Marshal French. As it was, this action was delayed until another year had passed and a great number of lives had been lost, but the British Army is notoriously reluctant to sack failing or incompetent commanders and for now Field Marshal French remained in post.

He was also nursing a new range of resentments. Six days later, in the middle of the Battle of the Marne, when he might have had more important matters to worry about, French was writing to Winston Churchill, again expressing his resentment at Kitchener for wearing uniform and wanting to see the troops.

While this matter was being settled the retreat from Mons continued. On 1 September, as related, while Kitchener and French were at odds in Paris, the cavalry and RHA were in action at Néry and I Corps clashed with the enemy at Villers-Cotterêts. On that day also the two corps of the BEF, separated for almost a week after passing the Forêt de Mormal, finally regained contact – another boost to morale. Many of the problems the BEF experienced at this time – not least the supply of food and ammunition – may have been due to the chronic lack of reliable communications.

Lieutenant-General Sir William Robertson, then QMG of the Expeditionary Force, refers to the problem in his memoirs:

> The maintenance of communications on the Western Front, particularly in the forward areas, was very difficult owing to heavy shellfire, mud and exposure and as no one means could be relied on many alternative methods had to be provided. Telegraph and telephone by wire and cable, wireless telegraphy, telegraphy through the ground, (power buzzer), visual signalling with electric lamps, helio and flags, carrier pigeons, messenger dogs, message-carrying rockets, firework signals, despatch riders, mounted orderlies, cyclists and finally runners, were all employed in turn, according to circumstances.[14]

Robertson is describing the situation after the Western Front settled down, but during the retreat from Mons the problem was compounded by the fact that GHQ moved frequently and the various Corps and Division HQs moved daily – if not more often – while the front-line units were widely dispersed and the roads crowded with refugees. Since good communications are vital to command and control, this problem may account for some of Field Marshal French's various errors and confusions, but he made no real effort to find out what was going on – and appeared particularly uninterested in the affairs of II Corps, unless they provided an excuse for criticizing Smith-Dorrien.

Even his own memoirs contribute to an impression that the size and violence of this war exceeded the field marshal's ability to command, and there can be no doubt that far too much attention was devoted to brooding over the presence of his unwanted sub-ordinate. Where Smith-Dorrien is involved, even tactical victories such as Mons should be discounted. According to French's mem-oirs, the German forces opposing Smith-Dorrien at Mons – two army corps and a cavalry division, six full divisions by the German count – are fictitious; the battle becomes a mere skirmish with German cavalry patrols. Smith-Dorrien is criticized for evacuating the Mons salient, though a glance at any map reveals that this position was untenable once the enemy advanced.

It is also interesting, and somewhat ironic, that the pages of French's regrettable memoir, spattered with complaints about Horace Smith-Dorrien, devote considerable praise to the actions of Douglas Haig and I Corps, a unit that was hardly troubled during the retreat from Mons – certainly not in comparison with the problems encountered by Smith-Dorrien's troops.

The irony is that French's main internal enemy in 1914 was Lieutenant-General Sir Douglas Haig, who was keeping a con-stant and critical eye on his wayward superior. On hearing of French's appointment to the BEF, Haig's first – and entirely justifi-able – reaction was that French was not the man to command Britain's only field army in this kind of war. By September, with a month's experience of French in the field, Haig was openly informing anyone who would listen that French was not up to the job; if unaware of this in 1914, French must have known of Haig's perfidy by 1918 when he started writing his memoirs, but none of this mattered. In his antipathy, if in nothing else, French was con-sistent; if destroying the reputation of Horace Smith-Dorrien required showering praise on the slippery Douglas Haig, so be it.

On 1 September 1914, Joffre made the decision that was to reverse French fortunes and give the generalissimo his enduring rep-utation as the saviour of France. Joffre has had numerous critics, but not even the most dedicated will deny that by keeping his nerve in the midst of apparent disaster, by remustering his forces and biding his time, Joffre saved France from defeat in 1914. A general's true abilities often arise from a combination of competence and character. It was Joffre's character – steady, dour, unflappable –

which saved the situation in August 1914, when the Germans were powering forward in unexpected numbers and threatening to prise the French armies apart

As for his decision to attack the German forces on the Marne, this must rank as one of the most critical in any war. Indeed, according to Liddell Hart, 'Germany lost the war when she lost this battle'.[15]

Given that the war went on for another four years and consumed a great number of lives, this claim seems a little extreme, but Liddell Hart makes a good point. Germany's entire strategy required a rapid victory and, as related, that depended on defeating France in six weeks and then turning on Russia. If the Schlieffen Plan could deliver that outcome Germany would avoid 'encirclement' – a war on two fronts – and achieve mastery of Europe. Now, clearly, the Schlieffen Plan had failed, the French, Russian and British armies were still in the field, and the French, far from being defeated, were about to strike back on the Marne.

As with the Schlieffen Plan, the essence of the Marne offensive was time – or timing. Joffre had to wait until the Sixth Army was in position, his front stabilized, the German supply lines fully extended – all this aided by von Kluck's decision to abandon the plan and turn east north of Paris. While waiting until the time was ripe was essential, the Marne counter-stroke, delivered on 6 September, could not have been delayed much longer. On 2 September the French government fled to Bordeaux, and with the French armies falling back everywhere and Paris threatened the crisis point of the war had arrived.

It can be argued, with the benefit of hindsight, that the French situation was not as desperate as it then appeared, for the enemy too were failing. The German soldiers were exhausted, at the limits of their endurance, and could not keep up the pace of recent days; they had been marching and fighting for five weeks without rest. The weariest of all were the soldiers of von Kluck's army on the far west wing, who had marched over 480 kilometres (300 miles) in that time and fought at Mons, Le Cateau, St Quentin and Guise, and in large and small skirmishes almost every day. 'The men stagger forward, their faces coated in dust, their uniforms ragged, like living scarecrows. They march with their eyes shut, singing to keep themselves from falling asleep on the march. The prospect of victory and of a triumphal entry into Paris alone keeps them going; without this certainty of victory they would fall exhausted.'[16]

From its inception the Schlieffen Plan had placed too heavy a burden on the German infantry. It had been pointed out to von Schlieffen that heavily laden soldiers could not march so far without regular rest and resupply but since – to make the timings work – they *had* to cover that distance within that time, the problem was simply ignored by von Schlieffen. It surfaced again on the cobbled roads of France in August 1914.

Quite apart from the requirements outlined above, Joffre was holding back because he was still not fully aware of what the German armies were doing. One thing the Germans were not doing – an omission that would have dire consequences later – was to extend their front as far as possible to the west and come south, sweeping all before them. 'Let the last man on the right brush the Channel with his sleeve,' von Schlieffen had declared. The German right wing had failed to follow this precept, partly because of the necessity to leave several divisions at Antwerp, partly because of a desire to round up the BEF and the French left wing. The result left a large area of north-west France untaken and available for exploitation, and von Kluck compounded this strategic error, this departure from the plan, by swinging his army to the east.

Allied aircraft had been following the divergent paths of the German First and Second Armies for some days, and Joffre's decision to attack was finally initiated on 1 September – that day of dramatic events – when a cavalry patrol found documents on the body of a German officer revealing the dispositions and intentions of the German First Army. These were rushed to GQG and Joffre learned for the first time exactly what the German armies were trying to do.

Joffre's previous shift of forces to the left wing and the creation of the Sixth Army under General Michel-Joseph Maunoury were now about to pay off. Joffre had also ensured total cooperation and a rapid response to his attack order by placing General Maunoury under the command of General Joseph-Simon Gallieni, the Military Governor of Paris. This shrewd move stopped Gallieni's constant complaints to President Poincaré that the defence of Paris was being neglected, and obliged him to support the Sixth Army with the men and resources of the Paris garrison when the counter-attack began on the Marne.

However, it is important to understand that even before von Kluck swung his army east, Joffre had intended to group several corps from the Third and Fourth Armies on the left flank and, together with the Fifth Army and the BEF, strike hard at the inner flanks of the German First and Second Armies, hoping to split them in two. The newly captured documents from the German staff officer revealed that von Kluck was about to abandon the Schlieffen Plan, and this offered Joffre a far more tempting prospect – that of striking these forces in the flank as they moved across his front.

By 2 September, von Kluck was faced with a stark choice. There was a widening gap between his army and the Second Army on his left; he could carry out his orders and continue to the west of Paris or follow his military instincts by maintaining contact with von Bulow's army. Moreover, as related, on 1 September his forces had bumped into the British at Villers-Cotterêts and it was abundantly clear that the gap between the two German armies was providing – or soon would provide – the BEF or the French with an opportunity to advance and split the German right wing in two. This must not happen so, opting for the second course – a decision that Helmuth von Moltke promptly endorsed – von Kluck started to swing east to maintain contact with von Bulow, thereby exposing his flank to the French counter-attack. This attack took place between 6 and 9 September, either side of the River Marne.

In retrospect, the dismissal of General Lanrezac just before this decisive attack seems somewhat unfair; Lanrezac should have been part of this victory. From the first days of the war – amazingly just four weeks previously – he had been warning GQG that the major German effort would come with a massive attack on the Northern Front, and his warnings had been ignored. He had also been ignored by Field Marshal French and had been denied British support for his highly successful counter-attack at Guise.

It can be fairly claimed that Lanrezac had done as well as any other commander and better than most, but by 1 September his Fifth Army was on the point of collapse and Lanrezac's nerves were in shreds. The Fifth Army crossed the Aisne in some disorder and a dangerous 40-kilometre (25-mile) wide gap had developed between the Fifth Army and the BEF. Reports had also reached GQG that Lanrezac had been heard crying *'Nous sommes foutus'* (politely, 'we are ruined') in moments of crisis. Joffre did not tolerate pessimistic officers so Lanrezac had to go and General Louis Franchet d'Esperey took command of the Fifth Army.

One of Franchet d'Esperey's first tasks was to make contact with Field Marshal French. As we have seen, French had promised to keep the BEF in the line – but would he go farther and support this counter-stroke against the enemy, which d'Esperey was preparing to make on 6 September? This question was also exercising General Joffre, and with reason, for on 4 September Joffre had been advised that French was dithering yet again.

French had now received a drubbing on Anglo-French cooperation from Kitchener and a written appeal for help from General Joffre and two of his aides, Murray, his Chief of Staff, and Henry Wilson, the Sub-Chief of Staff, were now at odds over strategy and giving him conflicting advice. French and Murray had had a meeting with Generals Gallieni and Maunoury at GHQ, during which French insistence on the importance of BEF participation on the Marne had clearly fallen on deaf ears; no sooner had the French generals departed than Murray issued an order for a further BEF retreat that night.

However, while Gallieni and Maunoury were with French and Murray, Wilson had held a separate meeting with Franchet d'Esperey. At that meeting he had agreed that, provided he could convince the Field Marshal, the BEF *would* support the Fifth Army attack. Then came a difficulty; according to Wilson's diary:

'When I got back I found that Sir John had already ordered a retirement, having this morning specifically stated to the Governor of Paris [Gallieni] that he would remain on the Marne unless turned out and also that he would co-operate with the Fifth or Sixth Army, or both. It is simply heartbreaking.'[17]

There is an Army expression for this sort of problem: 'order, counter-order, disorder'. Deluged with conflicting advice, even from his own staff, the Field Marshal elected to do nothing, telling Colonel Victor Huguet that he 'needed to re-study the situation before deciding on action'.[18] When news of this further prevarication reached Joffre's ears it drove him close to despair. In an attempt to change the Field Marshal's mind he sent French another copy of his Order No. 6, detailing the counter-attack, but by the time the order arrived at GHQ later that night the BEF were again retreating.

Joffre needed every available asset for his Marne attack, including the BEF, and now Joffre wondered whether the Field Marshal would indeed, as promised, commit the BEF to this assault on the Marne when the time came. He therefore decided to visit French at GHQ, which had now – worryingly – moved even farther south, from Compiègne to Melun, a town on the Seine, south-east of Paris. On 5 September, less than twenty-four hours before the Marne attack was due to begin, Joffre was obliged to leave his headquarters and motor the 160 kilometres (100 miles) to Melun to explain yet again the details of his plan to the Field Marshal. That done, Joffre then made a personal and very emotional appeal to French on behalf of France, adding that the honour of England was at stake. This appeal reduced French to tears but proved effective. Turning to Henry Wilson, he said, 'Damn it, I can't explain. Tell him all that men can do, our fellows will do.'[19]

The Battle of the Marne was largely a French affair. The onslaught involved the Fourth, Fifth, Sixth and Foch's Ninth Army, plus the BEF, pushing north and east on a 200-kilometre (150-mile) wide front with the Third Army standing firm in the east, all pivoting on the fortress of Verdun. Over a million men were committed to the Marne offensive and the BEF, positioned between the Fifth and Sixth Armies, therefore played only a minor, if vital, role.

The events of the battle can be briefly described. Maunoury's Sixth Army opened the offensive on 5 September with an attack on von Kluck's army along the River Ourcq, between Senlis and Reims. The first attack fell on the rear of von Kluck's army but, as the battle continued, corps after corps of the German First Army became involved – and were duly ground down as the advancing French tide swept over them. Von Kluck was then obliged to break off his march east in order to repulse the Sixth Army, and so the gap between the German First and Second Armies reopened – to provide a path north for the BEF.

Joffre sent the Fifth Army and the BEF into this gap, both tasked to prise the German armies apart. The Battle of the Marne went on for the next week and the outcome depended on whether Foch's Ninth Army and Maunoury's Sixth Army – holding the gap open – would be crushed before the Fifth Army and the BEF broke through. This was in doubt for some days, and at one point General Gallieni was obliged to send out 6,000 men of IV Corps from the Paris garrison, transporting the soldiers in taxi cabs, the famous 'taxis of the Marne', to shore up Maunoury's line against a German counter-attack. However, once the German retreat began it kept going, closely pressed by the advancing French and British – but not pressed closely enough.

By 8 September, French pressure was also having its effect on von Bulow's army, which was being slowly levered back towards the Aisne; on that day von Bulow admitted to a staff officer from von Moltke's headquarters that a retreat was now inevitable. Nor was the news much better at von Kluck's headquarters, and later that day a general order was given for the German armies in the west to withdraw to the line of the River Aisne, astride Soissons, and take up defensive positions; the Schlieffen Plan had been abandoned.

During the Battle of the Marne it gradually became apparent that the high-water mark of the German advance had been reached; now the *feldgrau* tide would ebb steadily back to the north, at least until the German generals found a place to dig in, make a stand and defy eviction. This ebbing of the Germanic tide was a withdrawal, not a rout; the German armies fell back without panic or confusion. One by one, starting on their right wing, one German army after another attempted to disengage, gain a little distance from the advancing Allied armies and the time necessary to find a defensible position and develop a defence line. That they were allowed the time to do this was an Allied defeat.

Otherwise the Battle of the Marne was a great French victory. By the end of the battle on the evening of 10 September,[20] the French armies, with some useful assistance from the BEF, had driven the German armies back some 100 kilometres (60 miles), to the steep-sided valley of the River Aisne. The BEF's contribution to this massive offensive could only be small but it was useful.

On 5 September the BEF was mustered south of the Grand Morin river, just east of Paris, 24 kilometres (15 miles) – or a day's march – to the rear of the flanking Fifth and Sixth French Armies. That day marked the official end of the retreat from Mons – at least according to the *British Official History*.[21] The previous day the first four divisions of the BEF had received their first reinforcements, some men arriving from the UK, others supplied by units hitherto kept in reserve but now deployed to top up those battalions or brigades seriously reduced in the recent fighting. The men were very welcome, but the BEF urgently needed supplies of food, clothing and artillery ammunition. Replenishment was difficult at this time for the northern supply bases had been closed and all stores and shipment of stores from the UK transferred to the port of St Nazaire at the mouth of the Loire in Brittany. Boulogne had been closed on 27 August, Rouen on 3 September. Le Havre, currently being emptied, would close on 5 September.

This was a staff failure; any transfer of essential supplies to the Loire should have been stopped on 1 September when French was obliged to keep the BEF in the line. The *Official History* records that on 29 August 60,000 tons of stores, 15,000 men and 1,500 horses were at Le Havre.[22] It does not explain why these men and supplies were sent south-west to Brittany instead of being dispatched north to the BEF, commenting instead that the movement of supplies from Le Havre to St Nazaire was 'a very considerable feat of organization'.

The very next paragraph[23] states that 'the arrival of the first reinforcements was only secured by the extraordinary exertions; and it was obvious that the III Corps must enter the new operations with its ranks still much depleted and lacking one third of its artillery'. Perhaps there is some logical explanation for the dichotomy between the statements in these adjoining paragraphs, but if so it is not supplied.

Field Marshal French had kept his promise to remain between the Fifth and Sixth Armies but the BEF was not in line with them; when the Marne offensive opened, the BEF was still south of its allies. Henry Wilson's diary entry for 1 September describes this as 'A ridiculous position, as it is neither one thing nor the other, and it makes the two French flanks ragged and insecure.'[24] The BEF were echeloned behind these flanking armies, but when news of the coming counter-attack filtered down to the rank and file, morale soared. A copy of General Joffre's order for the Marne counter-offensive beginning on 6 September reached French's HQ at 0300 hours on 5 September and his Operation Order No. 7 was issued at 1715 hours. All was quickly made ready for a general advance the following day; the men cleaned their weapons, loaded up with ammunition and tobacco and put on clean socks. Long before daylight on 6 September the men began to fall in, by platoon and company, by battalion and brigade.

Operation Order No. 7 stated:

1. The enemy has apparently abandoned the idea of advancing on Paris and is contracting his front and moving south-eastward.
2. The Army will advance eastwards with a view to attacking. Its left will be covered by the 6th French Army also marching east and its right will be linked to the 5th French Army marching north.

The BEF, now three corps and a cavalry division, were to march in the general direction of Montmirail, forcing a passage across the high plateau west of Champagne, driving the enemy before it. Sir John's orders required the BEF to wheel to the east, pivoting on its right flank, and then push on towards the north-east, east of the River Ourcq, towards Soissons and the River Aisne, which lay 100 kilometres (60 miles) to the north.

This terrain is not good campaigning country; the ground is rolling and dotted with extensive belts of woodland and the Allied advance had to cross several deep river valleys, those of the Grand Morin, the Petit Morin, the Ourcq and the Marne, before reaching the steep-sided valley of the River Aisne and moving across that river into Picardy. These are all wide, deep, unfordable rivers which could only be crossed at bridges, and each river provided the retreating enemy with a viable defence line – if he was given time to occupy it. This became the crux of the Battle of the Marne; defeating the enemy in the field and driving him back was one thing, but it was equally important to stay close on his heels and prevent him digging in.

The march began at around 1000 hours on 6 September, led by Allenby's cavalry division and two independent cavalry brigades under Brigadier General Hubert Gough which would eventually form part of the 2nd Cavalry Division. As the advance continued throughout 6 and 7 September the men realized, with considerable gratification, that the Germans were retreating before them. This fact was confirmed by patrols of the Royal Flying Corps, which reported by 1800 hours on 6 September that there were no major German units south of the Petit Morin. During the day, the advance was contested only by a few enemy cavalry patrols and occasional bursts of artillery fire.

The BEF advance therefore continued, but slowly – somewhat too slowly. On 7 September, the BEF marched up to the Grand Morin, two battalions of the 3rd Division, the 1st Wiltshire and the 2nd South Lancashire Regiment, getting across the river before being counter-attacked by the enemy; the Wiltshires beat off the attack without difficulty but the South Lancashires had a stiff fight with German cavalry before their crossing was secured. General Joffre's General Order No. 7, issued at 1720 hours, directed the armies on the Allied left to continue pushing the enemy north and east but to bear in mind the possibility of enveloping the enemy right wing if the chance arose; this order directed the BEF to 'get a footing in succession across the Petit Morin, the Grand Morin and the Marne'.[25]

Frank Richards was marching north with his battalion of the Royal Welch Fusiliers:

> We had finished with our retirement and were facing in the right direction. We marched up some rising ground. Down in the valley in front of us was the river Marne. On each side of the river was a village. A fine bridge spanned the river but it was now in half, the enemy having blown it up. We advanced down the hill in extended order. The enemy were supposed to be holding the two villages and we had to take them. We were met by a hail of fire. The men on the right and left of me fell with bullet wounds in the legs and a sergeant just behind me fell with one through the belly. We were having heavy casualties, but couldn't see one of the enemy.[26]

The BEF advance continued along the road from Sablonnières to Château-Thierry, now the boundary between the British and the Fifth Army, the BEF heading north-east now, in the direction of Rebais. As they advanced, the BEF discovered signs that seemed to indicate that the enemy – to quote the *Official History*[27] – were 'demoralized': empty wine bottles littering the verges, looted houses and, here and there, drunken Germans asleep in haystacks and barns. A better word would be 'undisciplined', but even that applied to only a few; the great mass of German soldiers were neither demoralized nor defeated.

The Germans fell back slowly and the Allied advance was neither as swift nor as close as it might have been. Douglas Haig certainly thought that the BEF should have pushed harder. 'I thought our movements were very slow today,' he recorded in his diary on 7 September, ' in view of the fact that the enemy were on the run.' Fortunately, the enemy did not make a determined stand on the

Petit Morin, which runs through a narrow, steep-sided valley, with only six bridges across the stream at the bottom, but strong parties of German infantry remained behind to contest the BEF's crossing.

The two bridges at Sablonnières were found to be defended and an attempt to rush across by the 4th Dragoon Guards was beaten off with rifle and machine-gun fire, as was an attempt to outflank the enemy with a push via Bellot. At Gibraltar, three kilometres (two miles) south-west of Orly, the cavalry detected a jäger battalion and a cavalry brigade at breakfast and brought up a battery of the RHA to drench their unsuspecting foes with shellfire, but in general the enemy had the best of it. By 0830 hours the British cavalry had been brought to a halt and were waiting for the infantry to come up.

The infantry were still moving slowly, mainly because the lanes were narrow and movement across wooded country difficult; on the extreme left the infantry of the 4th Division reached a ridge overlooking the Marne – a much wider valley than that of the Petit Morin – where the enemy greeted their appearance with a hail of shells. The 19th Infantry Brigade soon discovered that the enemy were holding the north bank of the Marne in considerable strength and maintaining a bridgehead on the south bank at La Ferté sous Jouarre. Meanwhile, over on the right, the BEF advance, covered now by artillery fire, had reached the Petit Morin, which was crossed near Bellot by the recently arrived 1st Battalion, The Cameron Highlanders; this success proved decisive and Sablonnières was in British hands by the early afternoon.

By that evening the Petit Morin had been crossed and the troops of I Corps had advanced as far as Basseville, midway between the Petit Morin and the Marne, though General Haig, the corps commander, still felt that the advance might have been made more quickly or taken more ground.

Forcing the Petit Morin line cost the BEF fewer than 600 men killed and wounded. More than 500 German prisoners were taken, along with at least a dozen machine-guns; the number of German killed and wounded is not known precisely but units of the German Guards, 2nd and 5th Cavalry Divisions, recorded heavy losses, some companies of the Guards' jäger battalions coming out of the action with only forty-five men.[28] The German positions along the Petit Morin having been reduced, the BEF moved up to the heights overlooking the Marne.

It had been expected that the enemy would make a stubborn defence on the Marne, which seemed to offer the ideal terrain for a rearguard action, but by the evening of 8 September RFC patrols reported that, on the contrary, while the enemy might still fight a delaying action, his retreat to the north appeared to be continuing. This being so, Sir John French elected to press on, but the pace of the BEF advance remained slow. On 9 September Haig was again urging his troops forward. 'A little effort now might mean the conclusion of the war! The enemy was running back. It was the duty of each of us to strain every effort to keep him on the run.'

This is true, so one might wonder why the advance of Haig's I Corps beyond the Marne stopped at 0830 hours and did not resume until 1500 hours – and stopped again before 1700 hours. II Corps were greeted with heavy shellfire and broken ground, so the advance of the 5th Division was 'consequently slow'.[29] The artillery problem was tackled by two companies of the 1st Lincolnshires in the 3rd Division, which made their way through the woods to the enemy gun line and shot down the German gunners, 'almost to a man', as they served the guns. Unfortunately, while taking the enemy guns, the Lincolns were hit by counter-battery fire brought down on the enemy guns by the 65th Howitzer Battery, RFA. Four infantry officers and around thirty men were killed or wounded; 'friendly fire' was not unknown to the soldiers of the BEF. The fighting beyond the Marne that day followed a similar pattern for every BEF corps, infantry advances supported by artillery being held for a while by German infantry and artillery; even so, the *Official History* claims that the pressure exerted by the BEF that day was the prime factor in forcing back von Bulow's Second Army.[30]

September 9 is generally regarded as the end of the Battle of the Marne. In three days the Franco-British armies – forty-nine infantry divisions and eight cavalry divisions – had forced forty-six German infantry divisions and seven cavalry divisions into a 100-kilometre (60-mile) retreat and fought one of the most decisive battles in history. The Marne battle is unusual because, while the enemy was certainly retreating, he had not been fought to a finish or indeed soundly defeated. Nevertheless, according to General Franchet d' Espery of the Fifth Army: 'Held on the flank, his centre broken, the enemy is now retreating towards the east and north by forced marches.'[31]

A significant part of the credit for this German reverse goes to the BEF. 'At the Marne,' says Spears, 'it was the British who were to be the only force available to march into the gap in the enemy lines. It was the wedge the British drove into the heart of the enemy's array that made the German retreat inevitable.'[32] Henry Wilson for one was delighted with the BEF advance: 'I believe the Germans are in retreat although I think that they may give us some shrewd knocks in the process. It is only three days ago that I had to fight all I could to prevent us retiring behind the Seine for three weeks' rest.'[33]

The Marne ended German hopes of a quick victory, but to ensure a decisive French victory the Allied forces needed to keep the enemy moving back, all the way to the Rhine if possible, and this they failed to do. The Allied advance stalled on the Aisne, where the Germans were given time to dig in and beat off their attacks. However, the German High Command also seems to have lost the plot at this time, failing to see that the failure of the Schlieffen Plan was a truly devastating blow. Indeed, von Moltke persisted in trying to rework the plan, not realizing that all the delays and errors since the Battles of the Frontiers had combined to render it useless. He did appreciate the more profound effect of the Marne reverse, writing to his wife on 9 September: 'Things are going badly and the battles east of Paris will not be decided in our favour. This war which began with such hopes will go against us and we must be crushed in the fight against East and West . . . and we shall have to pay for all the destruction we have done.'

So the first phase of the Great War, the war of movement, ended on the Aisne. The Battle of the Marne also marked the end of the Schlieffen Plan, which alone offered Germany the chance to win the war and avoid the perils of encirclement. Someone had to pay for this failure; on 14 September, six weeks after he had sent the German armies into Belgium, von Moltke was replaced as Chief of the German General Staff by General Erich von Falkenhayn, who took up his command while the opposing armies were locked in combat on the Aisne.

10

On the Aisne

13 September–2 October 1914

It seems as if the enemy is once more going to accept battle, in prepared positions north of the Aisne.
> Telegram from General Joffre to Field Marshal French,
> 15 September 1914, cited in *British Official History, 1914,*
> Vol. I, p. 367

On the night of 12/13 September the German First and Second Armies ended their retreat and dug in along the high ground above the River Aisne, a tranquil stream flowing through one of the greenest and prettiest valleys in northern France. Given time to do so, the German armies were able to occupy a line along the escarpment high above the north bank, a few miles south of the hilltop town of Laon. On the top of this escarpment lies a seventeenth-century carriage road, built by Louis XV as a place where his court ladies could take the air, and therefore known as the Chemin des Dames.

The arrival of the opposing forces on the Aisne marks the effective end of the first phase of the Great War. The change from a war of movement to static trench warfare on the Western Front would not happen overnight, but it began here on the Aisne, when the awesome power of defence, and especially of heavy artillery, first began to dawn on the opposing commanders. However, when the armies began to draw up along the Aisne on 13 September, there was still a great deal of open, undefended country available to the west, and every possibility that the war of movement would continue on the flanks.

In order to grasp the detailed complexities of the Great War on the Western Front it is helpful to understand the broad picture and keep in mind the general progress of events. Matters had not gone to plan in the east either, but during the first month of the war the two strategic plans, Schlieffen's and Plan XVII, had both gone awry in the west. As a result the balance of advantage by mid-September lay with the French. This can be attributed to four facts: the Schlieffen Plan was too ambitious; Prince Rupprecht had abandoned it in Lorraine and Alsace by advancing instead of retreating; von Kluck had turned east–north, rather than south, of Paris; and Helmuth von Moltke had agreed to these alterations and made a major contribution to the collapse of German strategy. As a result, although the French armies and the BEF had been driven back, they had not been surrounded and crushed and German hopes of a quick victory had slipped away.

However, the Franco-British victory on the Marne had also gone somewhat awry. Instead of keeping hard on the heels of their retreating foes and hustling them out of any possible defence line, the French armies and the BEF had allowed the retreating German forces to gain a little time and space in which to find a defensive position and dig in. The *Official History* points out[1] that several French writers allege that the BEF's advance was both slow and hesitant, a point confirmed by Haig's diary.

The BEF began at a disadvantage, for on 5 September the BEF was at least a day's march behind the two French armies on its flanks. Nor did the BEF make much ground thereafter. On 6 September the British units advanced a maximum of 18 kilometres (11 miles) and on 7 September 14 kilometres (9 miles), though this included crossing the Grand Morin. On 8 September, the BEF covered 16 kilometres (10 miles) crossing the Petit Morin, and on 9 September 11 kilometres (7 miles), including crossing the River Marne. This was, perhaps, all that could be expected, but it hardly added up to hot pursuit.

Nor was that all. When the German units found a defensive position it naturally offered certain advantages – good visibility over the front, ground suitable for the rapid creation of a trench system and reverse slopes to conceal artillery positions and supply lines. From its very inception, the advantage of ground on the Western Front lay with the Germans.

Giving the enemy time to find and occupy such positions was a fundamental error, one that would cost the Allies dearly in the months and years ahead, but in mid-September 1914 all was not yet lost. In spite of von Schlieffen's point about brushing the Channel coast, the advance of the German armies from Mons had not covered all the ground as far west as the Channel – far from it. West and north of the Aisne position a wide expanse of open country was still available for flanking movements, a process that began on the Marne. This turning movement, north and west, by the Franco-British armies, the so-called 'Race to the Sea', an attempt to outflank the German defensive line and roll it up, would provide the genesis of the Western Front, and the process began on the Aisne under the direction of the new German Army commander, Erich von Falkenhayn.

General von Falkenhayn was fifty-three when he took up this command in 1914 and was therefore one of the younger commanders on either side. His comparative youth was useful, for the exercise of command in war requires good health, strong nerves, a sense of detachment and a flexible mind. Von Falkenhayn was certainly no 'by the book' Prussian officer, the usual product of the *Junker* class; he had an analytical brain and was fully capable of evaluating facts and making difficult decisions. It might be added that the results of his analysis did not always produce the required results, a fact that would become apparent at Verdun in 1916.

Von Falkenhayn owed much of his advancement to the favour of the Kaiser. The Emperor had been much impressed – it has to be said that the Kaiser was easily impressed – with von Falkenhayn's dispatches from China during the Boxer Rebellion in 1900, when he commanded the German contingent. Appointed Prussian War

Minister in 1913, he had played a major part in formulating the plans for the attack on Belgium; now he had replaced the overall commander of the German armies and was responsible to the Kaiser for their operations in the field.

However astute politically and however shrewd his brain, von Falkenhayn was somewhat less than capable as a field commander. His strategy, orders and actions over the next few months, as the fighting began to concentrate around the Belgian town of Ypres, would cause severe losses to the cream of the pre-war German Army. It is also possible that he had taken on too much work for one man to handle competently; after taking command of the armies, he retained his post as Prussian War Minister and was therefore responsible for German strategy in forthcoming battles in the east as well as in Champagne and at Ypres, in which great losses were inflicted on either side for no worthwhile territorial gain. For the moment, however, von Falkenhayn was seen as the coming man and a great improvement on the hesitant von Moltke.

His first orders were for a widespread renewal of the offensive. The German armies were to attack at all points, hold back the advancing allies and press on with the siege of Antwerp. On 9 September, in an attempt to keep the Germans from shifting forces into France, the Belgian Army in Antwerp made a strong sortie, which saw Belgian cavalry patrols entering Louvain the following day. Then the Germans reacted as desired, bringing up the 6th Reserve Division and halting the movement of the IX Reserve Corps to France.[2] The Belgian sortie was quickly halted, and by 13 September, the opening day of the Battle of the Aisne, the Belgian Army retired within the fortifications of Antwerp. This sortie had, however, prevented the enemy from rapidly reinforcing the units retiring from the Marne.

Von Falkenhayn ordered the formation of a new German army, the Ninth, and the mustering of six and a half new reserve corps, but his immediate aim was to prevent the Marne reverse resulting in a long retreat of the kind recently experienced by the BEF and the French. He was too late to prevent a major reverse on the Marne but the subsequent withdrawal of the German armies was of short duration and came to a halt on the heights above the Aisne.

The Allied pursuit of the German forces to the Aisne was the last major movement on the Western Front until the German Michael offensive of 1918. This was the sort of war Field Marshal French was used to, and during it he handled his men well, pushing them on behind a thick cavalry screen, levering the enemy out of position with artillery fire and flanking attacks. After those weeks of retreat the British infantry and cavalry marched at their best speed, winkling the enemy out of his rapidly prepared positions, taking plenty of prisoners and a quantity of guns. It was good but not good enough, for the enemy gradually gained ground. 'As fast as we retired on our retirement,' wrote Frank Richards, 'the Germans were equally as fast on their feet from the Marne to the Aisne.'[3]

In the six days between the start of the Marne offensive on 6 September and their arrival on the Aisne on 12 September, the German First and Second Armies were driven back 100 kilometres (60 miles); on their eastern flank the German forces fell back as well, their front bending like a bow and pivoting on the fortress city of Verdun. The night of 12/13 September marked the end of the retreat for the German First and Second Armies. Blowing the bridges behind them, they withdrew across the Aisne to the escarpment overlooking the river and dug in there for the next phase of the struggle, the First Battle of the Aisne, which took place between 13 and 15 September, an attempt by the Allies to cross the river, take the Chemin des Dames ridge and continue pushing the enemy back; very little of this was actually achieved.

When this battle opened the BEF were at once confronted with a serious problem, a shortage of artillery ammunition. On 13 September, II Corps informed GHQ that it had not seen a supply column for the last two days – the advance was clearly inhibiting the movement of supplies. On 15 September, III Corps used up all its remaining stock of 60-pounder and 4.4-inch howitzer ammunition, and no more was available for another three days. These problems – supply shortages, particularly of artillery ammunition, and railway delays – were to plague the BEF for some time to come.

The dates given here for particular battles are those which appear in the *Official History*, but they should not be taken as definite limits; they are, at best, simply a historical convenience. They should not be understood to mean that no preliminary moves were made before the 'battle' or that nothing much happened thereabouts after it. The First Battle of the Aisne was a sideshow compared to the constant fighting that took place along the Chemin des Dames in the coming years; a host of French graveyards and the Caverne de Dragon museum now bear testimony to the duration and intensity of the continual fighting on the Aisne. Battles are simply points in a campaign; they are the result of what happened before and a cause of what follows, but the fighting continues all the time. One feature of this Aisne battle was the appearance on the front line of German heavy artillery.

Field Marshal French mentions in his memoirs that the first indication that the enemy had halted on the Aisne came when 'Jack Johnsons', heavy shells from German eight-inch howitzers, began to explode among the soldiers, 'our first experience of an artillery much heavier than our own'.[4] These heavy howitzers had been hurried down to the Aisne after completing the reduction of the fortress of Maubeuge, which had surrendered on 8 September.

French established his headquarters at Fère-en-Tardenois on 12 September and went forward the next day to the River Aisne, south-east of Soissons, where the 4th Division of Pulteney's III Corps were assisting an attack of the French Sixth Army. From a ridge above the south bank of the Aisne, the field marshal looked down on the valley and was astonished by the intensity of the shellfire; ' the river seemed to be ablaze, so intense was the artillery fire on both sides'.[5]

French was witnessing a change in the balance of power on the battlefield. Heretofore, victory usually depended on a mastery of the 'all arms' battle, finding the correct combination of artillery, infantry and cavalry. Now the artillery piece was beginning to dominate the battlefield and dictate the progress of events, and the guns would continue to do so until the end of the war; more than 60 per cent of all casualties during the Great War were caused by shellfire. The infantry answer to shellfire was entrenchment, so the battle for the Aisne marked the start of 'trench warfare', which became and has largely remained the abiding image of the Great War engagements, conflicts in which men in trenches, up to their knees or waists in mud, endured the relentless pounding of the guns.

Trench warfare began – and the Western Front developed – not from any deliberate strategic plan but for two simple, understandable, tactical reasons. On the heights above the Aisne the Germans found a position they could defend. To hold it they dug trenches and artillery positions. When the Anglo-French armies came up to assault these positions, they came under intense artillery and rifle fire. Unable to advance and taking losses, they too dug trenches and dugouts to shelter in while preparing for another attack and to resist any counter-attack. From this point on a further series of understandable actions caused the trench lines to extend.

The Allied soldiers first tried frontal assaults. When these attacks failed, the Allied units, French and British, attempted flanking attacks, hoping to edge round the enemy defences. From the Aisne there was an open flank to the south and east, terminating at the Swiss border, and running north and west towards the North Sea. Seeking the advantage of ground, and anxious to prevent any renewal of the Schlieffen attacks, the Allies hooked north and west in short tactical bounds – only to find that the Germans had meanwhile extended *their* flank, found more high ground and dug in to beat them off yet again. Impasse.

And so, with the Allies launching flanking attacks and digging in to hold any ground gained while the Germans extended their line and dug in to oppose any Allied attack, the trench lines crept north and west towards the North Sea. They also crept south and east, up to the frontier with Switzerland, but in September 1914 both sides were attempting to get round the 'open' or western flank of their foe, both still hoping to 'roll up' the enemy's line, a process that ended, as we shall see, when the BEF and the Germans finally collided head on at Ypres.

During this time, as Field Marshal French had noticed, the defensive elements of war – steep terrain, dugouts and trenches, artillery using indirect fire from behind hills and ridges – were beginning to dominate the battlefield and stifle the war of manoeuvre. Later on, when this combination was enhanced by barbed wire, the 'Old Front Line' of the Western Front gradually came into being as a means by which soldiers of all armies could hold their ground and protect themselves from shellfire and infantry assaults.

Overall, the Germans gained the greatest benefit from this procedure. They had the initial choice of ground, and although neither side had visualized a war of fixed positions the Germans also had an adequate supply of trench stores – barbed wire, spades and duckboards, and useful close-quarter assets such as hand grenades and trench mortars. At first the French and British had none of this equipment – and lacked heavy guns with which to reduce the German positions and support the infantry assaults. Rather more to the present purpose, they lacked ammunition.

In 1915 artillery ammunition of every calibre was in very short supply in all the armies; the consumption of ammunition in the first weeks of the war had exceeded the wildest pre-war estimate. Many batteries were taken out of the line simply because there was no ammunition for the guns, and an artillery piece without ammunition is no more than a bulky, heavy, useless piece of metal. The probable consumption of artillery ammunition in the British Army had been calculated on the basis of previous colonial wars; in practice these calculations proved wildly out of line with the artillery war now developing along the Western Front.

Nor was this all. The first weeks of campaigning in France revealed this underestimate, but the means to replace front-line ammunition as it was fed to the guns was limited; UK stocks were slender, and the British arms factories were not big enough, or numerous enough, to produce more.

William Robertson, then Quartermaster General (QMG) of the BEF, confirms this point in his memoirs:

Shortly after our arrival on the Aisne the enemy brought up more heavy artillery from Maubeuge and the period of trench warfare destined to last for nearly four years set in. With it arose demands for heavy artillery on our side, more gun ammunition, more machine-guns, bombs [grenades], barbed wire and other artillery and engineering stores, none of which could be even approximately met, so defective had been our wartime preparations.

When first sent out the Expeditionary Force had only two machine-guns per battalion, about 150 in all, while of 490 pieces of artillery only 24 were of medium type, the rest being light field guns or field howitzers. There was no heavy artillery. The twenty-four 'medium' guns were supplemented on the Aisne by 16 6-inch howitzers of an inferior kind and some rather old guns of 4.7in. calibre.

As regards artillery ammunition, no one, either before the war or in the early part of it, dreamt that the demand would reach the colossal figure it eventually did reach. At any rate no adequate provision was made to reach it.[6]

These facts and this general picture of the situation should be borne in mind as we consider the actions of the BEF on the Aisne. Field Marshal French's orders for the Aisne battle were issued to corps commanders at 1945 hours on 12 September. After crossing the river, the three corps should make an advance of some eight kilometres (five miles) from the north bank to the foot of the Chemin des Dames escarpment that occupied the high ground between the valleys of the Aisne and the Ailette. The advance to the escarpment from the river would not be easy; various spurs run down towards the Aisne from the heights and the entire country between the ridge and the river, a mixture of fields, woods and copses, was completely overlooked from German positions on the heights of the Chemin des Dames.

On the left of the BEF line, Pulteney's III Corps, reinforced from 16 September by the newly arrived 6th Division, had established a bridgehead across the Aisne by 0300 hours on the morning of 13 September. Brigadier A. G. Hunter-Weston's 11th Infantry Brigade, crossing at Venizel, just east of Soissons, took the German outposts on the heights beyond the river at the point of the bayonet, the defenders falling back to their main position some hundreds of metres to the rear. This was useful, but did not put the BEF on or anywhere near the crest of the Chemin des Dames.

On the right of the BEF attack, the Cavalry Division ran into stiff opposition from German riflemen positioned in houses along the north bank of the Aisne Canal, south of the river, and was not able to cross until the infantry of the 1st Division came up in support. At Vailly the advance of the 3rd Division of II Corps was checked by German heavy artillery firing from positions behind the Chemin des Dames, and when the divisional artillery opened fire in support it was promptly subjected to heavy counter-battery fire and forced to withdraw out of range. On the III Corps front, the 1st Royal West Kents of the 4th Division met resistance from German infantry at Missy but managed to force a passage over the bridge, which the divisional cyclists had seized soon after midnight.

Although all the Aisne bridges had been destroyed and the morning was wet and miserable, both wings – III Corps on the left, I Corps on the right – followed by II Corps in the centre, managed to get across without undue difficulty, some units using rafts and small boats, others clambering over the remains of demolished bridges, repairing the gaps with rafters and floorboards from nearby houses, but this still left the leading units some miles from the foot of the Chemin des Dames ridge. Once they were across the river, though, the ranging Germany artillery fire did little damage. The British troops were advancing on a broad front and in open order or 'artillery formation', whereby even heavy shelling had little effect. On 13 September, Hauptmann Walter Bloem watched the advance of Haig's corps from the Aisne:

> From the bushes bordering the river sprang up a second line of skirmishers, with at least ten paces from man to man: the second line pushed nearer and now a third line, two hundred lines behind that and then a fourth wave. Our artillery fired like mad, but all the shells could hit were single men, all in vain; a sixth line appeared, a seventh,

all with good distance and intervals between the men. We were filled with admiration.

The whole plain was now dotted with khaki figures, coming ever nearer, the attack directed on the corps on our right. Now our infantry fire met our attackers but wave after wave flooded forward and disappeared from our view behind the woods.[7]

By dawn on 14 September, GHQ were aware that a number of narrow bridgeheads had been established across the river – but it was also becoming evident that the BEF advance on 13 September had not been made without cost. The 6th Division had a bloody baptism, losing 1,500 men in its first engagement. Other units of III Corps crossing the river at Venizel were greeted with heavy fire from German 8-inch and 5.9-inch guns hidden behind the heights to the north. British heavy batteries engaged these guns but German counter-battery fire soon forced the British guns to withdraw; German guns outranged all the British guns except the 60–pounders. German artillery was therefore able to dominate the battlefield and bring the entire Aisne front under effective artillery fire.

The fact that the German retreat had ended on the Aisne had yet to dawn on General Joffre. His Special Instruction No. 23, issued on 12 September, was based on a belief that the enemy was still retreating. Confident in this belief, Joffre had already ordered an 'energetic pursuit' by the BEF between Athies, east of Laon, and the River Oise, while General Maunoury's Sixth Army matched their advance west of the Oise. This order required the Sixth Army to send the bulk of its forces to the west of the Oise, so outflanking the Germans, but to remain in close contact with the BEF as it moved north between Bourg and Soissons; meanwhile the Fifth Army, also keeping in close touch with the BEF on the left, would cross the Aisne east of Craonne.

Field Marshal French followed this GQG instruction to the letter, ordering his forces, now clinging on between the Aisne and the Chemin des Dames, to press on to the line Laon–Fresnes, 20 kilometres (12 miles) west of Laon – and some 24 kilometres (15

miles) north of the river. This required an advance of up to 20 kilometres, up and over the German defences on the Chemin des
Dames, which now became the next objective for Haig's I Corps.

The British divisions came up to support those advance guards
already across the river in three widely dispersed bridgeheads;
there was, for example, a five-mile gap between the 3rd Infantry
Brigade and the 8th and 9th Brigades on the north bank, and four
infantry brigades and two cavalry brigades were still on the south
bank, striving to cross the river.

Such a major advance could never have been easy, but the
Germans were now being reinforced. Von Falkenhayn was creating yet another new army, the Seventh, composed of units culled
from Alsace and Antwerp. He intended to place it on the far west
of the German, line so outflanking Maunoury's Sixth Army. Some
of these units, notably the VII Reserve Corps, were diverted to the
Aisne front, arriving there just in time to stop the German line
being outflanked by Haig's I Corps; the following day the German
XV Corps stopped a similar outflanking movement by one of
Maunoury's corps.

General von Bulow, commander of the Second Army on the
Aisne, had been placed in command of the German First and
Seventh Armies and had formed a continuous line, east to west for
some 48 kilometres (30 miles) above the Aisne, from west of
Soissons to beyond Craonne, from which he intended to advance
on the Allies below. The Battle of the Aisne was not simply one in
which the Franco-British forces assaulted the Germans in prepared positions; this was partly an 'encounter battle', in which the
Germans were fully determined not only to stem the Allied
advance to the Chemin des Dames but also to drive their opponents back across the river.

The *Official History*'s account of the fighting on 14 September,
the second day of the Aisne battle, records a day of 'thick weather,
fog, fighting at close-quarters and heavy casualties . . . a day of
great confusion'.[8] A study of events would reveal those comments
to be an understatement; it would be more accurate to say that
chaos reigned during the BEF attack.

The divisional and brigade commanders were unable to 'grip' the battle owing to the chronic lack of field communications, compounded here by fog and a wide dispersal of forces. In such a situation the outcome depended on battalion COs, company officers and NCOs, and the guts and tenacity of private soldiers. Those British divisions not yet across the river came across and attempted to advance through the bridgeheads established the previous day, but found the enemy alert and waiting, their heavy artillery ranged to the inch, fully determined to drive the British back across the river.

This they never managed to do, but, as at Waterloo ninety-nine years previously, this second day of fighting on the Aisne was a close-run thing. This was another Inkerman, says the *Official History*,[9] a 'soldiers' battle', with close-quarter fighting, the combatants advancing in small parties controlled by the company officers, fighting from behind cover, advancing or retreating in short rushes, contesting every piece of ground hard, often out of touch with the units on their flanks.

Various accounts emerge from the confusion. A party from the 1st Battalion, The Cameron Highlanders, fifty strong, hung on grimly to the ground they had taken, fighting until their ammunition was almost exhausted and then falling back behind the crest of the ridge; here they were attacked by a great number of the enemy and overwhelmed in one final fight in which many of the Camerons were killed and most of the survivors wounded. The 1st Coldstream Guards in the same brigade managed to get through a thick wood and across the road bed of the Chemin des Dames, Lieutenant Colonel J. Ponsonby lining his men up along the steep banks to repel the inevitable counter-attack.

They were then subjected to a heavy and accurate artillery bombardment – the German guns knowing their positions to the inch – and suffered severely until Colonel Ponsonby rounded up every man still able to move and led them forward to the village of Cerny, well behind the German front line, where they took up a position and opened fire on enemy troops debouching up the steep slopes from the Ailette valley. Here the Coldstreamers hung on until late in the afternoon, beating off counter-attacks with rifle and machine-gun fire.

Every available unit was fed into the line to hold these slender gains across the river and on the heights until, in the 1st Division, only two companies of infantry remained in divisional reserve. At dusk it was necessary to pull the advance units, including Ponsonby's Guardsmen, back to the main line, giving up the hard-won ground they had held all day. This day on the Aisne was not a battle of infantry against artillery, as at Mons and Le Cateau. German infantry, backed by plenty of artillery, were engaged here in force, and the day became one of attack and counter-attack along the entire BEF front; 14 September was the hardest day's battle for the BEF as a whole since the force landed in France a month before.

The *Official History*[10] records that the results of 14 September were 'disappointing' and that the positions the BEF held on the north bank of the Aisne were 'not secure'. They had also been costly; casualties that day in Haig's corps alone came to around 3,500 men, killed, wounded or missing. The 1st Cameron High-landers lost 600 men that day, almost 80 per cent of the battalion, and six other battalions in Haig's corps – including Colonel Ponsonby's 1st Coldstream Guards – lost more than 300 men apiece. Casualties were fewer in the 4th and 5th Divisions but the 3rd Division lost over 1,000 men.

As a result, the Allied advance beyond the River Aisne was checked and General von Bulow, now the overall commander of all three German armies on the Aisne front – the First, Second and Seventh – had every reason to be pleased. Had it not been for the pressure exerted by this strong BEF attack, he might well have succeeded in driving the Franco-British armies back across the Aisne but, suspecting that the strong British attack indicated the existence of BEF reserves, he was content to hold his ground and take a heavy toll of the attackers.

By 15 September the BEF's gains north of the river were restricted to those three bridgeheads, one across the river bend between Bucy and Missy, another in a loop around Vailly, and a deeper one established by Haig's corps, running from Soupir in the west up to the Chemin des Dames at Cerny. This last advance marked the only part of the Allied advance that had so far reached the top of the escarpment. These bridgeheads did not form a continuous line; they were footholds on the north bank of the Aisne, and the Germans, pivoting on their strong positions along the Chemin de Dames, were able to fend off further attacks here as the Allies attempted to outflank the defenders and the trench lines were gradually pushed north.

Constantly improved and reinforced, this German defence line on the Chemin des Dames became impregnable and remained so for much of the war; the Chemin des Dames became a German bastion of the Western Front and the fighting there a byword for slaughter. As the Allied attacks revealed any weaknesses in the German line, more men were brought up, more wire, guns and dugouts employed to strengthen it; the more the Allies attacked, the stronger the German line became. Breaching that line would not have been easy at any time, but the main reason for this Allied failure to push through on the Aisne in September 1914 – when a breach was possible – was excessive caution on the part of the Allied army commanders.

During the advance from the Marne, Field Marshal French became obsessed with keeping the BEF in line with the French Sixth and Fifth Armies on his flanks, writing in his memoirs: 'My intention to close at all speed with the enemy had to be tempered by consideration for the French Armies on my flank, both of which were opposed by much larger forces.'[11] French returns to this point again and again; his actions may have been prompted by a desire to show Kitchener that he intended to do what he had been ordered to do at the meeting in Paris – keep in line with the French – or by understandable fears of a German counter-attack.

Whatever the reason, the effect was to slow the Allied advance. This was not entirely French's fault. The Fifth and Sixth Army commanders also seemed reluctant to keep up the pressure on the enemy, so the three armies acted like men in a three-legged race and the overall pace became that of the slowest. As a result the

Germans were given the chance to find and prepare their strong position on the Aisne with the results described above – stalemate, heavy casualties and the start of trench warfare.

Not everyone was dismayed at the present situation or this slow advance. Henry Wilson, for one, remained optimistic, convinced that the war was in its final stages and victory in sight. He wrote in his diary on 9 September: 'Berthelot asked me when I thought we should cross into Germany, and I replied that unless we made some serious blunder, we ought to be in Elsenborn in 4 weeks. He thought 3 weeks.'[12] A few days later, in a letter to his wife, Wilson remarks: 'If we drive in the force in front of us, we won't have any more trouble until we get to the Meuse.'[13]

Henry Wilson's powers of divination were clearly in decline at this time, for the Allied pursuit had actually stopped. After some probing attacks up the southern spurs running off the Aisne crest, Field Marshal French ordered his men to dig in and hold their positions against German counter-attacks and the ever increasing shellfire; the situation on the Aisne was deadlocked.

That done, French fell silent. No operational orders were issued to his command for two whole weeks, from 16 September to 1 October, the period during which 'trench warfare' with all its attendant horrors began to create the fortified complex of the Western Front.

The official account of the Aisne battle concludes that the BEF frontal assault on the Aisne was a very remarkable feat of arms, and draws particular attention to the actions of Haig's I Corps, not least for its considerable tenacity in retaining its ground against shellfire and counter-attacks. II and III Corps actually got somewhat farther forward, even to the lip of the escarpment, but dared not put their heads over the top. Most of the German casualties were caused during their counter-attacks; when they chose to sit tight there was little the Allies could do to harm them. With the Germans holding the high ground and their positions getting stronger every day, it soon became clear that the Allied armies could not break through on the Aisne.

Joffre therefore opted for that series of left-hand attacks which provoked counter-entrenching moves by the enemy and has since become known in Great War history as the 'Race to the Sea'. This move to the north and west began in early October and went on until the BEF and the German Fourth Army collided frontally at Ypres in November.

By the time this race began the French and their British allies were already facing the Germans across a line of trenches that ran north for over 150 kilometres (90 miles) from Soissons to Béthune and La Bassée in the mining country between Arras and Ypres. Though it led to other problems, the development of the trench system disproves one of the popular myths about the Great War generals, that they used only frontal attacks and never attempted to outflank the enemy line. The trench system on the Western Front was created by *weeks* of flanking attacks, each halted by a rapid enemy movement opposing any progress round the end of their line.

While the French and German forces angled off to the north-west, the BEF remained on the Aisne. The *Official History*'s verdict on the BEF's advance from the Marne to the Aisne and its performance in the subsequent Aisne fighting seems accurate – and points the finger of blame at Sir John French: 'The race [from the Marne] was lost mainly owing to a failure to make a resolute effort to reconnoitre the enemy's dispositions on the river . . . and to push forward parties to seize the bridges on September 12/13. When the divisions made a rather cautious and leisurely advance they should have been reminded of the old adage that "*Sweat saves Blood*". In GHQ orders there was no hint whatever of the importance of time.' The account goes on to add that, after the Germans were known to have dug in, 'There was no plan, no objective, no arrangements for cooperation, and the divisions blundered into battle.'[14]

The *Official History* describes the situation on the Aisne front after 15 September as 'The Deadlock'[15] and notes that, at a meeting at Fère-en-Tardenois on 14 September, French had ordered all three corps commanders to entrench their troops and concentrate the heavy guns of all five BEF divisions in an attempt to subdue the powerful German batteries. French's gloomy view of the situation was confirmed by a communication from General Joffre at 0115 hours that day: 'It seems as if the enemy is once more going to accept battle in prepared positions north of the Aisne. In consequence it is no longer a question of pursuit but of a methodical attack, using every means at our disposal and consolidating each position in turn as it is gained.'

This note tacitly confirms a change in strategy and the introduction of another expensive Great War tactic, 'bite and hold', an attempt to seize part of the enemy line and hold it while preparing for another bite. The usual result of any 'bite and hold' attack was to create a small salient, which the enemy promptly brought under fire from three sides. The war of movement had given way to a 'war of offensives', in which the power of the offence would be pitted against the depth and tenacity of the defence.

Joffre's assessment of the immediate future was correct, but the day of the fully planned and prepared offensive – the set piece battle – had yet to dawn; there was still a little time for a better solution, one that avoided the risks and losses inherent in frontal assaults on well-prepared positions. With their flanks still open to the north and west, flanking attacks by either side were still possible. If only one side could get ahead of the other, the chances of success, of rolling up the opposing line from the flank, could be considered high.

Joffre certainly thought so, but in his Special Instruction No. 29, dated 17 September,[16] he notes that where the enemy had already entrenched, 'it is essential to maintain an offensive attitude in order to keep the enemy under threat of attack and prevent him from disengaging and transferring portions of his forces from one point to another'. In other words, the chances of winning this 'Race to the Sea' depended on speed *and resources*. It would be necessary to maintain the pressure on the Aisne and all other parts of the expanding Western Front, while still finding sufficient forces to hook round the end of the enemy line.

This steady shift of the French armies north and west towards the Channel coast soon led Field Marshal French to review the position of the BEF. This force was now in the centre of the Aisne front with French armies on either flank – and at some distance from those comforting ports on the Channel coast. This position pleased General Joffre since it prevented any radical actions by his British allies, but it was less than satisfactory to the Field Marshal, who wanted to shorten his supply lines and move the BEF closer to the sea and the Royal Navy. Therefore, at the end of September, French suggested to Joffre that the BEF should resume its designated pre-war position, on the extreme left flank of the French armies.

This dictated a move to the north of Arras, beyond the current French line, which ended effectively at La Bassée. The area north of this was lightly held by cavalry units, but once up there, aided by the Belgian Army, the BEF could fill the gap between La Bassée and the Channel, a distance of some 60 kilometres (40 miles), beat off any German movements to the west and – perhaps – mount an offensive towards the east and outflank the German line, creating a situation the French armies to the south-east could exploit.

French urged this action on the generalissimo but Joffre was unenthusiastic. Joffre preferred to keep the BEF between the French Fifth and Sixth Armies because he would then be in a position to dictate what the BEF would do. French's hesitation before the Marne had left a deep scar in Joffre's mind – and it appears that the Field Marshal was worrying yet again about his flanks.

On the evening of 16 September, French had been visited by Colonel C. B. Thompson, the British liaison officer with Maunoury's Sixth Army. Thompson informed the Field Marshal that the French XIII Corps had been checked that day west of Noyon by the sudden appearance of the German IX Corps, brought down from Belgium. 'Here', said French, 'was another incident in that continual flanking and outflanking manoeuvre which would only cease at the sea . . . Again the IV French Corps arriving east had been arrested on finding the German force entrenched on its left [or northern] flank . . . It was from this particular evening of 16th September that I date the origin of a grave anxiety which then began to possess me.'[17]

French refugees on the road to Paris and the south, September 1914

Battle of the Marne: 1st Bn, the Middlesex Regiment, 19th Infantry Brigade, struck by shrapnel. Nine horses were killed, several men wounded

Field Marshal Sir John French inspects a motorcycle section

A lancer unit retires from Mons, August 1914

The Queens Bays at Néry with two German prisoners, September 1914

Infantry in trenches during the Battle of Armentières, October 1914

Argyll and Sutherland Highlanders dig support trenches, Erquingham, October 1914

oyal Field Artillery (RFA) 18-pdr guns in action at Messines, October 1914

French cavalry observes German movements on the Aisne, October 1914

inter in the trenches: 11th Hussars in the line at Zillebeke in the Ypres Salient, 1914–15

Henry Wilson and Douglas Haig (right) as Field Marshals in 1918

As if he did not have enough current worries, French had now began to brood on some pre-war discussions at the Committee for Imperial Defence, concerning 'the importance that the Channel ports should be held by a power in absolute friendship with us'.[18] With the start of the Race to the Sea, 'what was to prevent the enemy launching a powerful movement for the purpose of securing the Channel ports whilst the main forces were engaged in practically neutralising one another?'[19] – the recent stalling of the French IV and XIII Corps attacks being a particular example.

The Field Marshal's solution was to shift the BEF north, mainly to defend the Channel ports and to be 'in a better position to concert combined action and cooperation with the Navy'. The *Official History* endorses the Field Marshal's opinion, stressing that the British were indeed very anxious to retain Antwerp and protect the Channel ports.

Inevitably, General Joffre did not like it; he thought that French was anxious to position the BEF close to the Channel ports, the better to arrange an evacuation should the war again turn sour. In his reply to French's suggestion he stated that 'the Commander-in-Chief cannot share the view of Marshal French as to the time at which this movement should be carried out'[20] and would prefer that any such move be delayed.

Anglo-French cooperation was clearly fragile at this time, and on 28 September Wilson's diary records: 'The fact is, and I think there are some grounds for it, that the French are dissatisfied with us. It is very unfortunate.'[21] So it was but, unfortunately for General Joffre, Field Marshal French had in reserve that part of his orders which stated that the BEF was an independent command. Therefore, on 1 October, the Field Marshal told Joffre that he had now decided to exercise this prerogative and intended to remove his force from the Aisne to a new position north of La Bassée – whether Joffre liked it or not.

In the event this blunt statement met with very little actual opposition from Joffre. The Allied front north-west of La Bassée was held only by French cavalry and Territorial troops; they needed bolstering as the trench lines crept towards them and the strategic dangers inherent in this open flank became ever more obvious. Therefore, if French wanted to go north, why not? There would be plenty for the BEF to do up there, in preparing defensive positions, supporting the French and Belgians, fending off any major German attack to the west or securing a line from La Bassée via Ypres to Dixmude, covering the Channel ports and establishing a 'start line' for any Allied attack to the east.

Joffre therefore did not oppose French's ultimatum, and on the night of 1/2 October 1914 the BEF began to move north. The units left their line on the Aisne in great secrecy, with the enemy unaware that they had gone. First to move was Gough's 2nd Cavalry Division, by road. This was followed by Smith-Dorrien's II Corps, which began to move by rail from Compiègne to Flanders on 5 October. Next to depart was Pulteney's III Corps, followed by Haig's I Corps, which concentrated at Hazebrouck on 19 October and was in position near Ypres two days later. GHQ moved to Abbeville on 8 October and was established at St Omer five days later. As these British units came into line in the north, so German units arrived in line to the east, just in time to oppose them. The stage was now set for the first engagements of what came to be the First Battle of Ypres.

11

The War in the North

2–18 October 1914

It was therefore judged necessary to halt and arrange a general, combined attack on a five-mile front . . . the first formal British attack of the war.

> The capture of Meteren, 13 October 1914, *British Official History*, 1914, Vol. II, p. 96

Shortly after Field Marshal French set up his headquarters at St Omer, he received a visit from Colonel à Court Repington, the military correspondent of *The Times*. In his memoirs[1] the normally shrewd Repington wrote an eulogistic account of the Field Marshal during this visit, one in which Repington's opinions seem somewhat at variance with the facts.

Writing of the advance from the Marne, Repington declares that 'Sir John's decision to cross the Aisne in pursuit was one of the boldest moves ever taken by a commander'.[2] Writing of the Race to the Sea, he continues: 'Our Army then moved to the west and began that series of wonderful actions which culminated in the defeat of the second great German effort to overwhelm us in the west and eventually ended in the establishment of rival lines of defence, and in the crystallisation of the fighting lines into the trench warfare which endured throughout the years 1915, 1916 and 1917.'

That most of these moves and 'wonderful actions' were a result of *force majeure* by the enemy rather than any sagacity on the part of Field Marshal French has clearly escaped Repington's notice, but the eulogy continues:

> Most days when I was at GHQ I had at least two long talks with the Field Marshal alone, and was impressed with his complete grasp of the whole military situation and by his intimate knowledge of all the details of his troops and their services. He possessed the sacred fire of leadership in a rare degree. I never knew him to be depressed. He was the incarnation of confidence and he inspired confidence in all. Nothing escaped him and the rapidity of his decisions was remarkable.[3]

A veritable Alexander, it seems – and how fortunate for the BEF were any of this true! Unfortunately, these views of the Field Marshal's character and competence are at variance with the facts, and since Repington was neither a fool nor under the pressure of events when he wrote these words – in 1920, when Sir John French's failings had long since been obvious to all – one can only wonder what inspired them. Whatever it was, these glowing opinions were not borne out by subsequent events.

One of the reasons advanced by Field Marshal French for the BEF's rapid move to the north was to help the defence of Antwerp, which was now on the brink of collapse. Antwerp was important for various reasons; not only was it a major port, but any troops there were in a position to threaten the German lines of communication across Belgium, while the Royal Navy was most anxious that Antwerp should not fall into German hands for use as a submarine base.

The Belgian Army and the Belgian king and government had been holding out in Antwerp since mid-August, receiving periodic assistance from the British but coming under steady and increasing pressure from the German Army. During his first advance into Belgium, von Kluck had sent four divisions and some infantry brigades plus a great deal of artillery to maintain the siege of Antwerp in spite of the pressures elsewhere. The Germans had now decided to reduce the Antwerp bastion completely, and on 28 September they began a heavy bombardment of the outer forts. By

1 October, this defensive ring had fallen and French was informed that the defences of Antwerp were on the point of collapse.

In an effort to stave off this disaster, the British government offered to send the 7th Division, the 3rd Cavalry Division and a small number of heavy guns under Lieutenant-General Sir Henry Rawlinson to the relief of Antwerp; the hope was that this force, together with the Belgian Army, could hold Antwerp until the BEF came up from the Aisne and drove off the besiegers. Given the urgency of the situation the first British troops dispatched to Antwerp on 3 October were a small brigade of Royal Marines, some 2,000 men with twelve machine-guns, with the 7th Division and the cavalry to follow the next day. This force would land at Zeebrugge and Ostend and march to Antwerp, being joined on the way by a French contingent of similar size; their joint strength would increase the garrison of Antwerp by some 53,000 men.[4]

However, on 3 October the Field Marshal was further informed that the Belgian government had already left Antwerp for Ostend and that King Albert, with the six-division-strong Belgian field army, intended to withdraw from the Scheldt and head in the direction of Ghent, partly to protect the coast, partly in the hope of linking up with the Allied armies close to the Franco-Belgian frontier. With this message came the dire news that the remaining defenders of Antwerp were unlikely to hold out for longer than another week.

From then on the collapse of Antwerp was rapid. The intervention of Rawlinson's force was both too little and too late, and the Royal Marine Brigade, which arrived on 6 October, was withdrawn on 8 October. Major-General T. Capper's 7th Division arrived at Zeebrugge on 7 October and was followed into Ostend by Major-General Sir Julian Byng's 3rd Cavalry Division. Their commander, Sir Henry Rawlinson, then arrived from the Aisne, where he had been in temporary command of the 4th Division after General Snow had been accidentally injured. The promised French contingent failed to arrive at all, but these British units were in position at Ostend or Bruges on 8 October, when the Belgian government decided to evacuate Antwerp.

This evacuation was not accomplished without loss. The Royal Naval Division, three light brigades composed of sailors and marines, lost a total of 2,558 men; many of these were interned in Holland for the duration of the war when they withdrew across the Dutch border and 1,000 men were taken prisoner by the Germans. The British effort to save Antwerp had failed and Rawlinson was now concerned with getting his corps out of Ghent and joining forces with the BEF at or around the town of Ypres. This move began on 11 October, and by the night of 13/14 October Rawlinson's force – Capper's 7th Division and Byng's 2nd Cavalry Division, now called IV Corps – were taking up an outpost position around Ypres in trenches currently held by the French 87th Territorial Division.

Field Marshal French was now nursing a new grievance, once again with Lord Kitchener, but largely over General Rawlinson. 'Lord Kitchener did not make things easy for me,' French complains in his memoirs.[5] 'Keenly desirous to influence the course of operations, his telegrams followed one after another, each containing directions regarding the local situation of which, in London, he knew little.' It does not seem to have occurred to French that telegrams can be sent in either direction and his original orders contained a specific requirement to keep Kitchener informed of events: 'You will kindly keep up constant communication with the War Office and you will be good enough to inform me as to all movements of the enemy reported to you as well as to those of the French Army.'[6] If Kitchener did not know what was going on at the front during this time, part of the fault lay with the BEF commander.

French also complains that Kitchener is dealing directly with Joffre and failing to tell him what they are talking about. He therefore 'repudiates any responsibility for what happened in the north in the first ten days of October', for, he adds, 'I explicitly told the Secretary of State for War that the British troops operating there were not under my command.' To underline this point he quotes a telegram from Kitchener that states: 'Have already given Rawlinson temporary rank. I am sending him instructions regarding his action Antwerp. The troops employed there will not for the present be considered part of your force.'[7]

It appears that French was telling Kitchener what Kitchener had just told him. On the other hand, French also quotes a telegram that he sent to Rawlinson on 11 October – two days *after* the date on which, according to the *Official History*, French took IV Corps under command: 'Your message 119, addressed to Lord Kitchener and repeated to me received. I really do not understand whether you regard yourself as under my orders or not; but if you do, please be good enough to explain your situation without delay ... Be good enough to answer me by some means at once as my own and General Joffre's plans are much put out and perhaps compromised by all this misunderstanding.'[8]

Here is another example of that common military situation: order, counter-order, disorder. One cannot help but feel sorry for Sir Henry Rawlinson, caught up in this telegraphic feud between the two field marshals while attempting to confront the enemy and extricate his command from a crumbling situation north of Ypres.

To avoid increasing this confusion here it is necessary to describe the situation of the BEF and the French armies in the north – basically astride the Franco-Belgian border – after the II Corps move from the Aisne had been completed and Rawlinson's IV Corps came under French's command; both these events took place on 9 October.

The German Sixth Army was on a line facing west between Menin and Arras. Between Arras and La Bassée the Sixth Army was opposed by two French corps, the XXXIII and XXI of General Maud'huy's Tenth Army. North of La Bassée, the Tenth Army had the 1st Cavalry Corps under Conneau and the 2nd Cavalry Corps under de Mitry, a total of six cavalry divisions, with General Conneau in overall command; these cavalry corps were positioned between the British II and III Corps when they came into the line. Apart from cavalry patrols, this part of the front was wide open up to Ypres until the arrival of the BEF in early October.

By the time Field Marshal French took his troops north the BEF had grown somewhat. The 6th Division (under Major-General J. L. Keir) had arrived on 12 September and joined III Corps and, as related, IV Corps under Rawlinson was about to arrive from Ghent. This increase in manpower would be useful for any attack to the east, for the Allied line north of the River Somme was currently very thin. The front of some 40 miles between the Somme and La Bassée was held by more units of the French Tenth Army, whose positions were 'scattered over a wide front',[9] and opposed by divisions of the German First and Second Armies.

The general strategy employed during the Race to the Sea is easily grasped. Each side was attempting to outmarch the other, get around the northern flank of the opposing force, and then turn south to 'roll up' the enemy line. The problem was that neither side could quite do it. Early-twentieth-century armies had weight but lacked mobility. They relied on the marching abilities of their infantry, on horse-drawn transport and where possible on railways. Neither side had any technological advantage and the use of motor transport – the 'taxis of the Marne', lorries, London buses, tractors and motor cars – was limited, not least by a shortage of drivers. Any rapid advance still depended on cavalry exploitation, hence the appearance of cavalry at the extreme end of the opposing lines.

The German cavalry moving up from Picardy had hoped to outflank the French by a rapid advance west towards Béthune and St Omer, but French cavalry and Territorial units had so far managed to hold them off. Clearly, the Race to the Sea would be won by the side that could disengage sufficient forces from the existing line and move them north in time to make a deep penetration before an opposing force arrived; in that sense it was a true race. General Joffre doubted that the cautious, pessimistic Field Marshal French would be able, or indeed willing, to attack east from the line La Bassée–Ypres, but he thought that the BEF would at least be able to stave off any German attack heading west until French forces came up in support.

Smith-Dorrien's II Corps detrained at Abbeville on 8 and 9 October and then concentrated on the banks of the River Authie,

20 kilometres (12 miles) north-east of Abbeville, close to the 1346 battlefield at Crécy. II Corps then advanced towards Béthune, being joined en route by the 1st and 2nd Cavalry Divisions. These had arrived from the Aisne by route march and were now formed into the I Cavalry Corps under Allenby and tasked to cover the II Corps' advance to the east.

III Corps arrived on 11 October, concentrated at St Omer and Hazebrouck and then moved east to Bailleul and Armentières on the Franco-Belgian frontier. A week later, on 19 October, Haig's I Corps arrived. Having concentrated at Hazebrouck, I Corps moved north-east to Ypres, where it linked up with Rawlinson's IV Corps. These BEF units now deployed between La Bassée and Dixmude and there linked up with the Belgian Army, so extending the Allied line to the North Sea coast. The Western Front of infamous memory was about to become a reality. It is important to note that ten-day gap between the arrival of the first BEF unit, II Corps, and the arrival on 19 October of Haig's corps; the Northern Front was not quiet at this time and many events took place in that period.

After the loss of Antwerp, Ypres was the only Belgian town still in the hands of its own people, a fact that gave it an emotional and political significance far in excess of its military utility and accounts for the various terrible battles that took place there in the following years. The First Battle of Ypres – or 'First Ypres' – in the autumn of 1914 was a long-drawn-out and very complicated engagement, which began around La Bassée, south of Ypres, and spread north to embrace the entire Northern Front, culminating in a major clash in early November. The *Official History* wisely refers to First Ypres as the 'battles' of Ypres, and to make any sense of it the reader must grasp both the overall picture and the general sequence of events.

The first point is the strategic opportunity, presented to both sides, of a breakthrough in the north; whoever could win this outflanking battle would be well placed to win the war. The second is the positions adopted by the BEF corps when they came north, gradually falling into line on the left flank of the French Tenth

Army. Between 8 and 19 October the BEF was extending the Allied line to link up with the Belgians, arriving just in time to stave off a German thrust towards the west. As these attacks came in and the BEF line crept towards Ypres, so the series of battles that came to be called 'First Ypres' began, beginning with the engagements at La Bassée, Messines and Armentières.

These three battles fall roughly between 11 and 24 October – 'roughly' because they did not end abruptly on that date but were continued by other battles around the Ypres 'salient', the line of low hills circling Ypres to the east. All these first engagements were attempts by the BEF to turn the right flank of the German Sixth Army and were followed by a short advance to the line of the River Lys which runs through Armentières.

II Corps was in position by 9 October, and on 10 October Field Marshal French agreed with General Foch – who on 11 October became commander of the Northern Group of French armies – that II Corps would support a push east by the Tenth Army towards the city of Lille, which was now some 16 kilometres (10 miles) east of the Allied positions but not yet occupied by the enemy – it is important to stress that the front was still fluid. II Corps' first task was to secure the railway centre at Hazebrouck, 20 kilometres (15 miles) north of Béthune, and to get them there quickly the French would supply sufficient buses to transport 10,000 men. By the night of 10 October II Corps was in touch with the left of Maud'huy's Tenth Army at Béthune and was ready to push east. Since there appeared to be little to oppose it west of Hazebrouck but some scattered German cavalry units, this thrust appeared simple.

Foch declared on 10 October that: 'I propose to advance our left [Tenth Army] by Lille to the Scheldt at Tournai or Orchies, the British Army forming a line from Tournai through Courtrai – in this way all the French, British and Belgian detachments would be united on the left banks of the Scheldt or the Lys. After that we can see.' This sounded a sensible plan but, unfortunately, the enemy got in the way.

On 11 October II Corps made good progress east of Béthune

while the French III Corps on their right reached the outskirts of Lille and Allenby's Cavalry Corps secured Messines and Wytschaete, two villages on the higher ground overlooking Ypres from the south. This move linked the cavalry with the British 7th Division east of Ypres, and with the Belgian troops now digging-in on the River Yser north of that city, by the evening of 11 October the Allies formed a loose but continuous front from the Swiss frontier to the North Sea coast, a distance of some 725 kilometres (450 miles).

However, the Allied attempt to push this line east and secure Lille quickly petered out. The Germans reacted quickly and countered the attempt with troops brought down from Antwerp and another four reserve corps, which were brought forward in an attempt to turn the Allied flank and break through to the sea; German troops occupied Lille on the evening of 11 October and they held it for the next four years.

The Tenth Army and the BEF's II Corps collided with the enemy at La Bassée, a small town on the Lys Canal east of Béthune, on the afternoon of 11 October; the French left wing ended at Vermelles, six kilometres (four miles) south of La Bassée, so the battle was mainly a BEF engagement with a six-kilometre (four-mile) wide gap between the Tenth Army and II Corps.[10]

The battle at La Bassée began with the commitment of a single infantry battalion, the 1st Royal Norfolks, at Annequin, tasked to cover the gap between II Corps and the French XXI Corps at Vermelles. The II Corps reserve, the 13th Infantry Brigade, was on hand should anything develop, and this proved wise. Soon after dawn on 12 October it became clear that the French had been forced back from Vermelles and II Corps' right flank was fully exposed.

This situation presented Smith-Dorrien with a now familiar problem. His orders from Field Marshal French were to move east, north of Lille, in the general direction of Brussels, but his flank was now open. Should he now follow French's orders and move north and east towards Lille – or obey the Field Marshal's other instruction, that he should, *at all costs*, keep in touch with the

French on his right? Smith-Dorrien, weighing up the odds, elected for the second course and chose to advance due east, so keeping in touch with the Tenth Army, rather than north-east towards Lille, which would have widened the existing gap with the French. This advance took II Corps across open country seamed with dykes and ditches and dotted with small farms and villages, towards a long, low mound, running north to south, 16 kilometres (10 miles) east of Béthune; this mound was Aubers Ridge, a slight rise in the ground that would see bitter fighting in 1915.

In October 1914, II Corps barely obtained a brief foothold on Aubers Ridge; German opposition, from infantry, artillery and cavalry, soon made itself evident and beat them back. These troops came from the German II Cavalry Corps, but German cavalry units contained jäger infantry, machine guns, cycle battalions and artillery, and these units were soon putting up a stiff resistance to the British advance. The five infantry brigades of II Corps were opposed by four cavalry divisions and eight infantry battalions, all well concealed or dug in. Even so, II Corps pressed on against steady opposition and by the evening of 12 October it had reached the village of Givenchy at the southern end of the corps line. The fighting on 12 October cost II Corps around 200 men, killed, wounded or missing, not a large total for a hard day.

The fighting on 13 October was considerably stiffer. Field Marshal French approved of Smith-Dorrien's decision to hang on to the left of the French XXI Corps and ordered III Corps, now detraining at Hazebrouck, to render Smith-Dorrien assistance if required. He also ordered the II Corps advance to continue – if the French were willing to proceed. Willing, perhaps, but not able; the French closed up on II Corps' right but no advance was made to the east and the Allied battle now developed into a struggle for Givenchy. The centre of the village was held by the 1st Bedfords, who lost 149 men that day in close-quarter fighting among the burning houses, with the Germans holding one end of the village street and the Bedfords the other.

Eventually the Bedfords were driven out and the fighting spread into the surrounding countryside and along the banks of a nearby canal. By the time the battle petered out at dusk, one battalion of II Corps, the 1st Dorsets, had lost their colonel and 400 men. Total casualties to II Corps on 13 October were close to a thousand men, and the Battle of La Bassée was only beginning. This situation provided the field marshal with another opportunity to criticize Smith-Dorrien:

> On the afternoon of the 14th I again visited Smith-Dorrien at Béthune. He was in one of those fits of deep depression, which unfortunately visited him all too frequently. He complained that the 2nd Corps had never got over the shock of Le Cateau and that the officers sent out to replace his tremendous losses were untrained and inexperienced; and, lastly, he expressed himself convinced that there was no fighting spirit throughout the troops he commanded.[11]

This is a typical French piece of fiction. There is no other evidence to support the allegation about Smith-Dorrien's frequent 'fits of deep depression' – but note the attempt to drive a wedge between Smith-Dorrien and his officers and men in the statements that the officers were untrained and the men unwilling to fight – two comments that Smith-Dorrien certainly never made.

In fact II Corps continued to fight, and fight hard. Over the next two days, while the fighting astride the Lys Canal continued, II Corps lost another 1,000 men, including Major-General Hubert Hamilton, GOC of the 3rd Division, who was killed by shellfire near Estaires. No progress was made along the north bank of the canal, and a notable feature of the fighting, something new in this war, was a series of German counter-attacks at night.

On the night of 14/15 October, the 2nd King's Own Scottish Borderers (2nd KOSBs) were attacked at Cuinchy by a battalion of German troops. This attack was pressed home hard but was eventually beaten off with loss. After that the 13th Infantry Brigade (2nd KOSBs, 2nd Duke of Wellington's, 1st Royal West Kents and 2nd KOYLI) moved north of the Lys Canal; from then on this waterway formed the southern boundary between the Tenth Army and the BEF. Heavy fighting continued along the Lys but the advance east was painfully slow and very costly; by the evening of

15 October II Corps had advanced just six miles in four days at a cost of nearly 2,000 men, ninety of them company officers.[12]

On 13 October, Foch wrote to Joffre, remarking that 'The Marshal [i.e. French] wishes at all costs to go to Brussels. I shall not hold him back'. [13] This intention again confronted Smith-Dorrien with his original dilemma – how to advance north-east, a point the field marshal kept pressing, while keeping contact with both the French on his right *and* the BEF's III Corps, which had now come into line on his left. II Corps was simply not big enough to hold this sector of the front and push ahead, especially after sustaining heavy casualties. However, over the next three days, until 18 October, II Corps pushed forward, retaking Givenchy and getting a footing on Aubers Ridge. The suburbs of Lille were only two miles away but the enemy was fighting hard for every metre of ground and II Corps' losses had now reached 3,000 men in this advance, which finally came to a halt when the German XIII Corps came up to assist the VII Corps.

For the moment II Corps could do no more. The *Official History* notes ruefully that, 'The high water mark had been reached and the 15th Brigade was nearer to La Bassée than any British troops were to be for the next four years.'[14] Inevitably, the enemy then counter-attacked. On 19 October II Corps suffered a severe setback when the 2nd Battalion, The Royal Irish Regiment in the 8th Brigade were overrun at Le Pilly, a hamlet on Aubers Ridge. The 2nd Royal Irish had already lost 200 men taking Le Pilly, a position beyond the rest of II Corps' line, and before orders to retire could reach them the battalion was attacked by two German infantry regiments. Only thirty of the Irishmen regained the British lines; losses at Le Pilly totalled 571 men, including the Royal Irish commanding officer, Major E. H. E. Daniell, who was killed in the final stand.

By 17 October the BEF, far from advancing, were being heavily counter-attacked, and any further advance on this part of the front was now impossible. Writing to his wife on 19 October, Wilson records: 'Our news tonight is not so good although there is nothing to be anxious about. But the Germans are crowding up against us and I am afraid that from the fact that we have not pushed as hard as we ought during the last week we are now going to find the boot on the other leg. We shall know more tomorrow. I still think the campaign will be over in the spring . . .'[15]

Wilson, that devoted Francophile, inevitably blamed French for these delays, in particular for not falling in with Foch's plans. Anglo-French *Entente* was not improved when, on 21 October, Field Marshal French asked Joffre to 'provide facilities to make a great entrenched camp at Bordeaux to take the whole EF'.[16]

On hearing this, says Wilson, 'Joffre's face instantly became quite square and he replied that such a thing could not be allowed for a moment. He would make some works to safeguard against a coup de main but an entrenched camp he would not allow. Sir John was checkmated straight away and said I was to discuss the matter with General Joffre. So that nightmare is over.'

On the II Corps front the nightmare continued. By the morning of 20 October, Smith-Dorrien's problems had, if anything, increased. His tired and much depleted ranks were now confronted by two fresh German divisions, both spoiling for a fight. These were able to come in on the left flank of II Corps, which had been exposed by the need to wheel right in support of the French XXI Corps. If II Corps could hold their ground here they would be doing well, but late on 20 October Field Marshal French called off this first BEF attempt to turn the German line. Clearly, the enemy had brought up enough troops to fend off the BEF's attack at La Bassée and their line would not be broken or outflanked here. II and III Corps were therefore to go on to the defensive and hold their ground – if they could – while Haig's I Corps renewed the turning effort at Ypres.

Whether II Corps could hold their current line was doubtful. The German counter-attack to II Corps' advance had begun at Le Pilly on the 19th and would continue on 21 October. On that day the French XXI Corps was strongly attacked south of the Lys Canal and the BEF's 3rd Division was struck by infantry attacks, backed with artillery, north of it. Once again the power of defence became apparent; the German infantry made splendid targets advancing across the open ground, and although their attacks were pressed home with great resolution, all had petered out by mid-afternoon, leaving the fields before the BEF line carpeted with enemy dead, the misty air loud with the cries of wounded men.

British losses on 21 October were also very high, mostly from artillery fire. In the 3rd Division 1,079 men had been killed or injured; the 1st Duke of Cornwall's Light Infantry lost 266, the 3rd Worcesters 83, the 2nd South Lancashires over 200. This division was therefore ordered to retire to a new line a mile west of their existing position and await reinforcements.

The advance of II Corps since 11 October placed it in a perilous position when these German counter-attacks came in. Fortunately, as at Mons in August, Smith-Dorrien had prepared another defence line to the rear of his front-line troops. When compared with Western Front entrenchments later in the war, this reserve position of 1914 was barely adequate, but it was still a great improvement on anything the division had had so far. The line of shallow trenches and dugouts – later known as the 'Smith-Dorrien Line' – ran from the east of Givenchy via Neuve Chapelle to Fauquisart. The Smith-Dorrien Line wavered behind the corps front; it was only a short distance behind the 3rd Division positions on the right, but some two miles behind the front line at Fauquisart on the left.

This position quickly came in useful when the French cavalry covering the left flank of II Corps suddenly fell back on 22 October. On the night of 22/23 October, French gave permission for II Corps to occupy this new position, a move screened by the newly arrived Jullundur Brigade of the Lahore Division, the first unit of the Indian Army to arrive in France. With their assistance, the withdrawal of II Corps to the Smith-Dorrien Line proceeded without any opposition from the enemy.

For the moment II Corps could do no more. On 25 October Wilson records Smith-Dorrien coming to GHQ and telling French that 'he was afraid his Corps might go during the night'.[17] Wilson adds that 'Sir John was rather short with him and I think fails to realise what it would mean.' The BEF's problems were no longer confined to halting German advances; the Germans were also improving their defences, so Allied attacks north of La Bassée were now meeting wire entanglements and well-prepared trench lines.

The Battle of La Bassée ended with the retirement of II Corps to their new defence line on 22 October. In spite of German pressure, the Smith-Dorrien Line was held. Meanwhile, farther north, III Corps were engaged in two battles: the Battle of Armentières (13 October–2 November) and the Battle of Messines (12 October–2 November). It will be noted that the dates of all three battles overlap; the fighting was continuous along the BEF line during this time (see map 4).

III Corps was at St Omer on the night of 11 October when, in accordance with Field Marshal French's directive for an advance in the direction of Lille, Pulteney's Corps was tasked to occupy the line Armentières–Wytschaete with Allenby's Cavalry Corps extending their left flank as far as Ypres. It was hoped that II Corps, shortly to be engaged at La Bassée, would be relieved by the French and move north into the position between the two BEF corps currently occupied by the two French cavalry corps of Conneau and Le Mitry. II Corps and these French cavalry would change places and the BEF would then form a continuous line between the French and the Belgians. However, owing to the difficulties encountered by II Corps at La Bassée, this transfer did not take place.

General Pulteney's Corps had a further problem – the ground. On the left of the line chosen for the III Corps advance and therefore directly across the line of advance of Allenby's Cavalry Corps, lay the 130-metre (400-foot) high range of steep-sided hills running from the Mont des Cats to Kemmel. Quite apart from the physical difficulty they presented to any assault, these hills offered the enemy superb artillery observation over the area of the proposed advance. Further problems existed in the series of steep ridges projecting south from the main line of hills, which provided the enemy with a perfect set of defensive positions and plenty of 'dead ground' for the deployment of artillery and the movement of reserves.

Clearly, the first task was to take the high ground before III Corps went forward. On 12 October the 3rd Cavalry Brigade was ordered to dismount and take the Mont des Cats, a task it accomplished that evening with very little opposition; it appeared that the enemy had not yet had time to occupy these positions in strength. Pulteney wisely decided to push ahead before the enemy did so, ordering his corps to advance on Bailleul while the Cavalry Corps on their northern flank completed the capture of the high ground east of the Mont des Cats. This advance duly began on 13 October – and ran into a strong German force entrenched along the ridge astride the village of Meteren, a mile west of Bailleul.

This position extended to the north, and the enemy were clearly determined to hang on to it; at 0900 hours RFC patrols noted the movement of a German battalion and two artillery batteries from Bailleul. The Cavalry Corps were unable to turn the Meteren position from the north and soon had their own problems; by early afternoon Allenby was asking Pulteney for infantry support. Pulteney therefore decided to put in a full III Corps assault against the Meteren position, sending in both divisions on a five-mile front – an assault which the *Official History* describes as 'the first formal British attack of the war'.[18]

Formal or not, this attack was quickly organized. The advance began at 1400 hours and in that close country rapidly developed into an infantry battle, to which the artillery observers, confused by the mixture of hop fields and small woods on a wet and misty day, could give very little assistance. Progress was therefore slow and costly; the German trenches, mostly occupied by dismounted cavalry troopers from four German cavalry divisions, were well sited and barely visible. The Germans also enjoyed the advantage of superb artillery observation from the church tower in Meteren, and when III Corps finally rushed the main German position that evening the enemy quickly disengaged and faded away into the dusk, having cost III Corps 708 casualties in a few hours of battle. German losses were later estimated at around a thousand.

Among the soldiers wounded that day was Lieutenant Bernard Montgomery of the 1st Battalion, The Royal Warwickshire

Regiment – 'Monty' to a later generation of British soldiers. Then aged twenty-six, Montgomery was shot in the chest leading his platoon into the attack and lay out in No Man's Land for many hours before his men brought him in; for his part in this action Montgomery was later awarded the DSO, a high award for a junior officer.

October 13 brought bad news for General Joffre and Field Marshal French: the Germans had now occupied Lille, one objective of this Anglo-French offensive in the north; RFC patrols reported that part of the town was in flames and that a large German column, presumably from the force that had taken Lille, was now marching in the direction of Armentières. General Pulteney therefore decided to push his troops on towards Bailleul and Messines before the enemy also occupied those places.

The morning of 14 October arrived with thick mist and a steady rain, which grounded all RFC patrols until the late afternoon. Autumn was now arriving in northern France and Flanders, bringing fresh problems for the troops, but cavalry patrols established that the Germans had withdrawn from Meteren and Bailleul to somewhere beyond the River Lys.

This withdrawal did not mean that the Germans had abandoned their strategic plan for a turning movement in the north; far from it. If the Anglo-French line could be turned at all the Franco-Belgian border was the place to do it. To this end the Germans had now put together a new army, the Fourth Army, which was to launch an attack between Menin and the North Sea and turn the Allied line at Ypres.

While the Fourth Army, composed of troops released by the fall of Antwerp plus four newly raised reserve corps composed of young civilian volunteers, was forming and coming up, the German forces currently on this front, the VII, XIII, XIX and Cavalry Corps of the Sixth Army, were to go on to the defensive and hold the line La Bassée–Armentières–Menin against anything the Franco-British armies could throw against it. This was the final stage of the Race to the Sea; these German corps had already checked the advance of II and III Corps but both sides were about to extend their flanks to the north and try again. The French and British hoped to attack east from Ypres before the Germans consolidated a front line running all the way from Belfort on the Swiss frontier to the North Sea.

Frank Richards recalls the creation of the Western Front by his battalion:

> We moved off at daybreak and relieved some French troops on the further side of the Belgian frontier; two days later we retired back through Fromelles and dug our trenches about four hundred yards this side of that village. Little did we think when we were digging those trenches that we were digging our future homes; but they were the beginnings of the long stretch that soon went all the way from the North Sea to Switzerland and became our homes for the next four years.[19]

This trench system was not yet a continuous line, and in many places it never became one. Richards records: 'Each platoon dug in on its own, with gaps of about forty yards between each platoon . . . We dug those trenches simply for fighting; they were breast high with the front parapet at ground level and in each bay we stood shoulder to shoulder.'[20]

For a brief moment in mid-October the advantage lay with the *Entente* powers at the northern end of the line. North of Armentières the British had Rawlinson's IV Corps, two strong, fresh regular divisions, one infantry, one cavalry, with Haig's I Corps coming up to join them, plus two French Territorial divisions and the six divisions of the Belgian Army. Estimates of enemy strength were not complete – and the existence of the Fourth Army as yet unsuspected – but they seemed to have just two corps at Ypres, the III Reserve Corps and the XIX Corps, totalling five divisions. With support from the French and Belgians, surely two BEF corps could overwhelm this German force? Perhaps, if III Corps to the south could get forward and cover their flank.

Pulteney's next task was to occupy Bailleul and beat off any German attempt at eviction, but on the night of 13/14 October word came that II Corps had been obliged to evacuate Givenchy and would appreciate some assistance. Pulteney decided that the best way to assist II Corps was by pushing on, in step with the cavalry and IV Corps, and enveloping the enemy left in front of Smith-Dorrien's troops. With French's agreement, III Corps duly advanced during the afternoon of 14 October and entered Bailleul about 1630 hours. That evening the 19th Infantry Brigade took up a position south-east of the town astride the Bailleul–Armentières road.

The next BEF task in this push to the east began on 15 October, with an advance to the line of the River Lys by Allenby's Cavalry Corps, tasked to move up to the river between Estaires and Menin. The river line was duly reached but the Germans were found to be in firm possession of the bridges. However, at 1200 hours, French held a conference with Pulteney and Allenby at Hazebrouck and ordered Pulteney to occupy Armentières, clear and if necessary repair the Lys bridges, and push on north and east, towards Lille.

Orders for this advance were issued on the afternoon of 15 October and the advance began that night when the 6th Division secured bridges over the Lys at Sailly and Bac St Maur against light opposition. Though these bridges and those as yet untaken were still under German fire, Field Marshal French issued orders for a general advance across the Lys and on to north of Lille. His orders encompassed Rawlinson's troops around Ypres, and this general BEF advance was to be supported by an attack east from Ypres by the French and Belgians. At last, or so it appeared, the Allied armies were acting in concert.

The Field Marshal had found the recent actions and advance of III Corps very gratifying. It appeared that the enemy was falling back steadily before this corps, while only three German divisions were threatening Ypres. This being so, he now intended to move east with all his power, 'attacking the enemy wherever met'.[21] With Foch supporting this move, the chances of a breakthrough in the north had never been better.

French's orders for this attack were as follows. The Cavalry Corps on the left (north) of III Corps were to cross the Lys between Armentières and Lille and screen the left flank of the advance. III Corps was to move north-east, astride the Lys, and make contact with Rawlinson's troops – now IV Corps – near Ypres. The 7th Division of IV Corps was to move east between Courtrai and Roulers, keeping ahead of III Corps but in contact with the Belgian Army; Field Marshal French was always very careful about his flanks. As for II Corps, Smith-Dorrien was directed to shift its left flank north towards III Corps, a move he was unable to make. Otherwise, the BEF advance was carried out as ordered; led by the cavalry, the BEF began to push east at 0600 hours on 16 October . . . and quickly ran into trouble.

The first problem was the ground. The Lys is a narrow, fairly shallow stream, around 15 metres (50 feet) wide and two metres (seven feet) deep. This created a barrier passable only at the bridges, which had already been destroyed by the enemy. The ground before Armentières was marshy, a mix of small fields and scattered farmhouses, cut about with dykes and streams, fences and hedges, all of which impeded the cavalry. The enemy defending this ground fell back steadily, contesting the BEF advance with artillery and machine-gun fire. The German strongpoints in houses overlooking the Lys bridges could not be reduced by the 13-pounder guns of the cavalry. This task had to wait for the arrival of III Corps' infantry, which was able to force a passage over the Lys by nightfall, but not without loss.

Rawlinson's IV Corps also made steady progress, reaching a line from Zandvoorde via Gheluvelt to Zonnebeke, two miles due east of Ypres, and on the crest of the surrounding ridge. There the 7th Division halted and began to dig in, covered by two French Territorial divisions in Ypres and Poperinge and Sir Julian Byng's 3rd Cavalry Division to the north-east of Ypres around Roulers. The German reaction to these early moves created the general impression among the British commanders that the enemy was on the defensive and would fall back farther if pushed hard.

This hopeful impression did not survive the first day. At around 1600 hours a heavy bombardment was opened on the Anglo-French lines followed by a strong infantry attack on the French positions at Dixmude, north of Ypres. This was beaten off, but

German attacks on Dixmude, a point at the junction of the French and Belgian line, continued throughout the night of 16/17 October and petered out only at dawn. Unperturbed by this hold-up, French ordered the BEF advance to continue, and by midday on 17 October III Corps had a brigade of the 4th Division in Armentières and other units of the 6th and 4th Divisions occupied a line from the Bois Grenier, south of Armentières, north to Houplines and Ploegsteert Wood, just inside the Belgian frontier. This advance brought the BEF to positions the British Army would occupy or fight over for the next four years – and which would become the graveyard of the original BEF.

October 17 was spent consolidating these positions, and by 18 October the BEF was established on a jagged line, circling Ypres to the south, east and north, with the various corps and divisions deployed as follows: II Corps was south of Ypres on a line from Givenchy to Herlies. III Corps, positioned astride the Lys, had the 6th Division screening Armentières, with the 4th Division line running north from Frelinghien to Messines. Here the Cavalry Corps took over the front between Messines and Hollebeke and held it to the east, past Zandvoorde to Kruisecke, where IV Corps took over, facing east, while, running north, the 7th Division held the line from Polygon Wood to Zonnebeke. Here Haig's newly arrived I Corps took over the front, the 2nd Division extending the line north to Langemarck, where the 1st Division of Haig's corps, currently en route from the Aisne, would take over the line as it ran north-west to link up with de Mitry's four-division-strong cavalry corps, the 84th Territorial Division and the Belgians at the Ypres Canal.

The line now occupied by the BEF ran along the low hills surrounding Ypres, a position that was later to become known as the Ypres salient. These hills, low as they are, at around 75 metres (200 feet), provided the troops holding them with a strong defensive position, good views over the ground to the east and perfect observation over the low country surrounding Ypres; whoever held the salient had the town of Ypres in their gift.

On 18 October, Field Marshal French issued orders for the

renewal of the BEF advance. II Corps were again to move on La
Bassée while III Corps were to push along the Lys and IV Corps
to capture Menin. The units of I Corps already in position at
Ypres were to hold their ground until the rest of Haig's troops
arrived, while the French and Belgians, acting in concert with the
BEF, would move on Roulers. Plotting these moves on the map, it
is clear that French was aiming to swing the Allied line east and
south, pivoting on Ypres and rolling up the German line from the
north.

There was, inevitably, a snag. To move east down the Lys valley,
III Corps had first to clear the Perenchies Ridge and secure the
village of Frelinghien, five kilometres (three miles) east of
Armentières, where there was a useful bridge. The attack by Keir's
6th Division went in at 0630 hours on 18 October and quickly ran
into stiff opposition on the Perenchies Ridge and in the nearby villages of Premesques and Perenchies. The 6th Division was held up
here by heavy fire, but by mid-morning III Corps HQ had convinced itself that there was little opposition in front of the 6th
Division and ordered Keir to push on, over the ridge to the Deule
stream, driving the enemy before him.

Keir tried; indeed he and his men kept on trying for most of the
day, without success. Losses mounted; the 2nd Yorks and
Lancaster Regiment and the 1st Buffs were held up by machine-
gun fire and counter-attacked when they went to ground, suffering 174 casualties; on their left, in the 18th Infantry Brigade, the
1st East Yorks and the 2nd Durham Light Infantry lost 175 men,
and none of these battalions had made much ground. When night
fell, the 6th Division was only two miles east of Armentières and
its right-hand battalion from the 17th Infantry Brigade, the 2nd
Leinsters, says the *Official History*, 'had got nearer to Lille than
British troops were to be for many a long day'.[22]

Meanwhile, to the left of the 6th Division, the 4th Division had
been tasked to move out of Armentières astride the Lys and capture the village of Frelinghien. This attack was led by Brigadier
General Aylmer Haldane's 10th Infantry Brigade supported by the
entire divisional artillery. This support proved useful, for it quickly

became apparent that Frelinghien was part of the main German defences west of Lille, and the Sixth Army had no intention of giving it up. As farther west, the country here was threaded with streams and dotted with barns and farmhouses, each one a German strongpoint. The leading battalions of the 10th Brigade – the 2nd Seaforths, 1st Royal Irish Fusiliers and 2nd Royal Dublin Fusiliers – soon ran into machine guns and a determined, well-entrenched enemy. With a dug-in enemy to its front and right flank, the 4th Division could make little progress; by 2000 hours on 18 October III Corps was ordered to hold any ground already gained and dig in.

Matters had not gone much better for the Cavalry Corps. The enemy defences to their front proved 'too strong and too well organized' [23] for the forces sent against them, and Rawlinson's IV Corps was equally short of success. Following GHQ's order, to 'advance on Menin', the 7th Division moved out at 0600 hours and, finding no opposition, soon reached a line three kilometres (two miles) to the east and in front of the main German positions covering Menin.

Here the 7th Division halted. General Capper somehow believed that GHQ did not intend them to advance into Menin that day, and that his division was to take up a defensive position prior to an all-out attack by IV Corps the following day. Further orders arrived at around 1400 hours, for the advance to continue into Menin, the 7th Division keeping in line with the French to their left. Unfortunately, by the time this order reached the forward units it was too late to attack again that day and the advance was put off until the following morning. The overall picture on 18 October is of the BEF attacking strongly, but making little progress.

Although the autumn days were growing shorter and the morning mist did not usually lift until around 1100 hours, RFC reconnaissance was proving its worth and providing some vital information. Some roads to the east were clear of enemy troops while others seemed to be filled with long columns of marching men, artillery and wagons, all heading west towards the front. On

the morning of 18 October, these reports suggested that a new formation, actually three divisions of the German III Reserve Corps,
was moving into position opposite the Belgians north of Ypres.
This was correct, and when these divisions were in position they
promptly launched a most determined attack on a line between
Dixmude and the sea. This attack was held off, the Belgian
defence being aided by naval gunfire from a British cruiser squadron under Admiral Hood, which shelled the German troops north
of Nieuport.

This RFC information, when combined with the stiff resistance
offered around Ypres and Armentières, seemed to suggest that the
enemy strategy was for the Sixth Army to hold around Ypres as a
pivot for another heavy attack between Dixmude and the sea, so
turning the Allied flank in the north. The newly-formed Fourth
Army, commanded by Duke Albrecht of Württemberg, consisting
of four reserve corps, would mount the attack. According to the
Official History,[24] this army was to win the war 'by successfully
closing with the enemy who was still engaged with the concentration and reorganization of his forces and by gaining Calais, the
aim and object of the 1914 campaign was to make a decisive
breakthrough against the Allied left flank from Menin to the sea'.

The second crisis of the 1914 campaign was now at hand. The
opposing armies were both attempting the same strategy, a breakthrough the enemy line followed by a turning movement to the
south. The 'revolving door' principle suggested by the Schlieffen
Plan was about to be tried again, but before it got going the Allied
and German armies would collide violently in the shell-torn
country east of Ypres.

12

Ypres

19–31 October 1914

Not Mons or the Marne but Ypres was the monument to British valour, as it was also the grave of four-fifths of the original BEF.
         Barbara Tuchman, *August 1914*, p. 425

The *British Official History* opens its account of the Battles of Ypres – and note the plural form – by admitting that 'it has been found impossible, in describing the fighting around Ypres in October and November 1914, to adhere rigidly to the limits fixed in the "Report of the Battles Nomenclature Committee"', adding that according to this report 'four battles took place simultaneously during October–November'.[1]

This statement is quite true; the engagements between La Bassée and Ypres during that period were continuous and do not fit neatly into any convenient timescale. There is a considerable amount of overlap in events, and the problem in describing these battles of La Bassée, Armentières and Messines between 10 October and 2 November, and the main Battle of Ypres which began on 19 October and is further subdivided into the battles of Langemarck, Gheluvelt and Nonne Böschen, is to avoid confusion. The solution taxes the resources and understanding of both writer and reader.

And yet it could be argued that the inherent difficulty in describing these battles merely reflects the situation on the ground at the time. The battles for Ypres *were* confusing, and those who find the situation confusing now might consider how much more confusing it must have been for the Allied generals and their subordinate commanders at the time. These men were forced to make vital decisions with only the vaguest idea of what was actually going on and very little to help them in the way of accurate information or effective communications.

Therefore, in the interests of clarity and with the inestimable benefit of hindsight, this chapter will follow up the events already described, those taking place from 10 to 18 October, and move north towards the salient to deal with events at and around Ypres during the period between 19 October and 2 November.

However, it has to be understood that the first part of this battle for Ypres was not a discrete engagement. The battle for La Bassée, Armentières, Messines and the other battles hereabouts at this time all form part of the general struggle for Ypres. All had the strategic object of turning the enemy flank – 'enemy' in this case referring to the Franco-Belgian-British forces as well as to the Germans. The first phase is accurately described in the *Official History*[2] as the Encounter Battle, which occurred when the German Fourth and Sixth Armies pushing west encountered the BEF, French and Belgians pushing east. This last point too should be noted; although this book concentrates on the BEF, the battles for Ypres were never an exclusively British affair.

Ypres is usually described as a 'cloth town' and, like most of these Flemish towns, it had indeed been a centre for the cloth trade in medieval times. By 1914 Ypres was best known for the manufacture of ribbons, lace, cotton and soap. The town had a population of some 17,000 and retained its medieval cloth hall and its strong earth ramparts and moat.

The importance of Ypres to the armies of 1914 arose from a number of factors. It was a road, rail and canal centre and the nearest large town to the North Sea coast; the port of Dunkirk was just 30 miles away. Surrounded by an encircling ridge to the north, east and south, the Ypres salient was a bastion for any force that held both the city and the ridge. To the west was the Ypres–Yser Canal, which might have provided a far better defence line. However, as related, the true importance of Ypres to the Allies, or at least to the British and Belgians, at this time and later, lay in political and emotional factors. It was the last major Belgian town still in Belgian hands; the small amount of territory between Ypres and the North Sea was all that remained of 'poor little Belgium', and the Allies were determined to hang on to it. Many of the British soldiers' comrades had died defending this place and they would not lightly give it up.

On 18 October 1914 the BEF front lay between the La Bassée Canal and the Yser Canal, just west of the village of Langemarck, eight kilometres (five miles) from the northern outskirts of Ypres. On the way north it ran east of Armentières to Messines, then turned sharply east, around the salient ridge to Zandvoorde, before turning north again across the Menin road to link up with the French cavalry divisions of de Mitry's corps at the canal and so with the Belgian divisions holding the line to the sea; in short, the BEF encircled Ypres to the east like a shield. East of the BEF line two German armies, one a new formation, the Fourth Army, in the north-east, its existence as yet unknown to the Allied command, the other the veteran Sixth Army in the south-east, the two together mustering eleven corps, were slowly converging on Ypres.

When the battles at Ypres began on 19 October the Allied forces on the northern front were disposed as follows. The French Tenth Army, under General Maud'huy, were holding the front from south of Arras to Vermelles, six kilometres (four miles) south of the La Bassée Canal. Then came Smith-Dorrien's II Corps and the Indian Corps, two French cavalry divisions of Conneau's corps and then Pulteney's III Corps. North of III Corps Allenby's Cavalry Corps held the line up to the Menin road, then the two divisions of Rawlinson's IV Corps, the 7th Division and the 3rd Cavalry Division, held the line east of Ypres with Haig's I Corps linking up with de Mitry's cavalry and two French Territorial divisions, which in turn linked up with the Belgian Army, thus completing the Allied line from Dixmude to the sea. A look at map 6 will be helpful at this point; again it should be noted that the French and Belgians also had units defending Ypres.

On 11 October, at the start of the II Corps battle for La Bassée, General Foch was appointed Commandant Groupe des Armées du Nord (GAN). This army group included the Tenth Army and all the French forces north of Arras. The British and Belgian forces were obliged to cooperate with Foch's army group but there was still no unity of command. Foch could send the French and Belgian commanders copies of his orders to French units but could only hope that his allies would support him. Usually they did so; Foch had the major force on this part of the front and the advantage of numbers dictated the strategy.

Foch's strategic plan, as noted, called for the Allied armies – French, BEF, Belgians – to advance north-eastward from the Ypres–Nieuport start line, drive the German III Reserve Corps away from the coast and break through the German line in the north. These breakthrough forces would then wheel south-east, on a line running from Menin to Ghent, before crossing the River Lys and taking the German Sixth Army in flank and rear. Unfortunately for General Foch, the German armies were working to a similar plan but heading in the opposite direction; the opposing forces were set on a collision course.

Battles do not come in handy packages, sealed at both ends. They arise from what has happened before and contribute to what follows. First Ypres started on 10 October when II Corps bumped into the Germans around La Bassée; after that the battle spread north as more Allied troops came into the line to confront the Germans farther east, and this process continued until battle was raging all along the northern front, from La Bassée to the sea. There is little evidence of a strategic plan, and when it finally developed First Ypres provided little opportunity for superior tactics or great feats of generalship. The battles around Ypres were, in the main, 'soldiers' battles', attempts to take ground, hang on to any ground occupied or recapture any ground lost, the weight of responsibility resting on battalion commanders and company officers.

Although both sides were attempting to push forward, as the battle developed the weight of these attacks came from the

German Fourth and Sixth Armies. The German armies had the most men and heavier guns but they were on the offensive, and the great lesson of the Western Front – that the balance of advantage lay with defence – was made fully apparent at Ypres, *after* the Allies were forced on to the defensive. Even so, German pressure was so strong and constant that the Allies were forced to throw in battalions and brigades wherever they were needed, simply to shore up the line; First Ypres rapidly became a battle of attrition, most costly in lives.

To understand the fighting around Ypres it is also necessary to understand the terrain. Flanders is generally thought of as flat country, seamed with waterways and drainage ditches, heavy with mud, and there is truth in this assessment. There are two significant rivers, the Lys, which runs south-west from Menin, and the Yser, which runs from Cassel to the North Sea at Nieuport; the Belgian Army's part in the battles for Ypres is known as the Battle of the Yser. Another notable feature is the Yser Canal, which runs south from Dixmude and passes just to the west of Ypres.

Flanders is not entirely flat; though most of the ridges around Ypres are low and the valleys between them shallow, some steep hills begin just to the south-west, around the town of Cassel. East of here the Mont des Cats, the Monts Rouge and Noir and steep-sided Mont Kemmel overlook the Ypres plain and offer views to the south as far as the slag heaps at Loos. Beyond Kemmel this high ground drops away to lower ridges at Messines and Wytschaete, and in turn these ridges fall away east towards the villages of Gheluvelt and Passchendaele. Ypres is best imagined as lying in the centre of a saucer; the eastern rim of this saucer is the low ridge that runs from Messines to Passchendaele.

The most significant physical factor in Flanders is the high-water table. When it rains, any undrained land floods quickly, and with most of the drainage ditches destroyed by shelling, the country around Ypres rapidly became a quagmire in the autumn months of 1914. Soldiers digging trenches struck water after a couple of feet; in many parts of the line trenching was impossible and it was necessary to build sandbagged breastworks – the snag was that at this stage in the war there were no sandbags. A lack of every kind of trench equipment – shovels, duckboards, sandbags, buckets, barbed wire and the rest – simply added to the problems the BEF faced at Ypres. Once these trenches and dugouts were excavated, they rapidly filled up with water, until the men were standing for hours or days, knee or waist deep in chilly, muddy water.

The major logistical problem, a now familiar one, was a grave shortage of artillery ammunition. On 23 October, General Sir William Robertson wrote:

> An enormous expenditure of ammunition has been expended over the last few days by the RHA and they appear to have shot, say, two or three of their guns entirely away. There has of course been a good deal of waste and a certain amount of sharp practice in units trying to pinch things in different ways but I do not think there has been any great excess of the latter although there certainly has been excessive waste. But when troops are fighting very hard one does not like to worry them about administrative matters. The chief thing is to beat the enemy and we must be lenient to some extent when fighting is taking place. I have no anxiety and never had any worth mentioning about food supplies but from the very first I have had a very great deal of anxiety with respect to ammunition.[3]

The artillery commanders' problems were also compounded by the matter of terrain. Small elevations are often important to military commanders. This is especially so in battles dominated by artillery and the Great War was, above all, an artillery war. The ridges of the Ypres salient offered artillery commanders the opportunity to direct fire on to targets on lower ground and some protection for guns and gun crews on the reverse slopes. Between 1914 and 1918 this ridge around Ypres was vital ground. Whoever held the Ypres ridge dominated Ypres and the entire salient; most of the many battles around Ypres were battles for positions on the ridge.

When the first elements of the BEF – Smith-Dorrien's II Corps – arrived south of Ypres in early October, the German forces on this front consisted of four corps of the Sixth Army. These Sixth Army units were able to hold the line and capture Lille but were unable to push west, being forced to extend and thin out their front as more Allied units came north in an attempt to outflank them. However, and with similar intent, General von Falkenhayn was forming the Fourth Army of IV Reserve Corps, which took up position east of Ypres in mid-October on a line from Menin to Nieuport, with the Sixth Army covering its left flank and the city of Lille.

The Fourth Army was supported by a large amount of artillery and augmented by III Reserve Corps of three divisions brought down from Antwerp. By early October the Sixth and Fourth Armies east and north of Ypres amounted to eleven corps and the Fourth Army was tasked with 'successfully closing with the enemy, who was still engaged in the concentration and reorganization of his forces and, by gaining Calais, [achieving] the aim and object of the 1914 campaign'.[4] While the Fourth Army was thus engaged the Sixth Army would remain on the defensive, coming gradually into the fray as the battle developed.

The Fourth Army was entirely composed of reserve formations; very few of the men in the ranks were professional soldiers. They were peasants, artisans, clerks, students, schoolboys and factory hands, with a leavening of regular soldiers, officers and senior NCOs to provide guidance, training and leadership in the field. Given their enthusiasm and such leadership – and the fact that most of the men had already completed at least two years' military service as peacetime draftees – the Fourth Army was a formidable military machine.

The Fourth Army was also fresh, and that was crucial. The bitter fighting of the past two months had strained German resources quite as much as it had those of the BEF and the French. The fighting had been hard and the marching strenuous, but both sides still cherished the belief that one more effort, one more attack, one extra ounce of energy and sacrifice – and lavish amounts of courage and artillery ammunition – could still decide the outcome of this war.

Germany was certainly not yet ready to give up those early

ambitions. Their war plan had been based on victory in six weeks; this had not been achieved, so in a final attempt to bring the war to a rapid conclusion these eager volunteers, the last human resources of the German Empire, were sent into battle against the finest professional infantry in Europe, soldiers famed for a thousand years for their stubbornness in defence.

By mid-October the Germans could count on sixteen infantry divisions and five cavalry divisions in the line around Ypres, with another five divisions marching west to join them. Of these, ten infantry divisions and five cavalry divisions from the German Sixth and Fourth Armies were about to confront the BEF east of Ypres. The BEF now mustered four corps totalling seven infantry divisions, three cavalry divisions and one division of the Indian Corps. All these divisions were severely under strength – and the BEF had no reserves at all.

On 14 October the German High Command ordered the Sixth Army to halt their drive towards Givenchy, Armentières and Menin until the Fourth Army was in position on their right, north of the Lys. That done, and with two full armies in the line, the Germans would launch a major offensive aiming to drive the British out of Ypres, back to the Channel coast and into the sea. This German offensive and the Allied push to the north-east would both begin on the same day, 19 October.

In his memoirs, Field Marshal French dates the beginning of First Ypres to 15 October and admits that:

> I thought the danger was past. I believed that the enemy had exhausted his strength in the great bid he had made to smash our armies on the Marne and capture Paris. The fine successes gained by the cavalry and III Corps did much to confirm these impressions on my mind . . . in my heart I did not expect I should have to fight a great defensive battle. All my dispositions were made with the idea of carrying out effectively the combined offensive, which was concerted between Foch and myself.[5]

It is again noticeable that tributes paid to the 'fine successes gained by the cavalry and III Corps' omit any reference to Smith-

Dorrien's II Corps, which had surely performed as well as any such force could have done at La Bassée. The second point to note is that French was now clearly willing to assist his French colleague – Foch was not Lanrezac – though he was clearly influenced by Foch's ever-constant friend at GHQ, Major-General Henry Wilson.

Callwell notes that at this time, 'Wilson was seeing Foch almost daily'[6] and experiencing considerable difficulty in persuading French to fall in with Foch's plans and arrangements. On 20 October, for example, Wilson's diary notes: 'It is a tonic to have a talk with Foch. I brought all this back to Sir John who said he would not take orders from a junior, etc., but he accepted the inevitable. He still clings to the 1st Corps going to Bruges but I don't mind this, as Bruges is for all practical purposes as far as Berlin, and tomorrow's fighting will settle that.'

Wilson's problems in convincing the Field Marshal seem to have been exaggerated. As we have seen, orders to implement Foch's plan for the coming attack between Ypres and Nieuport – to advance and 'attack the enemy where met'[7] – were issued to the BEF on the afternoon of 15 October, so the BEF's part in the First Battle of Ypres began with the movements described in the previous chapter. The only significant change in recent days was the arrival of Haig's I Corps from the Aisne; the 2nd Division moved into the line north of Langemarck and the 1st Division into positions west from Langemarck to the Yser Canal.

Thus were the forces poised when the battle of First Ypres began on 19 October. French was convinced that 'the whole enemy force north of the Lys probably does not exceed three and a half army corps'.[8] In fact it consisted of five and a half army corps, and these forces were bearing down on the BEF line like a battering ram. On 19 October this line was not a carefully prepared 'defensive position' but the 'start line' for an advance to the east, and although their forces were much larger the German plan was roughly similar. The Sixth and Fourth Armies were to crush the Allied flank at Ypres and then wheel west and south to pin the British against the Channel coast, taking the ports of Dunkirk and

Calais before pressing on to the south and rolling up the Allied line.

On 19 October, General de Mitry's cavalry, advancing to the north-east, met elements of the German Fourth Army outside Roulers, 24 kilometres (15 miles) from Ypres. On that day the German III Reserve Corps, positioned on the coast, mounted an attack against the Belgians to begin what became known as the Battle of the Yser – a battle that the Belgians won only by opening the dyke sluices and letting the sea in. This flooded Belgium from the coast to Dixmude but secured the north flank of the Allied line for the rest of the war.

On the same day Rawlinson sent the 7th Division of IV Corps down the road from Ypres towards Menin. The 7th Division got as far as the village of Gheluvelt, ten kilometres (six miles) from Menin, where it was halted by heavy artillery fire from the guns of the German Fourth Army. On the left of the 7th Division, the 3rd Cavalry Brigade reached Ledeghem and the 6th Brigade reached Passchendaele on the rim of the salient. The cavalry brigades were meeting very little opposition, for von Falkenhayn was biding his time; the more the BEF moved east, the deeper its divisions would move into his trap. Therefore, as IV Corps advanced towards Menin it created a sharp salient, or bulge, in the German defences – a bulge that von Falkenhayn intended to cut off in due course.

Up to this point neither French nor Joffre had known of the creation, let alone the presence, of the German Fourth Army. Fortunately, General de Mitry, the French cavalry commander, quickly realized that he had a new and totally unexpected German army on his front. He therefore withdrew his forces from in front of Roulers – an action that had the unfortunate effect of exposing the left flank of the British 3rd Cavalry Division to attack – and informed French's GHQ that strong German forces were moving across their front. This was when French realized that the BEF was facing not just the Sixth Army – which would have been bad enough – but the strong, fresh Fourth Army as well.

Getting accurate information was difficult. The weather on the first day of the German offensive was misty and cloudy, restricting RFC patrols. It improved the following day when intelligence was received that large enemy forces – very large enemy forces – were on the northern front and about to smash into the Allied line. RFC reports were proving exceptionally useful as the Western Front trench line began to form and cavalry patrolling gradually became impossible. The Germans were starting to move their divisions at night to avoid RFC reconnaissance, but such large troop movements could not be entirely concealed and the build-up of German forces east of Ypres was soon obvious.

Even so, Field Marshal French was still clinging stubbornly to his post-Armentières conviction that enemy opposition on his front was negligible. Haig's corps had now come into the line east of Ypres, and on 19 October French sent for the I Corps commander and gave him his orders. The enemy, said French 'cannot have more than the III Reserve Corps between Menin and Ostend so I Corps were to advance via Thourout with the object of capturing Bruges'[9] – the objective French declared to Wilson on 20 October. In fact, the enemy had five corps between Ostend and Menin. However, French continued, having taken Bruges, 'if this is proved to be feasible and successful, every endeavour must be made to turn the enemy's flank and capture Ghent'.[10]

I Corps was to pass through Ypres and move out on the line Ypres–Roulers. On reaching the top of the salient ridge, Haig could assess the situation and decide whether to attack the enemy in the north, moving towards Ostend, or north-east towards Roulers – an attempt just abandoned by the French cavalry. Haig, said French, would be supported by de Mitry's cavalry to the north and by Byng's 3rd Cavalry Division from IV Corps in the south, while the rest of the BEF – III and II Corps – were to continue pushing east if possible but always 'leaning' against the enemy line to prevent the Germans moving forces across Haig's front.

Although these orders were based on a complete failure to 'read the battle', it is possible to see that French was trying to adhere to Foch's strategic plan. The BEF's II, III, IV and Cavalry Corps would soak up the enemy opposition and hold it in place while

Haig's corps, advancing at dawn on 20 October, broke through the German line in the north and rolled it up from the flank. The fact that military circumstances on the BEF front had changed completely with the sudden appearance of the Fourth Army seems to have escaped the field marshal's notice. As related, the enemy force on this line actually consisted of some five and a half corps – eleven full divisions – of the German Fourth Army. On 20 October this army and the German Sixth Army to the south flung all their strength against the Allied line.

Commenting on this point, the *Official History* remarks that: 'The Commander-in-Chief apparently either placed no reliance on the details of the strength of the enemy gathered by his Intelligence or else he considered the new German Reserve Corps [of Fourth Army] of small account.'[11] If so the Field Marshal was gravely mistaken.

It also appears that French took far too much advice from Henry Wilson. Wilson was now little more than a GHQ mouthpiece for Foch, constantly urging the Field Marshal to comply with Foch's strategy and press on to the east, however much the growing evidence of German strength and intentions indicated the need for a defensive posture at this time. Another commander may have considered the mounting evidence of German strength on 18/19 October, calculated the enemy's probable intentions and taken a different course. Instead, Field Marshal French pressed on blindly with his plan until disaster was confronting him and about to overwhelm him.

French's Operation Order No. 39 of 20 October begins: 'The enemy today made determined attacks on the II, III and IV Corps which have been successfully repulsed. The Commander-in-Chief intends to contain the enemy with the II, III and Cavalry Corps and the 7th Division of IV Corps and to attack vigorously with the I Corps.'

In fact, the German attacks were still mounting in strength and had not been repulsed; the Field Marshal's subordinates – his corps and divisional commanders – were actually worried that these enemy attacks could not even be *contained*. Fortunately for the BEF the various corps commanders were already using their initiative, adopting defensive measures more suited to the situation and digging in to resist further attacks.

Early on 20 October, Pulteney realized that the III Corps advance at Armentières had been checked. Anticipating a violent counter-attack, he ordered his men to dig in and prepare to hold on. This counter-attack duly came in later that day when the German XIII Reserve Corps pounded the 6th Division positions with artillery and then sent in their infantry covered by heavy machine-gun fire. It was noticeable that the Germans had now become wary of British rifle fire and were advancing in short rushes, some troops moving forward while riflemen, supported by machine guns, fired on the British positions to keep the soldiers' heads down – the basic 'fire and movement' tactic of trained infantry in the advance. These German attacks continued after dark, and by dawn on 21 October Pulteney realized that his single corps was opposed by no fewer than two full corps, the XIX and XIII, of the Sixth Army attacking on a front of 19 kilometres (12 miles). After the losses of recent weeks III Corps no longer had sufficient men to hold such a front against heavy attacks.

Nor was this all; a new hazard now appeared. In addition to the chronic shortage of artillery ammunition the infantry now discovered that the cartridges they were being issued with were a fraction too large for the breeches of their rifles. While the rifles were cool this was not a problem, but as the breeches heated up the cartridge cases began to jam.

Frank Richards writes: 'One by one our rifles began to jam. In a short time mine and Smith's rifles were the only two that were firing in the whole of our platoon. Then ours were done up too: the fact was that continual rain had made the parapet very muddy and the mud had got into the rifle mechanism, which needed oiling in any case, and continual firing had heated the metal so that between one thing and another it was impossible to open and close the bolts. The same thing happened all along the battalion front.'[12]

The soldiers could not flick open the bolt to eject the spent cartridge and reload; it was necessary to kick the bolt open and feed in rounds by hand, all this compounded by a lack of rifle oil to clean and lubricate the action. With large enemy concentrations moving against their positions, this was no small snag, but somehow the infantry fire was maintained and the enemy attacks halted.

It spite of everything, the BEF soldiers put up a stout fight; the much-reduced 2nd Sherwood Foresters in the 18th Infantry Brigade, though surrounded at La Vallée on 20 October, held out all night against three enemy battalions. Only the remnant of this battalion – two officers and some sixty men – were taken prisoner at dawn, after what the *Official History* calls 'forty-eight hours of continuous fighting'.[13] The same story is told in other accounts; the British infantry battalions were being pushed back or pinned down but they were fighting hard for every metre of ground.

Allenby's Cavalry Corps was also driven back on 20 October. This was simply a matter of numbers. Allenby's two-division corps contained only around 9,000 rifles while six German cavalry divisions, plus four jäger battalions, a total of some 24,000 men, were sent in against the BEF position; Allenby's corps fell back before this onslaught and dug in that night around Ploegsteert and Messines, from where Allenby sent appeals to III Corps for assistance. III Corps and the Cavalry Corps held their positions that night under heavy German artillery fire and a succession of infantry assaults. These attacks were driven off with casualties but a number of BEF positions were lost on the 6th Division front, and although the cavalry managed to hold the village of Messines, the château at Hollebeke, just to the north-east, was captured.

Rawlinson's IV Corps was effectively acting as the right-flank guard of Haig's I Corps in Ypres, the 7th Division holding positions on the Menin road while Haig's corps came up on their left flank. Major-General Capper's 7th Division then pushed strong infantry patrols up to Gheluvelt and towards Menin, followed by elements of two infantry brigades supported by armoured cars – the latter introducing a new element into this war. Strong German forces were then encountered and the left flank of the 7th Division was obliged to withdraw to positions *behind* those it had occupied the previous day. None of this frantic activity along the line seems to accord with French's assessment of the situation, but on 20 October Haig was still intent on obeying the instructions contained in French's Army Operation Order No. 39 of 20 October: 'to march in the direction of Thourout using the road Ypres–Passchendaele and roads to the north. This Corps will attack the enemy wherever met.'

Given that the enemy were now advancing towards Ypres, this meeting was not long delayed. By the evening of 20 October no real progress had been made by the BEF units, and although German attacks so far had been driven off, pressure was mounting all along the line. So begins the first day of the 'Battles' of Messines and Langemarck, which the *Official History*[14] dates to 21 October.

At the northern end of the BEF line the 2nd Division of Haig's corps crossed the Zonnebeke–Langemarck road, six kilometres (four miles) east of Ypres, and promptly ran into plunging artillery fire followed by an infantry attack from no fewer than five German divisions. The 2nd Division observed a large body of German infantry from the 52nd Reserve Division moving on their front; for once the British were able to stop the German infantry with artillery rather than rifle fire. One Royal Field Artillery battery of six guns fired no fewer than 1,400 shells on 21 October, but this abundance of shells would not last.

Those German soldiers who survived the shelling were stopped in their tracks by more rapid BEF rifle fire, which quickly carpeted the ground with German dead, but the pressure of enemy numbers then brought the 2nd Division advance to a halt. That evening the 2nd Division was forced to entrench around Zonnebeke, having made little or no progress during the day. The 1st Division also met stiff resistance from the outset but pressed on, and had managed to advance about a kilometre (half a mile) before it too was halted between Poelcappelle and Koekuit.

Farther south, at Armentières, III Corps, tasked to hold its positions as a pivot for I Corps, was heavily shelled, and the 12th Infantry Brigade was forced out of its forward positions at La

Gheer when the enemy renewed the attacks of the previous day. The La Gheer position was retaken by the evening, but not without cost; the 12th Brigade lost 468 officers and men in the fight for La Gheer on 21 October – and the battle was just starting. Meanwhile, at Messines, the Cavalry Corps had spent a day on the defensive, unable to reoccupy the ground lost the previous day in the face of strong attacks by superior enemy forces

Overall, the results of this first day were mixed; the German Fourth Army had suffered severe losses and had been halted but the position of Haig's corps between Zonnebeke and Langemarck was not secure – and became even less secure when de Mitry's cavalry on their left was observed withdrawing towards the Belgian positions along the Yser.

General de Mitry's action that day was yet another example of the chronic problems caused on the Western Front by a divided Allied command. If a French – or Belgian or British – general wanted to withdraw or was ordered to do so by his superior officer, the situation thus created for formations on their flanks was considered of no importance. Fortunately for General Haig, the commander of the French cavalry division to the left of I Corps realized that if he moved his troops a great gap would appear in the Allied line; he therefore elected to stay in position until again ordered to withdraw at dusk. This brief delay gave Haig time assess the situation and issue fresh orders and, like the IV and III Corps commanders to the south, he ordered both his divisions to stop attacking and dig in. I Corps had lost 932 men that day, and the German attacks showed no sign of diminishing.

The BEF – seven and a half infantry divisions – and five French and British cavalry divisions, all fighting as infantry and much reduced in numbers, were now holding a front of some 56 kilometres (35 miles) against eleven German infantry divisions and eight German cavalry divisions backed by a quantity of heavy artillery and well supplied with machine guns. Rather more to the point, the Foch–French plan had stalled and the British and French advance had been halted. In the face of strong enemy attacks, the corps commanders were now digging in, though Field Marshal

French was still convinced that the enemy 'is vigorously playing his last card and I am convinced that he will fail'.[15]

Fortunately, in spite of these misconceptions, reason was at last beginning to prevail, even at GHQ. The heavy fighting and losses of 20/21 October had at last persuaded French that his troops should halt at least until the German reaction had been 'contained'. An order was issued at 2030 hours on 21 October, placing the BEF on the defensive; the troops now had to dig trenches and prepare to hold on to them against whatever force the Germans could bring up. Joffre visited French that day and assured him that the French IX Corps would be sent up to Ypres in support, an essential step since the BEF had no reserves of any kind. Until IX Corps arrived, the only help available to the hard-pressed BEF would come from the Lahore Division of the Indian Corps, which was now detraining near Hazebrouck.

Joffre's offer of help was encouraging, but there was now another problem: artillery support. On the evening of 21 October the BEF had only ninety-three heavy guns (60-pounders, 4.7-inch and 6-inch guns and 9.2-inch howitzers) in France, of which fifty-four were deployed along that 56-kilometre (35-mile) front at Ypres. This in itself was not nearly enough for adequate support, but the real problem was a shortage of ammunition.

As these battles at Ypres progressed, limits were placed on ammunition expenditure until the batteries still in action were restricted to firing one shell every half-hour or eight shells per gun per day; some batteries were withdrawn from the line as there was no ammunition for the guns at all. Urgent requests for more ammunition sent to the UK by GHQ were regarded as unrealistic or simply ridiculous; one artillery general was bluntly informed that 'no army or nation could maintain supply at the rate asked for.'[16] It was becoming ever more obvious that the defence of Ypres would depend almost entirely on the infantry.

At 2030 hours on 21 October, a somewhat ambivalent order was issued from GHQ: 'Action against the enemy will be continued on general line now held, which will be strongly entrenched.' Quite apart from the contradictory nature of this order, exactly how the line could be 'strongly entrenched' without the necessary tools or equipment was not explained. The British defences at Ypres were now 'at best short, disconnected lengths of trenches, three feet deep; there was no wire, no dugouts, no communication trenches and no time to construct anything in the nature of a second defence line'.[17] The British and French soldiers were excavating their shallow trenches with bayonets, sharpened stakes, spades looted from farmhouses, and their bare hands.

The British defence therefore depended on the guns of the field artillery and the rifles of the infantry when the German attacks began again soon after dawn on 22 October. These attacks were concentrated on a north–south line between Messines and Bixschoote, just east of Ypres, though the Sixth Army kept battering north of La Bassée in the south and the Fourth Army pounded the Belgians and French along the Yser Canal.

The German tactic was simple: keep pushing forward, keep probing the Allied line for a weak spot, keep battering until something gave way. The fighting at Ypres went on for a full month, the longest battle yet in this expanding war. Attack and counter-attack succeeded each other and losses mounted steadily, but the fighting neither stopped nor diminished in ferocity. The Germans were always probing for that weak spot; the Allies continued doggedly keeping them out.

Among all this general action there were certain significant events. The Germans launched attacks at Langemarck on 22 October because this was the junction of the 2nd Division and the 1st Division, but any hope that the line would crack wide open here soon ended. Heavy fire from both divisions was brought down on the German infantry floundering across the muddy fields until their dead were piled up two and three deep before the British trenches.

If the German infantry suffered from British bullets, the British endured a hurricane of German shells. The Germans were also using up artillery ammunition at a furious rate, raining shells down continuously on the British outposts, taking a heavy toll of the infantrymen crouching in their shallow trenches – trenches that could not be made deeper because they then filled with water. Under this steel deluge the trench line, such as it was, began to disintegrate. 'The troops must be imagined as fighting in small groups scattered along the front in shallow trenches, often separated by gaps amounting to two, three or even four hundred yards.'[18] The trench line at Ypres was not continuous. During daylight the gaps between these trench positions could be covered by fire, but at night they could be penetrated by enemy patrols.

The German attacks on 22 October did not seriously damage the British line – somehow the ragged men in these muddy rifle pits contrived to hang on – but German attacks on the Yser just to the north forced the Belgians to withdraw to the west side of the Yser Canal. The divisions of IX Corps promised by Joffre were now coming into the salient, but the 17th Division, the first unit of IX Corps, did not take over the front of Haig's 2nd Division until the evening of 23 October.

Nor was Foch willing to accept that the Allied advance had been stopped or that Ypres was seriously threatened. With IX Corps up in the line, he now ordered that the attack to the east should be resumed. His resolve clearly had a tonic effect on Field Marshal French, who, on 23 October, had told Kitchener that 'the enemy are vigorously playing their last card' and the following day assured the Secretary of State that the current battle was 'practically won'. There is no evidence to support either claim; though enemy losses were high and mounting, their divisions were continuing to press forward.

German attacks on 22 October again concentrated on the Langemarck position, a small salient in the BEF line. On that misty morning the German infantry, advancing in solid clumps and silhouetted against the eastern sky, provided a wonderful target for professional riflemen. Some British soldiers later claimed that they fired 500 rounds that day, firing until their rifles were too hot to handle. October 22 was the day that German histories have come to call the *Kindermorde* – the Slaughter of the Innocents – of Langemarck. These German units were composed largely of volunteers, many of them students with little military training and no experience, who advanced on the British line with arms linked, singing. The *British Official History* account[19] of what happened to the German infantry before the rifles of the 2nd Green Howards, 2nd Royal Scots Fusiliers and 2nd Wiltshires makes grim reading:

> Struck by gun and machine-gun fire as soon as they came well into sight, the German masses staggered . . . their dead and wounded were literally piled up in heaps . . .
>
> Led by their officers, however, some still struggled on; a few got within two hundred yards of the Wiltshires and others actually penetrated a gap between the Green Howards and the Scots Fusiliers, only to meet their fate at the hands of a reserve company.
>
> The 54th Reserve Division, for to this the attackers appear to have belonged, recoiled; but after a pause, made one last effort against the flanks of the Wiltshires, again to be driven back by shrapnel and rifle fire.

These attacks on the BEF line continued all day until the fields before the British line were carpeted with dead or wounded men, some crawling to the rear, those unable to move crying out for help or for their mothers. The vast German cemetery at Langemarck, where most of these dead now lie, is still a place of pilgrimage for Germany.

The German attacks were not simply concentrated on I Corps at Langemarck. The 7th Division was heavily engaged farther south and kept under artillery fire throughout the night of 23/24 October, followed up by an even heavier bombardment at dawn and an infantry attack. This came from units of the German XXVII Reserve Corps, which was making a desperate effort to breach the BEF line at Polygon Wood, a position north-west of Hooge and just inside the British line.

This attack was at first successful. Three battalions of the German 244 Infantry Regiment overran the 2nd Wiltshires, killing or capturing 450 men; only 174 of the 2nd Wiltshires answered the battalion roll-call on 25 October. The German advance through Polygon Wood was then checked by the divisional reserve, the

Northumberland Hussars – a Territorial unit and the first to be seriously engaged – and the 2nd Warwickshires. The latter battalion lost almost 300 men, including their CO, in this engagement, but Polygon Wood was eventually cleared and the enemy hunted back to their own lines at the point of the bayonet.

The critical point of this battle was now coming. The British were fully determined to hang on to Ypres and would not be driven out; as at Polygon Wood, attack was met with counter-attack. Even Field Marshal French's ever-volatile nature was in one of its up-swings; on 23 October he issued an Order of the Day, congratulating his troops on their endurance, 'and reminding the troops that the enemy must before long withdraw troops to the east and relieve the tension on our front'.

Some relief or reinforcement was urgently required, but where was it to come from? The 8th Division, composed of regulars brought back from far flung garrisons, would not disembark in France for another two weeks, and the trickle of men reaching the front-line units was not sufficient to make up for the steady flow of losses. The 7th Division of IV Corps, which was not one of the most heavily engaged formations – the most losses in 1914 were incurred by the 3rd Division of II Corps – had already lost 45 per cent of its officers and 37 per cent of its men. A large number of rifle battalions had already been gravely reduced; the 2nd Scots Guards, the 1st Royal Welch Fusiliers and the 1st South Staffs, three battalions from 7th Division brigades, had already lost over 500 men apiece, more than 50 per cent of their strength. These losses are worse than they appear for they were concentrated among the rifle companies, among the 'fighting men' of the battalions; as the 'fighting men' were killed off, so the BEF line began to weaken.

This shortage of manpower was now acute and could not yet be eased; the Territorial units had to volunteer for overseas service, and though many did so, Territorial battalions were only now arriving in the field. The infantry brigadiers in the BEF were having to fight with battalions mustering a couple of companies, the divisional generals with brigades at half-strength – while the supporting artillery faced a shortage of ammunition and no signs of an increase in supply.

On the other hand, the German armies had also lost a great number of men and the British and their allies at Ypres were now fighting a largely defensive battle; this gave them a useful tactical advantage in what was rapidly becoming a battle of attrition. As with the Allied attack on 18 October, the German offensive had been held – just – and on 25 October French telegraphed Kitchener that the situation was 'growing more favourable by the hour', concluding on 27 October that it was 'only necessary to press the enemy hard in order to achieve complete success and victory'.

This belief was all French needed to order his offensive to continue. Unfortunately, the enemy was still present in great strength across his front and there was still that shortage of artillery ammunition. On the day he ordered a renewal of his attack, French warned Kitchener that unless fresh supplies of shells were soon available 'the troops will be compelled to fight without the support of artillery'.

This was the situation when Field Marshal French decided to renew the offensive. On the night of 24/25 October, the BEF held the southern half of the Ypres salient with the 17th, 18th and 87th Divisions of the French IX Corps holding the northern half and the Belgian Army continuing the French line to the North Sea. The dividing point between the French and British units was at the villages of Broodseinde and Zonnebeke, on the eastern edge of the salient.

French's Operation Order No. 40, issued on 24 October, required the Ist, IVth and Cavalry Corps to advance east in support of the French while II, III and the Indian Corps contained the enemy to their front from Messines to Neuve Chapelle. In this order, French directed that the three corps should 'dress by the left' or stay in line with the forces to the north – a repeat of his action on the Marne. This order naturally produced a similar result. Haig's advance was constrained by the progress made by the French IX Corps, while the IV Corps to his right had to wait for Haig's battalions to get forward . . . and so it continued to the Lys.

The assumption was that the French on the left flank would set the pace. Whatever happened elsewhere, no matter which units got forward or were checked, the BEF units must conform to the pace of the French on their left flank. In making this decision the Field Marshal threw away the potential to take advantage of any opportunities, should they occur – unless the left flank did indeed forge ahead. No one could tell what would actually happen before the battle started, but if any of the advancing corps could force a breach in the German line, such a breach should be exploited. As it was, the troops were compromised before their attack even began.

This being so, the situation of the BEF on this northern part of the front on 27/28 October can be described in one word: stalemate. Although orders for the French IX Corps advance remained in place and were repeated on both days, this corps, now reinforced by the 31st Division, failed to get forward at all, and this situation did not change over the next six days. Defence still dominated the battlefield and, as the *Official History* points out,[20] if the Germans with all their superiority in guns and numbers were unable to sweep I Corps out of the way, it was hardly surprising that these Allied divisions, three French, three British, three cavalry, without heavy artillery, were unable to make any progress either.

This was not for want of trying. At dawn on 27 October, IX Corps tried hard to advance but were met with a hail of enfilade machine-gun fire from the high ground around Passchendaele and were quickly brought to a halt. This in turn inhibited the action of the British 2nd Division on the French right; this formation pressed on to the bottom of the slope leading to Passchendaele before being halted, having lost almost 300 officers and men for no significant gain. On the 1st Division front, no progress was made either, but forward patrols and RFC contact patrols reported large German formations – the first of a new German striking force, Army Group Fabeck – massing across the Menin road east of Gheluvelt.

The Germans were about to renew their attack here in the north because with the battle south of the Lys petering out they now had troops to spare. The Indian Corps had taken over from the battered II Corps around Neuve Chapelle on the night of 29/30 October; the battered village had been captured by the Germans on 27 October and the BEF line redrawn on the western outskirts. By the time it ended the three-week Battle of La Bassée had cost Smith-Dorrien's much-reduced corps another 14,000 casualties; for a while Smith-Dorrien found himself without a command, but the line was still being held.

Pulteney's III Corps, battling around Armentières, were outnumbered and under unceasing attack, but here again the line held and the Battle of Armentières ended – at least officially – on 2 November. Allenby's Cavalry Corps also managed to hang on at Messines, on the southern side of the Ypres salient, so Field Marshal French had some reason to believe that this new attack from the salient would be successful.

Unfortunately for the Field Marshal, with the pressure off their line south of the Lys, the enemy were also preparing to mount a major effort farther north, a surge down the Menin road to Gheluvelt and so into Ypres. French remained ignorant of this pending assault, believing, as he said in a cable to Kitchener on 27 October, that the enemy had suffered such losses in recent weeks that they were now 'quite incapable of making any strong or sustained attack'. Three days later the enemy put in just such an attack, down the Menin road to Gheluvelt, a thrust that quickly endangered the entire British line in front of Ypres.

Von Falkenhayn was handling his two armies at Ypres with considerable skill, defending with part of his force while attacking with the other, transferring his efforts up and down the Allied line, always probing for that weak spot. It has been argued that the German armies should have attacked all along the Allied line, all the time, until something gave way, but artillery – and artillery ammunition – was the key to success on the Western Front, now and later, and like their opponents the Germans were now very short of artillery ammunition. However, by alternating their attacks the German commanders could use the artillery of both armies to support whichever army was attacking, hence those crushing bombardments that battered the Allied defences and caused such casualties to the defenders of Ypres.

This alternating strategy did not mean that the front before the holding force became quiet; attack and counter-attack continued all along the line. It was necessary for von Falkenhayn to keep up the pressure everywhere to prevent any transfer of Allied forces to the point of attack, a sound strategy that made the best use of existing resources but rapidly led to exhaustion among the troops at the front.

Unfortunately for General von Falkenhayn, there was a snag with this sensible strategy, and a simple one: it did not work. The attacks and counter-attacks of recent days had caused great losses to both sides, but after several days of hard fighting and constant pressure the Fourth and Sixth Armies had not achieved a break-through. The opposing lines held – with small advances to and fro – while the fighting continued and the losses mounted. Clearly, a breakthrough would require more men, more guns and units not yet shattered by weeks of battle.

Therefore, on 27 October, Von Falkenhayn decided to form a *third* army or army group before renewing the offensive. This would consist of three corps, six divisions in all, under General von Fabeck, who was currently commanding the German XIII Corps. Fabeck was also given a cavalry corps and a further six unbrigaded battalions of infantry, plus a quantity of artillery, over 250 heavy guns in all.[21]

This force, 'Army Group Fabeck', was deployed between the inner flanks of the Fourth and Sixth Armies. All three armies were tasked with pushing a way through the vital Messines–Wytschaete ridge and so on to the Gheluvelt plateau, cracking the front before Ypres. This attack was set for 30 October. The striking force would consist of the right and centre of Sixth Army, the whole of Fourth Army, and Army Group Fabeck. To keep the British on their toes while Fabeck's men were mustering, two German army corps and a Bavarian reserve division would launch a fresh attack on Gheluvelt on 29 October.

While the Germans seemed ever able to form more armies and find more men, Field Marshal French had no more units available – indeed, some BEF units now had to be temporarily disbanded. On 27 October French decided to place the 7th Division under Haig, so raising his corps to three much-depleted divisions, while Lieutenant-General Rawlinson returned to England to take command of the 8th Division; the 8th would eventually join the 7th Division to form a new IV Corps. In the meantime, the 7th Division went to reinforce I Corps and the 3rd Cavalry Division went to the much-depleted Cavalry Corps. Haig placed the 7th Division astride the Menin road, and it was moving in there when GHQ telephoned Haig with the news that they had intercepted a German wireless message ordering the XXVII Reserve Corps of Fourth Army to attack down the Menin road towards Gheluvelt on 29 October. The final phase of First Ypres was about to begin.

13

Gheluvelt

29–31 October 1914

The general situation in Flanders on the night of the 30th/31st October was disquieting. The BEF had been continuously fighting for ten days; it had suffered heavy losses; its reserves were exhausted . . .

British Official History, 1914, Vol. II, p. 299

In the long and glorious history of the British Army, few engagements have displayed the qualities of that army so clearly as the Battle of First Ypres. The BEF were not unsupported and due credit must be given to the French and Belgian units involved in this battle, but the ragged, hungry, professional soldiers of the BEF were the keystone of the arch defending Ypres; had they given in, had those scanty battalions failed to hold ground in the face of repeated attacks, the Yprcs position could not have been held.

To follow the battles around Ypres in the last months of 1914, the various stages need to be kept under constant review. The Race to the Sea became a race only towards the end, as the opposing armies drew nearer and nearer to the finishing tape on the North Sea coast. Then, instead of a series of flanking attacks – with those on the Allied side 'always twenty-four hours and an army corps behind the enemy' – the race became an attempt by both sides to muster sufficient forces at the northern end of the line to achieve a breakthrough.

This last stage took some time to develop. The Ypres battles at La Bassée and Armentières in early October can be presented as parts of the flanking attack process, largely because neither II Corps nor III Corps had the strength for a breakthrough. The battle for Messines, which followed, bridges the gap between these two strategies. Although all the engagements north of Béthune from 10 October form part of what became known as First Ypres, the turning point of that battle took place in the salient after Army Group Fabeck entered the fray on 29 October and struck out for Ypres down the axis of the Menin road.

The previous chapters have described the development of the battles for Ypres. The overall effect of these engagements was stalemate on both sides, but the Germans were strong and growing stronger every day, and now had three armies in the field – the Sixth, the Fourth and Army Group Fabeck. By 29 October they had succeeded in stopping the Allied advance everywhere and driving it back in several places, but they had not curbed Foch and French's enthusiasm for a breakthrough.

In accordance with Field Marshal French's orders, issued at 2015 hours on 28 October, Douglas Haig ordered the 2nd Division to push east soon after dawn, its attack being fully developed no later than 0930 hours. He also advised the I Corps divisions – which now included the 7th Division – that a strong German attack was expected to develop down the axis of the Menin–Gheluvelt road from 0530 hours, and all units were to be on the alert. Within the context of his orders, General Haig was behaving sensibly, sending the 2nd Division forward as directed but putting his entire corps on stand-by to fend off an enemy attack when it came.

It came, as expected, promptly at 0530 hours, when artillery fire began to fall on the BEF's positions on the Menin road. This deluge of shells was followed by a strong infantry attack from three battalions of the 16th Bavarian Reserve Regiment from the 6th Bavarian Division, which struck the junction of the 1st and 7th Divisions, held by the 1st (Guards) Brigade of the 1st Division and the 1st Battalion, Grenadier Guards of the 7th Division, both astride the Menin road.

None of these units was up to strength; the 1st Coldstream in the Guards Brigade had only 350 men, just over a third of its ration strength, and all the others were well below their establishment. Nevertheless, they stood their ground and greeted the enemy with rifle and machine gun fire. The problem was that their rifles and machine guns jammed, their trenches were little more than shell-scrapes, there was no wire, and not enough Guardsmen to hold this length of front. Nor did the British infantry enjoy a clear field of fire; the Great War image of an open, shattered landscape, totally devoid of life, had yet to become reality here. The Menin road was still lined with trees, houses and barns, the fields surrounded by thick hedges and deep ditches; all this offered cover for the German advance and restricted the fire of the British infantry.

As a result the enemy, pressing home their attack with considerable resolution, was able to break through, overrunning the trenches of the 1st Black Watch and the 1st Coldstream, then rolling up the defending battalions from the flank, pushing the survivors of the Coldstream and the Black Watch out of their trenches.

News of this breakthrough took time to get back to Brigade HQ – that chronic lack of communications again taking effect – but when he understood the situation, Brigadier General C. FitzClarence sent the 1st Battalion, The Gloucester Regiment forward to oppose the enemy advance and retake the positions near the Gheluvelt crossroads. The Gloucesters duly pressed forward, suffering heavy losses – by the end of the day this battalion had lost 167 men – but retaking the ground lost before they too were first held and then pressed back by the German advance.

At about the same time, the 1st Grenadiers of the 7th Division, positioned south of the crossroads and unaware of what was happening a few hundred yards away, were also being subjected to heavy artillery fire followed by an infantry attack, which came in through the drifting fog at around 0800 hours. This battalion was also taken in the rear by Germans who had broken through to the north and was gradually driven back, making counter-attacks to delay the enemy advance and finally taking up a position south of

the road and east of Gheluvelt, where they were joined during the
day by the survivors of the 1st Gloucesters and a fresh battalion,
the 2nd Border Regiment, sent up from brigade reserve.

Heavy fighting for the Gheluvelt position went on all day but
that mutual support and interlocking fire, so essential for defence,
was limited by the thick woods and the persistent fog. In some
respects, though, the weather and the terrain favoured defence,
providing good cover for the rifle platoons while concealing an
almost total absence of BEF reserves from the enemy. The outcome was that the conflict around Gheluvelt dissolved into a large
number of small, separate company or battalion battles where the
enemy's superior numbers gradually began to tell as British losses
mounted. These losses were severe; the 1st Grenadiers, the left-
hand battalion of the 7th Division, lost 470 men that day, two-
thirds of its parade strength that morning, and the 1st Scots
Guards lost 344. The already under-strength 1st Coldstream lost
another ten officers and 180 men, and on the night of 29 October,
'mustered only 80 men under the Quartermaster'.[1] The 1st Black
Watch lost five officers and 250 men, two companies being 'annihilated'.[2] German losses were also high; some 240 German dead
were counted in front of the trenches stoutly held by the 2nd
Gordon Highlanders.

All in all, the battle for Gheluvelt on 29 October did not go well
for Haig's command. By dusk, and in spite of putting in a strong
counter-attack with the 3rd Infantry Brigade, his corps had lost
460 metres (500 yards) of trench, the vital Gheluvelt crossroads and
the best part of three regular infantry battalions, 1st Coldstream,
1st Grenadiers and 1st Black Watch, either cut to pieces by shellfire or during hand-to-hand fighting in the foggy woodlands. Nor
was the battle for Ypres going well elsewhere. The advance of
General Dubois' three French divisions north of Ypres had been
held by German troops that 'were numerically strong and well
entrenched and whose heavy artillery becomes day by day unceas-
ingly stronger'.[3]

The fact that this new Allied advance had been halted so
quickly did not bother Field Marshal French; indeed, he seems

unaware of the true situation. In his memoirs[4] he records that by the evening of 29 October I Corps had 'recovered all the ground they had lost' and were occupying a line 'well to the east of Gheluvelt [which] consequently represented a considerable gain as compared to the ground held the day before'.

Were this so, one might ask why that evening he issued orders for any ground lost to be retaken and for the advance to continue the following day, cabling Kitchener that: 'If the present success can be followed up it will lead to a decisive result' and that 'slow but decided success is being made everywhere'.[5] In fact none of this was true.

I Corps had been halted or driven back, many men had been lost and the Germans had been able to improve their positions by taking the spur of land between Kruisecke and Gheluvelt, which offered both higher ground for the artillery observers and the perfect, concealed forming-up position for another infantry attack. Guns from behind this ridge were soon bombarding Ypres and pounding traffic on the Menin road. The *Official History* records that 'On the morning of 30th October the Allied commanders in the north were still totally unaware of the massing of important enemy reinforcements opposite, strategically, the most important and, tactically, the weakest portion of the line near Ypres. The night of 29/30 had been fairly quiet; the troops reported the sound of an unusual number of vehicles and trotting horses, but the direction of the movement could not be ascertained with any certainty.'[6]

While claiming success and ordering another advance on 30 October, French also claimed that more troops would be needed ensure this 'success'. He therefore decided to take the much-reduced II Corps out of the line at Béthune and send it north, but this could not be done until the II Corps position was secure and given into the care of the Indian Corps on the night of 29/30 October. The only troops available to reinforce I Corps or the Cavalry Corps at Ypres on the evening of 29 October were a Territorial unit, the 1st Battalion, The London Scottish, which arrived at Ypres that night. The London Scottish was the sole BEF reserve when the second phase of the German thrust began, an attack on the I Corps front by four and a half infantry divisions, three cavalry divisions and a jäger brigade of Army Group Fabeck supported by 260 heavy and super-heavy guns. This attack began at 0600 hours on 30 October.

General Haig's view of the situation on his front was considerably more cautious than that of Field Marshal French. Haig received and noted the GHQ order to resume the advance on 30 October but did not distribute it to his subordinates. Instead he ordered his three divisions to entrench on favourable ground, reorganize, improve their defences if possible – the 2nd Division were even able to string a little barbed wire – and carry out an active reconnaissance at daylight. Haig added that 'orders as to the resumption of the offensive will be issued in the morning, when the situation is clearer than it is at present'. This reconnaissance revealed an unusual amount of activity behind the enemy lines but the precise point or direction of this activity could not at first be determined – but there was plenty of it and it boded ill for any prospect of a further advance.

The situation became clear soon after dawn when von Fabeck's main thrust was delivered between Messines and Hollebeke and came up against the 7th Division, the three cavalry divisions of the Cavalry Corps – these three worth perhaps two infantry brigades in firepower – and two Indian infantry battalions.

This attack by the XIII and XV Army Corps, backed by most of the Fabeck artillery, should have breached the British defences with comparative ease. There was no deep or continuous trench line on this front, a shortage of men, very little barbed wire, and no heavy artillery to support the tired defenders; as the *Official History* comments, 'the British line was already all too thin'.[7] This fundamental fact, a shortage of troops, dictated much of Haig's policy in this battle; his line was too thin when the battle began and reserves were non-existent. His solution was to rest his units where possible and feed them into the line where needed, 'putting-up the front' in the jargon of the time, hoping thereby to beat off any local attacks and keep the enemy out.

The German tactics were a repeat of the previous day; a heavy artillery bombardment followed by infantry attacks, pressed home with considerable courage but a lack of tactical skill or field-craft. The Germans were determined to break the BEF line that day; orders for XV Corps attacking Haig's corps stressing that 'The breakthrough will be of decisive importance. We must and will therefore conquer, settle forever the centuries-long struggle against our most detested enemy. We will finish with the British, Indian, Canadians, Moroccans and other trash, feeble adversaries who surrender in great numbers if they are attacked with vigour.'

This order called for an attack all along the line but stressed that the main thrust would be made by Fabeck's group south-east of Ypres, aiming a five-division thrust at the village of Zandvoorde and the Messines ridge. This was held by the 7th Division and three cavalry divisions; a breakthrough here would – or might – carry the Germans through to the heights around Mont Kemmel and split the BEF line in two. With this intention, the German soldiers hurled themselves forward against the Allied line, relying on their heavy artillery and superiority in infantry of three to one – or more – to carry them through to victory.

In the face of this second onslaught all the BEF soldiers could do was hang on, hold their ground and flay the enemy with rifle fire while Haig and his commanders threw in a company here or a battalion there, wherever the line looked fragile, to hold back the German advance. The first German attack against the 1st and 2nd Divisions on the left at Zonnebeke did not succeed. This attack was made against another unit junction, this time between the 2nd Division and the French 135th Infantry Regiment, by two German divisions, the 54th Reserve and the 30th Division. It began at 0630 hours and went on until after 0900 hours, the British infantry shooting down the advancing German infantry in great numbers.

German pressure then built up around Zandvoorde at the southern end of the 1st Division line, again at the divisional junction with the French brigade of Brigadier General Moussy. Infantry attacks continued and artillery fire began to fell trees, flatten the inadequate British defences and cause heavy casualties. By midday this artillery fire had helped the German infantry into Zandvoorde, where they evicted the 1st and 2nd Life Guards of the 7th Cavalry Brigade; two squadrons of the Life Guards were virtually wiped out during a massed attack by the 39th Division and three jäger battalions, only a few wounded troopers surviving to fall into enemy hands.

An immediate counter-attack on Zandvoorde at 1300 hours by the 7th Division and 3rd Cavalry Division failed. By 1500 hours Haig feared that the enemy were on the Zandvoorde ridge and about to break through south of Ypres, where the Cavalry Corps were also in difficulties. He therefore asked the French on his left flank for assistance, pointing out that if the Germans succeeded in breaking through south of Ypres they could cut the Allied line in two. General Dubois reacted promptly, sending his IX Corps reserve of two battalions up to Zandvoorde. Other units also sent forces to Haig's assistance, General Allenby placing three cavalry regiments at I Corps' disposal. Nothing was of any avail; by midday Zandvoorde was in enemy hands and the 1st Royal Welch Fusiliers, dug in just to the north of the village, were under flanking attack and artillery fire; fighting hard but eventually overrun, this battalion was reduced to eighty-six men at the evening roll-call.

Attempts to retake Zandvoorde continued all day, but numbers would tell. By the time the German attacks south of Ypres petered out in the late afternoon of 30 October the Germans had taken Hollebeke, the Hollebeke château, Zandvoorde and much of the Zandvoorde ridge, and had forced the British centre back for more than a mile between Messines and Gheluvelt. The loss of Hollebeke also put the Germans within five kilometres (three miles) of Ypres, three kilometres closer than they had been on 28 October. Heavy casualties had been inflicted on the 7th Division and I Corps' grip on the line east of Ypres was growing increasingly loose.

On the other hand, the Germans had lost heavily, and as the day wore on their infantry became less inclined to press home their attacks. The 7th Division and the 3rd Cavalry Division, repulsed from Zandvoorde that afternoon, were now preparing a new defence line west of the Zandvoorde ridge and were already stemming any attacks across it. With reinforcement, this new line could be held . . . provided some reinforcements could be found.

The attacks against I Corps around Gheluvelt were matched with a strong thrust against the 1st Cavalry Division of Allenby's corps at Messines. This was launched by the 26th Division of XIII Corps and followed a now familiar pattern – drenching artillery fire from heavy guns followed by massed infantry attacks. The shelling and infantry probes went on all day but the British cavalry held their ground and seemed ready to go on doing so whatever force was sent against them.

The crucial point now was Zandvoorde and the Zandvoorde ridge, both of which had to be retaken or the line there shored up to prevent the enemy gaining more ground. That night Field Marshal French, who was still apparently unaware of the forces to his front, visited I Corps HQ and, having been briefed on the situation by Haig, sent a message to Foch asking for more French troops as soon as possible. Foch promised to send five infantry battalions and three artillery batteries into Ypres the following day.[8]

Haig had now established his HQ in the White Chateau at the Hellfire Corner crossroads, just east of Ypres and three kilometres (two miles) behind the front line. I Corps spent that night establishing a new defence line from the Ypres Canal at Hollebeke north to a point just east of Gheluvelt, forming the last viable defensive position in front of Ypres. Plans were also laid for a dawn counter-attack to retake Hollebeke and Zandvoorde by a force of six battalions under Major-General Bulfin (and therefore known as Bulfin's Force) – the 1st and 2nd Cavalry Divisions and three French battalions. Unfortunately, while this work was in progress, the Germans struck again at the village and ridge of Messines, eight kilometres (five miles) south of Zandvoorde.

At 2200 hours on 30 October, a heavy artillery barrage fell on Messines. A strong attack was clearly coming in at dawn, if not before, and Haig, who appeared to be issuing orders to the

Cavalry Corps as well as his own divisions at this time, requested that all available reserves be sent to shore up the Cavalry Corps position on his right flank. The snag was that there *were* no BEF reserves; the only significant force available in the entire BEF was that Territorial battalion, the 1st London Scottish, 750 strong and fairly fresh but as yet untested in battle. Even so, this unit was attached to the 2nd Cavalry Division and sent to assist the defenders at Messines.

Messines occupied a small salient projecting from the rest of the BEF line and was currently held by the 1st Cavalry Brigade, plus the 9th Lancers from the 1st Cavalry Brigade and two companies of the 57th Rifles from the Indian Corps. After hours of shelling the German infantry attack came in at 0430 hours on 31 October, overrunning some trenches at the southern end of the village before the enemy were driven back by a local counter-attack. The shelling then began again, concentrating on the village centre, and a further infantry attack on the northern end of the village succeeded in pushing the defenders out. Orders were therefore issued to abandon the eastern edge of Messines and withdraw to the western side. This at least eliminated the costly Messines salient, but it was clear that the cavalry units in Messines – in total about a thousand troopers strong – were now being attacked by no fewer than twelve German battalions. At 1000 hours, after another heavy burst of shelling, these German units came on again and the battle in Messines really began.

The rest of that morning in Messines was spent in house-to-house, hand-to-hand fighting with rifles, bayonets and pistols, fighting in which the vastly outnumbered defenders were gradually driven back, eventually forming a line along the main street. Half the village was now in flames and the Germans troops manhandled field artillery into the village to engage the dogged British defenders at close range, blasting them out of the houses. Even so, the cavalry troopers were still hanging on grimly in the blazing ruins of Messines in the early afternoon when infantry reinforcements began to arrive.

By now, like all the BEF battalions, these reinforcement units were much reduced. The 2nd Battalion, King's Own Yorkshire Light Infantry (2nd KOYLI), the 2nd Battalion, The King's Own Scottish Borderers (2nd KOSB) and the 2nd Battalion, The Inniskilling Fusiliers were down to 300 men each; only the London Scottish was anywhere near full strength with 750 men.

Led forward by their CO, Lieutenant Colonel G. A. Malcolm, the London Scottish went forward to take up a position at l'Enfer Wood, just west of the Messines ridge. However, owing to a mis-understanding, they came into the line believing that the cavalry units holding the ridge were in the process of attacking, and the colonel therefore deployed his battalion in support and led it out of cover. They were immediately spotted by the enemy and sub-jected to heavy shelling and forced to go to ground in the open, taking shelter in shell holes or abandoned trenches. The London Scottish remained forward, engaging the enemy to their front for most of the day, beating off at least one German attack at the point of the bayonet. Losses were inevitably high; by nightfall this fine battalion had had lost 321 men.[9]

With this assistance the cavalry were able to hold most of Messines village and even mount local counter-attacks, but German pressure was building up all along the line. More attacks were being mounted against the 2nd Cavalry Division at Wytschaete but these attacks petered out by dusk; a further German attack at 2230 hours lasted only half an hour before the enemy were again beaten back. Field Marshal French records that 'for close on 48 hours these troops [the cavalry] held the Wytschaete–Messines ridge against the utmost efforts of two and a half German Army Corps to dislodge them. Here was the centre of our line of battle and had it given way, disas-ter would have resulted to the entire left wing of the Allied line.'[10]

German pressure was not confined to the BEF front. So great was the pressure on the northern end of the Allied line on 30 October that the Belgians opened the sluices in their dykes and let the sea flood their country north of Dixmude, and the French units north and south of the BEF were also being pounded by the Fourth and Sixth Armies; the BEF fought hard and well at Ypres but it did not fight alone.

The basic problem for the British commanders was manpower. The BEF had now been fighting continuously for over two months, and although several new divisions – the 6th, 7th and the 3rd Cavalry Division – had come out, these had been quickly absorbed in this expanding war. Very few replacements had reached the battalions in the four original BEF infantry divisions, where the battalions were often down to company strength. The BEF was simply running out of troops, and the line it held around Ypres was too long. As a result, the BEF was now in serious trouble, and the critical point in this battle had not yet been reached.

Closer inspection of the situation reveals more problems. Not only were there too few men but those in the line were dog tired. They had been fighting continuously for ten days, and when they were not fighting they were digging trenches to improve their positions. Any assistance in holding the Ypres position must come from the French, but the French units on the BEF's left flank, though cooperating wonderfully with their British allies on a local level, currently had no more troops to commit. Little more than defensive fighting could be expected on the front north of I Corps where the 1st Division had been heavily engaged at Gheluvelt.

The *Official History* goes into some detail when describing the importance of the Gheluvelt position. This village astride the Menin road blocked the best route into Ypres and, standing on the high point of the encircling ridge, offered great artillery observation to whoever held it. On the morning of 31 October the British, who occupied a line on the forward, eastern, slope of the ridge, still held Gheluvelt. The troops holding this line came from the 3rd Infantry Brigade, supported by two battalions from the 2nd Brigade; as elsewhere, these units were very weary and under strength.

The 3rd Brigade, which should have had over 4,000 men – from the 1st Queen's, 2nd Welch, 1st South Wales Borderers and 2nd King's Royal Rifle Corps (KRRC), this last from the 2nd Brigade – mustered barely 1,000 men, most of these in the 2nd KRRC. Elements of other battalions were close by, including two companies of the 1st Loyals (North Lancashire Regiment) and a detachment from the 2nd Royal Scots Fusiliers.

Fully determined to crack the BEF front and force a break-through, General von Fabeck sent in thirteen battalions to overwhelm the British troops defending Gheluvelt. Six of these German infantry battalions were fresh, and they struck the BEF's forward positions at Gheluvelt like a hammer.

Astride the Menin road, the 2nd Welch held the forward position, with the 1st Queen's on their right and the 1st South Wales Borderers on their left. To the north of the Borderers the line was held by the 1st (Guards) Brigade – the 1st Scots Guards, the 1st Cameron Highlanders and the 1st Black Watch. In reserve west of Gheluvelt were two companies each from the Loyals and the 2nd KRRC. Artillery support was provided by the 34th Brigade, RFA, positioned some 460 metres (500 yards) west of Gheluvelt, where the fourth battalion of the 3rd Brigade, the 1st Battalion, The Gloucestershire Regiment, guarded the guns. On the face of it, the BEF line seems strongly held but, again, the units composing the defence were but shadows of their peacetime selves. The British front line was just 180 metres (200 yards) – within easy rifle range – of the German front line, so there had been no chance to rest or relax. Pinching and slapping their faces to keep awake, the BEF infantry stood to their line and watched to their front.

When the enemy attempted to rush across the narrow gap of no man's land at 0615 hours on 31 October, the result was another slaughter. The young German soldiers from the 102nd Infantry Regiment were singing as they advanced; some were seen strolling arm in arm towards the British line – insanity indeed. As they came, the weary, muddy, khaki-clad soldiers defending Gheluvelt adjusted their rifle sights, waited until the bulk of these enemy soldiers were out in the open, and greeted them with a terrible fire.

The hail of shot produced by the British infantry's 'fifteen rounds rapid' cut the enemy down in droves. Later German accounts, from observers unable to believe that bolt-action rifles could produce such a volume of fire, reported that the BEF were equipped with a great number of machine guns. The first infantry attacks were quickly repulsed with great loss but, as so often before, German artillery then began to pound the British line. This process, alternating infantry attacks with artillery concentrations, went on all day and, under this pressure the British line began to collapse.

By 0930 hours the 2nd Welch had been blown out of their shallow trenches and the survivors withdrew to the even shallower support line, closer to Gheluvelt. Unfortunately, news of this Welch withdrawal failed to reach the 1st Queen's on their right and these men were taken in enfilade when the Germans occupied the former Welch trenches. Even so, the Queen's held on, assisted by a company of the 2nd KRRC, but some idea of the situation east of Gheluvelt may be gained from the fate of a company sent from the 1st Gloucesters to fill the gap left by the Welch. Eighty strong when it went forward, this company was down to just thirteen men when it came up to contest the next German attack. Moreover, since communications had broken down and no runner survived the shellfire long enough to reach Brigade Headquarters, the fate of this company and the Queen's in those forward trenches remained unknown to higher authority.

At 1000 hours the enemy launched another strong attack, seven battalions pushing forward north and south of the Menin road, cheering as they came on, buoyed by the news that the Kaiser himself had come up to watch them take Gheluvelt. Again they ran into terrible rifle fire; again those grey-clad bodies littered the ground before the British line. This attack was pressed home with great courage but it was more than an hour before the Germans could prevail against the BEF rifles – and then only after their attack had been aided by field artillery, which came up to pound the British trenches at point-blank range. By 1115 hours, German artillery fire and numbers finally began to tell; the forward BEF units, the Queen's and the KRRC – or what was left of them – were forced back and out of the ruins of Gheluvelt. Only two officers and twelve men of the Queen's survived this fight and the 2nd KRRC, the strongest unit in the line, was reduced to 150 (all ranks) by the end of the day.

The loss of Gheluvelt was a major disaster. Gheluvelt was a bastion in the BEF line. From here the Menin road ran east, directly into Ypres, providing the enemy with the perfect axis of advance for a final thrust through the Allied line. Moreover, with the fall of this position the front of the 1st Division had been broken and many of the men were now retreating towards Ypres. This was not a rout – they were retreating in good order – but their losses had been severe and they were doing the sensible thing in falling back. Field Marshal French records that on his way up to I Corps HQ that morning:

> I had not gone more than a mile when the traffic on the road began to assume a most anxious and threatening appearance. It looked as if the whole of I Corps was about to fall back in confusion on Ypres. Heavy howitzers were moving west at a trot – always a most signifi-cant feature of a retreat – and ammunition and other wagons blocked the road almost as far as the eye could see. In the midst of the press of traffic and along both sides of the road, crowds of wounded men came limping along as fast as they could go, all heading for Ypres. Shells were screaming overhead and bursting with reverberating explosions in the adjacent fields. This spectacle filled me with misgiv-ing and alarm.[11]

Such sentiments are hardly surprising. With no reserves on hand, how was the position to be retrieved, and if it was not retrieved, what could prevent a breakthrough? Fortunately, the commanders of the 1st and 2nd Divisions had previously agreed on a scheme of mutual support for just such an emergency. At 1015 hours General Monro of the 2nd Division met General Lomax at the Hooge château and placed one of his reserve battalions, the 2nd Worcesters, at the disposal of the 1st Division. Lomax sent the battalion to Brigadier General FitzClarence of the 1st (Guards) Brigade, who ordered Major E. B. Hankey, the com-manding officer of the 2nd Worcesters, to 'counter-attack with the utmost vigour against the enemy in Gheluvelt and re-establish our line there'.

Then I Corps suffered another setback. The staff of the 1st and 2nd Divisions were conferring at the Hooge château at 1315 hours, when four heavy shells struck the house and exploded in the conference room. Major-General Lomax was mortally wounded, Major-General Monro was severely concussed, several members of the divisional staffs were killed, and other staff officers were wounded. In the space of a shell-burst the command echelon of two divisions was literally blown apart.

This disaster added to Haig's existing problems. Gheluvelt had been lost, the Germans were within five kilometres (three miles) of Ypres and were pushing hard all along the line . . . and now two of his division commanders were either dead or *hors de combat*. News of this fresh disaster reached Haig at the White Chateau at about 1400 hours, but Douglas Haig not easily ruffled. Major-General Bulfin was sent to command the 1st Division and more men, any that could be found – sappers, cooks, clerks, grooms, lightly wounded men, anyone who could hold a rifle – was sent up the Menin road.

As a rule a commanding general is well advised to keep out of the battle and direct his command from some safe central position. Personal heroics have to be abandoned above brigade level, but this was a time for personal leadership. Summoning his mounted escort, ignoring the steady rain of shells, Douglas Haig went forward to join his men. Accompanied by a mounted lancer, he rode up the road towards Menin, halting and turning back any formed group of soldiers heading towards Ypres, stopping to encourage the men he met along the way. The sight of their commanding general moving towards the front line did a great deal to encourage the troops. They turned back, more men joining in as the scattered units went back to the fight.

With that much achieved, Haig returned to the White Chateau. His first order was for the rapid construction of a final defence line in front of Ypres to which I Corps could retire if the line was broken again. When Field Marshal French arrived at the château later that afternoon he found 'Haig and John Gough, his Chief of Staff, in one of the ground floor rooms, poring over maps and evidently much disconcerted. But though much perturbed in mind and very tired in body and brain, Haig was as cool and alert as ever.'[12]

French had no help to offer, no men to spare. Any reinforcements must come from the French, so while Haig prepared to pull his troops back to the outskirts of Ypres, the Field Marshal departed for Foch's HQ in search of aid. Then, just as the field marshal was leaving, a staff officer, Brigadier General Rice, came galloping up to the door with wonderful news. At 1530 hours the 2nd Worcesters, another much-depleted battalion, mustering just seven officers and 350 men, had stormed across the fields from the Polderhoek wood and retaken Gheluvelt at the point of the bayonet.

The Worcesters had lost three officers and over 180 men retaking Gheluvelt, but this crucial position astride the Menin road was now back in British hands. Not only that; the left of the 7th Division had also advanced and the broken link between the 1st and 7th Divisions had been reforged. For the moment at least Ypres was secure.

The charge of the 2nd Worcesters at Gheluvelt, if rightly famous, was but one gallant deed among many in the BEF that day. The 2nd Royal Scots Fusiliers had hung on outside Gheluvelt and beaten off all attacks though reduced to just 151 men. The 1st Loyals did equally well, down to just eighty men before they were overwhelmed, while the 2nd Welch had hung on to the Gheluvelt château and counter-attacked the enemy when he came up.

All the other units in the line did well that day: the 1st Queen's, the 1st (Guards) Brigade, the 2nd Royal Scots Fusiliers, the 60th Rifles – every BEF unit in the line. The German attack was pressed home with courage and persistence but it was opposed by British Regular soldiers – tired and ragged men who somehow found the strength, and the sheer guts, to hang on to their positions and fight back. They needed no urging, no cheering on; that natural bloody-mindedness of the British soldier in defence was enough. They had been tasked with hanging on to Ypres and if they could not hold their line living they would hold it dead.

While his troops were gritting their teeth and hanging on, Field Marshal French was moving close to despair. After leaving Hooge he had gone to meet General Foch to ask for help. Foch promised a counter-attack by French troops at dawn the following day but, clearly, this might be too late to save the BEF line in front of Ypres. This being so, Field Marshal French told Foch that unless support was sent soon, 'There is nothing left for me to do but go back up and die with I Corps.'

Foch had no patience with this remark. 'You must not talk of dying but of winning,' he said, and promised to send up six battalions of the 32nd Division by the following day. French and Foch then sent messages to Douglas Haig, urging him to hold on at all costs until the French attack relieved the pressure. These exhortations were unnecessary; Haig's corps *was* hanging on, though later that night Haig decided that Gheluvelt should be abandoned and the line moved back to the reverse, western, slope of the ridge, slightly closer to Ypres. This was the only step back. 'For the next ten days,' says Liddell Hart, 'Haig's line remained without change and unshaken, save for a minor withdrawal on the right on the 5th to conform to a recoil of the French troops on his right.'[13]

The fighting that day had been equally severe in other parts of the line. The right wing of III Corps had been heavily shelled and Pulteney's corps was ordered to pull back to the defence line between the hamlet of Klein Zillebeke and the Frezenberg ridge. Before moving, Major-General E. S. Bulfin, still commanding his composite unit – Bulfin's Force – ordered his men to give the Germans a 'mad minute' of rifle fire, then charge with the bayonet on the enemy masses closing on their front. This last move proved decisive; the Germans fled and the British soldiers suddenly found themselves on an open battlefield, heaped with German dead and wounded; they therefore advanced another half-mile before pulling back and digging in for the night.

October 31 was a day of triumph and disaster for the BEF. They had held their lines but at a terrible cost, a further reduction of the shrinking ranks of the rifle battalions. Of the battalions engaged at Gheluvelt that day, the 1st Queen's were down to fifty men, the 2nd Welch had seventy, the 1st Scots Guards 105, the 1st South Wales Borderers 204, the 2nd KRRC 150. Other battalions were in a similar state – the 1st Loyals (North Lancashire Regiment) was 'practically non-existent'.[14] The BEF as a whole was now down to between a half and a quarter of its original strength.

On the other hand, the BEF had held the line everywhere until the commanders chose to withdraw; they were not defeated. The Kaiser sent a laudatory message to von Fabeck's army group on the evening of 31 October, but a later, official account of that day's fighting admitted that very little had been achieved; no ground had been taken except part of the burning village of Messines, until the British pulled back from Gheluvelt. Von Fabeck now decided to concentrate his army group's efforts south of the salient, on the line between Wytschaete and Messines; to avoid the losses inflicted by British rifle fire, his units would, where possible, attack at night.

Writing to his wife of this battle on 31 October, Wilson relates that: 'All yesterday we were heavily attacked on our left hand and had to fall back. This morning the attack recommenced with increased violence and as I write the fire is very heavy. All last night I was at work collecting reserves for today's fight, and Foch, who came to see me at 1 am this morning, only left me at 2.30 am and then lent Sir John 8 battalions and 6 batteries.'[15]

In his diary for 1 November Wilson writes:

At 5 am message from Allenby to say cavalry heavily attacked all night and being driven in. By 11 am Allenby retiring on Kemmel. Lord K called me up on telephone from British Consulate in Dunkirk and asked for situation. I told him. He was upset and asked if he could do anything. I replied, 'For the moment – no – but send more troops.' He telephoned the War Office to send five more battalions of Terriers. Foch has now taken over the cavalry line with the 32nd Division and he has the equivalent of another division coming up tonight and if the 1st and 7th Division can hold on I believe Foch will save the situation. He is a fine fellow. The German Emperor was down opposite us today, no doubt thinking to see Ypres taken. *But he won't.*[16]

Douglas Haig spent the night of 31 October–1 November re-forming his line. The 2nd Worcesters were pulled out of Gheluvelt and became part of the 2nd Division reserve around the village of

Veldhoek. The rest of the 2nd Division dug in around Polygon Wood, east of Zonnebeke, while the 1st Division dug in across the Menin road west of Gheluvelt with the 3rd Cavalry Division in reserve. These actions indicate that Douglas Haig was preparing for a renewal of the battle. The Battle of First Ypres was not over and would begin again at dawn.

14

Nonne Böschen

1–22 November 1914

The line that stood between the British Empire and ruin was composed of tired, haggard and unshaven men, many in uniforms that were little more than rags. But they had their guns, rifles and bayonets and plenty of ammunition.
British Official History, 1914, Vol. II, p. 304

The trench line east of Ypres had become a bastion, an Allied rock against which successive waves of German troops dashed themselves to pieces. German guns resumed their pounding of the Allied line soon after dusk on 31 October, concentrating most of their fire on the trenches along the ridge line between Wytschaete and Messines. At midnight the barrage intensified, a battery of 8-inch howitzers concentrating exclusively on Wytschaete, and an attack on that village by nine battalions of the 6th Bavarian Reserve Division came in one hour later, at 0100 hours on 1 November. The first battle for Ypres was now entering its second month with no sign of a conclusion.

Wytschaete was then held by a detachment known as the 'Composite Household Cavalry', made up of 'odds and sods' from the 4th Cavalry Brigade, just 415 in number – giving the enemy a numerical advantage of twelve to one. By 0300 hours the Germans had driven the 'Composite Cavalry' back to the edge of the village; there the troopers rallied and drove the enemy back again, counter-attacking through the streets, among the burning houses. This ding-dong struggle continued until the increasing German pressure drove the cavalry troopers to the western edge of the village – from where yet another counter-attack was mounted, again pushing the enemy back.

This attack was the last the cavalry troopers could make; by dawn the enemy were in full possession of Wytschaete and consolidating their positions among the smouldering ruins. Two battalions from II Corps, the 1st Lincolns and the 1st Northumberland Fusiliers, were then sent up in support of the cavalry and duly attacked the village, but were swiftly pounded by that dreadful combination – rifle fire, artillery and enfilading machine guns. Before they broke off their bid to retake the village, the Lincolns had lost 301 men and the Northumberland Fusiliers ninety-eight – in each battalion about 30 per cent of the men committed.

This German attack on Wytschaete was part of a general attack along the Messines ridge, a position held by 294 men of the 6th Dragoon Guards (The Carabiniers) and 300 men of the London Scottish. These units were also driven back, and by dawn on 1 November the Germans held the centre of the Messines ridge, the defenders falling back to the Spanbroekmolen position on the far side of the shallow Steenbeek valley.

French reinforcements then arrived and their 32nd Division retook Wytschaete, aided in the task by German heavy artillery, which, unaware that their infantry had recently captured the village, continued shelling the defenders even as the French infantry moved in. Here again, though, recapturing Wytschaete was as much as the French could do, and the battle for Messines continued. By 0730 hours on 1 November it became apparent that the enemy had total control of the ridge and the valley to the west of it, leaving General de Lisle of the 1st Cavalry Division no option but to withdraw, covered by the remnants of the London Scottish.

The 4th Division of III Corps, on the right of the cavalry, were also preparing to withdraw to a prepared defensive line – known as 'Torres Vedras' – but were then attacked by the German 1st Cavalry Corps and the 40th Division. In fact, the enemy would have been well advised to let the 4th Division pull back unmolested, for the 4th Division turned on the advancing enemy and drove them back with rifle, machine-gun and artillery fire, somewhat balancing the setback at Messines.

By the evening of 1 November the situation around Ypres was as follows. The northern flank from the Belgians to Broodseinde was held by the French. Then came I Corps, straddling the Menin road, then the French again, from the Ypres–Comines railway line to east of Messines, where the Cavalry Corps took over again, linking up with III Corps as far as Armentières, where the Indian division held the line to the south.

Along the Belgian line north of Dixmude – most of which was now behind spreading flood water – all was quiet. French attacks south of the Belgian line had been held by the enemy, but although the British had now lost Wytschaete and Messines, the BEF front was firm and in no acute danger of collapse. There were, however, several serious problems. Quite apart from a chronic shortage of men, those now in the line were exhausted; they had been fighting all day and digging all night for the past ten days – and now they were having to fight at night as well. The men were falling asleep as they stood to arms, unable to continue the endless labour of repairing their existing trenches and digging new ones.

Added to this was a serious shortage of artillery ammunition, vital to maintaining the defence. Some BEF batteries had already been taken out of the line, as there were no shells for their guns. Indeed, on 2 November French reported to Kitchener that he had only 180 shells per howitzer and 320 shells for every 18-pounder – and no shells at all for the 6-inch howitzers.

The Allies were on the defensive but shells were urgently needed, not least to engage German guns and break up any attack formations gathering on the BEF front. Going on the defensive was sensible because the Germans had not yet decided to abandon their push past Ypres – far from it. While continuing to batter the BEF with artillery, the enemy mustered forces for one more stab at Ypres, building this final thrust on the strong foundation of the elite Prussian Guard.

Nor was this all; signs of strain were also starting to appear at GHQ. The BEF's chief of staff, Lieutenant General Sir Archibald Murray, was suffering from nervous strain, and Henry Wilson was anxious to replace him, pressing the advisability of this move on the Field Marshal. French relayed this suggestion to Kitchener, who informed French that the Cabinet had not forgotten Wilson's intervention in the Ulster affair and were anyway dubious about him and totally opposed to any change; for the moment, Murray stayed in his post.

However, as Wilson soon discovered, an even more radical change was also in the offing. During a meeting with the French commanders at Dunkirk on 1 November, Kitchener had proposed to the French President and General Joffre that Field Marshal French should be removed and General Sir Ian Hamilton take his place. According to Callwell, 'Joffre said at once that he could not agree as he and French got on very well and M. Poincaré backed this up.'[1] Foch quickly passed this news on to Henry Wilson, and Wilson, ever keen on intrigue, passed the details to Field Marshal French.

The following day, according to Wilson's diary, 'Sir John and I went to Cassel at 3 pm when Sir John thanked Foch personally and in the warmest terms for his comradeship and loyalty.'[2]

One wonders why Kitchener felt it necessary to consult the French over this suggestion, rather than simply informing them that Field Marshal French must go. After all, the French did not consult the British before sacking Lanrezac, and there seems no pressing reason for the British to consult their allies over a decision that rested with the British Cabinet. French support for the Field Marshal is also interesting; Joffre can hardly have held the BEF commander in very high esteem after the events of recent weeks, so it would appear that the support came from Foch, who, with the aid of Henry Wilson, found the Field Marshal easy to manipulate. And so, with French also still in his post, the war continued.

One has to admire German tenacity at this time; whatever casualties the Allies were sustaining, far higher casualties were being inflicted on the enemy formations moving in the open as they swept into the attack. And yet, in spite of these casualties, in spite of the fact that vast losses were being sustained for no perceptible territorial gain, the enemy kept on mustering men, forming new divisions and pressing home the attacks.

Assembling another force for yet another push took the German commanders a little time. Meanwhile, the day-to-day fighting around Ypres continued unabated and BEF losses continued to mount. In I Corps, the 7th Division, with a ration strength of 12,672 soldiers, could now muster just 2,434; the 1st Division had been reduced to just 3,583 men. Other units at every level – brigades, battalions, cavalry regiments – were in a similar situation. This shortage of men could not be remedied, certainly not with regular soldiers; the regulars called from far-off garrisons were still at sea and such small regular reinforcements as reached the BEF from the UK were the scrapings of an already empty barrel. In this extremity the only answer was to send out Territorial units, but all these were currently ill equipped and mostly half trained.

On 1 November, during the meeting with Foch and Joffre at Dunkirk, Field Marshal Kitchener told the Allied army commanders and the French politicians – and told them very distinctly – that Britain had no more men to send, adding that 'to send untrained men into the fighting line was little short of murder, and that no very important supply of British effectives could be looked for until the late Spring of 1915 and that the British Army would only reach full strength, its high water mark, during the Summer of 1917'.[3]

Britain's Regular Army was now paying the price for the government's pre-war failure to introduce conscription and Kitchener's blunt declaration, however unwelcome to the French, was both honest and totally correct. So too was his comment that no significant numbers of trained troops could be expected in the line for another two years.

It takes time to raise and train troops from scratch and even longer to form and train armies. Even if the men could be found – and hundreds of thousands of men were now answering

Kitchener's famous call to arms – the weapons and kit needed to equip them were simply not available and would not be available for another two years. The small pre-war army had not needed a large armaments industry, so this too had to be created, again virtually from scratch.

Lord Kitchener, who had been appointed Secretary of State for War much against his personal wishes, was now discovering on a daily basis just how unprepared Britain had been for a European war – those extended 'conversations' and Henry Wilson's pre-war machinations notwithstanding. Britain had an army, and a very fine army, but it was not an army designed, manned or in any way equipped for the sort of war in which it was currently engaged. What made it formidable were the fighting qualities of its soldiers – and those soldiers were now being killed or wounded in large numbers.

'Did they remember,' he asked the Cabinet in September 1914, 'when they went headlong into a war like this, that they were without an Army, and without any preparation to equip one?' By 25 August 1914, just three weeks into his appointment, Kitchener had already envisioned a force of twenty-five divisions in the field, but recognized that a shortage of kit was the critical factor.[4]

The cabinet and the House of Commons seemed to have some difficulty grasping this point. As late as 1916, Kitchener was reminding Members of Parliament that:

> The pre-war theory worked out by the General Staff on instructions from the 'Government of the day' had been that, in certain eventualities, we should despatch overseas an Expeditionary Force, six divisions in all, or in round numbers, 150,000 men; that the Territorial Force should take over the defence of these islands; and that the Special Reserve should feed the Expeditionary Force. On this basis, the business of the War Office in the event of war was to keep the Army in the field up to strength and to perfect the arrangements for Home defence. My immediate decision was that in the face of the magnitude of the war, this policy would not suffice.

Kitchener had clearly been reading the minutes of those Cabinet subcommittee meetings of 1909, and was pointing out that, right from the start, the demands and ferocity of this war – its *sheer size* – had exceeded all previous calculations and created an unprecedented situation. Looking at the equipment situation in the autumn of 1914, John Hussey gives the example of the 2nd West Riding Division of the Territorial force. This division quickly raised no fewer than twelve battalions between August and October 1914, but finding the men was the easy part. Clothing and webbing equipment came in over the autumn and winter but horses and rifles did not arrive until the spring of 1915 – and even then these were only drill rifles, not suited to the field. The battalions received their .303 SMLE rifles only in May 1916 – more than a year and a half into the war, just in time for the Battle of the Somme.

True as all this is, it still seems likely that much more use could have been made of the Territorial Force. Although originally raised by Haldane for home defence, the Territorial Force contained many units that were willing to volunteer for general service and, like the London Scottish, would have given a good account of themselves in battle if allowed to do so.

The snag was that Herbert Kitchener, the War Secretary, had no faith in the Territorial Force. Kitchener had spent most of his career in Egypt or India and had little knowledge of the British Army and little interest in the Territorial force. He had seen Territorial troops before – the aged, unfit, ill-trained and unwilling French Territorial troops of the Franco-Prussian War – and that dire experience had coloured his judgement. Kitchener did not appreciate the young volunteers of Britain's Territorial Force and made the fundamental mistake of rejecting the expansion of the Territorial Force to concentrate on creating new armies, the 'Kitchener's Armies' of civilian volunteers. Many of these civilians were already in the Territorial Force, so expanding this and equipping it properly would have been equally effective and a great deal quicker than starting from scratch.

Desperate for men, Field Marshal French promptly queried Kitchener's Dunkirk statement of 1 November and was informed that there were no Regular units left in Britain. Indeed, Kitchener added, the total number of Regular Army reinforcements currently available in the UK amounted to just 150 officers and 9,500 other ranks, roughly sufficient for two infantry brigades, but these were mainly engaged in training the newly recruited volunteers; for the moment the BEF must soldier on as best it could.

During the first days of November, as the rains fell and the first signs of winter began to appear, the battered BEF continued to do just that. German artillery fire grew in volume and duration, but when German infantry attacks came in – and they came in constantly – they continued to dissolve under the fire of the British, French and Belgian soldiers, doggedly hanging on in their muddy dug outs and water-filled trenches.

The battles of Gheluvelt and Messines ended – at least officially – on 31 October and 2 November respectively, but these terminations were not apparent to the troops on the ground. Their battle continued; to the men in the front-line trenches it seemed that the Germans had an endless supply of men and shells and would continue to attack until the Allied defences were finally breached and taken and their bodies added to the hundreds that now lay out between the trench lines, slowly consumed by the mud.

In an age when military service is rare, the plight of these soldiers is very hard to grasp. The hard fact was that if this war continued most of them were going to die. Many had died already; men not killed at Mons had died at Le Cateau or in the retreat to the Marne or on the Aisne. Now many of those who had survived those early encounters were locked in yet another struggle, or had already died defending Messines or attacking La Bassée or Armentières. Even if they had survived so far, there was no escape in this war. If they did not die or were not hideously maimed in this battle, they would simply be committed to the next one, and so on, until death, shrieking from the sky, brought an end to their condition. And yet they endured.

How men coped with this situation remains a mystery to later generations. Perhaps a certain lack of imagination helped, or it could be that, in spite of all the evidence, men were still convinced that being killed or wounded was something that happened only to the other fellow. Perhaps, most of all, they were kept going by that combination of comradeship, regimental pride, ingrained discipline and a simple determination not to give in that is the hallmark of the British soldier. They would hang on, develop their defences and give the enemy another pasting when he came on again. There was no glory in such a situation, no glory in this kind of life, but these men gained a kind of glory, simply by enduring it.

It is important to stress that the French played a major part in the Battle of First Ypres and the Belgian Army also played its part; First Ypres was never a purely BEF affair. French reinforcements were coming up steadily and taking over more of the line. The British had no more men to send and the French had no option but to fill the gap. It is equally important to stress that the arrival of the French did not stem the German advance on Ypres. The German line crept forward steadily during the first days of November, and on 5 November the Spanbroekmolen position (Hill 75) on the Messines ridge was lost by the French. German pressure was unrelenting, and another major thrust somewhere was clearly in the offing.

On 5 November, the Allied positions from the north were as follows. The Belgian Army held the line from the North Sea to Dixmude, from where the French 38th Division occupied the line south as far as Bixschoote. The line then swung east across the edge of the salient, de Mitry's cavalry holding the front as far as the Ypres–Roulers railway line north of Langemarck. Here General Dubois' IX Corps took over as far as Broodseinde, where Haig's battered I Corps – the 2nd, 1st and 7th Divisions and Lord Cavan's detachment – held the front astride the Menin road and as far as Zillebeke, where the French XVI Corps took over. French units then held the line south to the River Douve, where the Cavalry Corps and the 4th Division of III Corps took up the defence as far as the link with II Corps – though many II Corps battalions were now at Ypres, reinforcing other units in the salient. On 6 November these detached II Corps battalions were formed into a new division – a rather small one – under the command of Major-General F. D. V. Wing.

Having already sent one third of his field artillery batteries out of the line owing to a shortage of ammunition, on 5 November General Haig was obliged to ration the supply of shells to the remaining guns. Until further notice they would receive no more that twenty rounds per day of 18-pounder ammunition and only ten rounds per day of 4.5-inch ammunition. If the Germans came forward now the defence must rely on their rifles and bayonets.

Accounts of the action around Ypres in the first days of November give an impression of heavy and continuous fighting but without much movement in the positions of either side – 'very little change in the situation at the front . . . no crisis and calm reigned at the Allied Headquarters', according to the *Official History*.[5]

The belief was gradually gaining ground at GHQ that the fighting in 1914, if not exactly over, was at least dying down. Indeed, at the Corps Commanders' conference on 5 November, General Haig was surprised that the main topic put forward for discussion by the staff was arrangements for winter leave, some of it to the UK. At this time Haig was pressing hard for the relief of the 1st and 7th Divisions and reported a steady increase – were that possible – in the enemy shelling of his positions in front of Ypres; his units had no men to spare for leave or any other leisure activity. The I Corps advance HQ near the Menin Gate had been hit three times in as many days, several members of Haig's staff being killed; according to Haig's appreciation of the situation, the enemy was both active and aggressive.

In his life of Henry Wilson, Callwell comments: 'the situation had become fairly satisfactory and the enemy attacks were dying away'.[6] There were, in fact, no grounds whatsoever for complacency, still less for the bland assumption that the battles of 1914 were over and the winter lull at hand – there would be few lulls in the killing in this new kind of war.

To be fair to Field Marshal French, there was little he could do to help the troops in the line, and he did attempt to rest some of the more reduced formations. On 5 November, two brigades from II Corps came up to relieve the 7th Division, which withdrew to billets behind the line. More II Corps units were put into the line here and there around Ypres to bolster existing units or afford some relief to tired formations until, for a while, Horace Smith-Dorrien was a corps commander without a corps. The Indian Corps now held the former II Corps positions at Neuve Chapelle with four II Corps battalions in close support.

One indication of the mood of the time comes from the visit to the BEF of the elderly Field Marshal Lord Roberts, who arrived at St Omer on 11 November and contracted a chill which swiftly turned into pneumonia; on 14 November, the much-loved 'Bobs' died in France, in the midst of his beloved soldiers, with the gunfire of the Battle of First Ypres raging again outside his windows.

The first stages of this final battle around Ypres – an engagement generally referred to as the Battle of Nonne Böschen – began on 5 November. On 6 November, Wilson records: 'Our news today is that the French are being violently attacked and are giving ground. I was out this afternoon, and have to go and see Foch again. The Germans have got up another corps and in spite of 230 guns they are pushing the gallant little Frenchman back. We are being attacked everywhere also, but not with any ferocity so we are holding our ground all right.'[7]

In fact, pressure against the BEF sector of the front was mounting steadily and the basic BEF problem, a lack of numbers – reserves – continued to haunt Field Marshal French as this pressure continued to grow. All he had out of the line was the wreck of the 7th Division and two or three newly arrived Territorial battalions, brought to France to work on the lines of communication. However, French's memoirs record that 'our Intelligence Departments and the French became very optimistic on the subject of a great withdrawal of the Germans from the Western Front'.[8]

This optimism proved infectious, in spite of the evidence. Three days later, on 9 November, French cabled Kitchener that Joffre 'now believed the Germans were in the process of withdrawing troops from the Western Front and sending them east to Poland where General Hindenburg was currently in full retreat before the Russian Army'. In reality the three German commanders in the west –

Crown Prince Rupprecht, von Fabeck and the Duke of Württemberg, urged on by von Falkenhayn – had been steadily building up their forces in Belgium for yet another massive thrust at Ypres. This followed von Falkenhayn's dictum on 3 November that 'only perseverance in the offensive [is needed] to obtain a complete success'. This massive thrust came in on 11 November 1914, four years to the day before the eventual armistice.

The enemy spent the intervening days reorganizing their forces around Ypres after the flooding of the coastal area by the Belgians. This flooding was not entirely detrimental to the German armies, for they were now sheltered from attacks on the northern part of their line; it therefore enabled them to thin out their units in the northern sector and send some south to thicken up the troops around Ypres. Crown Prince Rupprecht of the Sixth Army also elected to send any units and guns he could spare to von Fabeck, and between 5 and 11 November another six divisions, including a division of the Prussian Guard Corps, were added to von Fabeck's strength astride the Menin road.

The German High Command – von Falkenhayn – then decided to create yet another new 'Army Group' under General von Linsingen. Formed on the night of 9/10 November, this consisted of XV Corps and Baron von Plattenberg's Guards Corps supported by no fewer than 230 guns – the guns noted by Wilson in his diary. This powerful unit – not an army group, as the term is usually understood, but still a massive force – moved into position astride the Menin road, opposite Haig's much-depleted I Corps and awaited the order to push into Ypres.

This was not to be an isolated attack. Von Linsingen's group would merely form the centre of the attack on the BEF position. His orders were 'to drive back and crush the enemy lying north of the Comines canal [i.e. north of the line Comines–Warneton], delivering the main weight of the attack with the left wing'. Meanwhile, Army Group Fabeck would push forward south of the canal and all the other divisions of the Sixth and the Fourth Armies north and south of Ypres were to push west to the sea.

As will be seen, this was no small-scale, localized push, this was *it,* an all-out, hard-driving thrust, right into the centre of the Allied line – and the point of that thrust would come against I Corps of the BEF astride the Menin road. It would begin, as usual, with an artillery bombardment of the Allied line and more exploratory attacks, the Germans seeking weak points among the Allied positions.

This last battle of First Ypres – known later as the Battle of Nonne Böschen – the 'Nun's Wood' – began on 10 November with an attack on the French positions north-east of Ypres, a strike that gained the Germans a small bridgehead across the Yser at Dixmude. This attack convinced the French generals – incorrectly – that the weight of this new German attack would come north of Ypres and fall on their lines between Bixschoote and Zonnebeke. It fact, it fell on the BEF between Gheluvelt and Hooge on 11 November, and the heart of this final battle took place just north of the Menin road, at Nonne Böschen and Polygon Wood, positions held by the 1st and 2nd Divisions of the BEF.

The morning of 11 November was chilly and misty and dawn arrived with a heavy downpour and the start of what the *Official History* describes as 'the most terrific fire the British had yet experienced'.[9] This fire concentrated on I Corps and on Wing's 'division' of II Corps – which could muster only some 4,000 men – just south of the Menin road. The bombardment went on for several hours, the Germans marking the BEF line to establish the position of the British guns and the infantry defences prior to the infantry attack, which came in at 0900 hours.

Later on, 11 November became better known 'Remembrance Day' or 'Armistice Day', but that was after the war ended. Until then 11 November 1914 was noted by the soldiers of the British Army as one of the hardest days of battle in the entire war. On that day twelve and a half German infantry divisions, surging forward on a 14-kilometre (9-mile) front from Messines to Polygon Wood, smashed into the British line astride the Menin road, positions manned by McCracken's, Gliechen's and Shaw's brigades in Wing's division south of the road and Brigadier FitzClarence's 1st (Guards) Brigade in I Corps in the woods just to the north of it.

These scratch brigades contained some of the great fighting battalions of the war, the cream of the county regiments. McCracken's brigade mustered 1,764 men from the 2nd KOSBs, 2nd Royal Irish Rifles, 1st Gordon Highlanders, 1st South Lancashires and 1st Wiltshires. Gleichen's brigade numbered fifty officers and 1,550 men from the 1st Cheshires and the 2nd Bedfords. Shaw's brigade contained seventy-six officers and 2,638 men from the 1st Lincolns, 1st Northumberland Fusiliers, 4th Royal Fusiliers, 1st Royal Scots Fusiliers and 2nd Duke of Wellington's.

All three of Wing's brigades were well under strength; at full strength an infantry brigade in 1914 should have mustered 124 officers and 4,100 other ranks. To the north of the Menin road lay the 1st (Guards) Brigade under FitzClarence; this was a Guards brigade in name only since it contained the 1st Black Watch, the 1st Cameron Highlanders and only one Guards battalion, the 1st Scots Guards; this 'brigade' mustered around 800 men – less than that of a pre-war battalion.

The German bombardment, which felled trees, levelled trenches and collapsed dugouts, went on for over two hours before the German infantry attack came in. This was a thrust by twenty-five battalions of infantry; a force totalling 17,500 men against some 7,500 British infantry entrenched in the Nonne Böschen on a short line running north-east to Polygon Wood.

The advancing Germans – Pomeranians and East Prussians from the 4th Division – suffered terrible casualties as they came on, both from shelling and the rapid rifle fire of the British regular infantry; the *Official History*, while recording that the enemy had twelve battalions here against the British eight and a half, states that these attacks were 'broken by the steady fire of II Corps and were never dangerous'.[10]

Even so, the attacks against McCracken's and Gleichen's battalions kept coming and were pressed home with great resolution; the German battalions attacked again and again, but were always driven back with losses. They tried again at 1600 hours and were again cut down, pressing their attacks until the shell-pocked fields before the British line were carpeted with field-grey dead, piled two and three deep in places – and still the attacks continued. The German attacks were not broken off until 2100 hours that evening, when the battlefield was dark except for flares.

Astride the Menin road the Prussian Guard division was attempting to break through the centre of the British line at the point held by Shaw's brigade and FitzClarence's Guards. The *Official History* estimates that three German divisions, the 30th, 39th and 4th – thirty-seven battalions in all – moved against Cavan and McCracken and Moussy – odds of five to one. These German units included their 4th Guards Brigade, which engaged Shaw's weak battalions, and the German 1st Guards Brigade, which engaged Brigadier FitzClarence's 1st (Guards) Brigade. These were the crack troops of the German Army, the Kaiser's pride and joy, men determined to live up to their reputation as an elite force, unstoppable in attack. Their attack was duly delivered, and with considerable force.

Alas for the Prussian Guard! Regimental pride and élan were no use against the raking rifle fire of two stubborn county battalions, the 1st Lincolns and the 2nd Duke of Wellington's. The 1st Guards Grenadier Regiment of the 4th Brigade suffered such heavy losses before the British trenches that it came to a halt and went to ground. Farther north, the 2nd Guards Grenadier Regiment succeeded in breaking through the British line, its enfilade fire forcing the 1st Royal Fusiliers to fall back, but Brigadier General Shaw then counter-attacked with two companies of the 2nd Royal Sussex and the 1st Royal Scots Fusiliers and drove them out again. Brigadier Shaw was well forward and was wounded in this counter-attack, the command of his scratch brigade passing to Lieutenant Colonel W. D. Smith of the 2nd Royal Sussex.

This counter-attack did not prevent other German units breaking through the BEF line in places. Haig therefore committed the rest of the 2nd Royal Sussex to the front line; other units were also sent forward and the belief spread that the Royal Fusiliers' positions had been retaken. This turned out to be mistaken, and further attempts to evict the enemy during the afternoon met with no success. In this action the 1st Battalion, The Royal Fusiliers was reduced to 100 men led by two second lieutenants – the only officers left. German losses had also been high, and all they had to show in return was a brief success – and one short section of battered trench. All in all, the right and centre sections of the I Corps line had held up well against the German onslaught.

The encounter between Prussian Guard units and the BEF took place at Nonne Böschen around 0900 hours when the German 1st Guard Brigade – six full battalions – met the 800 men of the British 1st (Guards) Brigade just south of Polygon Wood – though it should be noted that the 1st Guards Brigade had the 1st Battalion, The King's Regiment of the 6th Infantry Brigade (in all 456 men) in close support on its left.

The attack at Nonne Böschen was undertaken with typical courage and disregard for casualties. The German Guards advanced across the shell-torn ground at the trot and crossed the first line of trenches in the face of heavy rifle and machine-gun fire, shedding men with every metre. This was a last flash of pride and élan; these German Guards came into the attack with bayonets fixed and rifles at the high port, the officers with drawn swords. Without stopping to return fire, they breasted the British line and attacked the defenders with the bayonet

British soldiers – and especially Highland soldiers – are not afraid of cold steel. The Scots soldiers quickly scrambled from their trenches and came out to fight the enemy in the open, bayonet to bayonet, but numbers soon began to tell. The chaplain of the German 4th Guards Division wrote later that the British were 'cold-blooded and tough and defend themselves even when their trenches are taken',[11] but the Scots could not hold back the German Guards for long.

Accounts of this violent action are not surprisingly confused. The British line was broken but in the process the German attack apparently fell apart, the forward units split by the stout resistance from FitzClarence's men. The Cameron Highlanders and the Black Watch were overwhelmed but the Scots Guards hung on to their last strongpoint in a farm and defied eviction as the German tide flooded past. The British artillery now began to flay the German advance, expending all available supplies of ammunition and putting a wall of shellfire between the German forward units and those coming up in support.

The 2nd Duke of Wellington's, north of the Menin road, had taken over some of the Guards Brigade trenches and was attacked by the fusilier battalion of the 2nd Guards Grenadier Regiment, which broke through and advanced 800 metres (500 yards) into the BEF position before they were checked; the *Official History* records that 'in the course of a long struggle the Fusilier Battalion gradually became a disorganized crowd and finally was practically annihilated'[12] – the remnants being driven from the woods by a bayonet charge from the Duke of Wellington's reserve company. In this engagement the German Guards lost seven out of twenty officers and 380 out of 826 men . . . and still the battle continued.

By midday, three hours after opening their attack, the Prussian Guard had fought its way into Nonne Böschen, its battalions much reduced and confused by the relentless British rifle and machine-gun fire that assailed them from every quarter, but still fighting hard. The battle in this close country – for as yet shelling had not obliterated the vegetation – was fought at very close range, often hand to hand. The heavy German artillery fire of previous days, which had felled trees and pitted the ground with shell holes, had provided the British infantry with an adequate amount of cover.

Moreover, being ordered to advance and penetrate the British line quickly, the German units failed to 'mop up' – to kill or capture any survivors of their first attack – before moving on. These survivors therefore went to ground, took up all-round defensive positions wherever they happened to be, and shot at any Germans that came before their rifle-sights. The result was a sprawling battle in the woods, with no one on either side having a clear idea as to what was going on. This fight for the Nonne Böschen and Polygon Woods was another 'soldier's battle', in which everything depended on the individual soldier's ability to 'stick it' . . . and keep fighting.

Therefore, although the German units were pressing forward relentlessly, most of the British line was still holding firm. In front of Polygon Wood the 1st Battalion, The King's Regiment beat off all attacks by the German 3rd Foot Guards Regiment and raised a wall of dead in front of their position; no Germans entered the wood, though at one time the King's battalion reported to Brigade that it was 'supported on the right by the Prussian Guard'. The Scots Guards position at Northampton Farm, north of the Menin road, also held out and was never taken. At Verbeek Farm, 100 men of the Black Watch plus the staffs of several battalion HQs – clerks and grooms and batmen – not only beat off any attacks on their position but were also able to open fire on German units moving west across their front.

In short, the British line was ragged in parts but it did not break; the Prussians were either kept out or rapidly evicted from the BEF line by the fire of the dogged infantry battalions backed up by men from the Headquarters companies, who snatched up their rifles and came running forward to join in the fighting and shore up the line. Even so, when the 'tail' of a battalion, those troops whose prime task is to support the fighting men, gets involved in the action, matters are getting desperate, and so it was here.

At one point during the day a wounded German officer captured at Nonne Böschen was being escorted to the rear when he asked a BEF artillery officer, 'Where are your reserves?' The battery commander pointed mutely to his guns. Unable to accept this amazing response, the German officer asked, 'And what is behind them?' On receiving the reply 'Divisional Headquarters', he said only, 'God Almighty' – as well he might. The BEF was hanging on to its position by its fingertips; had the Prussian Guards any real idea of the situation, had it been possible to restore any order to the fighting in the woods, one last coordinated attack would have broken through. As it was, the chronic problem of battlefield communications, common to all armies on both sides at this time, was taking effect yet again. The German attack was disintegrating and could not be put back together.

At noon the battle was still in the balance but it now appeared that the German advance had halted all along the front. The best intelligence seemed to imply that only one outstanding penetration remained, that of the Prussian Guard units in Nonne Böschen. In the early afternoon orders were therefore issued for the 2nd Battalion, Oxfordshire and Buckinghamshire Light Infantry to clear this wood, supported on the right by the 2nd Highland Light Infantry, which would drive the enemy out of the ground between Nonne Böschen and Polygon Wood.

Four companies of the 'Ox and Bucks' duly entered the Nonne Böschen wood at around 1500 hours and went through it at the double, driving the Prussian Guards before them: 'big men, some in helmets and some in caps, pell mell before them and killing or capturing all who resisted'.[13] These men proved to be from the 1st and 3rd Guards Regiments, and as the survivors emerged from the woods in full retreat they were fired on by the men of the Northampton and Cameron Highlanders in Glencorse Wood and exterminated. The Ox and Bucks suffered practically no casualties in this attack, and after a brief pause on the edge of the wood advanced again and took over the old trenches on the left of the 1st (Guards) Brigade. The account concludes: 'Although there were some gaps in it, the British line was now however secure, and every German who had crossed it in the morning had been accounted for.'[14]

The month-long Battle of First Ypres was effectively over when the Prussian Guard fell back from Nonne Böschen that night, but the fighting went on until the end of the month and the losses continued to mount. The First Battle of Ypres slowly petered out as winter drew on in December, more from sheer exhaustion and casualties than from any lack of will to continue.

During First Ypres, between 14 October and 30 November, BEF losses amounted to 58,155 men, with 614 officers and 6,794 British and 522 Indian other ranks being killed in the fighting. Those listed as 'missing' included men taken prisoner, but the bulk of the 'missing' died, their bodies never found. Their remains disappeared in the mud of Flanders and their names are now recorded on those monuments that dot the landscape in every part of the old salient.

To these BEF losses must be added those of their French and

Belgian comrades who fought at their side and took over more of the line as BEF strength declined. On 31 October, after two weeks of fighting, the British held 19 kilometres (12 miles) of the front, the French 24 (fifteen miles), the Belgians 10 (6 miles). By 5 November the French share had risen to 29 kilometres (18 miles) and the British share had shrunk to 14 (9 miles). Since the French had more men and all the reinforcements this is hardly surprising, but it should not be overlooked; if the defence of Ypres in 1914 was glorious, there is plenty of glory to spare.

German losses were very high: 134,315 German soldiers are listed as killed, wounded or missing between 15 October and 24 November.[15] The number of German soldiers killed during this period comes to 19,230, almost three times the BEF total. Given the massive losses sustained during those frontal assaults against entrenched British infantry, this may be an accurate figure; in August alone, German losses in the early battles along the frontiers exceeded 250,000 men, many more than the BEF could put into the field at this time.

First Ypres was only the first of three terrible battles that would take place around Ypres in the following years; the Second took place in 1915 and saw the first use of gas; the Third, in 1917, is better known as Passchendaele. None of these battles can be described as a victory, and the result of First Ypres was stalemate or at best a draw. Both sides were attempting a breakthrough, neither succeeded and both paid a terrible price in the attempt. However, since the Anglo-French and Belgian forces succeeded in hanging on to Ypres after going on the defensive, they might be awarded the palm of victory here – though retaining Ypres was to prove a great drain on the British Second Army in the hard years ahead.

And so they ended, the first four months of this four-year-long catastrophe that was to change Europe for ever – and kill no fewer than 9 million soldiers before it petered out in November 1918.

First Ypres is remembered as the graveyard of the original BEF, the old Regular Army. The battle left little room for generalship, strategic plans or much tactical skill. First Ypres was a 'soldier's battle' for the regular soldiers of the BEF and especially for the junior officers and the men in the ranks. The outcome depended, quite simply, on their ability to hang on and keep fighting; if they could stand their ground, keep their weapons clean and *keep fighting*, Ypres might be retained and Germany's only real hope of victory in this war would be extinguished.

The strategy of Foch, French and their subordinates boiled down to hanging on, doing one's best, putting in what men there were to 'putty-up' the front, trusting to the skill and courage of the soldiers; neither quality was in short supply. If those ragged, hungry men in those hastily dug trenches lacked reinforcement and artillery support, the fault lies with those pre-war politicians who had failed to anticipate the nature of this coming war and build up an army in peacetime.

The Germans had quantities of artillery and – most of the time – an abundance of shells, and yet they sent their men in mass attacks against entrenched British infantry and saw them cut to pieces time and time again by rapid and accurate rifle fire. These German attacks, all the way from Mons to First Ypres, usually had great weight, but there is little evidence of sensible tactics; it soon became clear that the German commanders also had a lot to learn about twentieth-century warfare. The tactic of battering the opposing line with shellfire and sending in massed infantry attacks was not sufficient to cause a breach; defence was master of the attack in this war and would remain so for some time to come. First Ypres was an example of the years of slaughter that would follow.

Now winter was coming to the Western Front. The men in the line had more hanging on to do, waiting in water-filled trenches for whatever fortune would bring them in the spring. On both sides of the line, those reservists who had rushed to the Colours back in August, expecting to be home 'by the time the leaves fall' or thinking that the whole business would be 'over by Christmas', could look across the drenched fields of Flanders and see beyond the opposing trench line the prospect of only more of this long, hard war.

Epilogue

He looked, and saw wide territory spread
Before him – towns, and rural works between,
Cities of men with lofty gates and towers,
Concourse in arms, fierce faces threatening war,
Giants of mighty bone and bold emprise.

John Milton, *Paradise Lost*, 1667

The enduring attraction of the First World War to military histor-ians is, it might be argued, largely due to the sense of what it cost. This cost cannot be measured only in terms of blood and treasure, though both were wasted in great quantity. The cost must also include the loss of the illusion, an end to the notion that man is perfectible, that humankind is capable of finding some way to settle disputes that does not involve the wholesale slaughter of brave young men. Nine million soldiers died in that war and a world died with them.

The nineteenth century, marked by decades of human progress in Europe, with advances in the arts and science, even in politics, between 1815 and 1914, finally foundered in the mud of Flanders and – again, it might be argued – such advances have never risen again. Follow the path of the BEF from Mons to the Marne and then north again to Ypres and you will pass a great number of graveyards on the way; the final emotion is one of great sadness and a sense of loss.

As for the human cost, the *British Official History*[1] gives the casualties from the start of the campaign in August 1914 to the end of First Ypres in November as 89,864 men, killed, wounded or missing. It notes also that 'the greater part of this loss had fallen on the infantry of the first seven divisions, which originally numbered only 84,000 men'.

German losses around Ypres from 15 October to 24 November are harder to compute but the *Official History*[2] estimates them at 134,315. This figure excludes the other losses since August; the total German casualties in the first five months of the war were in the region of half a million men, French losses on a similar scale. By the end of 1915 the opposing armies – British, French and German – had racked up over 2 million casualties. By the end of 1916, this total had risen to 4 million.

With the exception of Kitchener, all the main characters in this book survived the war, if not always for long. Field Marshal Sir Henry Wilson – as he eventually became – was appointed CIGS at the end of the war, and was murdered in London by the IRA in June 1922, soon after retiring from the army.

Horatio Herbert, Lord Kitchener, was drowned in June 1916 when the cruiser HMS *Hampshire*, in which he was travelling to Russia, struck a mine off the Orkneys. His work as Secretary of State for War in 1914 and 1915, not least in realizing that this would be a long war requiring large armies, has not always been appreciated.

Ferdinand Foch became Commander-in-Chief of the Allied armies in France in April 1918. After the war he was showered with honours by the Allied nations, including appointment to the rank of field marshal in the British Army. His statue outside Victoria Station in London recalls his comment that 'he was as conscious of having served Britain as he was of his own country'. He died in 1929.

Field Marshal Sir John French was sacked as commander of the BEF after the disaster of Loos in 1915 and replaced by General Sir Douglas Haig. He spent the rest of the war as C-in-C, Home Forces, and later as Lord Lieutenant of Ireland. Awarded an earldom – of Ypres – for his war service, he died in 1925.

Joseph Césaire Joffre was sacked as generalissimo and Commander-in-Chief of the French Army in 1916, after the losses of

Verdun and the Somme. Raised to the rank of Marshal of France, he had largely been forgotten by 1918 and died in 1931.

Had Sir Horace Smith-Dorrien not been finally brought down by Sir John French early in 1915, he, and not Douglas Haig, might have succeeded French as commander of the BEF the following December. Smith-Dorrien's career never recovered from his abrupt dismissal from the command of the Second Army. He was posted to a command in East Africa and went on to a series of second-rank appointments before the war ended. In 1919 he was officially refused permission to reply to the numerous libels made against him in French's memoir, *1914* – though he was one of the pall-bearers at French's funeral in 1925. He died in 1930 as the result of injuries sustained in a road accident.

General Sir Douglas Haig commanded the British armies in France from December 1915 until the end of the war. After the war he was instrumental in founding the British Legion and the Poppy Day appeal- once known as the Earl Haig Fund for Soldiers. He died in 1928 and has since been the vector for all the allegations – true and false – made about the competence of the British Army commanders of the First World War.

Helmuth von Moltke, the German commander on the outbreak of war, was dismissed in September 1914 and died two years later, in 1916. His successor, Erich von Falkenhayn, lasted a little longer but was destroyed by the terrible losses sustained by the German Army at Verdun in 1916. Sacked from the High Command in September 1916 and replaced by von Hindenburg and Ludendorff, he took command of the Ninth Army in Romania in 1917 and was then sent to command in Mesopotamia. He died in 1922.

As for the old British Army – the BEF – that, says the *Official History*, 'was gone past recall by the end of 1914, leaving but a fragment to train the new Armies; but the framework that remained had gained an experience that made those Armies invincible'.[3]

Notes

Chapter 1: The Continent Goes to War, 1871–1914

1. As featured in *The Prisoner of Zenda*, published 1894.
2. *The Proud Tower* by Barbara Tuchman (London, 1966), p. 340.
3. *History of the First World War* (London, 1970), p. 49.

Chapter 2: The British Go to War, 1898–1914

1. *Conflict on the Nile: The Fashoda Incident of 1898* by Patricia Wright (London, 1972), Introduction, p. ix.
2. *The Times,* 27 September 1898, p. 9.
3. Tuchman, *The Proud Tower,* p. 247.
4. *The Scramble for Africa* by Thomas Pakenham (London, 1992), p. 581.
5. Tuchman, *The Proud Tower,* p. 67.
6. The phrase was coined by Lord Goschen, then First Lord of the Admiralty, in 1896.
7. *The Chiefs: The Story of the United Kingdom Chiefs of Staff* by Bill Jackson and Edwin Bramall (London, 1992), p. 28.
8. *France and the Origins of the First World War* by John Keiger (London, 1983), p. 19.
9. *The Rise of Anglo-German Antagonism, 1860–1914* by Paul M. Kennedy (London, 1980), p. 464.
10. ibid., p. 191.
11. Tuchman, *The Proud Tower,* p. 316.
12. Kennedy, *The Rise of Anglo-German Antagonism,* p. 250.
13. *August 1914* by Barbara Tuchman (London, 1962), p. 16.
14. ibid., p. 16.
15. ibid., p. 17.
16. ibid., p. 17.
17. *Great Britain, Parliamentary Papers,* 1911, Vol. CCCIII, Cmd. 5969.
18. *British Official History 1914,* Vol. I, p. 18.
19. ibid., p. 21.
20. ibid., p. 19.
21. *The Esher Report, Part I,* p. 3.

22. *Britain and her Army* by Correlli Barnett (London, 1970), p. 359.
23. *The Supreme Command 1914–1918,* by Lord Hankey (London, 1961), p. 62.
24. ibid., p. 62.
25. ibid., p. 62.
26. *The Western Front, 1914–1918* by John Terraine (London, 1964), pp. 51–4.
27. Jackson and Bramall, *The Chiefs*, p. 42.
28. *The World Crisis* by Winston S. Churchill (London, 1923), Vol. I, p. 32.
29. Tuchman, *August 1914*, pp. 61–2.
30. Jackson and Bramall, *The Chiefs*, pp. 42–3.
31. Hankey, *The Supreme Command*, p. 68.
32. ibid., p. 70.
33. *A History of Germany 1815–1990* by William Carr (London, 1991), p. 196.
34. ibid., p. 197.
35. Churchill, *World Crisis*, Vol. I, p. 37.
36. ibid., p. 36.
37. *Haldane of Cloan; His Life and Times 1856–1928* by Dudley Sommer (London, 1960), p. 189.

Chapter 3: Wilson at the War Office, 1910–1914

1. *Field Marshal Sir Henry Wilson* by Major-General Sir C. E. Callwell (London, 1927), p. 189.
2. Hankey mss quoted in essay by Keith Wilson in 'Hankey's Appendix' in *War and History*, November 1994, pp. 85–6.
3. Callwell, *Field Marshal Sir Henry Wilson*, p. 79.
4. ibid., pp. 79–80.
5. ibid., pp. 78–79.
6. CID Paper, 109–B.
7. Sommer, *Haldane of Cloan*, p. 213.
8. Callwell, *Field Marshal Sir Henry Wilson*, p. 89.
9. WO 339/14401.
10. This is an error: WF means simply 'with France'.
11. Callwell, *Field Marshal Sir Henry Wilson*, p. 91.
12. ibid p. 91.
13. ibid p. 91.
14. ibid p. 91.
15. Churchill, *The World Crisis*, Vol. 1, p. 43.
16. ibid, p. 44.
17. *Memoirs of David Lloyd George*, Vol. I (London, 1928), p. 26.

18. *The Politics of Grand Strategy* by Samuel R. Williamson Jr (Cambridge, MA, 1969), p. 174.
19. *British Documents on the Origins of the First World War* by Gooch and Temperley, Vol. X (London, 1923), p. 629.
20. Tuchman, *August 1914*, p. 60.
21. Callwell, *Field Marshal Sir Henry Wilson*, p. 99.
22. ibid., p. 99.
23. ibid., p. 99.
24. Bramall and Jackson, *The Chiefs*, p. 46.
25. ibid., p. 47.
26. Callwell, *Field Marshal Sir Henry Wilson*, p. 102.
27. ibid., p. 104.
28. Terraine, *Mons*, p. 18.
29. Callwell, *Field Marshal Sir Henry Wilson*, p. 106.
30. Tuchman, *August 1914*, p. 63.
31. *Military Needs of the Empire*, CID Paper, 109-B.
32. Tuchman, *August 1914*, p. 104.
33. Callwell, *Field Marshal Sir Henry Wilson*, p. 153.
34. Tuchman, *August 1914*.
35. Callwell, *Field Marshal Sir Henry Wilson*, pp. 158–9.
36. ibid., p. 106.
37. Williamson, *The Politics of Grand Strategy*, pp. 140–1.
38. Bramall and Jackson, *The Chiefs*, p. 46.
39. *British Official History, 1914*, Vol. I, pp. 10–11.

Chapter 4: Mobilization, Transport and Logistics, 1911–1914

1. PRO Files; WO 339/14401. Undated but clearly written after April 1922, when the first volume of the *Official History* was published.
2. *White Heat: The New Warfare 1914–1918* by John Terraine (London, 1982).
3. PRO Files: WO 106/49A/2, Appendix I.
4. 'Ready for the Greater Game: The role of the horse in the First World War', by Robert Grey, *The Field*, November 2002, pp. 89–90.
5. *British Official History, 1914*, Vol. I, p. 19.
6. Grey, 'Ready for the Greater Game', p. 90.
7. Interview with Robin Neillands, May 2003.
8. Information supplied by Lt.-Col. Will Townend, RA, Royal Artillery, Woolwich.
9. This information differs from that given in the *Official History*, Vol. I, p. 30, namely 120,000 horses in twelve days.
10. www.1914.net/logistics/loc.htm.

11. Ian Malcolm Brown, *British Logistics on the Western Front, 1914–1919* (Praeger, CT, 1998), p. 56.
12. 'The Logistics of the BEF, August to September 1914' by Roger G. Miller, *Military Affairs Journal*, University of Indiana, October 1979, p. 134.
13. 'The Supply of Ammunition and Motor Transport' by Major H. de Pree, RFA, *RUSI Journal*, August 1912, p. 1,154.
14. ibid., p. 1,154.
15. PRO Files, WO 339/14401, p. 5.
16. ibid., p. 7.
17. ibid., p. 7.
18. Callwell, Field Marshal Sir Henry Wilson, p. 149.
19. Miller, 'the Logistics of the BEF'.
20. PRO Files, WO 339/14401, p. 6.
21. ibid., p. 8.
22. *From Private to Field Marshal* by Sir William Robertson (London, 1921), p. 205.
23. *British Official History, 1914*, Vol. I, pp. 30–31.

Chapter 5: The BEF Advances, 9–22 August 1914

1. *British Official History, 1914*, Vol. I, p. 39.
2. Tuchman, *August 1914*, pp. 308–309.
3. ibid., p. 173.
4. *Old Soldiers Never Die* by Frank Richards (London, 1933), p. 11.
5. *The Life of Field Marshal Sir John French* by Major The Hon. Gerald French (London, 1931), p. 204.
6. John Hussey, letter to the author, 1997.
7. *Verdun: The Price of Glory* by Alistair Horne (London, 1964), p. 29
8. *British Official History, 1914*, Vol. I, p. 442.
9. *1914* by Field Marshal Sir John French (London, 1919), p. 36.
10. ibid., p. 37.
11. *Liaison 1914*, by E. L. Spears (London, 1930), p. 75.
12. Tuchman, *August 1914*, p. 238.
13. ibid., p. 239.
14. *British Official History, 1914*, Vol. I, p. 48.

Chapter 6: the Battle of Mons, 23 August 1914

1. *British Official History, 1914*, Vol. I, p. 63.
2. Spears, *Liaison 1914*, p. 73.
3. *British Official History, 1914*, Vol. I, p. 59.
4. ibid., p. 60.

5. ibid., p. 60.
6. French and German accounts habitually refer to the BEF as 'the English Army' and its soldiers as 'the English'.
7. Callwell, *Field Marshal Sir Henry Wilson*, p. 166.
8. *British Official History, 1914*, Vol. I, p. 68.
9. ibid., p. 70.
10. *Feldienstordnung, 1906*, paras 265–327, supplied to the author by John Hussey.
11. *British Official History, 1914*, Vol. I, p. 82.
12. Callwell, *Field Marshal Sir Henry Wilson*, p. 167.
13. ibid., p. 167.

Chapter 7: The Battle of Le Cateau, 26 August 1914

1. *British Official History, 1914*, Vol. I, p. 86.
2. French, *1914*, p. 70.
3. Quoted in the *British Official History, 1914*, Vol. I, p. 92.
4. ibid., p. 93.
5. Richards, *Old Soldiers Never Die*, p. 19.
6. French, *1914*, p. 71.
7. Smith-Dorrien, *Memories of 45 Years' Service*, p. 392.
8. See Tuchman, *August 1914*, p. 272.
9. Smith-Dorrien, *Memories of 45 Years' Service*, p. 396.
10. ibid., p. 398.
11. Quoted in Terraine, *Mons*, p. 139.
12. Charteris, *At GHQ* (London, 1931), p. 78.
13. *British Official History, 1914*, Vol. I, p. 135.
14. Smith-Dorrien, *Memories of 45 Years' Service*, p. 401.
15. Callwell, *Field Marshal Sir Henry Wilson*, p. 169.
16. *British Official History, 1914*, Vol. I, p. 141.
17. Terraine, *Mons*, p. 150.
18. *British Official History, 1914*, Vol. I, pp. 162–3.
19. ibid., p. 182.
20. ibid., p. 182.
21. French, *1914*, pp. 79–80.
22. FSRs Para 13, Section 12, Part I.
23. French, *1914*, p. 82.

Chapter 8: The Retreat to the Marne, 27 August–5 September 1914

1. Smith-Dorrien, *Memories of 45 Years' Service*, p. 414.
2. *British Official History, 1916*, Vol. I, p. 83.

3. ibid, notes, p. 244
4. ibid., p. 224.
5. ibid., p. 209.
6. ibid., pp. 208–12.
7. Spears, *Liaison, 1914*, p. 267.
8. ibid., p. 267.
9. ibid., p. 266.
10. Tuchman, *August 1914*, p. 366.
11. *British Official History, 1914*, Vol. I. p. 232.
12. ibid., p. 241.
13. ibid., p. 261.
14. Callwell, *Field Marshal Sir Henry Wilson*, p. 173.
15. French, *1914*, pp. 94–5.

Chapter 9: From the Marne to the Aisne, 5–12 September 1914

1. French, *1914*, p. 91.
2. ibid., p. 92.
3. ibid., p. 92.
4. ibid., p. 93.
5. ibid., p. 94.
6. ibid., p. 98.
7. Steel helmets were not issued to the British Army until 1916.
8. Richards, *Old Soldiers Never Die*, p. 31.
9. French, *1914*, p. 95.
10. ibid., p. 95.
11. ibid., p. 100.
12. *British Official History, 1914*, Vol. I. p. 245.
13. ibid., p. 245.
14. Robertson, *From Private to Field Marshal*, p. 244.
15. Liddell Hart, *The First World War*, p. 78.
16. A German report of 2 September 1914, quoted in Liddell Hart, *The First World War*, pp. 33–4.
17. Callwell, *Field Marshal Sir Henry Wilson*, p. 174.
18. Tuchman, *August 1914*, p. 416.
19. ibid., p. 421.
20. *British Official History, 1914*, Vol. I, p. 318.
21. ibid., p. 258.
22. ibid., p. 263.
23. ibid., p. 263.
24. Callwell, *Field Marshal Sir Henry Wilson*, p. 173.
25. *British Official History, 1914*, Vol. I. p. 279.

26. Richards, *Old Soldiers Never Die*, p. 23.
27. *British Official History, 1914*, Vol. I. p. 278.
28. ibid., p. 286.
29. ibid., p. 290.
30. ibid., p. 294.
31. ibid., p. 295.
32. Spears, *Liaison, 1914*, pp. 337–8.
33. Callwell, *Field Marshal Sir Henry Wilson*, p. 176.

Chapter 10: On the Aisne, 13 September–2 October 1914

1. *British Official History, 1914*, Vol. I. p. 296.
2. ibid., p. 322.
3. Richards, *Old Soldiers Never Die*, p. 27.
4. French, *1914*, p. 144.
5. ibid., p. 145.
6. Robertson, *From Private to Field Marshal*, p. 214.
7. Bloem, Notes in *British Official History, 1914*, Vol. I, p. 330.
8. ibid., p. 340.
9. ibid., p. 341.
10. ibid., p. 360.
11. French, *1914*, pp. 122–3.
12. Callwell, *Field Marshal Sir Henry Wilson*, p. 177.
13. ibid., p. 177.
14. *British Official History, 1914*, Vol. I, p. 465.
15. ibid., p. 367.
16. ibid., p. 373.
17. French, *1914*, pp. 154–5.
18. ibid., p. 155.
19. ibid., p. 156–7.
20. ibid., p. 168.
21. Callwell, *Field Marshal Sir Henry Wilson*, p. 180.

Chapter 11: The War in the North, 2–18 October 1914

1. *The First World War, 1914–1918* (London, 1920).
2. ibid., p. 25.
3. ibid., p. 29.
4. *British Official History, 1914*, Vol. II, p. 42.
5. French, *1914*, p. 177.
6. Instructions to Sir John French from Lord Kitchener, *British Official History, 1914*, Vol. I, Appendix 8, p. 443.

7. French, *1914*, p. 177.
8. *British Official History, 1914*, Vol. II, p. 65.
9. ibid., p. 403.
10. This is the date of the BEF's first engagement at La Bassée; the *Official History* records the La Bassée battle as lasting officially from 10 October to 2 November.
11. French, *1914*, p. 210.
12. *British Official History, 1914*, Vol. II, p. 83.
13. Quoted in Liddell Hart, *The First World War*, p. 119.
14. *British Official History, 1914*, Vol. II, p. 85.
15. Callwell, *Field Marshal Sir Henry Wilson*, p. 183.
16. ibid., p. 184.
17. ibid., p. 185.
18. *British Official History, 1914*, Vol. II, p. 97.
19. Richards, *Old Soldiers Never Die*, p. 34.
20. ibid., pp. 34–5.
21. *British Official History, 1914*, Vol. II, p. 103.
22. ibid., p. 113.
23. ibid., p. 115.
24. ibid., p. 121.

Chapter 12: Ypres, 19–31 October 1914

1. *British Official History, 1914*, Vol. II, p. 125.
2. ibid., p. 125.
3. Letter to General Maxwell, War Office.
4. *British Official History, 1914*, Vol. II, p. 121.
5. French, *1914*, p. 216.
6. Callwell, *Field Marshal Sir Henry Wilson*, p. 183.
7. *British Official History, 1914*, Vol. II, p. 108.
8. ibid., p. 137.
9. French, *1914*, p. 226.
10. ibid., p. 226.
11. *British Official History, 1914*, Vol. II, p. 157.
12. Richards, *Old Soldiers Never Die*, p. 46.
13. *British Official History, 1914*, Vol. II, p. 140.
14. ibid., p. 148.
15. Telegram to Lord Kitchener, 22 October 1914, 12.12 p.m.
16. *British Official History, 1914*, Vol. II, p. 165.
17. ibid., p. 173.
18. ibid., p. 175.
19. ibid., p. 178.

20. ibid., p. 253.
21. ibid., p. 259.

Chapter 13: Gheluvelt, 29–31 October 1914

1. *British Official History, 1914*, Vol. II, p. 270.
2. ibid., notes, p. 270.
3. General Dubois, quoted in *British Official History, 1914*, Vol. II, p. 275.
4. French, *1914*, p. 242.
5. *British Official History, 1914*, Vol. II, p. 276.
6. ibid., p. 278.
7. ibid., p. 279.
8. French, *1914*, p. 245.
9. Allenby claims that the London Scottish mustered twenty-six officers and 786 men when they entered the line and sustained 278 casualties, some 34 per cent on 31 October, adding in his report, 'rarely, if ever, have second line troops sustained unshaken so high a percentage of casualties'.
10. French, *1914*, p. 238.
11. ibid., pp. 248–9.
12. ibid., p. 249.
13. Liddell Hart, *The First World War*, p. 127.
14. Notes, *British Official History, 1914* ,Vol. II, p. 347.
15. Callwell, *Field Marshal Sir Henry Wilson*, p. 185.
16. ibid., p. 186.

Chapter 14: Nonne Böschen, 1–22 November 1914

1. Callwell, *Field Marshal Sir Henry Wilson*, p. 186.
2. Ibid., p. 187.
3. *British Official History, 1914*, Vol. II, p. 349.
4. John Hussey, *British Army Review*, No. 109.
5. *British Official History, 1914*, Vol. II, p. 375.
6. Callwell, *Field Marshal Sir Henry Wilson*, p. 187.
7. ibid., p. 186.
8. French, *1914*, p. 270.
9. *British Official History, 1914*, Vol. II, p. 421.
10. ibid., p. 427.
11. ibid., p. 434.
12. ibid., p. 481.
13. ibid., p. 441.
14. ibid., p. 442.
15. ibid., p. 468.

Epilogue

1. *British Official History, 1914*, Vol. II, p. 467.
2. ibid., p. 468.
3. ibid., p. 465.

Bibliography

What follows is only a small selection of the books and papers consulted for this book. Many are now long out of print but can still be obtained from libraries or in second-hand bookshops.

Arthur, Max, *Forgotten Voices of the Great War*, Ebury, London, 2002
Asquith, H. H., Prime Minister, *The Genesis of War*, Cassell, London, 1923
Barnett, Corelli, *The Swordbearers, Studies in Supreme Command during the First World War*, Cassell, London, 1963
——, *Britain and Her Army, 1509–1970*, Cassell, London, 1970
Bethmann-Hollweg, Theobald von, *Reflections on the World War*, Thornton Butterworth, London, 1922.
Blake, Lord, *The Private Papers of Douglas Haig, 1914–1919*, Eyre & Spottiswoode, London, 1952
British Commission for Military History (ed.), *Look to your Front: Studies in the First World War*, Staplehurst, Spellmount, 1999
Brown, Ian Malcolm, *British Logistics on the Western Front, 1914–1918*, Praeger, Westport, CT, 1998
Brown, Malcolm, *The Imperial War Museum Book of the First World War*, Sidgwick & Jackson, London, 1991
Callwell, Major-General Sir C. F., *Field Marshal Sir Henry Wilson, His Life and Diaries* (2 vols), Cassell, London, 1927
Carew, Tim, *The Vanished Army*, William Kimber, London, 1964
Carr, William, *A History of Germany, 1815–1990* (4th edn), Edward Arnold, London, 1991
Carver, Field Marshal Lord, *The War Lords*, Weidenfeld & Nicolson, London, 1976
Charteris, Brigadier-General John, *At GHQ*, Cassell, London, 1931
Churchill, Winston S., *The World Crisis, 1911–1914*, Thornton Butterworth, London, 1923
Collier, Basil, *Brasshat, A biography of Field Marshal Sir Henry Wilson*, Secker & Warburg, London, 1961
Corbett-Smith, Major, A. *The Retreat from Mons*, Cassell, London, 1916
Corrigan, Gordon, *Mud, Blood and Poppycock,* Weidenfeld & Nicolson, London, 2003

Crozier, Brigadier General F. P., *A Brass Hat in No Man's Land*, Jonathan Cape, London, 1930

De Watteville, Colonel H., *The British Soldier*, J. M. Dent, London, 1954

Edmonds, Brigadier General J. E., *History of the Great War: Military Operations, France and Belgium, 1914* (2 vols), Macmillan, London, 1922

Falls, Cyril, *Marshal Foch*, Blackie, Glasgow, 1939

Farrar, Martin J., *News from the Front: War Correspondents on the Western Front, 1914–1918*, Sutton Publishing, Stroud, 1998

Farrar-Hockley, Anthony, *Death of an Army*, Arthur Barker, London, 1967

Farwell, Byron, *Mr Kipling's Army: All the Queen's Men; Britain's pre-World War One Army*, Norton, New York, 1981

Fischer, Fritz, *Germany's Aims in the First World War*, Chatto & Windus, London, 1967

——, *War of Illusions*, Chatto & Windus, London, 1975

Foch, Marshal Ferdinand, *The Memoirs of Marshal Foch*, trans., William Heinemann, London, 1931

French, Major The Hon. Gerald, *The Life of Field Marshal Sir John French*, Cassell, London, 1931

French, Field Marshal Viscount French of Ypres, *1914*, Constable, London, 1919

Fussell, Paul, *The Great War and Modern Memory*, Oxford University Press, Oxford, 1975

Gilbert, Martin, *The First World War*, Weidenfield & Nicolson, London, 1994

Haldane, Lt. Gen. Sir Aylmer, *A Brigade of the Old Army, 1914*, Edward Arnold, London, 1920

Hamilton, Ernest, *The First Seven Divisions*, Hurst & Blackett, London, 1916

Hankey, Sir Maurice, *The Supreme Command, 1914–1918* (vol. 1), Allen & Unwin, London, 1961

Henig, Ruth, *The Origins of the First World War*, Routledge, London, 1989

Hobley, L. F., *The First World War*, Blackie, Glasgow, 1971

Horne, Alistair, *Verdun: The Price of Glory*, Penguin, Harmondsworth, 1964

Hunt, Barry, and Adrian Preston, *War Aims and Strategic Policy in the Great War*, Croom Helm, London, 1977

Jackson, General Sir William, and Field Marshal Lord Bramall, *The Chiefs: The Story of the United Kingdom Chiefs of Staff*, Brassey's, London, 1992

Joll, James, *Europe since 1870* (4th edn), Penguin, London, 1990

——, *The Origins of the First World War*, Longman, London, 1984

Keegan, John, *The Face of Battle*, Jonathan Cape, London, 1976

Keiger, John, *France and the Origins of the First World War*, Macmillan, London, 1983

Kennedy, Paul, *The War Plans of the Great Powers*, Allen & Unwin, London, 1979

——, *The Rise of Anglo-German Antagonism, 1860–1914*, Allen & Unwin, London, 1980

McDonough, Frank, *The Origins of the First and Second World Wars*, Cambridge University Press, Cambridge, 1997

Macksey, Kenneth, and John Batchelor, *Technology in War*, Arms & Armour, London, 1986

Maurice, Major-General Sir Francis, *Forty Days in 1914*, Constable, London, 1920

Miller, Stephen, Sean Lynn-Jones and Stephen van Evera (eds), *Military Strategy and the Origins of the First World War*, Princeton University Press, Princeton, NJ, 1991

Owen, Edward, *1914: Glory Departing*, Buchan & Enright, London, 1986

Pakenham, Thomas, *The Scramble for Africa, 1876–1912*, Weidenfield & Nicolson, London, 1991

Prior, Robin, and Trevor Wilson, *Command on the Western Front*, Blackwell, Oxford, 1992

Repington, Lt. Col. Charles à Court, *The First World War, 1914–1918*, Constable, London, 1920

Richards, Frank, *Old Soldiers Never Die*, Faber & Faber, London 1933

Robbins, Keith, *The First World War*, Oxford University Press, Oxford, 1984

Robertson, Field Marshal Sir William, *From Private to Field Marshal*, Constable, London, 1921

Sheffield, Gary, *Forgotten Victory: The First World War, Myths and Realities*, Headline, London, 2001

Snyder, Louis L., *Historic Documents of World War I*, Van Nostrand, Princeton, N.J., 1958

Sommer, Dudley, *Haldane of Cloan: His Life and Times, 1856–1928*, Allen & Unwin, London, 1960

Spears, E. L., *Liaison 1914*, William Heinemann, London, 1930

Steiner, Zara S., *Britain and the Origins of the First World War*, Macmillan, London, 1977

Taylor, A. J. P., *The First World War*, Hamish Hamilton, London, 1963

Terraine, John, *Mons: Retreat to Victory*, B. T. Batsford, London, 1960

——, *The Western Front, 1914–1918*, Hutchinson, London, 1964

——, *The First World War, 1914–1918*, Hutchinson, London, 1965

——, *White Heat: The New Warfare, 1914–1918*, Sidgwick & Jackson, London, 1982

Travers, Tim, *The Killing Ground: The British Army, the Western Front and the Emergence of Modern Warfare*, Unwin Hyman, London, 1990

Tuchman, Barbara, *August 1914*, Constable, London, 1962

——, *The Proud Tower: A Portrait of the World before the War, 1890–1914*, Hamish Hamilton, London 1966

Turner, L. C. F., *Origins of the First World War*, Edward Arnold, London, 1970

Van Creveld, Martin, *Supplying War: Logistics from Wallenstein to Patton*, Harvard University Press, Cambridge, MA, 1997

——, *Command in War*, Harvard University Press, Cambridge, MA, 1985

Wavell, General Sir Archibald, *Generals and Generalship*, Penguin, Harmondsworth, London, 1941

Williamson, S. R., *The Politics of Grand Strategy: Britain and France Prepare for War, 1904–1914*, Harvard University Press, Cambridge, MA, 1969

Wright, Patricia, *Conflict on the Nile; The Fashoda Incident of 1898*, Heinemann, London, 1972

Primary Sources

INTERVIEWS AND PRIVATE PAPERS

Interviews on horse management and artillery in 1914 with Captain Neil Cross, RA, The King's Troop, Royal Horse Artillery, London, and Lt. Col. William Townend, RA (retd), The Firepower Museum, Royal Arsenal, Woolwich, May 2003.

Papers of Field Marshal Sir William Robertson (Ref. GB99 KCLMA), Liddell Hart Centre for Military Archives, King's College, London.

The diaries of Field Marshal Sir Henry Wilson, Department of Documents, Imperial War Museum, London.

MANUSCRIPT SOURCES

The PRO sources on the First World War are enormous but the following documents were particularly useful:

WF Scheme (WO 339/14401). Action taken by the General Staff since 1906 in preparing a plan for rendering military assistance to France in the event of an unprovoked attack on that power by Germany. PRO. Undated.

Winston S. Churchill. *Military Aspects of the Continental Problem*, CID Papers, 132-B, August 1911.

Committee of Imperial Defence (CID) (Cab. 4/3), Minutes of the Meeting, 23 August 1911 – *Action to be taken in the Event of a European War*

R. McKenna, *Remarks by the Admiralty on proposal (b) of the Memorandum by the General Staff*. Cab. 4/3, p. 195.

BIBLIOGRAPHY

PRIMARY PRINTED SOURCES

Callwell, Major-General Sir C. E., *Field Marshal Sir Henry Wilson, His Life and Diaries* (2 vols), London, 1927.

Edmonds, Brigadier General J. E., *History of the Great War; Military Operations, France and Belgium, 1914*, vol. 1, London, 1922.

Gooch, George. P. and Harold Temperley, *British Documents of the Origins of the War, 1898–1914*, vol. X, London, 1938.

MAGAZINE ARTICLES

Bate, Brigadier-General T. R. F., 'Horse Mobilisation', *RUSI Journal*, November 1921, pp. 1154–8.

Buchanan Dunlop, Major C. N., 'Ammunition Supply', *RUSI Journal*, January 1913, pp. 88–9.

Coogan, John, and Peter F. Coogan, 'The British Cabinet and the Anglo-French Staff Talks 1905–1914; Who knew what and when did he know it?', *Journal of British Studies*, vol. 2, January 1985, pp. 110–31.

De Pree, Major H., RFA, 'The Supply of Ammunition and Motor Transport', *RUSI Journal*, August 1912, pp. 88–9.

Donoughmore, The Earl of, 'The National Horse Supply and our Military Requirements', *RUSI Journal*, February 1908.

Grey, Robert, 'Ready for the Greater Game; the Role of the Horse in the First World War', *The Field*, November 2002, pp. 89–90.

Hussey, John, '"Without an Army, and Without any Preparation to Equip One"; the Financial and Industrial Background to 1914', *British Army Review*, 109, April 1995.

Miller, Roger G., 'The Logistics of the British Expeditionary Force, 4 August to 5 September, 1914', *Journal of Military Affairs*, October 1979.

Tarle, Capitaine d'Artillerie A. de, 'The British Army and a Continental War', trans. from article in *Revue de Paris* (October 1912), *RUSI Journal*, March 1913.

Wilson, K. M., 'The Making and Putative Implementation of a British Foreign Policy of Gesture, December 1905 to August 1914; the Anglo-French Entente Revisited', *Canadian Journal of History*, August 1996, pp. 227–55.

Index